LIBRARY LIT. 19– The Best of 1988

edited by

JANE ANNE HANNIGAN

The Scarecrow Press, Inc.
Metuchen, N.J., & London
1989

ISBN 0-8108-2276-8
Library of Congress Catalog Card No. 78-154842

TABLE OF CONTENTS

iii

INTRODUCTION

The wealth of literature in librarianship and information science has been obvious to me throughout my professional career. I admire the convictions and the ideas that my colleagues share through their writing; and, as a library educator, I have a vital interest in highlighting and preserving the best of that literature. As editor, I was responsible for reading an entire year's work in library and information science and of bringing to the attention of the jury for this publication those articles that are exceptional and from which a final list was selected. The fact that the jury considered at least 150 articles in reaching its final decision is indicative of the quality of professional contributions of which we can all be proud.

Part I, Government, Access and Libraries, includes articles that alert us to issues of critical importance to librarians. Summers addresses the significance of the Constitution which, while never mentioning libraries, offers the very principles we as librarians support, that of free inquiry and citizen access. Privatization, both as a concept and as a political movement is affecting the federal information flow. Levin and Kranich both examine the impact of the Paperwork Reduction Act and explore the climate of restraint that privatization imposes. Line reminds us that it is the performance of library functions at a national level that is the crucial issue in examining national libraries. Stave presents a detailed account of the 1979 Public Lending Right Law of the United Kingdom with obvious implications for a comparable law here in the United States. It is an interesting paradox to read Richards' account of the gathering of scientific and technical information during World War II and note the recent pressures of the FBI to identify foreign users of similar materials in today's libraries.

Part II, Societal Concerns, contains those articles significant to us not only as professionals but as fellow human beings. Donelson gives an objective and scholarly analysis of creationism that is understandable and useful. Woodrum details a case study of the positive interaction of the library and the homeless. Morehead discusses topical concerns of ageism from bereavement, death and elderly prisoners to Alzheimer's and hospice care, identifying various journals that deal with these issues. Ndiaye argues that the traditional model for the operation of libraries may need modification in nations where the oral culture is dominant.

Part III, Professional Problems, includes articles that discuss a range of problems facing libraries, some relatively recent and others that have concerned librarians for a very long time. Otness examines the targeting of maps for theft and offers alternative solutions to this costly problem. Clancy focuses on a critical concern that has permeated our society, that of the invasion of computers with a virus that can cause enormous damage to data files. He offers an explanation of what happens and a series of preventive measures as well as remediation. Greenberg traces the history of concern about books as disease carriers which should prove thought-provoking in light of the unwarranted fear about AIDS. Horning discusses the problem of variant printings of award-winning children's books and questions whether the illustrations children see today are actually those which won the awards.

Part IV, Issues in Evaluation, presents various forms of evaluation of library materials and services. Mandel analyzes cost-benefit analysis and proposes a model for evaluation in technical services using that method. D'Elia presents his research on fill rates and argues that fill rates are not a valid measure for evaluation of library services. Giblin offers fascinating insights into and evaluation of the evolution of nonfiction for children from his personal perspective. Echelman suggests that knowledge about information behavior as well as expert systems designed to meet individual needs will be critical to the future success of academic libraries. Smith's research demonstrates that Black women have been consistently ignored or inadequately covered in encyclopedias.

Part V, Technological Applications in Libraries, focuses our attention on the ever-increasing impact of technology on libraries. Vandergrift considers the influence of science and technology on the literature and media for children. Krause discusses the difficulty of indexing picture collections and the complex questions that must be considered in that process. Van Hine and Pearse provide a case study of the ACOG IAMS Project with its mission to identify and put into electronic form the core of knowledge necessary for the practice of obstetrics and gynecology. Weinberg provides new insight in her analysis of why indexing fails the researcher, using the analogs of 'aboutness' and 'aspect' as a focus. Meadow reviews the history of the database industry and develops a time chart including major accomplishments from 1945 to 1988. Adams contends that decisions made about catalogs will influence the values of libraries and questions whether we increase managerial competence at the expense of access to information. Murphy offers a checklist in planning for an automated system and includes a report of her research on OPACS in schools.

Part VI, Library Professionals, looks at a range of concerns including the image and the day-to-day roles of librarianship. Johnson presents a scholarly and thoughtful case for comparable worth in libraries focusing on intraoccupational intentional wage discrimination and examines legislation and major legal actions related to this topic. Fisher examines psychological investigations into the personality of the librarian conducted over the last 30 years questioning the efficacy of the whole psychological enterprise. Land draws on research that discusses the image of librarians in popular culture, the importance of projecting a clear and positive image of reference librarians and ways to improve users' understanding and image of librarians. Swan suggests we are in the Age of the Librarian and ought to be engaged in information activism that offers access to the new technology as well as other forms of information and education. Traister's article, reviewed by the jury from those remaining from a previous year, details the precise nature of a rare book librarian's day as a personal case history. St. Clair revisits his 1976 article and examines the changes in managerial styles and educational approaches developed in the last decade.

No book is completed without the support and help of a number of people. I would like to thank the professional community who share their ideas, research and expertise in our journals and all those who nominate articles for the jury's consideration. The 1988 jury's diligence in reading all the recommended articles and their lively, sometimes argumentative, discussions before closure are greatly appreciated. I express my gratitude to Jana Varlejs who acted as recorder during the jury deliberations. I owe a special debt of gratitude to Betty Jean Parks whose patience was matched only by her care in typesetting this book and in preparing it for printing. Finally, I thank all of those contributors whose articles were selected for inclusion in this nineteenth volume of *The Best of Library Literature*.

Jane Anne Hannigan
Editor and Professor Emerita
Columbia University
New York, New York

Note: All those who wish to nominate articles for consideration by the jury should send them to the editor at 24 Starview Drive, Neshanic, New Jersey 08853.

THE BEST OF LIBRARY LITERATURE
JURY FOR 1988

John Berry, III
Vice President and Editor-in-Chief
Library Journal
New York, New York

Arthur Curley
Director
Boston Public Library
Boston, Massachusetts
Editor of *Collection Building*

Jane Anne Hannigan
Professor Emerita
Columbia University
New York, New York
Chair of 1988 Jury

Norman Horrocks
Vice President, Editorial
Scarecrow Press
Metuchen, New Jersey

Bill Katz
Professor
School of Information Science and Policy
State University of New York, Albany
Albany, New York
Editor of *The Reference Librarian*

Patricia Glass Schuman
President
Neal-Schuman Publishers, Inc.
New York, New York

NOTES ON CONTRIBUTORS

JUDITH A. ADAMS is Director, Lockwood Memorial Library, University at Buffalo, State University of New York, Buffalo, NY.

STEVE CLANCY is Associate Librarian/Reference Librarian, Biomedical Library, University of California, Irvine and System Operator (SYSOP) of the Wellspring Remote Bulletin Board System based at the Biomedical Library.

GEORGE D'ELIA is Associate Professor, Management Sciences Department, Carlson School of Management, University of Minnesota.

KEN DONELSON is Professor of English, Arizona State University, Tempe, AZ. Former Editor of *English Journal*, co-author of *Literature for Today's Young Adults*, Chair of the National Council of Teachers of English Committee that published *The Student's Right To Read*.

SHIRLEY T. ECHELMAN is a Consulting Librarian based in Alexandria, VA.

DAVID FISHER is Assistant Librarian (Sociology and Psychology), Trent Polytechnic Library Service, U.K.

JAMES CROSS GIBLIN is Editor and Publisher of Clarion Books, New York, NY. He is also the author of ten nonfiction books for young readers.

GERALD S. GREENBERG is Reference/Bibliographic Instruction Librarian, Ohio State University's Undergraduate Library, Columbus, OH.

KATHLEEN T. HORNING is Special Collections Coordinator at Cooperative Children's Book Center, University of Wisconsin–Madison; and Children's Librarian at Madison Public Library, Madison, WI.

NANCY P. JOHNSON, J.D., MLS, BA, is Law Librarian/Associate Professor of Law, Georgia State University, College of Law, Atlanta, GA.

NANCY C. KRANICH is Director of Public and Administrative Services, New York University Libraries and Chair of the Coalition on Government Information, New York, NY.

MICHAEL KRAUSE is Assistant Buyer at Morley Book Company, Ltd., U.K. He was formerly employed by Bradford Libraries and Information Services.

MARY LAND is General Librarian, Society and Recreation Department, North York Public Library, Ontario, Canada.

MARC LEVIN is Librarian for Administrative and Support Services, Institute of Governmental Studies, University of California at Berkeley, Berkeley, CA.

MAURICE B. LINE now a Consultant, was formerly Director–General, Science, Technology and Industry, The British Library, U.K.

CAROL A. MANDEL is Director, Technical Services, Columbia University Libraries, New York, NY.

CHARLES T. MEADOW is Professor, Library and Information Science, University of Toronto; formerly Manager of Customer Services and of Technology Applications at DIALOG Information Services.

JOE MOREHEAD is Professor, School of Information Science and Policy, State University of New York at Albany, Albany, NY.

CATHERINE MURPHY is Director of Library Media Services, Three Village Central School District, Setauket, New York.

RAPHAËL NDIAYE is Chairman of the Division of Regional Activities in IFLA.

HAROLD M. OTNESS is Collection Development Librarian, Professor of Library Science, Southern Oregon State College, Ashland, OR.

WARREN H. PEARSE, M.D. is Executive Director, American College of Obstetricians and Gynecologists, Washington, DC.

PAMELA SPENCE RICHARDS is Associate Professor, Department of Library and Information Studies, School of Communication, Information and Library Studies, Rutgers University, New Brunswick, NJ.

GUY ST. CLAIR is President of OPL Resources Ltd., New York, NY.

HENRIETTA M. SMITH is Associate Professor, School of Library and Information Science, University of South Florida, Tampa, FL.

THOMAS A. STAVE is Head, Documents and Public Affairs Service, University of Oregon Library, Eugene, OR.

F. WILLIAM SUMMERS is Dean, School of Library and Information Studies, Florida State University, Tallahassee, FL.

JOHN C. SWAN is Head Librarian, Crossett Library, Bennington College, Bennington, VT.

DANIEL TRAISTER is Assistant Director of Libraries for Special Collections, Van Pelt Library, University of Pennsylvania, Philadelphia, PA.

KAY E. VANDERGRIFT is Associate Professor, Department of Library and Information Studies, School of Communication, Information and Library Studies, Rutgers University, New Brunswick, NJ.

PAMELA VAN HINE is Head Librarian and Associate Director, American College of Obstetricians and Gynecologists Resource Center, Washington, DC.

BELLA HASS WEINBERG is Associate Professor, Division of Library and Information Science, St. John's University, Jamaica, NY and President of American Society of Indexers, 1988/89.

PAT WOODRUM is Director, Tulsa City–County Library System, Tulsa, OK.

PART I:
GOVERNMENT, ACCESS
AND LIBRARIES

LIBRARIES AND THE CONSTITUTION

F. William Summers

One searches in vain for any specific reference to or provision for libraries in the Constitution of the United States. This omission may, upon first glance, seem ironic since today we regard our libraries as one of the first lines of defense in protecting and defending the rights of people. We in the United States are not alone in this belief, for it has often been observed that one of the first concerns of totalitarian governments is to control the press and along with it the rights of access to and the contents of libraries.

Why then did our founding fathers, so farseeing in many ways, fail to make specific provision for the libraries as sources of information for the people. First, it must be noted that these people did not themselves come from a strong tradition of libraries. While one of them, Benjamin Franklin, had been responsible for founding a library in Philadelphia, it was not truly a public library. While some of them were college educated, they had probably encountered only the most limited of libraries in the schools in which they had studied. The one who might most likely have seen the need for some provision for libraries was not present. Thomas Jefferson was in Paris arranging for credit and representing the interests of the still frail and fledgling nation.

Nevertheless, the principles which motivated these men, their view of their fellow men, and their desires for free government are akin to the principles we hold forth for libraries today. They would have well understood the principles which librarians support; the rights of free inquiry and citizen access would have not sounded strange to their ears.

The coming together of the fifty-five men who wrote our constitution was in itself a strange event. In the first place, they had no authorization to write a new constitution. The convention had been called for the specific and strictly limited purpose of revising the Articles of Confederation. These Articles, which had been quickly assembled following the revolution, had

"Libraries and the Constitution" by F. William Summers in *North Carolina Libraries* Vol. 45 (Winter 1987), pp. 178-184; reprinted with permission from *North Carolina Libraries*.

produced a structureless and ineffective government which could not pay its own bills except by subscriptions to the states which they were free to ignore, and many did. There was no national currency, and money from one state was not necessarily recognized in another. States were in dispute about their boundaries and were even levying tariffs on one another's goods. Some states were considering negotiating their own treaties with foreign nations. Prisoners and criminals fleeing from one state to another were or were not extradited depending upon the whims and honesty of local officials. Who were these men then who dared to exceed their authority and to lay before their countrymen a plan for a new nation, a plan unique in the world at that time, a document which has endured for two hundred years with only twenty-six amendments (ten of which had been planned for in the beginning and one of which fortunately, repealed an earlier one banning the sale of alcohol)?

Catherine Drinker Bowen, in the opening of her wonderful book *Miracle at Philadelphia*, sets the flavor and tone of the meeting with these words, which I quote in part, "Over Philadelphia the air lay hot and humid; old people said it was the worst summer since 1750. French visitors wrote home they could not breathe. At each inhaling of air, one worries about the next one. It was May when the convention met, it would be September before they rose." Among the fifty-five delegates from twelve states (Rhode Island refused to attend) were some of the most luminous names in American history: Washington, Madison, Hamilton, Franklin, South Carolina's John Rutledge, and the two Pinckneys, Charles Cotesworth and Charles. Again quoting Bowen, "The roster reads like a Fourth of July oration, a patriotic hymn. It was a young gathering, Charles Pinckney was twenty-nine, Alexander Hamilton thirty. Rufus King was thirty-two, Johnathan Dayton of New Jersey twenty-six. Gouvenor Morris—he of the suave manners and the wooden leg was thirty-five. Even that staid and careful legal scholar, James Madison of Virginia, kinown today as 'father of the Constitution,' was only thirty-six. Benjamin Franklin's eighty-one years raised the average considerably but it never went beyond forty-three. Men aged sooner and died earlier in those days. John Adams at thirty-seven invited to give a speech in Boston, had said he was 'too old to make declamations.'"

It is perhaps ironic, given the traditions of free and open government which it has produced, that all deliberations of the convention were in secret. Many of the delegates, Madison among them, believed that to open the debates to public scrutiny and publicity would have doomed the Constitution from the beginning. It is to Madison's indefatigable note-taking that we owe most of the present-day knowledge of what actually transpired in the debates. Madison, it should be remembered, took these notes not for the benefit of posterity but to fashion arguments for others to make in refutation of points with which he disagreed, for he himself was a weak public speaker.

Anyone who studies the history of the Constitution will inevitably identify among those fifty-five men their favorites, people who stood for principles they hold dear. Madison is probably most everyone's hero. Madison, the shy, bookish person in constant real and presumed ill-health, arrived at the convention with a forty-one page notebook in which he had inscribed the lessons of history which should be reflected in the Constitution. He also brought an outline of a plan of government that the convention eventually adopted, an outline based upon the principle that the more people who are brought into the system on a free and equal basis, the safer are the liberties and lives of all.

Others may find themselves drawn to the more enigmatic Alexander Hamilton, who supported a strong central government for the nation, not because of concerns about liberty or the rights of citizens, but because he saw it as the only way to guarantee an economic system which could function for the benefit of all.

Many, including your speaker, are drawn to the crusty old Virginian, George Mason, who had written a Bill of Rights for Virginia which became the Bill of Rights in the new government and, indeed, is the basis of the bills of rights of most modern governments. Mason had a strong dislike and distrust for politicians, and his efforts were to empower the people with rights to protect themselves against politicians.

Despite the fact that this document makes no mention of libraries, it is the foundation upon which rests the structure of most of our social institutions. The Constitution makes no provision for public schools either; yet the necessity for an informed citizenry which it demands made the development of a public school system a mandatory condition for our society to function. So it is with libraries. We all like the implications in the title of Sidney Ditzion's study of censorship efforts in public libraries, *Arsenals of a Democratic Culture*. It is this view of the library as the place to which the citizen can go for unbiased, diverse, and current information which is our most fundamental claim to public support.

Despite this fundamental support which the Constitution gives to libraries, there are many places in which the document impacts directly upon our work. Despite the lack of specific language, a great deal of our library tradition and practice and some of our current issues are grounded in the language of the Constitution. We must remember that our Constitution, though written, is organic and changes over time. The recent hearings on the confirmation of Robert Bork demonstrated clearly the conflict between those who regard the Constitution as fixed and limited and those who look upon it as organic and flexible, changing over time in resposne to the beliefs, attitudes, and values of the people. That difference of opinion was present in Philadelphia, and it is with us today. Those who wish to see the Constitution as a fixed contract between the government and the people set in 1787 have great difficulty with the fact that our society and our government have changed enormously in the intervening two hundred years. There are many factors present in our world today that the framers could not have foreseen.

Let us examine that principle as we look at some of the ways in which the Constitution does impact today upon libraries and library services.

Copyright

One matter directly affecting libraries is specifically enumerated among the powers of the Congress, "to promote the Progress of Science and useful arts, by securing for limited Times to Authors and Inventors the exclusive Right to their respective writings and discoveries." A strict reading of that provision could suggest that only materials in the areas of science and the useful arts should have such protection. But in enacting the various copyright laws, Congress has used its power to extend copyright to works of fiction, religion, and history. It has also extended that right to television and radio programs, to motion pictures and now to such things as computer software programs. Libraries find themselves in the difficult position of having readily available technology in the form of copy machines, VCR's and microcomputers which can very easily permit them or users to violate the terms of copyright. We have wisely refused to be the policemen in the battles between technology and copyright. The real battleground for libraries has shifted, at least for the moment, from photocopying of books and journals to video-cassettes and computer software. There is a clear antagonism between the goals of libraries and those of copyright holders. Libraries exist to make materials as widely available to users as possible; copyright holders prefer that every use of a copyright item result from a purchase. Meanwhile, technology continues to provide the processes for duplicating copyrighted materials far in excess of the law.

The so-called "shrink-wrap" issue, which involves the rights of use of computer software, is a very thorny one. The copyright holder's contention that what is conveyed to the purchaser is not a piece of property but a license to use, is a new extension of the copyright principle. In all other instances, when a purchaser buys a piece of copyrighted material, it is theirs, and they may do with it what they please. They can lend it to others, they can destroy it, they can make an additional copy for their own use, but in the case of computer software, it is claimed that only the purchaser has the right to use. We will certainly see this issue tested in the courts in the future, but it is not the last such issue we will face. We can anticipate that copyright holders will continue to seek technological methods to control and measure the access of users to their copyright protected works. Now the library which buys the *World Almanac*, for example, is free to make it available to any users who want it, the only limit being that the format makes it difficult to serve more than one user at a time. It is likely that we will see this type of information soon put into an interactive format, CD-ROM for example, which has the capacity to monitor each use. The copyright holder may then wish to seek payment on a per use basis rather than simply for the cost of acquiring the information collection. As technology provides more and more ways to store, acquire, and manipulate information, we will see many future issues dealing with the constitutional powers given to Congress and the rights of "authors and inventors" as opposed to the rights of the people and their social institutions.

It would have been very helpful in today's world if the founding fathers had been as precise about setting out society's rights of access to information as they were in protecting those of author's and inventors. We librarians believe and argue that the purpose of copyright is for the benefit of society as well as for the benefit of the creators, but the language of the Constitution addresses only the rights of those who create and invent.

The Bill of Rights

The constituional issues which have most concerned librarians have been those relating to the Bill of Rights, that series of amendments to the constitution, promised by the drafters and adopted by the Congress at its first session in 1789. These amendments were quickly ratified by the states and became part of the Constitution on December 15, 1791, when ratified by the last necessary state, Virginia. (Ironically Massachusetts, Georgia, and Connecticut did not get around to ratification until 1939 when it was a symbolic act to have the last of the thirteen original colonies ratify the Bill of Rights.) It is also interesting to note that the questions of specifically what action by a state constitutes ratification and whether a state can rescind its ratification came up in the consideration of these amendments as it did in the recent considerations of the Equal Rights Amendment. The Constitution itself is silent upon both of these matters.

George Mason, who had drafted the Bill of Rights, did not originally support the Constitution and, in fact, refused to sign it because the Bill of Rights was not part of the document. Those who had supported the Constitution had committed themselves to the prompt submission of the Bill of Rights for approval. In fact, a number of the states made their approval of the Constitution contingent upon submission of a bill of rights, and many of them in their ratification resolutions contained provisions which should be included in such a statement.

The First Amendment

When as either citizens or librarians we think of the Constitution, it is most often the First Amendment which comes to our minds. These forty-

five clear and direct and, to many, unambiguous words have probably
provoked more debate, legislation, and court deliberations than all the rest
of the Constitution combined. The amendment says things rather simply:

> *"Congress shall make no law respecting an establishment of religion,*
> *or prohibiting the free exercise thereof; or abridging the freedom of*
> *speech, or of the press; or the right of the people peaceably to assemble,*
> *and to petition the Government for a redress of grievances."*

The First Amendment is a paradox in that it can force people to
change political colors in the face of its power. The late Justice William O.
Douglas is generally considered to have been a far left liberal; yet when
it came to the First Amendment, he was a conservative, strict constructionist who argued that when the Constitution said "Congress shall make
no law," it meant precisely that. The Reverend Jerry Falwell, on the other
hand, is generally a conservative strict constructionist, but when it comes
to the First Amendment, Rev. Falwell wants a more liberal position and
favors many restrictions on the right of free speech and a free press.

The First Amendment also produces paradox in that some, who stoutly
defend one right it grants, may be willing to permit tampering with another.
Thus, people who would die at the barricades defending their right to go
to the church of their choice are less sure that they want other people
to come to their community to write or speak about matters of which they
disapprove. The First Amendment hoists us on our own petard, and as
a nation we have frequently been uncomfortable with the cognitive dis-
sonance which it generates within us. We rejoice in the freedom it gives
us, but we are sometimes uncomfortable when we see others using those
same rights in ways of which we do not approve.

The First Amendment is under assault and public scrutiny today as
it has never been before. The government assaults it when it attempts to
stifle citizen access to government information. The press assaults it when
it intrudes on the privacy of citizens. We are not comfortable with the First
Amendment, but none of us would be comfortable living in a country
without it.

It is this amendment which comes into consideration whenever library
materials are criticized and when some citizens seek to have them removed
from our libraries. Because it receives the most publicity, we tend to think
that these efforts have most often been based upon issues of alleged
obscenity, which the Supreme Court has ruled does not have constitutional
protection. It is well to remember that the efforts at cleaning up library
collections are also directed against the alleged political affiliations of
authors and toward offenses which writings have given to various groups.
A recent issue of the ALA *Intellectual Freedom Newsletter* indicated that
objections had been raised to materials alleged to address the following
themes: the occult, eviction of tenants, abortion, sex education, AIDS

information, and secular humanism. Along with many books which had been challenged on grounds of obscenity, there also appeared *Rumplestiltskin*, *Macbeth*, and *The Diary of Anne Frank*. We must also remember that sometimes objections are raised in the name of obscenity when, in reality, some other less emotional principle is at stake. A clear example occurred when ministers who really felt that Sinclair Lewis's book *Elmer Gantry* was unflattering sought to have it banned on the ground of obscenity.

Librarians sometimes tell me that in censorship conflicts they feel ALA and, occasionally, they themselves are defending books, films, and people such as magazine publishers, dealers, and adult book store operators which really aren't very savory and with which they would rather not be associated. Let me reassure you that what is being defended in these cases is the First Amendment and, by so doing, we stand solidly with the founding fathers. The First Amendment is first because it is the foundation of our liberty.

The Right of Association

We seldom think about the right of association granted by the First Amendment. It is one of those rights which we use everyday. You are using it today to assemble here as a group of librarians representing the needs and interests of your state. You did not require any approval from state or local authorities for this meeting. You are free to take any positions you wish on matters of concern to you, and you may not be prohibited from participating or be punished for so doing. Your association is free under the Constitution to propose any changes you may wish other than the violent overthrow of the government. You may even advocate violent action in the future so long as you don't actively plan for it.

The right of association also protects you from being subjected to any kind of loyalty oath. If the American Library Association falls out of favor with the state, you may not be required to swear that you are not a member of it. That may seem far-fetched, but some of us can recall times when the NEA was out of favor at the local level, and people were pressured not to join.

The First Amendment also severely restricts the degree to which the government can interfere in the internal affairs of an association. You may set any membership requirements for this organization that you wish so long as you do not discriminate on the basis of age, race, national origin, religion, or physical handicap. You may notice that I did not include sex in that list because, due to the failure of the Equal Rights Amendment, discrimination on the basis of sex is not prohibited by the Constitution.

You may within reasonable limits have marches, demonstrations, and similar meetings for the purpose of presenting your views to government and to the public at large. Reasonable limits set by the government must relate to such matters as protecting the public safety and the rights of other people. You may, for example, picket a movie theater showing a movie of which you disapprove; but you may not picket in such a way as to prevent others from entering nor may you go inside and disrupt the showing. It is also important to note that, in the case of libraries, others have these same rights with respect to our activities. People may and have demonstrated against the library and picketed it.

The government may not deprive you of other rights solely because you have used your right of association. If Mr. Reagan gets mad at the ALA because we do not support his nominee to be Librarian of Congress, he may not deny you a passport to travel or deny you employment in a federal library.

The government may not require you to disclose the names of your members, and it may not require you to identify yourself as a member of an organization. That may not sound like much of a right, but it has been crucial to organizations which have not gained or which fall out of public favor. It was very significant in the early days of the labor movement and to groups like the NAACP, because disclosure of their members might well have resulted in substantial pressure against those individuals.

Government Information

As you all know, we are engaged today in a major struggle about information by and about the United States government. I am proud, as I hope you are, that the American Library Association is playing a major role in that struggle. The question of government information also bothered the Constitutional Convention, and they thus required that each house of Congress keep and publish a journal, but gave them the right in their judgment to keep parts of it secret. Patrick Henry, who opposed the Constitution, said of this provision—and it certainly pertains to all government information—"The liberties of a people never were or never will be, secure when the transactions of their rulers may be concealed from them. The most iniquitous plots may be carried on against their liberty and happiness." Those who watched and read the Iran/Contra hearings would today find it hard to disagree with Henry.

The issue of access to government information has, today, a number of manifestations, all of which are very serious. Perhaps the most far reaching is the government effort in the name of economy and efficiency to contract out to private contractors as many of its information functions as possible. At first glance, we librarians may be seen to be self-serving when we oppose such efforts; but who better than we can understand the implications of placing increasing control over the information activities of the executive branch of government in private hands which are outside the constitutional system of checks and balances. Again the Iran/Contra hearings give clear evidence of the perils of conducting the public's business under the cloak of "private operations." Fortunately, the Congress is growing increasingly aware of the possible perils in this area. In this year's hearings on the Appropriations Bill, the Senate Appropriations Committee, commenting on the administration's proposal to privatize the National Technical Information Service, a service which operates at no cost to the taxpayers, mentioned "turning over government scientific and technical information to private contractors which may be controlled by foreign interests or can be bought by foreign firms." It is encouraging that the committee concluded its report with these comments, "Given the dynamics of public policy development, the Committee believes that certain positions in nonrecreational library positions are presumptively governmental in nature . . . Therefore, the Committee fully expects the head of each Federal agency to notify the applicable appropriations subcommittee and other appropriate authorizing committees, using the proper reprogramming procedures, before initiating the contracting out of any Federal library." The struggle on this issue is far from over; but ALA's positions on the issue were early, they were clear, and they have been consistent. Isn't it ironic that those who have for decades called for government to be businesslike now seek to take out of government those activities which have succeeded in being businesslike?

We also face a major struggle to preserve the role of libraries as a principal component of the system for providing public access to the information which government itself produces and develops. From very early in our history the role of the public printer to ensure citizen access to government information was clearly established. Now, again in the name of efficiency, we are seeing increasing efforts to privatize, or place in private hands for public access, a wide variety of information collected, compiled, and paid for by the public. The public will have access only if it pays for access to value-added vendors or if libraries are able to pay the costs for them. The coalition of federal agencies seeking to lower their costs or transfer them to information users and private sector vendors anxious to increase their markets will be very difficult to resist. Patrick Henry's worst fears would be realized in some of the proposals we seek to resist today. We stand in the tradition of Francis Lieber, the great University of South Carolina faculty member and President who said, "Liberty is coupled with the public word and however frequently the public word may be abused it is nevertheless true that out of it rises oratory—the aesthetics of liberty. All governments hostile to liberty are hostile to publicity."

Again, I hope that you are as proud as I am of the great and energetic leadership which your professional association is providing in this issue. It is we who stand in the tradition of the framers of the Constitution and who believe that government information, like government activity, ought to be open and apparent to its citizens, not hidden in secrecy or made unavailable in the name of cost cutting. We may truly need to cut the federal budget, but curtailing citizen access to public information, information by and about the United States government, is far too high a price to pay. George Mason's argument against slavery in which he said, "as nations cannot be rewarded or punished in the next world they must be in this . . . [and] providence punishes national sins by national calamities" fits equally well a government which would control or limit the access of its citizens to information about its activities.

The Due Process Clause

The Fifth Amendment provides that no person may "be deprived of life, liberty or property without due process of law." For much of our history this provision was seen as relating to criminal matters and civil matters relating to the taking of real property for public purposes. In more recent years, however, statutes and court decisions have resulted in a broadening of the definition of "property" to include things other than real property. A tenured professor may now be seen as having a "property" interest in the position. A library staff member past a probationary period of employment may also have a property interest in his position and if those property rights are taken away or denied, then that individual must be given the rights of "due process." Due process, like beauty or privacy, is an elusive matter and is highly circumstantial in nature. It is clear that at least in the employment area, due process means that the person must be informed of the charges against him, i.e., what he has done wrong. He must be given the opportunity to inquire into those charges and to examine those who bring them, and he must be able to present testimony in his own behalf. Usually it means that, if requested, he must also have the opportunity for legal counsel in these processes.

The rights of due process have also entered into the education of students who are seen as having a property right in their education. School administrators, teachers, and media specialists now deal with the necessity of imposing discipline in the schools while insuring at the same time that students receive their due process rights.

Many library administrators, particularly those of the old school, chaff at the seeming rigidity of due process provisions in employment, but would we really want to have it otherwise? We know that not all decisions to terminate employees are fairly reached. There are administrators who are capricious, discriminatory, authoritarian, and in some instances downright mean. Should not employees have at least the minimal protection which the Constitution can afford them in the face of such actions?

It is certainly true that due process provisions make employee terminations and other kinds of actions much more cumbersome than they once were. But the United States Constitution is not about convenience and expediency. It is fundamentally about fairness and how government and its agencies may treat and interact with citizens.

Conclusion

The richness of the Constitution provides material for a much longer presentation than circumstances of today permit. We could talk, for example, about the librarian's concern for the privacy of circulation records and the Fifth Amendment's right to be protected against self-incrimination. It is an important topic now that we again have federal law enforcement officials going into libraries and asking librarians to spy on their fellow citizen's use of libraries.

It is clear that the Constitution is as fundamentally a part of our libraries as it is our lives. Our libraries play the role in our lives that they do because of our Constitution, just as we are the kind of people that we are because of our Constitution. I have lived long enough to see that Constitution sustain us in economic disaster, in several wars, in presidential succession, in the dismissal of a president, and in periods of great national embarrassment. It is a remarkable document and because we live under it, we are a remarkable people.

GOVERNMENT FOR SALE: THE PRIVATIZATION OF FEDERAL INFORMATION SERVICES

Marc A. Levin

Introduction

In the market for a dam? How about Grand Coulee Dam, the world's second largest concrete dam? Prefer an airport? Would you be interested in Dulles International Airport outside Washington, D.C.? Too far out of town? Well, Washington's National Airport is also available. For more information, contact the Reagan administration.

These properties are just a few of the federal government assets listed for sale to the private sector in the 1988 fiscal year budget that the President sent to Congress. National Weather Service satellites, Naval Petroleum reserves, Small Business Administration loans, and the National Technical Information Service can be found on an expanding list of public property destined for the auction block.[1] These proposed sales illustrate the current administration's long-term strategy of shifting public functions to private enterprise, commonly referred to as "privatization."

The effects privatization may have upon the delivery of federal information services remain uncertain and speculative. However, the privatization debate does raise several critical professional issues regarding public access to tax-supported information services, who controls public knowledge, the future direction of federal library programs, and the quality of government we might expect as a result of widespread implementation of this policy. This essay will explore the conceptual and practical aspects

"Government for Sale: The Privatization of Federal Information Services" by Marc A. Levin in *Special Libraries* Vol. 79, no. 3 (Summer 1988), pp. 207-214; reprinted with permission from *Special Libraries* © by Special Libraries Association.

associated with privatization to develop a framework for understanding these vexing public issues. Examination of two current examples of privatization in action—namely, the contracting out of federal libraries and the proposed sale of the National Technical Information Service—will provide a backdrop to analyze the declining federal role in the library/information sector and what this signifies for our profession.

The Concept Defined

"Privatization" has quickly become an important buzzword in the lexicon of public policy. What exactly is meant by the term? According to a 1983 report issued by the President's Private Sector Survey on Cost Control (a.k.a. the Grace Commission), privatization means:

> . . . to turn over an activity, or part of an activity, currently performed by the Federal Government to a non-Federal entity. It is an option for implementing Government programs and policies, allowing the Government to *provide* services without producing them.[2]

The Grace Commission, consisting of 161 high-level private sector executives, identified $28.4 billion potential savings for the federal treasury, over a three-year period, from increased reliance on a privatization strategy. In this country, privatization has come to mean mainly government's relying more on private producers for services for which government remains, in varying degrees, responsible. Federal information services, like other public "utilities," must confront the prospects of deregulation through reliance on the free market philosophy known as privatization.

Contracting, as a common form of privatization, is not new in American government. It is traditional in public works at all levels and has been common in the rapid growth of human services since the 1960s. What is new, however, is the proposal to radically expand the practice and apply it to service areas in which it has not previously been considered appropriate, including federal information services.

Privatization can be defined as the policy of handing over to the private sector functions that previously have been performed in-house by government employees. Thus, privatization represents a pragmatic policy choice that combines economy, efficiency, and effectiveness in designing service delivery systems. At its best, privatization creates competition, efficiency, and wealth. At its worst, it substitutes insensitive and unresponsive privately owned monopolies for reified public bureaucracies, and breeds corruption.

Privatization is an emerging conservative concept that evokes sharp political reactions. It covers a great range of ideas and policies, ranging from the eminently reasonable to the widely impractical. As a reaction to the modern regulatory and welfare state, privatization has been a part of the Reagan agenda since 1981, and demonstrates the administration's commitment to reduce "big government" and as a strategy to control domestic federal spending.

Public vs. Private Provision

According to Professor Paul Starr of Princeton University, the terms "public" and "private" are fundamental to the language of our "law, politics, and social life, but they are sources of continual frustration."[3] Many activities seem to be public and private at the same time in varying degrees or in different ways. The confusion arises partly because the public/private dichotomy is used to characterize number of other related oppositions in our thinking.

Historically, the private sector in the U.S. has long performed many services financed by public funds. Familiar examples are the purchasing of ordinary supplies that most governments buy in the marketplace, many professional services, design and construction of public works, and defense-related manufacturing. In pursuit of the public interest, for many years and in various ways, governments have undertaken an increasing range of activities that are by no means inherently governmental. The federal government, for example, ventured into many commercial activities with four main goals: 1) to remedy a perceived marketplace failure; 2) to capitalize on the government's unique ability to marshal the necessary economic resources to get the job done; 3) to obtain a desired national policy objective; and 4) for national security or legal reasons.

Since about 1980, the trend toward increased government spending, ownership, and intervention has been seriously questioned. This has sparked new debates about the merits of private versus public provision. Assertions that the private sector, as more efficient and effective, could do better have stimulated discussion of the desirability of government provision. Privatization, which is the transfer of assets or service functions from public to private ownership or control, has emerged as the focal point of this debate.

Proponents of privatization cite efficiency as a chief objective. However, while the leadership of business has strong ownership interests, there is no hard evidence that private sector employees work harder than their public sector counterparts. There are, however, persistent rigidities in public institutions (e.g., burdensome civil service rules, excessive legislative oversight, rampant proceduralism) that limit managerial flexibility and discourage efficiency. Conceivably, public management improvements and administrative reforms might achieve the same productivity objectives as privatization. Yet economy and efficiency, while worthy objectives for public managers to pursue, are sometimes insufficient criteria and must be tempered by values of equity, justice, and sense of community in serving the public interest.

An Overview of Federal Contracting

Interactions between government and the private sector have been widespread over the past few years, due to rising costs of providing services, shrinking revenues, and federal aid cutbacks. Contracting out is a practice as old as the Republic and is found at all levels of American government. When the government contracts out a public service, it retains its funding responsibility but hires a private firm to provide the service. The primary motivation for contracting out is to cut government cost by using a competitive bidding situation to drive down the expense for a particular good or service.

In recent years, there has been a marked trend toward increasing the scope of contracted services. According to the U.S. Office of Management and Budget, in 1980 the federal government spent about $100 billion for contracting services, and that figure reached $183 billion by 1984.[4] Pointing with pride to the successful efforts at the state and local levels, the Reagan administration has actively promoted contracting out as a means of pruning federal spending and taming the budget deficit. (Ironically, state and local governments have not considered information services as appropriate for contracting.)

The federal policy regarding reliance on the private sector for commercial activities was first addressed in U.S. Bureau of the Budget bulletins issued in 1955, 1957, and 1960. In 1966, the U.S. Office of Management and Budget (OMB) issued *Circular A-76*, which established implementation guidelines. OMB's principle was that the federal government should not engage in any activity that could be performed by the private sector. The 1983 revised circular contained even more precise language and provided definitions, tests, criteria, and other requirements for cost comparisons, including a suggested listing of activities deemed appropriate for contracting. Despite the strong protests by the American library community, "library services" was one of the commercial activities, along with laundry and janitorial services, found on OMB's list of federal activities deemed ripe for contracting.

Library Contracting

By the mid-1980s, several federal agencies (e.g., Department of Energy, Environmental Protectiuon Agency, Department of Housing and Urban Development), in accordance with the OMB's ambitious A-76 program, had transferred their libraries to outside contractors. Perhaps the most controversial case involved the National Oceanic and Atmospheric Administration's (NOAA) decision to contract for the operations of its Central Library located in Rockville, Maryland. In April 1987, under heavy pressure from several constituencies, Congress requested the U.S. General Accounting Office (GAO) to examine NOAA's contract and investigate several serious allegations.

The GAO report, issued in August 1987, provides insight into the problems engendered by this policy.[5] Apparently, NOAA management, relying on the assistance of outside consultants, had to rewrite its contract solicitation more than 10 times, and was still unable to devise an accurate statement of the library's work. In commenting on this situation, Congressman Gary L. Ackerman (D-NY), chairman of the House Civil Service Subcommittee on Human Resources (with jurisdiction over federal contracting), stated the following: "I am convinced that this effort has cost the U.S. taxpayer far more money for outside consultants to study the library than its privatization could possibly save."[6]

The GAO investigation revealed that, even after several years of contract preparation and study, NOAA management accepted a lowest bid that was inaccurate by virtue of its failure to include collection development costs. Even more astonishing was the fact that NOAA officials accepted a bid based on the bogus assumption that the winning contractor's costs would continue to decrease over the life of the contract because "volunteers" would come forward to help staff the library. This assumption raises two immediate serious questions. First, where do these volunteers come from, what are their qualifications, and who controls them? Second, is it not illegal for unpaid volunteers to replace federal civil servants to work unpaid for government contractors?

Poor contracting places an agency at risk. Federal officials confronted with today's complex challenges—such as cleaning up toxic wastes, ensuring air safety, containing terrorism, deterring insider trading, combatting the AIDS pandemic, promoting competitiveness, and fighting drug abuse—need reliable and high-calibre information services. Government libraries were originally established to help an agency fulfill its mission by providing professional in-house information services for busy federal officials. The NOAA case illustrates that the arithmetic of the marketplace does not always serve the public interest, since private firms are willing to cut corners to get higher profit margins at the expense of existing service levels.

There are other salient issues, primarily having to do with accountability and continuity of personnel, that are critical to managerial competence and must be considered before awarding a contract. For example, the library manager operating under a contract with a private firm faces a dual accountability situation, which presents a possible conflict. The library manager must please the corporate president while also serving the needs of the agency chief in Washington. The priorities of the two executives might be in conflict. The agency head, however, cannot easily dismiss the contractor and the library employees without the potential loss of key institutional memory. Thus, Ronald C. Moe of the Congressional Research

Service warns that privatization poses serious problems "in providing direct institutional support" for public managers.[7] Federal librarians with years of experience possess keen institutional memory and a sense of commitment and pride in an agency's work. They offer expertise and are key elements of the bureaucracy and serve as organizational assets not easily traded in the open marketplace.

Federal experience with contracting out library services is still in its infancy. Studies to evaluate contractor performance and compliance, client satisfaction, and real agency savings have yet to reveal the effect this policy has upon the capacity of public decision makers to achieve their information needs. Serious questions regarding contractor commitment to preserving the integrity of agency libraries, their willingness to permit public access to tax-supported library collections, and their ability to recruit and retain competent staffing still loom.

Will contractors, knowing that the life of the contract has a termination date, continue to invest adequate resources into agency libraries and encourage strategic planning? Various risks and rewards are just beginning to emerge as the federal bureaucracy searches for balance between often competing objectives of efficiency and effectiveness. A crisis could be developing. Government leadership in the library/information sector appears on the wane as federal library services become the first tragic victim of a system rushing to embrace a policy objective shrouded in uncertainty.

A Privatized NTIS

Federal budget deficits can be reduced either by cutting spending or by increasing revenue. Given the political difficulties of the former, and the President's opposition to tax increases, the sale of government assets would seem to provide an expedient solution. The recent decision by the U.S. Department of Commerce to sell the National Technical Information Service (NTIS) to the private sector provides an illuminating case in point. The outright sale of NTIS to the private sector is the purest form of privatization, and the most dramatic. NTIS was established by Congress more than 40 years ago to serve as the nation's "cornerstone" for scientific and technical publishing.[8] This unique federal agency was designed to foster wide and impartial public dissemination of specialized information critical to encouraging technical innovation and the open exchange of tax-supported research results. However ironically, the agency's strong financial and management condition makes it an excellent first candidate for privatization, especially in the eyes of federal budget managers eager to test their free-market philosophy.

Arguing that the federal government should not compete with the private sector, the OMB since 1981 has sought to convince the Congress that private firms should be permitted to operate NTIS under contract. This ignores NTIS' statutory mandate to operate on a self-sustaining basis, a requirement that has created an organization able to compete successfully with private operations. Numerous reviews carried out under the guidance of OMB's A-76 program attest to this. Yet the agency remains uncertain about its future as no compelling reason for privatization has been demonstrated by OMB.

After numerous meetings, public workshops, congressional hearings, and impartial studies—all demonstrating strong opposition—the President's fiscal year 1988 budget states: "in 1988, the private sector will be offered the opportunity to operate NTIS on contract, with the government retaining overall policy direction." In accordance with this budget language, in January 1988 the U.S. Department of Commerce issued a request for a proposal to privatize NTIS under the Federal Employee Direct Corporate Stock Ownership Plan (Fed CO-OP) concept.

The Fed CO-OP idea was introduced by the director of the U.S. Office of Personnel Management in 1986 as an innovative means to overcome long-standing in-house employee resistance to contracting out.[9] This form of untested privatization requires a winning contractor to fund an employee stock ownership plan at a level equal to one-half the savings expected to result from private management. This fund would be managed for the benefit of the former federal workforce that would, under this plan, be transferred to the new entity for a minimum of 180 days of guaranteed employment.[10]

Significant questions remain about where the money for the stock purchase would come from, as well as about how to place a fair market value on the stock, since the winning contractor might not publicly trade stock. An additional impediment to this idea would be the existing federal conflict-of-interest laws, designed to protect the government from corruption and graft, which prohibit public jobs from being used for private gains.[11] This plan raises questions about how many public employees would opt to share in the risks and rewards of ownership over the security provided by the civil service, all in exchange for just six months of assured employment?

In economic terms, whether a particular activity should be carried out by the private or public sector depends on the relative efficiency of the two sectors and the presence or absence of market failures. Simply changing the ownership of an existing public asset, such as the NTIS, has no meaning or impetus unless the new owner's efficiency in operating the asset differs from that of the original owner. Thus, in the case of NTIS, a private producer must, at a minimum, be able to improve or enhance the existing operations to justify the change. The proposal to sell NTIS does not even require a private operator to match or exceed existing service levels. In fact, it is doubtful that a private provider would be able to improve services, given the fact that NTIS already operates as a high

performing (efficient) and client-centered (responsive) organization.
Privatization as government policy might on the surface seem like a good and politically correct notion. However, a closer analysis reveals several unattractive opportunity costs. Privatization of NTIS represents a major federal policy shift away from a constitutional and legislative tradition that embraces the concept of an open and free exchange of public information to ensure an informed citizenry. A privatized NTIS, as one facet of the federal information dissemination system, promises to have a grave impact on other, remaining channels of public access to federal information. For example, it is no secret that the U.S. Government Printing Office (GPO) and NTIS often compete with one another in marketing the same government publications; however, the GPO version is usually more reasonably priced to encourage wider public distribution. What would happen to GPO's deliberately reasonable pricing policy if it were suddenly forced to compete against a private provider in an unregulated commercial marketplace?

The possibility that private operation of NTIS might increase the price of materials is a serious concern to the scientific community since the loss of access to NTIS documents would hamper research. It is conceivable that the massive federal investment in research and development would be wasted if the information generated by researchers were not readily shared with other members of the scientific community. The ability of the nation to meet global competition, to provide for national security, and to improve the quality of life for all citizens depends in part upon national investments in science and technology. Thus, the nation's future position in global markets depends upon the sustained generation of new knowledge and the open transfer of this knowledge to the people who need it most. Privatization of NTIS appears to be in conflict with these articulated national policy objectives since it places at risk a vital link in the process of technological innovation and scientific advancement. Serious questions about the ability of the federal government to maintain policy direction over a dismantled NTIS, accountable only to a private board of directors, linger.

Limits on Privatization

As a concept and as a political movement, privatization is profoundly altering the shape of the public sector in the United States. Too often the relationship between the public and private sectors is viewed as a zero-sum game in which increased prosperity for one sector is achieved at the expense of the other. The reality of the modern nation state, however, is that the prosperity of each of the two sectors is inextricably linked to that of the other. To understand the potential of privatization, it is, therefore, first necessary to understand its limitations. To accomplish that requires an investigation of the dialectical tensions raised by the legal, economic, and value dimensions of this policy.

Although the U.S. Constitution provides many protections for citizens against arbitrary governmental action, it provides little or no protection from abuses by the private sector on infringement of individual liberties. This realization has prompted Professor Harold J. Sullivan of the City College of New York to assert: "privatization does threaten our constitutional rights." [12] By turning public services over to private groups, the government can effectively evade constitutional restraints. For example, a private contractor delivering library services may, without having to follow the due process of law, legally determine who will receive what level of tax-funded services. Thus, if private flexibility and discretion are among the advantages promised by privatization, they may come at the expense of citizens' rights.

Perhaps the most potent factor limiting the spread of privatization is the spectre of corruption. A high percentage of the instances of corruption that have occurred over the two centuries of American administrative history has involved contracts with private providers to perform a public service. [13] This is perhaps understandable since the letting of contracts generally involves substantial sums of money accompanied by considerable discretion on the part of contracting officials. The stakes for private parties are often high, and they may be willing to go to the edge of the law. Thus, the potential for corruption during the contract stage is considerable.

Among the arguments for contracting is that contractors are more efficient than civil servants. There is, however, little evidence that the contract bureaucracy is a model of efficiency. Moreover, contracting has tended to breed inefficiency in the civil service, requiring many public employees to administer contracts instead of carrying out governmental programs. At the same time, contracting expands the powerful spending coalition that lobbies Congress to increase the federal budget in support of contractor special interests. Thus, while contracting might lead to more efficient government, it does not guarantee smaller government.

Economic return is not the sole measure of public benefit from privatization. The fact that the private sector seeks it suggests that the economic return is most likely to benefit the private sector. A frequently made charge against privatization is that it will result in service going just to the easy and profitable customers, called "creaming," resulting in the neglect of difficult and/or unprofitable customers. [14] In the case of public information services, this practice would create an uneven "playing field," pitting the information "rich" against the information "poor."

Public managers must face the unpleasant prospect of the hidden costs of privatization. The costs of disruption associated with transition, labor unrest, vendors' failure to deliver, or poor management are potential pitfalls of a privatization venture. Hostile takeovers, bankruptcies, mergers, divestitures, and business failures are common market occurrences that could play havoc with contractor services. Estimating market value of a public asset is another significant problem. Is the government obtaining private sector efficiency or merely subsidizing a private firm by selling public assets at below market value?

The determination of public benefit requires a more complex formula, one that considers other values. What serves the public interest does not always provide the highest economic return. A major danger of bringing the private sector into the provision of public services is that it risks bringing cost considerations into the forefront of the decision-making process to the detriment of other values held by our society. The private sector is more concerned with doing well (making a profit) than with doing good (advancing the general welfare). In a democracy, a major social value is the idea that public officials are accountable for their actions to elected officials and, ultimately, to the public. When a public function is assigned to a private entity there is a weakening of the lines of political accountability. What then occurs is the emergence of "third-party government," allowing the government to operate by remote control, held captive by influential and invisible non-federal actors.[15]

Conclusion

At present, there is no evident reason to believe that the spread of privatization will stop. Looming budget deficits and mandated expenditure limitations will encourage federal policymakers to consider all privatization options. However, privatization should be applied only to things the American people are not willing to risk. Is the American public willing to place the future of federal information services in the hands of the lowest commercial bidder, rather than the "best and brightest" public servant? Information professionals, as the collective voice of expertise, should remain skeptical about a program with no verifiable record of expenditures and savings, and should mobilize to protect our public information infrastructure from the vagaries of the marketplace.

References

1. U.S. Executive Office of the President, Office of Management and Budget. *Budget of the United States Government, Fiscal Year 1988*. Washington, D.C.: GPO, 1987.
2. U.S. President's Private Sector Survey on Cost Control. Report on Privatization. Washington, D.C.: GPO, 1983. 209 pp.
3. Starr, Paul. "The Meaning of Privatization." *Privatization*. Working Paper no. 6, Washington, D.C., Project on the Federal Social Role, National Conference on Social Welfare, 1985. 49 pp.
4. U.S. Congressional Budget Office. *Contracting Out: Potential for Reducing Federal Costs*. Washington, D.C., 1987. 31 pp.

5. U.S. General Accounting Office. *Contracting Out: National Oceanic and Atmospheric Administration's Central Library.* GAO/RCED-87-184, Washongton, D.C., 1987. 13 pp.
6. Ackerman, Gary L. "Going Private Can Hurt the Taxpayers." *USA Today* (January 15, 1986): 10A.
7. Moe, Ronald C. *Privatization: An Overview From the Perspective of Public Administration.* Report no. 86-134 GOV, Washington, D.C.: Congressional Research Service, 1986. 63 pp.
8. U.S. Office of the Federal Register. *The United States Government Manual, 1987/88.* Washington, D.C.: GPO, 1987, 891 pp.
9. "Federal Workers: Competing in the Private Sector." *Government Executive 19:* 37-38 (March 1987).
10. U.S. Office of Personnel Management. *Federal Employee Direct Corporate Ownership Opportunity Plan: Fed CO-OP, and Alternative Contracting Out Approach.* Washington, D.C., 1987. 4 pp.
11. Guttman, Daniel. "Organizational Conflict of Interest and the Growth of Big Government." *Harvard Journal of Legislation 15:* 297-364 (1978).
12. Sullivan, Harold J. "Privatization of Public Services: A Growing Threat to Constitutional Rights." *Public Administration Review 47:* 461-467 (November/December 1987).
13. American Federation of State, County and Municipal Employees. *Passing the Bucks: The Contracting Out of Public Services.* Washington, D.C., 1983, 116 pp.
14. Kolderie, Ted. *What Do We Mean by "Privatization?"* Contemporary Issues Series no. 19, St. Louis, Mo., Center for the Study of American Business, Washington University, 1986. 16 pp.
15. Salamon, Lester M. "The Rise of Third-Party Government: Implications for Public Management." *Third-Party Government and the Public Manager: The Changing Forms of Government Action.* Washington, D.C.: National Academy of Public Administration, 1987. 57 pp.

NATIONAL LIBRARIES IN A TIME OF CHANGE

Maurice B. Line

National Libraries have received a great deal of discussion in the last 20 or 30 years. Not only have numerous articles been published on their nature and functions,[1,2] but there have been several major conferences on National Libraries, some with a worldwide representation, some restricted to a particular region of the world. National Libraries are not only of interest to librarians; they are of concern to politicians as national symbols or institutions of national significance. From the debate has emerged a partial consensus as to the role and functions of National Libraries, and a general view that no country is complete without one.

During this period of intensive discussion, how much progress has actually been made with National Libraries? If we look first at a continent where there were very few at the end of World War Two, Africa, we find that only one or two have been created since then. Some of the countries have national archives, but very few have National Libraries. Perhaps the most ambitious plans have been in Nigeria, the most populous country in Africa, where a National Library with quite wide powers was not only planned but actually set up and opened in 1964. Progress has however been very slow in the last 20 years, and the National Library has been unable to fulfil at all adequately several of the roles that it was empowered to perform.[3]

In other African countries, the view now is probably different from what it would have been 20 years ago, when there was optimism that National Libraries could in fact be established. In an implicit recognition that the funds required to set up an adequate National Library are not likely to be forthcoming in the near future, librarians have been debating not so much what a National Library should do but how national library functions can be performed without a National Library. One writer suggests no fewer than eight different alternative systems.[4]

"National Libraries in a Time of Change" by Maurice B. Line in *IFLA Journal* Vol. 14, no. 1 (1988), pp. 20-28; reprinted with permission from K. G. Saur Verlag, Munich, West Germany.

Reasons for this lack of progress—if progress is assumed to consist of the creation of a National Library—are obvious enough. Many countries in Africa are faced with serious crises—economic, climatic, agricultural, or political. In such circumstances it is not surprising if the government gives priority to production, agriculture, and political stability. It may give lip service to the importance of information in the future economy, but there are immediate problems that demand attention, and libraries are not one of them.

At the opposite extreme from Africa, National Libraries in developed capitalist countries have not had an easy time either. While libraries have long been accepted in these countries, they are no longer taken for granted in all of them as worthy of a large continuing public subsidy. Government funding for National Libraries has tended to decline in real terms, partly because of a radical shift in thinking on the part of many Western governments. They accept the importance of information as an economic resource, but in the same way as they see steel manufacture or the clothing industry as an economic resource: information should earn its own keep, in the same way as other resources do. Commercial information interests in such countries as the United States are now powerful, and they are effectively threatening some of the traditional functions of libraries. There has also been an emphasis on information services, databases and "added value", rather than on the basic resources of publications on which these activities are often based. It is not surprising therefore if National Libraries, which in most countries are fundamentally resources and not services, should be in a rather vulnerable position. In some countries they are for the first time having to justify themselves in terms of cost-effectiveness. The bigger and more prominent the National Library, the greater the pressures on it are likely to be.

In truth, very few countries have been able to realize an "ideal" National Library. They may adopt one of several positions. They may go off the idea altogether, and settle for a diluted form of National Library, having a wide range of functions but not fulfilling any of them in the way they would desire. Another option is to reduce the range of functions and try and do one or two really well. A third main option is to maintain or even extend the range of functions, supplementing government grants by earning money or by joint arrangements with the private sector.

Even with level funding, National Libraries would be faced with severe challenges. Not only is the cost of published material rising faster than the general level of inflation, but the number of publications issued per year is still growing, so that to maintain acquisitions at the present level National Libraries need to have an increase in funding in real terms each year. Not only that, but the range of published material is expanding. Whereas 20 or 30 years ago the majority of published output was in printed form, the proportion of "grey" literature has grown gradually, and there has been a spectacular growth in the output of various forms of non-book material—sound recordings, video recordings, etc. The "etc" includes computer software and publications that are made available only in electronic form, and never issued as printed pages at all. Legal deposit covers non-print materials to varying degrees in different countries—in some countries not at all. In other countries their collection is the responsibility of another institution than the National Library, for example a national sound and visual archive, or of no institution at all.[5] Quite apart from the problems of collecting such materials, especially if they are not subject to legal deposit, there are the problems of making them available, since a characteristic common to all of them is that they require some machinery in order to be used. This would not matter so much if there were a small number of standard and permanent formats, so that only a few different kinds of machine were needed; but this is far from the case. Not only is there a wide variety of formats, but they keep changing, so that there may be a number of items published in a particular form that goes out of fashion in a year or two, when the machinery becomes obsolete. Unless they can be converted to another format, a process which is often costly and not always easy, the library or archive has to maintain an ever-growing collection of machinery, some of which is obsolete but all of which has to be kept in working order.

The question whether such material should be collected nationally is not one that National Libraries can ignore. Even if they do not have, or do not wish to have, the responsibility themselves, they certainly have some responsibility to ensure that the materials are collected, for they are just as much part of the nation's culture and heritage, not to mention its information resource, as printed materials. In the UK the British Library has taken the lead in gathering together a small number of senior people in the main institutions involved in collecting such materials to try and ensure between them comprehensive coverage; the British Library itself has responsibility only for printed materials and sound recordings, and the latter are (like other non-print materials) not subject to legal deposit.[6]

If comprehensive collecting of the nation's publications is one traditional and accepted function of the National Library, conserving them is another. Only in the last decade have librarians generally been awakened to the scale and rate of deterioration of their collections.[7] The resources required to preserve a total collection in satisfactory condition are so vast that it is unlikely whether any library other than perhaps the Library of Congress can make them available. Whether the materials are preserved in their existing form or converted to some other form, for example microform or digital form, there are no quick or easy solutions. The advantage of conversion is of course that copies once made can be made available to other National Libraries (and indeed libraries of other kinds), so that the cost and labour can be shared among countries. Whatever solution is adopted, it is hard to believe that it will not be a selective one and that some materials will not be left unconserved, uncopied, and possibly unkept.

Conservation should include of course not only printed materials but also non-book materials and electronic publications. These give rise to special problems. Some of these have been mentioned earlier with reference to non-book materials. Publications in electronic form are amenable to constant revision—indeed, that is one of their advantages. If a copy is to be placed in the National Library, which version or versions should be deposited?[8]

To fulfil their traditional functions of comprehensively collecting the nation's publications and conserving them, then, National Libraries require far more resources than any but one or two are likely to be able to expect. Nor are such problems confined to countries with large outputs of published materials. In Africa, for example, the historical culture and even present day culture is very much an oral rather than a written one, and there is a responsibility to ensure that this culture is recorded for posterity, the more so as many of the countries are undergoing rapid social change.

Moreover, although the volume of published output is usually small compared with most developed capitalist countries, the problems of ensuring that legal deposit is observed or of collecting material in other ways are much greater, and certainly conservation is very much more difficult in tropical and subtropical climates.

A third traditional function is the recording of the nation's output of published material. In some countries an activity that was manageable a few years ago has become an increasing burden as a result of the increase in output, and possibly also of an extension of coverage of the national bibliographic record to other forms of publication than printed material. It might have been hoped that the expansion of activity could have been self-sustaining from the sale of records to other libraries, but this has not always proved to be the case. Nor is the conversion of existing records to form an exploitable database an operation to be undertaken lightly. All these activities are very demanding of resources.

At the same time as the fulfilment of traditional responsibilities creates serious problems for National Libraries, new opportunities arise. National Libraries have traditionally been resources of published material, available for consultation rather than exploitation in a more positive sense. That is, few National Libraries play a major role in document supply, whether by photocopy or loan, or in information services, whether from bibliographic databases or by serving particular client communities with information derived and processed from the collections. Some National Libraries that have moved some way in this direction have resisted the imposition of charges for such services, on the grounds that this would create a dangerous precedent—also perhaps because of a feeling that, whatever other kinds of library might do, National Libraries should be the last to charge. Others, such as the British Library, have embraced or at least accepted charges, on the equally valid grounds that it would be impossible to give the services at all unless they recovered all or most of their costs. In many cases National Libraries, even if they charge for services, cannot keep the income earned, so that there is little point in charging; they therefore either give rudimentary services free—rudimentary because they cannot be provided without more staff—or opt out of providing services altogether. This too can make them vulnerable, since governments may be reluctant to fund large and very expensive resources that are not exploited to the full.

It should be said that not all governments appear to think clearly about or act consistently towards National Libraries, in that they expect them to behave more efficiently and cost-effectively without giving them any incentives such as the ability to retain revenue earned—and if they do, they may reduce the money they give to the National Library. The negative incentive of reduced funding may achieve good results up to a point, but positive incentives are also needed. A low-achieving National Library may justifiably be able in some circumstances to blame its government.

This dilemma—whether to retreat into one's shell or break out of it, and if the latter how to do so in a practical way—is one that many National Libraries will have to face in the near future. On the one side lies the prospect of a passive collection with inadequate funds even to carry out traditional functions fully (a shrinking shell); on the other lies the possibility of a range of dynamic services based on the collection, with money earned from the services not only paying for the services but being used also to help maintain the collections. This bold statement of the alternatives simplifies them both; in particular, it does not tackle the practical difficulties of developing information services, quite apart from the question of retaining income. For example, is it right and proper that a publicly funded National Library should "go commercial" in such a way? Will not the services compete in some way with the private sector? If they are allowed to compete at all, must they not compete on fair and equal terms —and if so, will they not lose the contest? Where does the National Library, with all its traditions, find the right staff to offer positive and competitive information services? How does a publicly funded body, unable to borrow money or obtain extra resources to pump-prime services, bring them up to a level where it is sensible even to start charging? Even the exploitation of the national bibliographic record, profitable though it might be in a few years' time, cannot be achieved without committing resources to it first.

One possible solution would be to offer the exploitation of the National Library's collections to the private sector, which would generate from them commercial information products. This already happens to a certain extent, because private firms can and do use national libraries in the same way as other users, but it is very unlikely that the resources of most National Libraries are exploited to more than a fraction of their potential. Would it really be sensible or appropriate for a National Library to offer one or more private enterprises use of its resources for commercial exploitation without some form of return? Shall we see National Libraries entering into contracts with commercial organizations, or offering franchises? These are not hypothetical questions; they are all facing several National Libraries now, partly because of government pressures and partly because National Libraries themselves perceive the need for more self-help as an alternative to gradual erosion.

The questions just discussed are of interest at present mainly to certain highly developed capitalist countries, but it is impossible to believe that the policies they adopt will not have some impact, however indirect, on National Libraries in less developed countries and in socialist economies. Whether this impact will be good or bad is a matter for speculation. Certainly, the road along which some National Libraries, including the British Library, are travelling is not without its own dangers; but at least the dangers are interesting and challenging, and they are probably less than the dangers of erosion and dilution that would be our lot if we did not travel at all. To travel hopefully is better than to stay at home.

There is another major question that needs to be addressed, though there seem to be very few writings that touch upon it. This is the role of National Libraries in science and technology. It is related to the question of information services and exploitation because science and technology collections offer much more scope for these. In most countries, the National Library tends to have a strong bias towards the humanities and social sciences; and this is reflected and reinforced by the government ministry under which it comes, often a ministry of culture. This is in no way surprising. When the great National Libraries were created the vast majority of published output was in the humanities, and to a lesser extent in the social sciences; it is only in the years since World War One that science and technology have leapt ahead. As they have done so, scientists and technologists have demanded different services from what the National Library as constituted could provide—information services, good document supply services, indexing and abstracting services, and so on. As a result, national documentation centres for science and technology have been set up in many countries, usually under a different ministry from the National Library. The result tends to be a poorly funded National Library concentrating on the humanities and social sciences, and a relatively well funded national documentation centre performing rather different but related functions for science and technology. The documentation centres may or may not have substantial collections; in many countries the National Library still has legal deposit of publications in science and technology. This leads to a relationship that is often uneasy and sometimes antagonistic. At worst, the National Library can get left far behind the documentation centre, since it does not have nearly such a demanding clientele nor, usually, such a powerful ministry.

This raises the question of whether the requirements of the humanities are so different from those of the sciences that they cannot be provided by the same body. Certainly if they are to be provided by the same body, many National Libraries will have to change radically. One possibility is to have a National Library organized in two main divisions, working very closely together but offering rather different services and having rather different priorities in accordance with their different clienteles. This is the solution that was adopted for the British Library when it was restructured in 1984. It does not mean that there is no longer any tension or competition, but this occurs within the same body; given goodwill and suitable machinery for coordination it can be creative rather than destructive. Indeed, because of the much greater earning capacity of the Science, Technology and Industry division of the British Library, it has been able indirectly to help the Humanities and Social Sciences division; the gross expenditure of the two divisions is very nearly the same (in the current year 1987-88, the expected figures are £26.44 million ST&I, £25 million H&SS), but the net expenditure (gross minus earnings) is very widely different (respectively £14.3 million and £22.86 million).

Probably because of the history and tradition of National Libraries, some of them have tended to see humanities and social science publications as somehow of more "importance" than scientific and technological publications. In support of this, they might argue that most science and technology literature goes rapidly out of date, that anyway a great deal of it is rubbish, and that humanities literature represents the national culture in a way that science does not. It is doubtful whether the percentage of rubbish in different subjects differs all that widely, and there can be no objective way of testing this. Social science literature dates as quickly as science and technology literature; admittedly there are some sociological and economic classics, but in some science subjects such as botany, geology and zoology obsolescence is in fact very slow. As for the "cultural" argument, we are living in a scientific and technological society: this is our culture, and the national collection must surely represent it. Finally, yesterday's rubbish is today's sociology, and the day before yesterday's rubbish is today's history. If a culture produces a lot of rubbish, so be it; the national collection must reflect this, just as a national museum consists as much of everyday artifacts as of precious objects—it must have the contents of a medieval midden as well as of Tutankhamen's tomb.

A question that concerns all National Libraries is the problem of maintaining collections of whatever range and scope up to date with current acquisitions without adequate resources. As mentioned earlier, in some less developed countries, particularly in Africa, some writers are advocating the "distributed national library"—in effect, the national collection (however defined), including legal deposit materials, divided among several libraries. This solution is a novel one insofar as it does not have at the centre a National Library as such, but versions of it which include a National Library are quite common;[9] the Nordic countries offer notable examples. Even in countries where national library functions have been highly centralized, there is now more active thought being given to sharing responsibilities with other libraries. The British Library, for example, has encouraged the use of Conspectus to measure collection strengths in British research libraries, and the results will be used to explore whether and how far the British Library can reduce or even opt out of collecting in specific areas. This is unlikely to be a serious possibility in most of science and technology, but it is difficult to see how the country's total collections of humanities and social science material can be maintained otherwise. The days of the would-be comprehensive all-dominating National Library have gone. The National Library will retain a leading role, in the sense both of being the most significant library in the system and of guiding the management of national research collections, but that may become its main role. In smaller countries, such as New Zealand, the "total national resource" is likely to become an even more important concept.[10]

One possible role of the National Library is what might be called a residual one—doing the things that other libraries or bodies cannot or do not want to do. The collection of such a National Library would consist largely of material that no other library had acquired because hardly anyone ever needed it; its information services, if any, would be the kind that no commercial body would touch; and so on. This could be called the cost-ineffective model—a sort of bibliothecal hyena, picking up bits of meat that the lions had left. It leaves the bush tidy, but there is little else to be said for it as a main (rather than supplementary) activity.

What is happening is that the debate over the role and functions of the National Library is gradually changing its nature, though this has yet to be fully recognized. What we are really concerned with is *the performance of national library functions*—that is, library functions that must be, or are best, carried out at a national level. If one looks at functions such as legal deposit, bibliographic control of the nation's publications, conservation, document supply and so on, one can then explore alternative ways of carrying them out and decide on the best option for each.[11,12] Obviously this should be done as a total exercise, otherwise a variety of incompatible solutions may be produced in place of an overall solution. For example, if it were decided that a single National Library was the best means of maintaining the total national resource, but it were also decided that the best way of achieving national document supply was by cooperative methods, it would probably be undesirable to do both, since a national collection could if properly organized achieve an effective national document supply system. The functions themselves would not remain unchallenged; for example, it would not be assumed that all national imprints should be acquired, still less that they should all be retained permanently; nor that all publications should be described by records of equal level and quality in the national bibliography. The next step in national library planning should be to look at the various functions that have been put forward for the National Library—and possibly add some other functions to them—to consider whether they are necessary, and to analyze how they might best be carried out. The answers will differ from country to country, but the approach is surely valid for all. In carrying out this exercise one would of course bear in mind strengths and weaknesses in the existing system; and one would also look at the economic and practical realities, rather than design an "ideal" system that could never be achieved.

The priorities for national library functions will also differ from country to country, not only in scale but in importance. For example, the creation of the national bibliographic record is an important but very small function for a small less developed country, but leadership, training and planning of the nation's library system must be regarded as both important and major functions. This kind of analysis would help to show whether in fact African countries could manage without a conventional National Library, but might instead have a unit responsible for, say, legal deposit (as an archive only), the construction of the national bibliographic record, and national library planning, including a national acquisitions policy, as well as acting as a focus for relations with other countries. This would not be a National Library in the usually accepted sense of the word—its collection would be very small, for one thing—but rather a central unit and focus.

The various efforts that have been made to establish standard guidelines and generally agreed functions for National Libraries have perhaps been misplaced. There is no one model that can be applied to all countries. More than any other type of library, National Libraries do and must vary; they must reflect the culture, and relate to the needs, of their countries. Some of the older National Libraries did just this when they were set up, others grew out of private, often royal, collections; these may need to reconsider their nature and functions no less than newer National Libraries. Perhaps a National Library is no more than a library that carries out some national functions.

At the beginning of this article was mentioned the general view that no country is complete without a National Library. But, as we have seen, some countries do not have one, and are perhaps never likely to have; and in others a debate that might have been thought closed is being forcibly reopened. We cannot even assume that National Libraries are permanent institutions. Some have lost major parts (in Australia the visual and sound archive is now separate, as is the General Assembly Library in New Zealand), and in one country (Papua, New Guinea) the National Library was at one point actually threatened with closure. Others seem likely to shrink, though the shrinkage will probably be concealed under the respectable cloak of "resource sharing". To date debate has tended to be greatest where the National Library has been smallest, but debate is likely to grow in both volume and intensity in countries where the National Library is large and well established.

National Libraries may have a choice between being regarded as a prestigious but ultimately expendable cultural luxury or as a vital element in the nation's information system, and therefore a vital contributor to the nation's future economic health. Fewer and fewer countries may be willing to pay for expensive symbols of nationhood unless they are more than symbols. Not all National Libraries seem to be aware of the threats and dangers that face them—or are conscious of the opportunities that present themselves. Nor is it at all clear how well prepared they are to react to the threats and opportunities, or whether they can make the adjustment, perhaps a massive one, that may be required; size and dignity do not always go with adaptability. (Any comparison with dinosaurs should be avoided; they were around for 120 million years and are better known than they ever were 70 million years after they disappeared). Perhaps the debate needs to be brought down to a yet more fundamental level, and we should ask ourselves not simply what National Libraries should do but whether National Libraries are necessary, what they are *for*, and *why* they should do what everyone says they should do.

References

1. Line, Maurice B. and Joyce Line (eds.). *National libraries I.* London: Aslib, 1979 (Aslib Reader Series, 1).
2. Line, Maurice B. and Joyce Line (eds.). *National libraries II. 1977-86.* London: Aslib, 1987 (Aslib Reader Series, 6).
3. Aguolo, C. C. "The Evolution of the National Library of Nigeria". *Journal of Library History* 15(4): 393-426 (Fall 1980).
4. Mchombu, K. J. "Alternatives to the National Library in Less Developed Countries". *Libri* 35(3): 227-249 (September 1983).
5. Pinion, Catherine F. *Legal Deposit of Non-book Materials.* London: British Library, 1986 (Library and Information Research Report 49).
6. "The British Library and Non-book Materials". *Audiovisual Librarian* 12(1): 32-34 (February 1986).
7. Wilson, Alexander. "Moving to Planned Deterioration: Library Preservation Strategy at the National and Local Level, *in* Line, Maurice B. (ed.). *The World of Books and Information: Essays in Honour of Lord Dainton.* London: British Library, 1987, p. 197-207.
8. *Archival Aspects of Electronic Publications and Their Availability. Report on a . . . Seminar . . . November 1983.* London: British National Bibliography Research Fund, [1984].
9. Humphreys, K. W. "The Principles of the Relationship between National and University Library Collections as a Basis for a Network". *IFLA Journal* 9(1): 20-27 (1983).
10. Line, Maurice B. "The Total National Resource: Reflections on Document Provision and Supply in New Zealand". *New Zealand Libraries* 45(3): 45-49 (September 1986).

11. Line, Maurice B. "National Library and Information Planning". *International Library Review* 15(3): 227-243 (July 1983).
12. Line, Maurice B. "Performance Assessment at National Library Level". *In*: Blagden, John (ed.). *Do We Really Need Libraries? Proceedings of the First Joint Library Association/Cranfield Institute of Technology Conference on Performance Assessment*. Cranfield: Cranfield Press, 1983, p. 25-45.

PAY AS YOU READ

Thomas Stave

Last February 11,000 British authors found a royalty check in their mail. There is nothing unusual about that, except that this check was not for books bought in bookstores but borrowed from public libraries. Later this year Canadian writers, too, will receive checks for the use of their books in libraries. Americans have only recently become aware, if at all, that in some foreign countries authors are paid when library users read their books. It was a minor event for us when in 1979 British authors were given this right by Parliament, and when Canadian writers followed suit in 1986 there were only small ripples even in the American library press. The Canadian program of library royalties is the first manifestation in this hemisphere of what has been until now primarily a European phenomenon. The fact that American authors are also eager for this right, the so-called Public Lending Right, is therefore apt to be a surprise to American librarians—but not to the readers of the *Authors Guild Bulletin*.

The *Bulletin* always rewards a librarian's perusal. Authors, after all, share many of our concerns. They are interested in censorship, copyright, concentration in the publishing industry, government secrecy, and even libraries. And their opinions on these issues usually match our own. But in addition to matters of principle, authors are also interested in economic survival.

This fact is the first thing to understand in considering the authors' interest in Public Lending Right. The second thing to remember is this: authors know well that the ability to make a living from their work is possible only because society considers their continuing interest in their writing to be a matter of right, a form of property right called copyright. These two facts underlie a phenomenon that cannot be missed by the reader of the *Authors Guild Bulletin*: that for the past four years Public Lending Right has been its constant front-page topic.

"Pay As You Read" by Thomas Stave in *Wilson Library Bulletin* Vol. 62 (October 1987), pp. 23-28; reprinted with permission from *Wilson Library Bulletin*.

PLR Primer

Public Lending Right is the concept, recognized in some form by twelve countries, that the loan of a book by a public library constitutes a use for which the author should be paid. As a descriptive label, "Public Lending Right" is so lacking in precise meaning that nothing is sacrificed when, as is usually done, it is shortened to its initials, PLR. In Canada and among Authors Guild members PLR is more accurately known, respectively, as Payment for Public Use (PPU) and Authors Lending Royalty (ALR), but "PLR" still elicits more nods of recognition in English-speaking countries. Countries with PLR programs, in addition to the U.K., are the five Nordic countries, West Germany, the Netherlands, Australia, New Zealand, Canada, and (most recently) Israel. If the Belgian government introduces PLR legislation as expected, Belgium may soon become the thirteenth. There is much variety among these national plans in their specific details. Some, for example, base their payments on annual loans, while others are indexed to yearly bookstock censuses; some make only direct annual payments to authors, while others fund a sort of authors' social security as well. The essential common feature is that authors receive monetary payments from the government for the library use of their books.[1]

Historically, three arguments have been used, in varying strengths, to justify enacting PLR legislation: 1) Authors have a right, related to copyright, to be paid for the repeated use of their books by library users. 2) As most authors cannot make a living from their writing, the state has an interest and an obligation to help them maintain a living income. 3) PLR payments to national authors can be a useful means of bolstering the production of a national literature. Adding emotional warmth to all three claims is the suspicion, probably in the end not testable, that free library lending actually undermines book sales and royalties.[2]

American authors have officially attached themselves only to the first claim: the right to compensation. They do not wish to be seen as asking for state patronage, though they admit the additional income from PLR could mean for some authors the difference between writing and not writing. Nor do they see reason to fear for the survival of American letters in the way that the Scandinavian countries and Israel, for example, must fear for theirs. But they assert strongly that library borrowings of their works, like dramatization or photocopying or publishing in translation, are a form of repeated use of an intellectual creation that in justice ought to work to the advantage of the creators.

Efforts in the U.S.

News of the enactment in 1979 of Public Lending Right in the United Kingdom took American authors by surprise, most never having heard of it. But within four years the Authors Guild had decided PLR was both desirable and attainable. They took courage from the publication in 1981 of an issue of *Library Trends* on PLR (Spring 1981), which in turn stimulated a symposium at the Library of Congress in 1983.[3] If PLR legislation ever succeeds in this country, that event may be seen as seminal. Most of the interested parties—authors, librarians, and publishers—as well as the U.S. Copyright Office, the British Public Lending Right Office, and Senate Judiciary Committee staff were represented. Senator Charles Mathias (R-Md.) used the forum to have his intention announced to introduce a bill (S. 2192, 98th Cong.) establishing a commission to "study and make recommendations on the desirability and feasibility of compensating authors for the lending of their books by lending institutions." Two days before, the Guild had taken the tactical move of passing a council resolution in support of the PLR concept, in order to announce that at the LC meeting.

Since then the Guild's announced strategy has had two thrusts: to educate its members and opinion makers, and to get the Mathias bill passed. Two Guild members have pursued the education campaign by publishing articles where they are likely to reach a larger audience: Herbert Mitgang in the *New York Times Book Review* and William Goldman in the *American Scholar*. Apart from these articles, there has been little appearing before the general public on PLR.

On the legislative front progress has been slow as well. Senator Mathias's first bill received no action, though it seemed for a time that a similar bill in the 99th Congress (S. 658) might have a hearing. In the last months of the 99th Congress an identical bill (HR 5571) was introduced in the House by Representative Robert W. Kastenmeier (D-Wis.), chairman of the subcommittee of the House Judiciary Committee with responsibility for copyright matters. At this writing it is not clear whether new bills will be introduced in the 100th Congress. Senator Mathias retired at the end of the last session, and at that time no new PLR champion in the Senate had stepped forward.

The Mathias/Kastenmeier bill was carefully drafted for smooth passage. In the first place, it did not propose to enact PLR, merely to create a study commission. And in outlining the commission's charge it made certain assumptions about PLR very clear: the "reading public" must not be adversely affected, the funds must come from the government, and libraries must not have to deal with "burdensome administrative requirements." These are all principles learned the hard way over a three-decade struggle in the United Kingdom, during which British authors had to overcome accusations that their library royalty proposal would undermine the principle and practice of free public libraries.

American authors are in the position of their British counterparts in the pre-PLR years before 1979. In fact the British experience has a great deal to tell us about the "desirability and feasibility"—and the likelihood— of Public Lending Right in the United States.

The British Experience

Beginning in 1951, and heavily through the 1960s and 1970s, the topic of Public Lending Right dotted the pages of the *Author*, the journal of the U.K.'s Society of Authors, and the *Bookseller*, the magazine of the British book trade. Eric Leyland, librarian turned children's author, and novelist John Brophy, probably unaware of the young Scandinavian PLR movement of the late 1940s, were the first to protest what they saw as the unfairness to authors in free library loans. Brophy's particular contribution was to give the infant movement a catchword by proposing that a fee of one penny be levied on the reader for each book borrowed. Thus the "Brophy penny" became the first of many campaign slogans. What followed were twenty years of false starts, frustrations, fraternal squabbles, official studies, government promises, and constantly adapting strategies.[4] The leadership of the Society of Authors was challenged in the 1970s by two novelists, Maureen Duffy and Brigid Brophy (daughter of John Brophy), who founded a vigorous single-issue alternative called WAG, the Writers Action Group. With the boost from WAG's single-minded fervor the authors eventually won the day, when in 1979 with the backing of all major parties the Labour government's PLR bill was adopted. This was primarily enabling legislation, and after further delay Parliament approved the full implementing regulations, or "scheme," in 1982 (*The Public Lending Right Scheme 1982, Order 1982*, Statutory Instrument 1982 No. 719). The first payments were made to authors in 1984.

The authors' antagonists in this extended drama were the Library Association and the associations of local governmental authorities, which fund public library service in Britain. The local authorities behaved predictably, their job being to protect their treasuries from incursions. They reasoned, as did librarians, that as PLR money would have to come from somewhere, it might come from library budgets or increases in local taxes. Librarians, while just as protective of their own budgets, offered more wideranging arguments that reflected concerns for their users, for the libraries, for (in a rather different way) writers themselves, and about the justice of the asserted right itself. Some librarians strongly supported the authors' cause, but most who wrote about it challenged its basic assumptions: that authors were in fact hurt by library loans, or that their property rights in their books were not exhausted in their original purchase by a library. Some argued that a program of grants to authors or even subsidies for library book budgets would serve the authors better. In the end, of course, the philosophical question of a newly discovered right became a political one. The LA withdrew effective opposition when it became clear that the political question had been decided, taking some comfort in the knowledge that they had forced enough changes to make the legislation palatable.

The authors' strategists eventually recognized that the government was not prepared to accept a bill that laid the burden of PLR funding on libraries, their borrowers, or the local authorities. So whereas early bills enshrined the "Brophy penny" concept, the later versions insisted upon a central government fund. They also took care to eliminate from their proposals any method of measuring use that appeared to overburden library staff. The loans-based method of computing payments had for years been dismissed as requiring far too much library labor. Not until it was demonstrated that this could be accomplished by electronic data capture equipment, with little attention from library staff, did the authors put their weight behind this method. Loans being a more accurate measure of use than annual purchases or stock counts, this method was more attractive anyway for those who held strongly that PLR was not patronage, but payment for actual use. Another shift was away from a basis in copyright. The early bills had simply added PLR to the list of uses protected by copyright, until legal advice discouraged the approach. Under international copyright agreements such a program would have to be extended to nationals of other countries. And the benefits would accrue to the copyright holder, who was not necessarily the author.

Throughout the course of its development there was a gradual progress in the authors' understanding of the PLR idea, a movement away from patronage and toward what was often called "simple justice." Whereas early campaigners had drawn attention to the writers' poverty, this approach was eventually abandoned as self-demeaning and unconvincing, and "payment for use" became the emphasis.

How Public Lending Right Works

Stockton-on-Tees, in England's depressed Northeast, was the government's choice as the site for the Public Lending Right Office, now in the fifth year under its original registrar, John Sumsion. The Stockton office has three essential tasks: 1) to build a register of eligible authors and books, 2) to estimate the annual public library loans of each book, and 3) to distribute a fixed fund of money to authors in proportion to their loans. The PLR Office's work is primarily computer number-crunching, which does not need to be done in London. But the distance from the center of the writing and library communities is real. So the registrar receives advice on his operations through an advisory committee, with representatives of the principal organizations of writers, agents, publishers, librarians, and local authorities, as well as the firm of J. Whitaker and Sons (ISBN agents in the U.K.), and the government's Office of Arts and Libraries, which oversees PLR.

According to the scheme, an "eligible author" may be a writer, illustrator, compiler, editor, revisor or translator, who resides in the United Kingdom or West Germany (which has a reciprocal program), and who files a PLR registration form. An author need not be the copyright holder, but his or her name must appear on the title page of the book. Books are excluded if they have more than three authors or illustrators, or if they were written for hire or by a corporate body. Nonbooks such as periodicals or musical scores are also ruled out. From the information on their registration forms the PLR Office creates a computerized database of registered authors and titles. This database is enriched by the addition of bibliographic records from the London and Southeast Library Region (LASER). The LASER records permit the PLR Office to check on the accuracy and completeness of the authors' information, and also to discover editions the authors themselves had overlooked. On top of all this the PLR Office adds any additional records for books reported as loans by its sample libraries.

The PLR Office estimates annual loan figures by totaling up circulation records from computer tapes supplied by a representative sample of twenty public libraries. In 1985-86 these libraries accounted for 1.35 percent of all public library loans, and were selected to represent seven geographic regions, urban and rural sites, and various library sizes. The sample is rotated about every two years, ten libraries being replaced each year, to give greater sampling variety over time. Only books issued across the counter are recorded; on-site use, as in reference sections, does not count. And no other library types, such as academic, special, or school libraries, are currently within the scheme. In counting up loans, the PLR Office actually measures lending activity for each edition rather than for each title, to assure proper payments in cases where the contributors may vary from one version to another. Using the ISBN as its standard book record identifier makes this distinction relatively simple. By multiplying up the sample figures to national lending levels, adjusting for varying sampling strengths within different regions, the office produces an estimate of total British loans for each book (that is, for each edition).

By comparing the registration file with the loans file, the PLR Office can then compute the authors' payments. £2.75 million (about $4 million) was appropriated for 1985-86, which after expenses was reduced to £2.4 million. Of the 622 million total loans from British public libraries 223 million (35.9 percent) qualified for PLR. After adjusting for the upper and lower limits specified in the act—no payments over £5000 per author or under £1 per book—a basic rate per loan is calculated. This rate fluctuates from year to year, but has hovered around one penny. In 1985-86 each estimated loan earned 1.2 pence (about 1.8 U.S. cents). Of the 12,990 authors registered, 11,003 had some earnings, with the median payment being just under £50.[5]

Learning From Experience

Public Lending Right is now an accepted fact of life with British authors,

librarians, and publishers, and a good deal of experience has been gained
against which to evaluate the predictions that ushered in PLR five years
ago. It is especially useful for Americans to examine what was both hoped
and feared of PLR in the light of what has actually happened, because
many of the same assertions heard in Britain in the years leading up to
1984, on both sides of the question, are beginning to be heard in the
United States.

Will PLR compensate authors adequately for the library use of their
works? It is clearly true that British authors have achieved the right to
receive "some recompense"; and just as clear that some think it not
enough. The *Author* repeatedly urges its readers to press MPs for more
than inflationary improvements to the fund. The government continually
says it can afford nothing more than inflationary increases, and even that
not every year. The description of financial justice in this case will always
be a compromise between the authors' notion of the worth of a book loan
and the government's estimation of what can financially and politically be
afforded. John Brophy's 1951 penny would be worth four pence (six U.S.
cents) in today's decimal currency, or about four times what authors now
receive.

Will PLR promote authorship? In the Mathias bill this question is the
test to be used in judging the desirability of Public Lending Right. And
yet of all the questions it is the hardest to evaluate. The simplest answer
is to cite figures. Authors who clocked up loans from the sample libraries
are from £1 to £5000 richer this February. Of the 12,990 registered authors
15 percent got nothing but 4 percent received more than £1000. The
average payment was £219. But from the information available we cannot
know whether that additional income has permitted any more books to
be written, or any more authors to undertake or continue to write. Even
if there were a pure measure of literary productivity, it is hard to believe
that a mere £2.4 million annual infusion into the authors' economy could
by itself explain any improvement.

If we accept that improvements in author morale, however brief or
small, are good for the writing profession, then there is by now a small
body of testimony by which to judge. But unless the money available for
PLR is dramatically increased, the annual boosting of spirits is likely to
be the most visible effect of Public Lending Right on British authorship.
Even so, PLR is presently the government's largest program of financial
support for authors.

Will PLR only make the rich richer? It has been assumed that those
authors receiving large publisher royalties will be the ones to receive large
PLR payments. In general, this complaint is well founded, and comparing
best-seller lists with a PLR "best-lender" list provides some highly suggestive confirmation. Authors who sell well in bookstores—Barbara Cartland,
Catherine Cookson, Dick Francis, Victoria Holt—also issue well from

libraries. But the comparison also points out significant areas of difference, as the following exercise shows.

The *Sunday Times* produces weekly best-seller lists (reprinted in the *Bookseller*) based upon reports from a selection of bookstores. For the period July 1985 through June 1986 the PLR Office published its own list, "PLR Estimates," of the 100 most often lent editions (usually the main hardback version: loans clocking up on other editions would not be figured into this list). Only ten of these titles found themselves on the *Sunday Times* lists as well: two were hardbacks, two were hardback fiction, and eight were paperbacks (two titles appeared on more than one best-seller list).

This sort of comparison is a simple and in some ways misleading one, especially as it focuses on only the most active titles. But it does suggest a relationship between book sales and library loans that is not so simple. In the first place, books remain "on-shelf" in libraries far longer than they stay "in-print" with publishers. Consequently, many of the best-lenders are older titles. Of the 100 most heavily loaned editions in 1985-86, half were first published in 1981 or earlier. That means that PLR payments in some cases continue to come in long after royalties have dried up. And, too, some categories of books do far better in libraries than in bookstores, and vice versa. Of the eighty *Sunday times* best-sellers, fully half were reference books or nonfiction of some sort, whereas the PLR list consists exclusively of middle-brow fiction.

When patterns of this sort began to emerge from PLR statistics the registrar, John Sumsion, made inquiries with publishers. He learned that 60 to 80 percent of the sales of some types of books are to libraries. High-quality, highly priced children's books, serial hardback fiction, and literary novels by unknown authors fit into this pattern.[6]

By the lights of the pure PLR principle, though, this answer misses the point. If, as its proponents argue, PLR is merely the rightful recompense for actual library use, and some of the rich are thereby further enriched, no one should worry. But the drafters of the scheme made a compromise between the aims of right and patronage, and set a top limit of £5000 per author (originally £1000 per title), to give less well-off authors a larger piece of the pie. Fifty-nine authors exceeded the maximum payment in 1985-86. The money not paid them—£272,000, or 11 percent of the sum appropriated—was plowed back into the fund, increasing the other authors' payments by nearly 15 percent.

Will PLR be perfectly just when not all categories of books, authors and libraries are included? The scheme as first adopted seems by hindsight to have chosen fairly narrow categories. This approach was intended to make the scheme as simple and workable as possible. After several years' experience, a number of exclusions proved to be false efficiencies and were dropped. In amendments to the law these types of authors were let in: editors, compilers, translators, authors whose co-authors (or illustrators) were dead, and nationals of foreign countries with reciprocating PLR programs. Illustrators had been in from the start. Co-authors or illustrators ordinarily work out among themselves their individual shares of PLR, but fixed percentages were established for editors and compilers (20 percent) and translators (30 percent). Publishers, who supported the authors in their campaign, and who might with equal reason claim a right to PLR, have not been included.

Most of the remaining exclusions—corporate authorship, works for hire, nonbook formats, works with more than three contributors, works by nonresident authors (except, currently, West Germany)—are not at the moment controversial. But the next revision of the act may bring into consideration books used in other types of libraries, specifically academic libraries and the reference sections of public libraries. There is no logical reason why they should not be included, but different counting techniques will be needed. Reference books, not being controlled through circulation systems, have no accurate record made of their use. And academic libraries, with their reserve collections and varying loan periods, have use patterns sufficiently different from public libraries that a simple measure of loans may be less useful than say, an annual census of the titles in their collections.

Will PLR place an unacceptable administrative burden on libraries? Out of 6,500 library service points, PLR relies upon 20 each year for its sample data on book loans. Two relatively recent developments have made this sort of sampling feasible: the almost universal adoption by publishers of the ISBN as a unique edition identifier, and the installation in some libraries of computerized circulation control systems. By 1983 enough libraries were computerized that the registrar could select from them a sample representing the main geographic regions, urban and rural settings, and "principal" and "ordinary" service points. In all but four instances existing systems could be modified to supply monthly tapes in the format PLR required.

At the beginning of a sample library's participation, its existing loans system must be modified to produce monthly tapes for the PLR Office, to weed out non-qualifying materials (such as sound recordings or musical scores), and to produce a file of book records needing additional identifying data (such as missing ISBN, author, or title) for later checking. A library's ongoing involvement usually includes running the monthly PLR tape program, supplying book details if missing or conflicting with the PLR Office's own database records, and working out system bugs should they occur. A small side-benefit to the library is that in the process of having its records run against the PLR Office's, its own bibliographic data can be cleaned up over time.

The PLR Office reimburses expenses to its sample libraries. In 1985-86 the cost of setting up ten new sample libraries and running all twenty was

£49,000 with starting-up costs taking about half of that money. It could be objected that money reimbursed an organization is rarely applied to the actual expense incurred. And libraries might conceivably complain that staff are being asked to postpone their own work in order to do the PLR office's. But my conversations with both the registrar and with many participating librarians have turned up no major dissatisfactions. In fact, there seem to be some compensations for participating librarians above the monetary reimbursement. Some librarians have found PLR statistical reports interesting, as they can compare their own lending rates for various categories of books with those calculated for the full sample.

Might PLR restrict libraries' freedom to select books according to their usual policies and practices? It is difficult to detect the specific cause for worry in this complaint, but it was voiced in the U.S. as recently as 1982.[7] There may be at least two thoughts at the root of it. One is the concern that if circulation figures became well known, pressure might be exerted on libraries either a) to tie collection development policies more closely to actual circulation patterns, or conversely, b) to change collection development policies to try to reverse disturbing circulation trends. In fact, the first publication of PLR statistics showing the remarkable popularity of certain authors of light romantic fiction caused one librarian to wonder whether public libraries had not already given themselves over to the "give-them-what-they-want" school of librarianship.[8] These same statistics brought other, more alarming comments from an unexpected source. The conservative Adam Smith Institute published in 1986 a report strongly challenging the very notion of a publicly supported library system. The anonymous author of *Ex Libris* (now known to be one Douglas Mason) based a part of his argument on conclusions he drew from PLR loans data: "In the light of the claim that libraries are essential to encourage education and learning, it is significant that the great bulk of the [PLR] money is going to the writers of popular fiction." The *Sunday Telegraph* newspaper seconded Mason's criticisms after PLR's 1986 results were publicized in January.[9] All these responses were in their own way superficial and misleading, as they looked at little more than the list of 100 most borrowed titles, and did not take into account the use patterns of even those; very light fiction can be read rapidly and such books can clock up circulation figures far out of proportion to their numbers on the shelves. Nevertheless, they showed how suggestive even these figures can be, how much interest there can be in the library's role in society, and how important it is for librarians to try to extract the real significance from available data such as that produced by PLR.

There is a second reason some librarians worried about PLR interference with the book selection freedom of the sample libraries. They feared that librarians' knowledge of the effect their decisions could have on author's PLR payments might become a subtle new influence on their selection and weeding decisions. Since the scheme went into operation there have been no such doubts expressed, either by sample libraries or by others. What is, perhaps, more interesting is that the authors have not raised the question themselves. They have a very personal interest in the sampling process, but seem also to have an implicit faith in the integrity and fairness of library book selectors. A more real possibility is that authors may try to influence their ratings by donating copies of their books to sample libraries. The advice of the PLR Office has been that if sample libraries choose to accept such books under usual gift policies, they do so on behalf of the entire library system, with no promise the books will be placed in that particular library. To deal with the possibility of conspiratorial mass borrowings, the PLR Office built an "overlimit" check into its own system. Any title borrowed more than six times from a library in a month is kicked out for questioning. While these overlimit reports do occur, a few actually represent legitimate heavy borrowing. The others can be traced to a problem in a library's system or practices, and not to deliberate cheating. So the feature has been useful, not in detecting tampering, but in spotting other errors that might raise a book's score.

Will PLR be too expensive to administer? In 1985-86 the Public Lending Right Office employed 14.5 FTE staff and spent £248,000 on operating costs, including the money reimbursed sample libraries. Operating costs are currently 12.7 percent of the total appropriation, but the relative costs of administration would, of course, diminish with any improvements to the fund itself.

An increase in the number of libraries sampled would of course increase administrative costs. Analysis of PLR figures has shown substantial variation between libraries and for individual authors from year to year. So statisticians are currently studying those variations to see whether a larger sample or an even more frequent rotation is called for. The fact that a large number of libraries and vendors have already made PLR modifications to their circulation systems means that adding libraries to the sample can now be done at much less expense.

Making it Work in the U.S.

If American authors are to get PLR they will have to take to heart the lessons of their British counterparts, at least those that can apply to their circumstances, avoiding what failed and emulating what worked. Naturally, not all the lessons apply. American authors will not, for example, be able to exploit with equal force the alarming and heady perception British authors had of the enormity of their injury from library loans. Lord Willis observed during the 1975 parliamentary debates that in Britain thirty-eight books were borrowed for every four bought, while in the United States the ratio was thirteen to fourteen. More recent studies examining library use from a slightly different angle have shown that in 1983 19 percent of American adults got their current book from the library, while in 1980 38 percent of British adults used the library as their source. Nor can American authors focus on a centralized public library system operating under national legislation. While public libraries in Britain are run by local governments, they receive their mandate and legislative framework from the Public Libraries and Museums Act of 1964. Because Parliament governs libraries in this way, authors could use Parliament as the forum in which to air their grievance.

Those were some of the favorable preconditions the British authors faced. But they succeeded finally because they did the important things in the right way. Strategically, the best course seems to have been to hold firm on a small number of non-negotiables (e.g., a loans-based scheme, central funding) and be flexible on all else. They produced a handful of dedicated leaders, well informed about parliamentary procedures, the British book world, foreign PLR programs, information technology, and public libraries; and having the skills to carry their case to the public as well as to the government. These were supported by a large grassroots army of campaign workers. At its peak the Writers Action Group had about 1,000 members. Brigid Brophy acknowledges the significant help of scores of supporters, including such well-known writers as Ted Hughes, John Fowles, Kingsley Amis, Lady Antonia Fraser, and Graham Greene. That numbers like this could be recruited says as much about the willingness of British writers to organize for collective action as it does about their desire for PLR. Whether American writers are able to muster such corporate discipline remains to be seen.

One great mistake in the PLR campaign was made by authors and librarians alike. For perhaps the first time in their experience, their normally congenial relationship was tried by an issue that put them on opposite sides of the table; and the response of many (not all) on both sides put an important and fruitful alliance in jeopardy. Librarians, for their part, responded with a massive opposition that now seems far out of proportion to their reasonable interests. Although the two communities now appear to have repented of their differences, the amount of good left undone because of the prolonged bad feelings is an imponderable that Americans would do well to ponder. If the authors' initiative amounts to anything, librarians would be far better served by a system creatively designed to meet their needs as well as the needs of authors. Public librarians, for example, now frustrated by the shortage of detailed statistical information on library use, could find that a carefully structured loan sampling system, enhanced by the addition of other variables, would go a long way toward making up those deficiencies. That can happen only if librarians and authors find a way to make common cause in a matter of common interest.

Notes

1. The most up-to-date comparison of various European programs is Per Kogeson, "Authors' Lending Royalty Plans in Europe Detailed," *Authors Guild Bulletin* (Spring 1986): 1, 22-23.
2. For opposite opinions, see Brigid Brophy, *A Guide to Public Lending Right* (Aldershot, England: Gower, 1983), 52-57; J. G. Cullis and P. A. West, "The Economics of Public Lending Right," *Scottish Journal of Political Economy* 24 (June 1977): 169-174.
3. John Cole, "Public Lending Right: A Symposium at the Library of Congress," *Library of Congress Information Bulletin* 43 (December 12, 1983): 427-432.
4. For historical treatments from several perspectives, see Raymond Astbury, "The Situation in the United Kingdom," *Library Trends* 29 (Spring 1981): 661-685; Victor Bonham-Carter, *The Fight for Public Lending Right, 1951-1979* (London: The Society of Authors, n.d.); Brophy, 105-130; R.J.B. Morris, *Parliament and the Public Libraries* (London: Mansell, 1977), 170-175, 190-96 and passim.
5. Great Britain, Public Lending Right Office, *Information on Fourth Year's Results* (Stockton-on-Tees: Public Lending Right Office, 1987), p. [4].
6. John Sumsion, "What the Figures Show," in *Back to Books*, ed. Peter Mann (Report No. 44) (Loughborough: Centre for Library and Information Management, Loughborough University of Technology, 1985), 77.
7. Edith McCormick, "PLR Could Cost Libraries Millions," *American Libraries* 14 (February 1983): 107.
8. "Pushing Pap," *Assistant Librarian* 77 (December 1984).
9. Bill Jamieson, "Should Libraries Be Privatized?" *Sunday Telegraph*, 11 January 1987.

GOVERNMENT INFORMATION: LESS IS DANGEROUS

Nancy C. Kranich

As last year's Iran/Contra hearings demonstrated, denial of information precludes participation in the governmental process. This is no less true when it is the public that is denied than when it is Congress or cabinet members. Yet, although the erosion of government information has been underway for seven years, we are only now seeing public recognition that basic democratic values are at risk. Until Oliver North and Fawn Hall revealed how they shredded and concealed documents, "the already stricken and worsening national information situation" was probably "the best-kept secret since the U.S. Air Force bombed Cambodia." [1]

Since 1981, the federal government has consistently reduced its publication and other information dissemination activities. Such reductions are of particular concern to university faculty who rely heavily upon the federal government to fund research, collect data, publish reports, disseminate information, and promote access to scholarly resources.

These reductions are of equal concern to university librarians who work closely with scholars and students in locating data and other resources provided by government agencies. The government information policies that have emerged over the last seven years are less than sympathetic to the academic tradition of free access to information. They result from specific administrative directives, interpretations and implementation of the 1980 Paperwork Reduction Act, recommendations of the Grace Commission, the pursuit of privatization, the increasing use of security classification, and agency budget cuts.

Information about the government's own activities is of crucial importance if citizens are to make judgments about public policy. The philosophy underlying the federal government's responsibility to disseminate information about its activities was articulated in 1787 by James Wilson, a delegate to the Constitutional Convention, who stated, "the people have

a right to know what their agents are doing or have done."² Recently,
Representative Glenn English, chair of the House Subcommittee on Government Information, reaffirmed this principle in a response to a draft
circular on the management of federal information resources from the
Office of Management and Budget:

> Informed public debate is the basis of our form of government and
> is the bedrock of the First Amendment to the Constitution. These values
> are reflected in numerous laws guaranteeing citizens a right of access
> to government information, such as the Freedom of Information Act,
> the Government in the Sunshine Act, and the law establishing the Federal
> Depository Library Program.³

Since the earliest days of the Republic, our federal government has
made provisions to inform the public of its acts and to collect information
essential to its operation. Today, the federal government is the largest
collector and largest publisher of information in the United States. It is
also a major consumer and subsidizer of information resources. Government funding for education and libraries has provided major markets for
the publishing industry while several federal agencies have underwritten
the production of information products on massive scales. In fact, the
largest scientific, technical, and medical databases have been created and
maintained by the government.⁴

When the Reagan Administration took office, it cited budgetary constraints as an excuse to eliminate one-fourth of the government's 16,000
publications. Among the rich sources of information totally eliminated
were: several subject reports of the decennial census including *Black Population, Persons of Spanish Origin and Surname, Labor Force Status and
Work Experience, Education, Occupational Characteristics,* and *Household and Family Composition; Health Resources Statistics; Housing and
Urban Development Trends; Unemployment Rates for State and Local
Governments; Weekly Petroleum Status Report;* and such periodicals as
Housing and Urban Development Trends, the *Quarterly Journal of the
Library of Congress* and *Labor Literature.*

In March 1987, the Office of Management and Budget boasted about
the elimination of government publications. "Unnecessary spending on
the printing and distribution of government publications can and has been
eliminated," said OMB, and "procedures have been established to tightly
control agency plans to create new publications or expand distribution of
existing ones."⁵

Through its directives, the Reagan Administration has stressed "maxi-
mium feasible reliance on the private sector" as a rationale to privatize
and commercialize the dissemination of documents.⁶ This has resulted in
consistently higher charges even though the taxpayers have already paid
the basic costs of gathering and organizing the information. Further-

more, federal documents are no longer distributed through the Depository Library Program, a nationwide system of 1,400 libraries that provides access to government information. The Administration has, at the same time, drastically increased the amount of information kept secret. According to Thomas Blanton of the National Security Archive, the number of decisions to classify information grew from 17 million in 1982 to nearly 22 million in 1985.[7] Moreover, under new uniform fee schedule guidelines issued by the Office of Management and Budget on March 27, 1987, obtaining information through the Freedom of Information Act may become prohibitively expensive. This would occur if an agency decides not to waive the fee for search costs in addition to fees for the reproduction of records. In order to waive the extra fee, a requestor must reveal the purpose of the search, thereby violating the confidentiality of the research process.[8]

The Administration has also greatly restricted the release of scientific and technical information. Federal research grants have contained pre-publication review clauses. Scientists and engineers have been pressured into withdrawing contributions from open technical conferences. Foreign students have been barred from attending meetings or conducting research in the United States and denied admission to certain university classes. Each government agency is required to review regularly all research grants, contracts, or cooperative agreements for potential classification.[9]

In 1984, the President signed National Security Decision Directive 145, "National Policy on Telecommunications and Automated Information Systems Security," which authorizes the government to protect sensitive non-government information, the loss of which could adversely affect the national security. The Administration claimed that unclassified data available in commercial databases could be pieced together like a mosaic that "can reveal highly classified and other information when taken in aggregate."

Over the last few years, representatives from the Defense Department, the Central Intelligence Agency, and the Federal Bureau of Investigation have visited such private information companies as Mead Data Centers, purveyors of the full-text databases Lexis and Nexis, and Dialog Information Services, an abstract and full-text deatabase vendor with users in some 80 countries. The government agents sought information about the security of the databases and about their users, and attempted to place the companies in a position of limiting access and policing their customers.[10]

FBI agents also visited several libraries to determine how foreigners were using databases. At the State University of New York at Buffalo, the FBI served a subpoena to divulge the nature of an online search request that had been performed in the library for a foreign student. In June 1987, government officials approached Columbia University librarians, inquiring about "materials being used by foreign nationals in [their] science libraries." The librarians did not cooperate with the FBI, citing their policies in regard to privacy, confidentiality, and respect for academic freedom.[11]

Donna Demac, a professor at New York University who has written extensively on information policy issues, views such efforts to exclude foreign students—who represent one third of all graduate students—from various projects and technologies on campus as self-defeating in the long term.[12] Such attempts to control private and federal information flow, fears Herbert B. Landau, the president of Engineering Information, Inc. and the National Federation of Abstracting and Information Services, "will backfire and lead to a major decline in our domestic information industry, loss of control over its own information infrastructure, and retaliation by other nations."[13]

In November 1986, in yet another attempt to expand its secrecy campaign, the Reagan Administration ordered everyone with access to classified information, including university professors, scientists, medical researchers, and others conducting government-sponsored research, to sign a Classified Information Nondisclosure Agreement—Standard Form 189A—that is "binding forever unless revoked by an 'authorized representative' of the U.S. government."[14] The form that university researchers must sign has two intentions, according to Steven Garfinkel of the Information Security Oversight Office: "to remind people not to disclose, and to provide evidence, should the Justice Department decide to prosecute, of a person's knowledge and consent that disclosure could result in criminal penalties."[15] Demac adds that such actions "clearly jeopardize both the basic groundwork of communication in our society and the competitiveness of American society."[16]

The Department of Energy made another noteworthy attempt to curtail access to unclassified scientific and technical information in August 1987. Its Technical Information Division asked organizations receiving their reports to sign a document that states: "By electing to receive this material, you are agreeing to limit access to the microfiche to only those persons and organizations authorized to receive them . . . [i.e.] government agencies and their contractors, and Department of Energy offices and contractors."[17] This agreement which, in effect, requires libraries to act as the government's agent in restricting access, is plainly inimical to the very purpose of research libraries and universities.

The Office of Management and Budget's decision to privatize the National Technical Information Service (NTIS) is of equally grave concern to research universities and librarians. This service was created more than 30 years ago to "make the results of technical research and development readily available to industry and business, and to the general public."

No one can deny that NTIS has done this job admirably, and at no cost to the taxpayer. The service makes available federally-funded scientific and technical reports that are free from copyright restrictions. NTIS also prepares indexes and abstracts of federally-supported scientific and technical reports and makes them available through the Depository Library Program, as well as provides a centralized source for the sale of such reports at reasonable prices.

In congressional testimony, Harvard University Vice President for Government, Community and Public Affairs John Shattuck, speaking for the Association of American Universities and the Association of Research Libraries, told Congress that privatization is likely to result in:

• the elimination of documents with low sales potential.
• the probable loss of a permanent archival collection of older reports.
• the probable loss of foreign research reports.
• increased prices for documents.
• the establishment of proprietary rights over NTIS products.
• commercially driven decisions about all collections and services.
• increasing pressure to delete "sensitive" but unclassified information.[18]

In the long run, Shattuck concluded, restrictive federal information policies would lead to a stagnation of basic sciences. He cited several relevant National Academy of Sciences reports, one in 1986 that claimed the continued health of U.S. science depends on openness and communication. He also referred to the long-term negative effects on national security if broad communications restrictions retard rapid technological development.[19] Shattuck concluded that "overbearing restrictions on the flow of scientific and technical information can severely hurt the process of discovery, invention, research, and development no matter what one's view of the role of government may be." [20]

Government censors have devoted extensive attention to science and technology, but Administration officials have also heavily scrutinized other subject fields. Under the Paperwork Reduction Act of 1980, the Office of Management and Budget received the authority to review all data collection efforts of executive branch agencies. These agencies as well as various congressional committees have charged OMB with obstructionism: "Allegations of improper use of its powers include OMB's hostility to any data collection dealing with minorities and discrimination, questions concerning the environment and public health, and social science generally. In matters calling for medical or other scientific expertise, unqualified OMB officers are charged with overruling agency scientists." [21]

Jurisdiction questions were again raised in August 1987 when the Joint Economic Committee of Congress held a hearing on the potential effects of OMB's last-minute proposal to drop from the 1988 Census Dress Rehearsal roughly 30 questions scheduled for inclusion. Committee Chairman Paul S. Sarbanes began that hearing by noting that "Access to accurate, comprehensive and timely data is indispensable to sound decision-making." [22] Added Sarbanes:

The Committee is deeply concerned about the impact these severe cuts will have on the federal statistical infrastructure. OMB is proposing the elimination and curtailment of essential statistics in critical areas, including housing, transportation, and employment. This could have a crippling effect on the decision-making process in both the public and private sectors. Reliable statistical data does not guarantee good policies, but it is a vital factor in making good policies more likely.[23]

The erosion and restriction of government information clearly threatens libraries. At greater risk is the Depository Library Program that assures citizens access to government information through the donation of non-classified information to 1,400 libraries around the country, many of which are at universities and colleges.

Protests by librarians and intervention by concerned members of Congress may have temporarily thwarted attempts by the Government Printing Office (GPO) to discontinue hard copy for all dual format (microfiche and paper) documents sent to depository libraries. But with GPO appropriations cut from $29.9 million in 1985 to $23.6 million in 1987,[24] GPO may eventually have no other budget-cutting options than to eliminate more and more paper items. Unfortunately, microfiche is not favored by library users because it is cumbersome to read, expensive to reproduce in hardcopy, and takes much longer to reach libraries.

A parallel development has been the accelerating tendency of federal agencies to utilize computer and telecommunications technologies for data collection, storage, retrieval, and dissemination. In the process, the government has increasingly turned to contractual arrangements with commercial firms for the dissemination of information collected at taxpayer expense. User charges for government information have risen, and a growing amount of government information has become available in electronic format only.

Because much of this information is essential for research, the Congressional Joint Committee on Printing, which has oversight responsibilities for the Government Printing Office, has urged the GPO to initiate pilot projects to test the dissemination of federal information in electronic format to depository libraries.

Some 16 federal agencies have agreed to participate in the program, but the House Appropriations Committee has denied the transfer of the $800,000 necessary for these pilot projects in 1988, indicating that prospective participants should include the private sector. This decision came after information industry groups complained to Congress that they have not been involved in pilot project development, despite the presence of their members on the Joint Committee's task force that recommended the pilots.

Continued delays in implementing these pilot projects may result in the eventual loss of information to depository libraries, particularly if the privatization of databases ensues. With the bulk of publications such as the census expected to be distributed only electronically in the future, scholars may ultimately lose affordable access to essential research tools. The Depository Library Program is not the only endangered library service, and the decreasing availability of government information is not the only Administration-initiated threat. Other attacks on library services have included Presidential budget proposals to eliminate the Library Services and Construction Act, Title II of the Higher Education Act (which supports academic library programs), and postal subsidies for fourth class (library rate) mail. These assaults are creating a precarious environment for assuring library users their right to know.

Librarians are on the warpath against attempts to limit access to government information. To protect the interests of their users, librarians have become the most outspoken opponents of every action that diminishes information access. To better chronicle Reagan Administration moves, the American Library Association (ALA) is publishing a semi-annual report entitled "Less Access to Less Information By and About the U.S. Government." [25] The 1981-1984 report contains 71 entries in 18 pages, while the 1985-86 report contains 116 entries in 34 pages, clear evidence that the trend toward restrictions on access is accelerating.

This alarming and continuing pattern spurred ALA to establish a Coalition on Government Information. The Coalition, formed in 1986, is focusing national attention on efforts to limit access to government information and developing public awareness and support for improvements in access to government information.

Among the more than 50 groups that are either members or supporters of the Coalition are the American Association for the Advancement of Science, the American Civil Liberties Union, the Association of Research Libraries, and the National Newspaper Association. The NEA center in Washington has hosted some Coalition meetings. Interested organizations are welcome to join the Coalition.[26]

ALA is not the only group organizing efforts to protest Regan Administration action. The Advocacy Institute in Washington has recently assembled a "Right To Know Committee of Correspondence" to rally broad-based national support. This group intends to increase communication with those interested in Right to Know issues and develop strategies to draw attention to them.

Congressional interest and concern about diminishing access to government information is also growing. Hearings on various information topics are now underway in both the Senate and the House. Bills to curtail Administration efforts have been introduced, most recently from Representative Doug Walgren of Pennsylvania. Walgren's bill would prohibit the contracting out of NTIS services. The Senate took a similar action. Congress has also passed legislation to transfer responsibility for developing a government-wide computer security program from the National Security

Agency to the National Bureau of Standards.

On other fronts, the American Federation of Government Employees and the National Federation of Federal Employees have filed a suit to broaden a legal challenge to the Reagan Administration's use of secrecy pledges governing classified information. And the Occupational Safety and Health Administration has expanded its "right-to-know" regulations to all employers who must inform workers about any potential hazardous substances on the job.

Today, government information is fast becoming an endangered resource. Without the vigilance and concern of organizations interested in protecting their own informational interests and preserving the public's right to know, access to government information could deteriorate still further. At risk is far more than the scholar's freedom to pursue research and the student's ability to discover.

As Donna Demac has so aptly concluded in her book *Keeping America Uninformed*: "If government abandons its basic information functions, how will progress be measured? How will history be remembered?" [27] More important, how can we expect a system of government based on the ability of an informed citizenry to determine the conduct of public affairs to survive?

Notes

The author gratefully acknowledges the assistance of Donna Demac, Anne Heanue, Eileen Cooke, Ira Mothner, and Jaia Barrett in preparing this article.

1. Herbert I. Schiller, "Information, Important Issues for '88," *The Nation* (July 4-11, 1987), 1.
2. Statement made August 11, 1787, as recorded by James Madison. *Debate on the Adoption of the Federal Constitution in the Convention Hall at Philadelphia in 1787.* Rev. and newly arranged by Jonathan Eliot. (Philadelphia, Pa.: J.B. Lippincott and Co., 1845).
3. Rep. Glenn English, Chairman, Subcommittee on Government Information, Justice and Agriculture, U.S. House of Representatives, letter to Douglas H. Ginsburg, Administrator for Information and Regulatory Affairs, Office of Management and Budget, May 15, 1985.
4. Patricia Schuman, "Social Goals vs. Private Interests: Players in the Information Arena Clash," *Publishers Weekly* (November 23, 1984), 56.
5. U.S. Office of Management and Budget, *Management of the United States Government, FY 1988* (Washington, D.C.: Government Printing Office, March 1987), 76.
6. Perhaps the most significant single attempt to control government information is the promulgation of the Office of Management and Budget Circular A-130: *Management of Federal Information Resources*, which provides a general policy framework for the management of federal information resources. Other OMB directives that affect publications and privatization efforts are Circular A-3: *Government Publications*, which requires annual reviews of agency publications and detailed justifications for proposed periodicals, and Circular A-76: *Performance of Commercial Activities*, which encourages the contracting out of certain commercial activities and includes libraries in its list along with laundries, dry cleaners, motor pools, and refuse collection. OMB has recently issued

proposed rules, "Controlling Paperwork Burdens on the Public: Regulatory Changes Reflecting Amendments to the Paperwork Reduction Act," *Federal Register* (July 23, 1987), 52: 27768, which would give it three-year "sunset" review power over all federal regulations requiring information. Yet another set of new rules affecting government printing is the government-wide procurement regulation implemented July 1, 1987: *Federal Acquisition Circular 84-25,* which removes the requirement that executive branch agencies obtain approval of the Congressional Joint Committee on Printing to use non-government printing operations, thereby further privatizing government printing activities, and removing still more publications from the Depository Library Program.

7. Sara Frankel, "Library for FOIA Papers," *Mother Jones* (December 1986), 11: 18.
8. For a comprehensive review of the Reagan Administrative's campaign to increase government secrecy and censorship during his first term, see Donna A. Demac, *Keeping America Uninformed: Government Secrecy in the 1980's* (New York: Pilgrim Press, 1984), and Eve Pell, *The Big Chill* (Boston: Beacon Press, 1984).
9. The American Association of University Professors issued several reports on these topics in 1982-83. See "Federal Restrictions on Research: Academic Freedom and National Security," *Academe* (September/October 1982), 68: 18a-20a; "The Enlargement of the Classified Information System," *Academe* (January/February 1983), 69: 9a-14a; and "Government Censorship and Academic Freedom," *Academe* (November/December 1983), 69: 15a-17a. Also, the Association of American Universities has prepared for the Department of Defense-University Forum, "National Security Controls and University Research: Information for Investigators and Administrators," August 1987, which offers background materials on government policies as they affect university research.
10. Charles L. Howe and Robert Rosenberg, "Government Plans for Data Security Spill over to Civilian Networks," *Data Communications* (March 1987): 136-152.
11. Robert Pear, "Washington Feeling Insecure About Non-Secret Information," *New York Times* (August 30, 1987): E5.
12. Federal Library and Information Center Committee, "Federal Information Policies, Views of a Concerned Community: Fourth Annual Forum, Summary of Proceedings," Prepared by Douglas Price (Washington, D.C.: Library of Congress, 1987), p. 9.
13. *Ibid.*, p. 25.
14. Donna Demac, "Sworn to Silence: If You Work for the Government Leave the First Amendment Behind," *The Progressive* (May 1987): 29-32. Demac discusses the far reaching effects of the directive on university research and campus policies toward such restrictions.
15. As reported by Donna Demac at the Fourth Annual Forum of the Federal Library and Information Center Committee, "Federal Information Policies," p. 9.
16. *Ibid.*
17. U.S. Department of Energy, Office of Scientific and Technical Information, "Memorandum to Recipients of DOE Microfiche," (Oak Ridge, Tennessee, August 4, 1987).
18. John Shattuck, "Statement on Behalf of the Association of American Universities and the Association of Research Libraries on Federal Policies Relating to the Collection and Dissemination of Scientific and Technical Information Before the House Subcommittee on Science, Research and Technology," July 14, 1987. The positions of other organizations are well documented in: U.S. Department of Commerce, National Technical Information Service, *NTIS Privatization Study Responses to April 28, 1986 Federal Register Notice Request for Public Comment* (Springfield, VA: NTIS, June 1986); and *Public Workshop to Discuss Alternatives and Issues Associated with Privatization of the National Technical Information Service, July 30, 1986* (Springfield, VA: NTIS, March 1987).
19. *Ibid.*, pp. 7-8.
20. *Ibid.*, p. 11.
21. "GAO Investigating OMB Meddling with Data Collection," *Library Journal* (January 1987), 112: 28.

22. Paul S. Sarbanes, "Opening Statement Before the Joint Economic Committee Hearing on OMB Proposal For Severe Cuts in the 1990 Census," August 7, 1987, p. 1.

23. U.S. Congress, Joint Economic Committee, "Senator Sarbanes Announces Hearing on OMB Proposal for Severe Cuts in the 1990 Census," Press Release, August 5, 1987, p. 1.

24. Donald E. Fossedal (Superintendent of Documents) statement before the Federal Library and Information Center Committee, "Federal Information Policies," p. 6.

25. Copies of "Less Access" are available from the American Library Association Washington Office, 110 Maryland Ave., N.E., Washington, D.C. 20002.

26. For membership information, contact the Coalition on Government Information, c/o The American Library Association Washington Office, 110 Maryland Ave., N.E., Washington, D.C. 20002.

27. Donna Demac, *Keeping America Uninformed*, p. 11.

INFORMATION SCIENCE IN WARTIME: PIONEER DOCUMENTATION ACTIVITIES IN WORLD WAR II

Pamela Spence Richards

The early history of organized information science in the United States was dominated by the influence of a world readying itself for war and then fighting it. Much of the enormous progress made in the techniques of documentation during this period in this country, as well as in England and Germany, was a result of the perception of the various governments of the military importance of improved scientific information dissemination. The government's attitudes stemmed from the altered relationship between science and military technology by 1939: The weaponry of previous wars had tended to be the result of fairly mature science and technology rather than of newer, evolving areas of technology or derivations from fundamental science itself. World War II was novel in three important respects: First, its military technology was involved with an area of science still at the level of fundamental science, namely atomic physics; second, its military technology was linked to several areas of rapidly developing technology based on known but incompletely elaborated scientific principles, notably electronics, rocketry, and jet turbines; and third, the scale on which outstanding scientists and technicians were mobilized was unique and resulted in a historically unprecedented productivity[1] To sustain this vast new scientific mobilization required both the input of the world's most current scientific and technological information as well as the organization and dissemination of its (largely classified) production. Inevitably, the skills of those men and women already involved in the United States' embryonic documentation movement were harnessed into this effort, and a number became distinguished both by their war work and by their postwar con-

"Information Science in Wartime: Pioneer Documentation Activities in World War II" by Pamela Spence Richards in Journal of the American Society for Information Science Vol. 39, no. 5 (September 1988), pp. 301-306. Copyright © 1988, The American Society for Information Science; reprinted with permission from John Wiley & Sons, Inc.

tributions to the American Documentation Institute (ADI). In this article I will describe the world of documentation on the eve of World War II and demonstrate how subsequent events shaped information science developments in the United States and Europe, where documentalists working for the U.S. Office of Special Services (OSS), England's Association of Special Libraries and Information Bureaux (Aslib), and the German Society for Documentation played seminal roles in enemy scientific information procurement. As we will see, some of the most important trends in American postwar scientific and technical information procurement, organization and dissemination had their roots in wartime developments.

The diverse elements of wartime information science, which defense needs would fuse and further develop into an efficient system in the U.S. between 1942-1945, were all present on the eve of the war. These were: mechanisms for acquiring foreign scientific and technical publications, and technologies permitting both the reduction in size of these publications for clandestine and/or air transport and their subsequent republication after import into America. However, the most critical element for success was the existence of a small but energetic group of individuals who recognized the importance of swift and targeted information provision and who had the imagination to exploit the new techniques and technologies for that purpose. The story of U.S. information science in wartime is essentially that of how the U.S. federal government, which for the four war years assumed the characteristics of a highly centralized organization, encouraged these individuals to build, at the taxpayers' expense, a number of scientific and technical information systems, several of which proved so essential that they survived—albeit in altered form—into the postwar years.

Allied Enemy Scientific Information Procurement

In 1941, America was still dependent on foreign fundamental science for much of her technological development. German research laboratories and universities in particular had long been at the most advanced level of inquiry in certain fields, notably chemistry and physics, producing pioneering research papers and attracting students worldwide. (U.S. atomic physicist J. Robert Oppenheimer's Ph.D., for example, was from Göttingen). Book trade channels for the importation of German scientific journals existed in the U.S. since the nineteenth century. *Chemical Abstracts* had indexed and abstracted German chemical information since its founding in 1907, and German reference books (like Beilstein's *Handbuch der organichen Chemie*) were staples of American scientific and technical collections. American science librarians were so fearful of the consequences of being deprived of German publications that immediately upon the outbreak of the war between England and Germany in 1939 they organized a Joint Committee on Importation to coordinate purchases through the booktrades of neutral countries such as the Netherlands and Switzerland. The importation of German scientific publications was lent a greater sense of urgency when dramatic scientific events unfolding in Germany were brought to the attention of powerful Americans with defense responsibilities. Otto Hahn's splitting of the uranium atom in Berlin in 1938 had led to the famous August 2, 1939 letter of Albert Einstein to President Roosevelt warning of the possibility of German atomic weapons development. American fear of German science was later cited as one of the reasons that U.S. science itself was so well organized during the war; and in 1945 Under Secretary of War Robert Patterson revealed that the fundamental priority accorded German over Japanese defeat in the Anglo-American strategy was the fear of the new weapons that German science might develop in the course of the war.[2] The fact that fear of German science at the highest levels of the U.S. government was translated into federal support for the acquisition of German publications was due to Germans' record before the war of publishing findings of considerable strategic value. At the end of the war, members of the Atomic Scientists of Chicago were quoted in *Life* magazine (29 October 1945) as saying that "If Hitler had prevented the publication in 1939 of the first papers on atomic fission, Germany might have remained for a certain time in exclusive possession of a fundamental secret of atomic power." Since Hitler's government had not restricted publication of the Hahn papers, it was hoped that it might be equally lax in other cases, even after the war broke out. It was on this basis that the first efforts in U.S. history were made by the federal government in the systematic acquisition and processing of foreign scientific information for military and civilian use.

The individuals who spearheaded the U.S. government's wartime documentation efforts were largely drawn from the relatively small group of Americans knowledgeable about the young technology of microfilm, which dominated information science thinking from 1935-1945. Microfilm had been used to record banking transactions since 1929, but by 1935 it was being used in a small number of libraries both for preservation and interlibrary loan purposes. Watson Davis, the pioneer microfilm enthusiast, and in 1934 founder of the Biblio-film service at the Department of Agriculture Library, set up the American Documentation Institute (ADI, ASIS's predecessor) to serve as a national clearinghouse for information on bibliographic networks using microfilm technology. He was convinced that the widespread use of microfilm would revolutionize scientific communication, and even envisioned microfilm as the basis of a world science bibliography. A more market-oriented approach was that of Eugene Power, founder in 1938 of University Microfilm Inc. Power recognized early the commercial potential of the new technology as a method of preservation, and in 1935, while still an employee of Edwards Brothers' publishing company, he began the microfilming in England of all the books listed in the *Short Title Cata-*

logue (those printed in England before 1600), the first of this century's mammoth scholarly reprint programs. Positives were sold to about twenty U.S. libraries on a subscription basis. By 1937, the year of the ADI's founding, there was research in microphotographic documentation going on in laboratories at a number of research libraries, including the Library of Congress, the National Archives, and the University of Chicago under Herman Howe Fussler. When the first World Congress of Documentation was called by the League of Nations Institute of Intellectual Cooperation in Paris in March, 1937, it was Fussler who organized the American exhibit of a small microprocessing lab actually at work copying French Revolutionary journals. From this meeting of 460 documentalists representing thirty-one governments, at which H. G. Welles waxed euphoric about microfilm as a preserver of "the brain of mankind, the race brain",[3] Watson Davis returned to the U.S. convinced that while the Europeans had as "much more advanced and comprehensive appreciation of the possibilities" of documentation their "technology for providing services was less ready."[4] In other words, American microfilm procedures were the best in the world. By 1938, there was even an American scholarly journal specifically devoted to the use of microfilm in documentation: First edited by Vernon Tate of the Library of Congress, the *Journal of Documentary Reproduction* was published by the American Library Association (ALA) until the war forced its cessation in 1943 (in 1950 the ADI assumed responsibility for its republication as *American Documentation* until 1968, when its title was changed to the *Journal of the American Society for Information Science*, reflecting the new name of the ADI).

After Pearl Harbor, when the first steps were taken by the federal government to insure the flow of foreign (most importantly, German) scientific and technical publications to government agencies, it was logical to turn for key personnel to microfilm experts; the enemy scientific journals acquired in the European theater of war were too bulky to airlift over the Atlantic in hard copy. It was clear, upon America's entrance to the war in 1941, that methods employed to secure German journals during World War I could not be used. From 1917 to 1919, the ALA's Importation Service had operated under Department of State aegis to buy enemy journals through neutral countries such as Holland. Hitler's invasion of Western Europe in the spring of 1940, stepped-up submarine warfare in the Atlantic, and British (and eventually, U.S.) aerial bombardments of continental ports made this solution impractical in 1941. The library associations' Joint Committee on Importations set up in 1939 was having increasing difficulty with hard-copy imports.

It was under these circumstances in December, 1941 that William Langer, the Harvard historian, convinced the head of U.S. intelligence operations, William J. Donovan, to organize a unit specifically to concentrate on the import of enemy printed information. This unit, the Interdepartmental Committee for the Acquisition of Foreign Publications (IDC), operating after June 1942 under the Office of Special Services (OSS), became one of the chief foci of American information science in World War II. Langer planned to have microfilm units situated in neutral Stockholm and Lisbon, both accessible to the German mails. Adele Kibre was dispatched to Sweden, but Herman Fussler turned down the offer of the Lisbon job to stay at Chicago and eventually become head of the Manhattan Project's library division (thus laying the groundwork for the Atomic Energy Commission's later information activities). A twenty-eight-year-old microfilm expert from the Harvard Library's newspaper microfilm project, Frederick G. Kilgour, joined the IDC in March, 1942, and, upon Langer's resignation as chairman, took over supervision of the IDC as executive secretary.

Meanwhile, Eugene Power, whose work for the American Council of Learned Society's project to microfilm war-threatened British manuscripts brought him to England frequently, was asked by the Office of the U.S. Coordinator of Information (COI)—the forerunner of the OSS, which was not founded till June, 1942—to help film enemy documents obtained by the British so that they could be shipped to the U.S. Power's University Microfilm was interested in setting up a retail service for hard-to-get foreign scientific periodicals, and he agreed. Since January, 1942, the (British) Association of Special Libraries and Information Bureaux (Aslib) had been running a commercial service to microfilm and disseminate to subscribers hard-to-get enemy periodicals received by British government agencies. It was immediately apparent to both Power and Aslib that it would be more efficient to merge U.S. and English efforts and have the Aslib Microfilm Service (ASM), strengthened by whatever technical resources the Americans could offer, supply both the British and American markets, with Power being the U.S. agent for the product. But Power knew that the COI was also interested in enemy newspapers, an area in which Power had no personal business interest; the COI was planning to open enemy newspaper procurement stations in Lisbon and Berne, but its present needs were urgent. While Aslib was not in the business of microfilming newspapers, Power learned that the British Ministry of Information was launching a plan to collect, film, and distribute copies of the continental press to pertinent government agencies. It was Power's accomplishment, before leaving London in May, 1942, to bring all of the different Allied agencies interested in enemy publications import together and to establish a group, formalized as the Executive Committee of the Aslib Microfilm Service. Here American intelligence and the British Ministry of Information shared with Aslib a concern in the enterprise, one of the war's most successful examples of joint Anglo-American intelligence work. The enterprise was also profitable for Power; of the three films made of the foreign journals, one stayed in England, one went to the IDC in Washington, and one went to University Microfilm in Ann Arbor.[5]

The existence of the Aslib operation was, according to Kilgour, what got the IDC's publications gathering "off to a flying start." The first film shipment of German periodicals arrived in Washington on July 4, 1942, and until late that fall, Alsib's Kodak Microfile cameras at the Science Museum Library—after April 1943 relocated to the Victoria and Albert Museum—were responsible for almost all the enemy material available to U.S. agencies. By fall 1942, other IDC outposts were becoming active, and Kilgour's reliance on London steadily declined. In the course of the war, the IDC shipped large microfilm cameras—250-exposure magazine Leikas— to outposts in Stockholm, Cairo, New Delhi, and Chungking, so that enemy periodicals could be photographed in place and flown directly to Washington. The delivery from Stockholm was the riskiest, entailing flight over German-occupied Norway, but the IDC never lost a shipment as a result of enemy action.[6]

From the records of the IDC and the OSS's London post in the National Archives (declassified in 1975 and 1985, respectively) we are able to learn something about the IDC's sources of supply. The British connection gave Washington access to the many foreign titles traditionally collected by the British ministries (the Foreign Office, and the Air, Information and Economic Warfare Ministries being the most important). Additionally, at the IDC outposts located along the periphery of enemy territory in the European and Pacific theaters of war, U.S. agents, in coordination with the British, subscribed to hundreds of enemy periodicals, sometimes through neutral subscription agencies and sometimes under cover names. In Europe, Lisbon and Stockholm were key stations for German journals, especially after communications with Switzerland broke down following the Nazi occupation of Vichy, France in November 1942. Japanese journals, though less valuable,[7] were harder to get hold of, though the Soviets were a valuable source: An ally in the European war after June 1941, but neutral in the war on the Pacific till the summer of 1945, the USSR had an active diplomatic post in Tokyo dispatching Japanese publications back to Moscow, and eventually to the IDC. Other Japanese materials were acquired by bribery, smuggling, or simple purchase along the border between Chinese- and Japanese-controlled sections of Northern China. Microfilmed in Chungking, these journals were translated by Koreans, whose country had been occupied by the Japanese since 1910.

The saga of the OSS's enemy periodical program does not end with the periodicals' final availability to government agencies on microfilm, however. Microfilm was never popular with users; and besides, there was an acute shortage of microfilm readers due to war conditions. In late 1942 the U.S. Alien Property Custodian (APC), who had been issuing licenses for the reprinting of German books whose copyright had been seized by the U.S. for the duration, began a venture with Edwards Brothers in Ann

Arbor, Michigan, to reprint enemy periodicals from the IDC's microfilms. The periodicals were available by subscription to U.S. research libraries. Not all the journals collected in Europe and Asia by the IDC were reprinted; an Advisory Committee on the Periodical Republication Program was set up in October 1942 to assist the APC in choosing titles for reprint. Of the eleven committee members, eight were top librarians or documentalists in the country, including E. J. Crane (editor of *Chemical Abstracts*), Watson Davis (president of the American Documentation Institute), Sarah Jones (librarian of the Bureau of Standards), Keyes Metcalf (president of ALA), Luther Evans (assistant librarian of Congress), and Paul North Rice (executive secretary of the Association of Research Libraries). The make-up of the committee was meant to insure that the literature needs of the most important scholarly disciplines would be met.

By the war's end the Alien Property Custodian had sent to a group of selected U.S. and British research libraries seven circulars announcing the availability of reprints of a total of 116 separate continental journals. (All seven circulars were marked "NOT FOR PUBLICATION! If any publicity is given, it will mean cessation of the supply of copy and total failure of the enterprise.") The journals were principally German and Austrian, but also included sixteen French, three Dutch, and one Belgian titles. They covered almost every subject of scientific and technological importance to a nation at war, including acoustics, aviation, biochemistry, electronics, engineering, enzymology, explosives, mathematics, pathology, petroleum plastics, rubber, and research viruses. A survey done by the ADC at the end of the war revealed that 94% of the over 900 subscribers to the reprints used them for war purposes, and that 58 of the subscribers were in the British Empire.[8]

Given the effort and money spent by the Allies on the procurement of enemy scientific and technical publications, do we have any evidence that the publications contained material of importance to the war effort? A number of the technical periodicals did contain material of immediate practical value; *Nachrichten für Seefahrer* (*Sailors' Bulletin*), for example, reported to German ships exactly where the German Navy was laying mines. It was, however, in the pure sciences, notably atomic physics, that the periodicals made their most dramatic contribution. According to Niels Bohr, the atomic physicist who escaped from Denmark in 1943, the Germans were indeed working on an atomic bomb at least through 1941. At some point in 1942 the project was abandoned as impractical, for a variety of reasons, including both the loss of Germany's heavy water supply in Norway through enemy action, and because the Germans badly over-estimated the amount of enriched uranium necessary.[9] In any case, the Germans' conclusions about the impracticability of atomic fission for war use resulted in the declassification of the project and the release of valuable research: eight articles in the 1942 and 1943 issue of *Die Naturwissenschaften*, by

Otto Hahn, Fritz Strassmann, H. J. Born, W. Seelmann-Eggbert, and their associates at the Kaiser Wilhelm Institut für Chemie and the Radiologische Abteilung der Auergesellschaft gave detailed descriptions of experiments with the fission of the uranium atom, the gaseous and other byproducts obtained, and the energies released. These articles, all of which were reprinted by the APC, produced much excitement among members of the Manhattan Project (Kilgour recalls being able to get some idea of the importance of atomic energy from the titles of the chemistry and physics articles that were in great demand) who were able to skip certain proofs of their own as a result of the German findings. At the end of the war, the articles were credited as having been factors in making the American bomb possible by 1945.[10]

German Enemy Information Procurement

The Germans had emerged from the terrible financial difficulties of the 1920s with a highly developed mechanism for the central acquisition and dissemination of (costly) foreign publications, so less adjustment was necessary than in the United States to wartime circumstances. The *Beschaffungsamt* of the German Research Association at the Prussian State Library in Berlin (now the German State Library in East Berlin) handled a large proportion of the country's foreign purchases, with the Berlin Technological University acting as an acquisitions and documentation center for foreign science and technology information. The Reich ordinance of 1936 requiring library orders for foreign materials to be submitted to the Gestapo for approval tended to centralize foreign acquisitions further.

The documentation movement emerged in Germany in the late 1930s under the leadership of H. A. Krüss, director of the Prussian State Library, and the aborted 1940 Conference of the International Federation of Documentation was scheduled to be held in Mainz. By 1941 the importance of efficient documentation for the war effort had so impressed the National Socialist government that it backed the formation of the Deutsche Gesellschaft für Dokumentation (DGD); representatives of Goebbels' Ministry of Propaganda, the Ministry of Education, and the Army High Command were all present at the inaugural conference.[11] The Reich Chancellery ordered all government agencies (which included Germany's academic research libraries) to report their current foreign subscriptions to the DGD, which issued a union catalog in 1943 of all German holdings of foreign periodicals issued after September 1, 1939. The DGD also collaborated, with the Information Center of the Berlin Technological University and the Hamburg World Economics Institute, in the publication from 1942 of a monthly abstracting bulletin (*Referatenblatt*) of foreign journal articles, of which copies of the originals could be ordered from Berlin. (Paper shortages ruled out the possibility of any kind of reprinting program being launched in wartime Germany.) In spite of the total destruction of Berlin Technological University and the fire bombing of Hamburg, both in the summer of 1943, the *Referatenblatt* continued to appear until the end of 1944.[12]

The procurement methods used by the Germans paralleled in some respects those of the Allies, with subscriptions to hundreds of enemy journals placed with booksellers in neutral countries. However, the role played by private industry in the German acquisitions network had no Allied counterpart; the huge chemical and weaponry firms of I. G. Farben and Krupp, for example, had branches all over the world which before and during the war dispatched to Germany scientific, technical, and patent material. Right up to Pearl Harbor, Chemnyco, an I. G. Farben subsidiary with headquarters on Fifth Avenue, maintained an American subscription list costing $4,000 annually, all of which was forwarded to Farben's huge library on Unter den Linden in Berlin, whence numerous items were made available to government agencies. Krupp used its Delaware subsidiary, Krupp-Nirosta, for much the same purpose. After America's declaration of war on Germany, the firms moved their subscription activities to their Mexican or South American branches.

With its outstanding optical industry, Germany was swift to apply advanced microfilm technologies to documentation. As it became increasingly difficult to mail U.S. periodicals openly from the Western Hemisphere, German agents in Mexico resorted to sending issues by "microdot," whereby a film is so reduced that it can be inserted in the period hole made by a typewriter, or, more difficult to detect, in the gum of an envelope flap. After D-Day, when Allied information access became more difficult for Germany due to its loss of overland access to Lisbon, procurement became more of an ad hoc and irregular process. Probably the most colorful example of the various methods utilized was the aborted November 1944 submarine landing on the coast of Maine of two German agents with a microfilm camera with orders to proceed to New York Public Library to photograph technical journals. Agents and camera were apprehended quickly by the Federal Bureau of Investigation.[13]

The Germans continued to exert extraordinary efforts for procurement for the same reasons as the Americans; the rewards were high. In 1939, for example, before censorship was imposed on such matters, the *Reviews of Modern Physics* published a description of a gas centrifuge that scientists in Hamburg later tried to adapt to work with uranium hexafluoride gas. Through notes put in the March and April 1940 issues of *Physical Review*, experimental proof was given that slow neutrons had a greater probability of fissioning U-235, and in the June 1940 issue of the same journal, the discovery of plutonium was announced. Thus German scientists learned the results of physical investigations they lacked the resources to conduct themselves.[14]

Eventually the Germans' efficient perusal of Allied publications led to their discovery of the IDC's republication program. On June 29, 1944, the British periodical *The Bookseller* carried an advertisement of the H. K. Lewis firm for German books reprinted in America. The advertisement led to a flurry of correspondence at the Reich Chancellery reconfirming Martin Bormann's 1943 decree banning the export of German printed matter damaging to the Reich and instructing German agents in Sweden to obtain a catalog of the "Jewish firm H. K. Lewis." While the advertisement did not mention reprinted periodicals, by December 1944, suspicions in Berlin were grave enough to produce a Chancery memorandum suggesting that periodicals be removed from the booktrade altogether.[15] But, by that time, there were relatively few important German journals still being printed; the gigantic Royal Air Force attack of December 3, 1943 had destroyed 90% of the publishing center's publishers, paper manufacturers, and type founders. By October 1944, German periodical publishing was reduced to 10% of its prewar production. Thus, even had the Germans exercised more effective export restrictions after December 1944 —and there is no indication that they did—it would have made little difference to the Allied republication program. The APC never did reprint any 1945 issues of German journals, reporting that "the upper limit for their republication has already been established by the action of B-17s . . ."[16]

The procurement of enemy scientific information was only one example, if perhaps the most dramatic, of documentation at war. In the United States, a variety of other information activities advanced during the emergency; there was a more urgent need for scientific and technical translations, for example. Thus, in 1941, Watson Davis set up an Oriental translation service within the American Documentation Institute to abstract Japanese and Chinese scientific journal literature, and from April 1941, to March 1943, it published the mimeographed abstracting journal *Far Eastern Science Bulletin*.[17] Further, the unprecedented pace of innovation during World War II (radar, jet aircraft, guided missiles, proximity fuses, and the atomic bomb all appeared *during* the fighting) led to the accelerated development of numerous government-supported, mission-oriented information centers, the most elaborate of which was probably the library and documentation network of the various Manhattan District Project laboratories.

What interests us here, forty years later, is principally the extent to which wartime developments affected subsequent documentation patterns in this country. Certainly the value to both U.S. industry and the U.S. military of imported German information during the war and occupation was a prime factor in the establishment by the federal government of permanent agencies to supply foreign technical information to both the civilian and defense sectors in peacetime. Thus, after the invasion and surrender of Germany, and the capture of literally tons of German research documents by scientific intelligence troops, the desire to process and disseminate their contents to American industry led to the forming of the interdepartmental Publication Board in 1945, and in 1946 the Department of Commerce's Office of Technical Services, the forerunner of the National Technical Information Service (1971). Similarly, the Air Documents Centers set up in 1945 by the Army Air Force in London and at Wright Field in Dayton, Ohio—direct forbears of the Defense Documentation Center (1965) —were examples of the military's parallel efforts to keep its researchers supplied with the most advanced foreign technical information. Like the wartime foreign information acquisition mechanisms, some of the mission-oriented information services proved too valuable to be jettisoned in peacetime. In 1945, the Manhattan District Project established an Editorial Advisory Board to evaluate and publish the Project's records; consisting of, among others, Alberto Thompson from Oak Ridge and Herman Fussler from Chicago, the board published a "Weekly Title List," the prototype for the later *Nuclear Science Abstracts* (1950). A year later, the Library Unit of the Research Division at Oak Ridge, under Bernard M. Fry, began centrally to control information exchange among all units of the Project. All of these activities eventually became part of the Atomic Energy Commission's Technical Information Service (1950).[18]

The documentation legacy of World War II is visible in the private sector as well. The scholarly reprint industry has its roots in Edward Brothers' wartime publishing of enemy books and periodicals,[19] and Eugene Power's collaboration with Aslib from 1942-1945 accelerated the growth of American micropublishing. Academic libraries' postwar interest in cooperative acquisition of foreign publications, embodied in the Farmington Plan of 1948, can be traced to the perception, heightened by the wartime information emergency and the measures taken to overcome it, of the critical importance of foreign publications to research of all kinds.

The forty years since the war, and the powerful American traditions of individualism and minimal government, have eroded some of the cooperative and centralized trends in documentation that resulted in our four-year communal effort for victory in World War II. It is unquestionable, however, that the war made it permanently impossible for the U.S. government—or indeed any government—to ignore the military importance of scientific and technical information. When new military crises arose—Sputnik, for example—it was an automatic response on the part of government to seek some of the solution in improved information supply. The burgeoning of the information industry during the postwar era, the increase in size and importance of the scientific and technical societies and their publications, and even some of the self-esteem of ASIS, is an outgrowth of information's evolution during World War II into a national defense priority.

References

1. Rostow, W. W. *The United States in the World Arena.* New York: Harper; 1960:59.
2. Rostow, W. W. *The United States in the World Arena.* New York: Harper; 1960:150.
3. Rayward, Boyd. "The International Exposition and the World Documentation Congress, Paris 1937." *Library Quarterly* 53:263. 1983.
4. Farkas-Conn, Irene. "From Documentation to Information Science—The Origins and Early Development of the American Documentation Institute; American Society for Information Science." Ph.D. thesis. Chicago: University of Chicago; 1984.
5. "War Diary of the Research and Analysis Branch, OSS, London." Records Group 226, Military Records Division, U.S. National Archives, Washington, D.C.
6. Kilgour, Frederick G. Interview: Columbus, Ohio, May 31, 1979.
7. Bush, Vannevar. *Modern Arms and Free Men.* New York: Simon and Schuster; 1949:23.
8. U.S. Office of Alien Property Custodian. "Report to the President on Periodical Republication Program." Washington, D.C.; 1 November 1945:7.
9. Jones, R. V. *The Wizard War: British Scientific Intelligence 1939-1945.* New York: Coward, McCann and Geoghegan; 1978:483.
10. Alien Property Custodian: 6.
11. *Dokumentation und Arbeitstechnik: Zwanglose Mitteilungen des Fachnormenausschuss für Bibliotheks-, Buch-, und Zeitschriftenwesen.* July 1941:2-3.
12. Richards, Pamela Spence. "German Libraries and Scientific and Technical Information in Nazi Germany." *Library Quarterly* 55:151-173. 1985.
13. Richards. "Aryan Librarianship: Academic and Research Libraries under Hitler." *Journal of Library History* 19:231-258. 1984.
14. Irving, David. *The German Atomic Bomb.* New York: Simon and Schuster; 1967:70-72.
15. File NS 6/440. Archives of the Federal Republic of Germany, Coblenz.
16. U.S. Office of Alien Property Custodian. "Withdrawal by the Custodian from the Periodical Republication Program." Washington, D.C.; 25 May 1945.
17. Farkas-Conn, Irene. "From Documentation to Information Science—The Origins and Early Development of the American Documentation Institute; American Society For Information Science." Ph.D. thesis. Chicago: University of Chicago; 1984: p. 289.
18. Adkinson, Burton. *Two Centuries of Federal Information.* Stroudsbourg, Pa.: Dowden, Hutchinson and Ross; 1978:42.
19. Nemeyer, Carol A. *Scholarly Reprint Publishing in the United States.* New York: Bowker, 1972.

PART II:
SOCIETAL CONCERNS

THE CREATIONISM CONTROVERSY: IT'S ONLY THE BEGINNING

Ken Donelson

I'd hardly settled into work Friday morning when I heard from the radio news commentator that the U.S. Supreme Court has tossed out Louisiana's creationist law (in *Edwards v. Aquillard*). A student came by to fill me in on some details of the decision. Others stopped by, and all agreed that the decision was a victory for the good guys (us) against the bad guys (them). As one woman left my office, she said, "Well, that takes care of *them*, doesn't it? At least *they* can't do *that* again."

The decision pleased me. But those pronouns bothered me then, and they worry me even more today. They allow us to believe—or invite us to pretend—that the long, bitter, divisive, social and religious controversy is over—another historical curiosity to be filed—and then forgotten. I'm sure someone in 1859 must have said something similar when Charles Darwin's *On the Origin of Species* was published. I'll bet someone also said something like it in the mid-1920s when Tennessee's Supreme Court threw out the *Scopes* decision.

But the evolution/creationist debate won't go away—and that's not surprising. True believers in creationism are impervious to Justice William J. Brennan Jr's argument that Louisiana's act advanced a religious doctrine and thereby violated the First Amendment's Establishment Clause. States with heavy fundamentalist constituencies may shy away from creationist litigation, but only for the moment. Creationists in state legislatures are certain to keep careful tabs on the health of older justices and possible changes in Supreme Court personnel. Some desperate politicians may seek support from conservatives by embracing creationism. Other public figures may prove again that Americans are often happily indifferent about their scientific ignorance. It was only seven years ago when Ronald Reagan, on a campaign swing through Texas, was asked what he thought about the teaching of evolution. He replied, "It is a scientific theory only, and it is

"The Creationism Controversy: It's Only the Beginning" by Ken Donelson in *School Library Journal* Vol. 34 (March 1988), pp. 107-113; reprinted with permission from Reed Publishing, USA, copyright © Reed Publishing, USA. This article is based on a project supported, in part, by the National Science Foundation.

not believed in the scientific community to be as infallible as it once was believed. But if it is going to be taught in the schools, then I think the biblical story of creation should also be taught."

Assuming that Reagan meant that creationism should be taught in science classes and not in classes on comparative religions, the scientific community was shocked. But the words shouldn't have surprised either scientists or the educated populace. Newspaper polls, over the years, have consistently shown that one-half to three-fourths of the public believe that both evolution and creationism should be taught in public schools, even though, as Ohio State's Professor of Genetics, Paul Fuerst, has said, such surveys show how high schools have failed to teach "what science is and is not. Creationism is not science at all." [1]

Delos McKown, Auburn University professor of philosophy, with a degree in theology and a background in evangelicalism, is even less kind about our national mania for scientific illiteracy.

> We're [Americans] the biggest class of know-nothings in the civilized world. How we could have so many people going to school for so many years and coming away with so little beggars the imagination. [2]

It's not enough that we teachers and librarians know of the recent Supreme Court decision or a little about the Scopes trial in 1925. It's important that we know the literature about the controversy, including the documents that most accurately present both creationism and evolution and that relate the most critical attacks. More important, we need to get all this in the hands of students. Scientists have long been concerned about a public that is scientifically illiterate, but which is increasingly being asked or forced to make public policy decisions on atomic energy, the Star Wars program, the space shuttle program, disarmament, evolution, and the science curriculum in the public schools by voting for Representative Smith or Jones or for Grey or Brown for the school board. Yes, we can joke about educating kids for tomorrow, to make them better-informed citizens, and all those cliches of graduation speeches, but cliches sometimes have an uncomfortable way of being true.

Teachers and librarians have something in common—a drive to educate young people and to expose them to all sorts of ideas, a hatred of indoctrination into any one truth (no matter how immediately appealing it may be), and a belief that all of us should be treated as professionals in control of our own professions. For teachers, this means determining the proper content of subject matter and the most-efficient way to present that material. For librarians, this means determining budgets and purchasing priorities and the right to stock and recommend many books of many different kinds with many ideas.

As teachers or librarians, we are responsible to the public, but we are not public servants. We must educate the public, which is not the same as giving in to public whims. But the positions of librarians and science teachers are not always identical. I don't expect that science teachers will pay any attention to creationism or to their own personal religious experiences in their classrooms. I do expect that librarians will stock and recommend many books on science and religion of many different persuasions, including books specifically on creationism. These books may or may not reflect the personal religious experiences of the librarians, but that is not the reason for stocking or recommending them.

What should we know about the evolution/creationism dispute? I've included a rather long bibliography at the end of this article because the topic is complex. But let me briefly sketch out some topics we ought to know about as educated citizens and reasonably well-informed teachers.

Informative Topics

1. A history of Darwin's ideas and influence:

Few of us are likely to read Darwin directly, but we can learn much about him and his ideas from Jonathan Miller and Borin Van Loon's *Darwin for Beginners* (Writers & Readers, England, 1982). At first this book seems little more than a grotesque comic book, but it's a brilliant presentation of Darwin's major ideas, what led to the ideas, and what the ideas led to. For a bit more, Ronald W. Clark's *The Survival of Charles Darwin: A Biography of a Man and an Idea* (Random, 1985) is recent and readable. Clark is excellent in discussing Darwin's influence and why evolution divided early American scientists, particularly the work of Asa Gray, Darwin's enthusiastic believer, and the more famous Jean Louis Rodolphe Agassiz, who wrote in the margin of *On Origins*: "This is truly monstrous."

2. The rise of fundamentalism in America—what the fundamentalists believed about evolution and why:

Although Curtis Law, editor of the Baptist's *Watchman-Examinor*, popularized the term "fundamentalist," fundamentalism began in 1910 with the publication of ten small pamphlets under the title of *The Fundamentals. A Testimony to the Truth. Compliments of Two Christian Laymen.* Given or sent to anyone who requested them, three million copies were distributed.

The five points or basics of fundamentalism were the infallibility or inerrancy of the Bible, Christ's virgin birth, Christ's substitutionary atonement, Christ's resurrection, and Christ's second coming. The first point alone would conflict with Darwin's evolutionary concepts, or as George McCready Price wrote in *Back to the Bible, or the New Protestantism*, "No Adam, no fall; no fall, no atonement; no atonement, no savior. Accepting evolution, how can we believe in a fall?"[3]

Soon churches across the country, but especially in the South, attacked evolution because it contradicted the creation story (or stories) in the first chapters of Genesis. Maynard Shipley's *The War on Modern Science: A Short History of the Fundamentalist Attacks on Evolution and Modernism*, still highly readable and inflammatory, even after 60 years, notes one such attack:

> A church convention was told by a Texas clergyman that the higher schools are teaching "blasphemous, Bible-undermining, God-denying, Christ-cursing, and faith-robbing evolution." His tirade was followed by an anti-evolution resolution, unanimously passed.[4]

Schools, colleges especially, but also high schools, soon came under increasing attack as fundamentalists worried about the influence of this newfangled idea on the souls of their children. In 1927, a visiting minister at the Raleigh, North Carolina, Baptist Tabernacle declared, "Teach a child often that he is only a high class monkey, and you lay the foundations for confidelity, pessimism, and suicide."[5]

It was only a short step between attacking schools that taught, or might teach, evolution to creating laws to save the children from this Godless influence. Americans have always had faith that the best way to fight an idea is to pass a law prohibiting the idea. It doesn't work. However, the 1920s saw many such laws, and many educators lambasted evolution and its teaching. At its 1925-26 midwinter session, Henry Noble Sherwood, Indiana's State Superintendent of Public Instruction, told the National Education Association: "only those teachers should be employed who are active in church work."[6] Governor Miriam Ferguson of Texas went a step further in declaring, "I'm a Christian mother who believes Jesus Christ died to save humanity, and I'm not going to let that kind of rot go into Texas textbooks."[7]

Texas then, as it did recently, pressured textbook publishers like Macmillan, Allyn & Bacon, Ginn, and Holt to change or delete offending passages that presented evolution at all, much less favorably. In an Allyn & Bacon text, whenever the word evolution occurred, "development" was substituted. In a Holt text, the phrase, "Evolution is a slow and gradual process," was deleted. And, in a Ginn book, editors deleted ". . . mutations give rise to new species."[8]

Between 1921 and 1932, a total of 45 anti-evolution bills were introduced into 20 state legislatures, mostly in the Bible-belt South, but hardly exclusively. Among these states, for example, were California, Delaware, Oregon, New Hampshire, Washington, and Minnesota. The first bill to be introduced was in Kentucky in 1921; it was narrowly defeated 42 to 41. The honor, such as it is, for passing the first education anti-evolution bill belongs to Oklahoma, which passed legislation in 1923. In California in 1925, the State Board of Education ruled that evolution be taught "only as a theory"—a point that deserves comment a bit later on.

The case most associated with evolution began in March, 1925 when Tennessee Governor Austin Peay signed a bill making it illegal "for any teacher in any of the state universities, normal, and all other public schools of the state, to teach any theory that denies the story of the divine creation of man as taught in the Bible and to teach instead that man has descended from a lower order of animal." Later that year, in a friendly test case, John Thomas Scopes was charged with teaching evolution in the Dayton (Tennessee) High School. Though the disposition of the case was never in doubt (Scopes had used Hunter's *Civic Biology* with its references to evolution for several years), it brought Dayton national attention when William Jennings Bryan headed the prosecution and Clarence Darrow headed the defense. The trial was brief, and more circus sideshow than law, but Darrow cared little since he knew that the point of the trial was to appeal the conviction. Bryan got his conviction, lost his public appeal, and died. Darrow lost the case, appealed to the Tennessee Supreme Court, and didn't get what he wanted. The Court overturned the conviction on a technicality (the lower court had erred in the amount of the fine it levied on Scopes), and the chance to chase the appeal higher was lost.

The South, particularly Tennessee, appeared foolish and ignorant, but this didn't keep other states from adding anti-evolution laws to their statues and from making the teaching of evolution unpopular and largely illegal. But then, know-nothing laws have always appealed to people eager to make the difficult and abstract simple enough for anyone to understand (either that or ban it altogether). Howard K. Beale cited one state where the revolt against science took the form of an attempt to prescribe by law that "pi" should be changed from 3.1416 to 3.000, partly because it was simpler to use, partly because the Bible describes King Solomon's vases as three times as far around as across.[9]

3. What fundamentalists, the chief source of attacks on contemporary evolution teaching and theory, think about evolution today:

If you think that anti-evolutionists of the 1920s were wild-eyed and prone to exaggeration, the modern anti-evolutionists are even more so. In 1972, Henry M. Morris, the house intellectual of the creationist movement, wrote, "Evolution is the root of atheism, of communism, behaviorism, racism, economic imperialism, militarism, libertinism, anarchism, and all manner of anti-Christian systems of belief and practice."[10] By 1974, Morris had grown even less happy about evolution:

> Satan himself is the originator of the concept of evolution. In fact, the Bible does say that he is the one "which deceiveth the whole world" (Revelation 12:9), and that he "hath blinded the minds of them which believe not." (II Corinthians, 4:4). Such statements as these must apply

especially on the evolutionary cosmology, which indeed is the world view
with which the whole world has been deceived.[11]

The winner of the purple-prose award for colorful attacks on modern
evolution must go to Judge Braswell D. Deen, chief justice of the Georgia
State Court of Appeals, who said:

> It's bigotry to teach only evolution. Right now we're financing permis-
> siveness by teaching only that man evolved from a purposeless past of
> a barnyard beginning . . . I say that creationism teaches you to have a
> responsibility to a creator and that it will help reduce our state's high
> crime by stressing human values . . .[12]

> [The result of teaching evolution is] permissiveness, pills and drugs, pro-
> phylactics, perversions, pregnancies, abortions, pornotherapy, pollution,
> poisoning, and a proliferation and geometric generating increase of
> crimes of all types.[13]

4. The effects of these attacks on evolution in the public schools:

In an article in *Science Education*, Gerald Skoog, who surveyed
references to evolution in high school biology texts in 1979 and 1984,
noted that while evolution was treated cursorily and generally non-contro-
versially prior to the 1960s, texts since then have decreased attention to
evolution or even evidence that evolution exists or is highly regarded by
most scientists.[14]

In its more-rarified form, that attitude produced a heightened ignorance, best illustrated by a comment published in the August 9, 1983 *USA
Today*. The opinion page was given over to columns and comments on
textbook censorship. In the "Voices from Across the USA" feature at the
bottom of the page were responses to the question, "Do you think school
boards should be allowed to censor or reject textbooks?" The first reply
came from a 16-year-old girl who attended an Alabama school:

> My biology teacher refused to teach us about evolution. He said if we
> wanted to learn about it on our own time, fine. But he didn't believe it,
> so he skipped right over it in the book. Most of the other teachers did,
> too. I'm in favor of censorship, and I'm glad he decided not to teach it.
> Certain things I just don't want to know about.

A finer, more-complete justification for ignorance, of science (or anything else that might be dangerous) would be hard to find.

Evolution, per se, wasn't the only thing caught up in the drive toward
educational know-nothingness. In 1977, the Invisible Theatre of Tucson,
Arizona, became controversial when "Ancient Ooze and All That Moves,"
an elementary school play was cancelled in one town because the "evolution theme was offensive." In another town it was cancelled because it was
now considered "controversial."[15]

Jerome Lawrence's and Robert E. Lee's widely produced *Inherit the Wind* caused problems for two Maryland middle school teachers who wanted to produce the play with their gifted students. The county school superintendent announced that *Inherit the Wind* was "an entirely inappropriate play for impressionable youngsters [and they should not] be placed in the middle of a controversy on the teaching of evolution." He noted also that he wouldn't approve of a production of the play in a public high school.[16]

Given all that, it's not surprising that evolution has been widely attacked in many states. The only new feature has been the pseudo-democratic/ fair play effort to ram through creationism as a requirement wherever evolution is to be taught. States like Arkansas and Tennessee and Louisiana and Mississippi were hardly surprising in their drive to kill modern science. Far more surprising, with far less publicity, were attempts to bring creationism into states such as Oregon, Colorado, Michigan, New York, Connecticut, Iowa, New Mexico, Arizona. Utah, Wisconsin, Minnesota, Idaho, Illinois, Ohio, and Indiana.

5. What, exactly, is creationism and creation-science?

In the 1940s, the American Scientific Affiliation was formed by scientists eager to bring their Christianity closer to their scientific work. Because its stand on evolution was considered by some members to be weak, these members broke off to form the Creation Research Society in Ann Arbor, Michigan. In 1970, Henry M. Morris helped found Christian Heritage College at El Cajon, California. The Creation Science Research Center (CSRC) was closely tied to the college. Later, the CSRC, directed by Kelly Segraves, became independent of the college. The Institute for Creation Research (ICR) was started at Christian Heritage College to replace the CSRC, and most of the books by ICR members, especially Henry Morris, have been published in San Diego by Creation-Life Publishers.

The catalog for Christian Heritage College states that the faculty supports inerrancy of the Holy Scriptures, particularly on four points: (1) the creation of the world in six days; (2) the biblical account of the introduction of sin into the world; (3) the Noachian flood, and (4) the origins of language and nations at the Tower of Babel.

The Creation Research Society has three types of membership—voting, student, and sustaining. All three must sign applications agreeing to the following points as stated:

1. The Bible is the written Word of God, and because we believe it to be inspired throughout, all of its assertions are historically and scientifically true in all of the original autographs. To the student of nature, this means that the account of origins in Genesis is a factual presentation of simple historical truths.

2. All basic types of living things, including man, were made by direct

creative acts of God during Creation Week as described in Genesis.
Whatever biological changes have occurred since Creation have accomplished only changes within the original created kinds.
3. The great Flood described in Genesis, commonly referred to as the Noachian Deluge, was a historical event, worldwide in its extent and effect.
4. Finally, we are an organization of Christian men of science, who accept Jesus Christ as our Lord and Savior. The account of the special creation of Adam and Eve as one man and one woman, and their subsequent Fall into sin, is the basis for our belief in the necessity of a Savior for all mankind. Therefore, salvation can come only thru accepting Jesus Christ as our Savior.

Creationists usually begin their explanation of creation-science (an oxymoron) by attacking evolution. Indeed, one of the problems with reading creationist material is sifting through the attacks on evolution to find what creationists believe, not what they do not believe. For most scientists—and for many lay people—creationism founders on its assumption and requirement that all science must jibe with a literal reading of the Bible, especially the first eleven chapters of Genesis. Even the best known creationist author, Henry Morris, seemed to have a bit of trouble with this when he spoke at the Congress of the Bible in 1982. At one point, Morris told the large and attentive audience: "Science means knowledge and truth . . . If we are really searching for truth, we ought to go where it leads us." Moments later, he said: "If the Bible teaches it, that settles it, whatever scientists might say, because it's the word of God."[17]

Francis J. Flaherty summarizes the feeling of most scientists about creationism:

> The best way to define creation science is the best evidence that it is not a science at all; it is an amalgam of assertions whose only common denominator is their consistency with a literal interpretation of the *Genesis* story of creation. True science asks: "What theory of origins best accords with the facts?" Creation science, in effect, asks: "What theory of origins best accords with *Genesis?*" One needn't be a scientist to realize the unneutrality of the latter approach.[18]

6. What objections do creationists have about evolution?

Ignoring the most obvious and fundamental objection, that creationism is Bible-based and evolution is presumably not, creationists argue that: (a) evolution is "only a theory" nothing more, and (b) in all fair play, if evolution is going to be taught, shouldn't creationism be taught as well. "What," sneer the creationists, "do the evolutionists have to hide? What do they fear by allowing young people to choose the system that seems most logical to them?"

The "it's only a theory" syndrome is a good example of untruth in advertising, and the problem starts with that word, *theory*. Most non-scientists assume that theory means to scientists what it means to the rest of us. A word, unless you're in Alice's Wonderland, should mean the same to all of us. But it doesn't. To most of us theory means an educated guess, a hypothesis, something less than a fact. But scientists use theory in terms of the theory of gravity or relativity. In other words, it's used as a statement in accord with all the facts as we presently know or understand them. A theory is a widely accepted idea, not someone's wild-eyed and farfetched notion. Obviously, a theory can be disputed, as different approaches to and ideas about evolution are constantly in dispute, not because the disputants do not accept evolution, but because they disagree about details. Theories can be disproved—and have been over the years. This makes science and scientists fallible. Creationists need not worry about developing or justifying theory, for they deal in certainties based on the Bible. As Stephen Jay Gould wrote:

Creationists play upon a vernacular misunderstanding of the word theory to convey the false impression that we evolutionists are covering up the rotten core of our edifice. . . . In the American vernacular, theory often means "imperfect fact," part of a hierarchy of confidence running downhill, from fact to theory to hypothesis to guess. Thus the power of the creationist argument: evolution is "only" a theory, and intense debate now rages about many aspects of the theory. . . . Well, evolution is a theory. It is also a fact. And facts and theories are different things, not rungs in a hierarchy of increasing certainty.

Facts are the world's data. Theories are structures of ideas that explain and interpret facts. Facts do not go away when scientists debate rival theories to explain them. . . . Moreover, *fact* does not mean *absolute certainty*. The final proofs of logic and mathematics flow deductively from stated premises and achieve certainty only because they are *not* about the empirical world. Evolutionists make no claim for perpetual truth, though creationists often do (and then attack us for a style of argument that they themselves favor). In science, *fact* can only mean "confirmed to such a degree that it would be perverse to withhold provisional assent." [19]

Even if evolution is right, wouldn't it be the American way to play fair and allow creationists to have their time in classrooms? After all, when Darrow defended Scopes, he only asked for equal time in the classroom. Evolution ultimately got that time. Isn't it fair that creationism be accorded equal time now?

The argument has a specious fairplay overtone. What could be more democratic, more decent, more inherently all-American than allowing, maybe even encouraging, creationists to have equal time? But fair or decent as it sounds, there are several built-in problems. First, no matter how much they pretend, creationists are really dealing in Christian creationism, not creationism as such. The first 11 books of Genesis do not have a stranglehold on all creation myths, though creationists might disagree. Other religions sincerely believe that their creation myths or legends or stories or revealed truths are accurate and historic.

Second, creationism is, by definition, predicated on a creator, recent state legislative acts not withstanding. Whether we call that creator God (or Creator or something else) is unimportant for the moment. Soon, no matter how we treat the matter, we're almost certain to be talking about and teaching a religion. Whether or not the religion moves us, it's still a religion, a body of beliefs inappropriate to a science class.

Finally, life is rarely fair, and teachers have not yet signed agreements that parents or school boards or administrators should determine what should (or should not) be included in the science curriculum (or any other for that matter). Lawrence Welk is rarely accorded much time in a music appreciation class anymore than Elvis Presley movies are given much time in a cinema class. But both Welk and Presley are certain to be more popular than many other people who are studied in detail. Similarly, in science classes, a teacher trained in the subject is qualified to determine what belongs and what is extraneous. And, according to scientists, creationism is clearly the latter.

7. What court battles have creationists fought with evolutionists?

A lot of them . . ., but the creationists have ultimately lost all so far. In 1977, in Sellersburg, Indiana, a creationist biology text used in a public high school, *Biology—A Search For Order in Complexity*, was forced out of school when a superior court judge wrote, "The prospect of biology teachers and students alike, forced to answer and respond to continued demand for correct Christian doctrines, has no place in the public schools."[20]

In Texas in 1982, a young Republican state representative ran for office to do one thing—to sponsor a bill requiring public schools to teach the biblical theory of creation whenever evolution was taught. In 1984 the State Board of Education ruled that biology texts did not have to mention the name of Charles Darwin—a bone tossed to conservatives who opposed the ruling. Later that year, the State Attorney General ruled that teaching evolution as "only one of several explanations" for the origin of humanity was unconstitutional. So the Texas State Board of Education, admittedly pressured by People for the American Way, repealed the ruling, frustrating the many educational conservatives in Texas.

If Texas is confusing, the California situation has, at times, bordered on chaos. In 1981, a Superior Court Judge ruled that the state's guidelines for teaching evolution were adequate if two insertions were made, both aimed at making clear that evolution should not be taught dogmatically. But, by 1985, the State Board of Education had begun rejecting science texts that had "watered down" treatments of evolution. Superintendent of

Public Instruction Bill Honig commented:

> First of all, the issue is not one of whether evolution should be taught. Instead, it was how well evolution should be taught. Nor was this a fight between science and religion; it was a fight for quality.[21]

The major battles have been, as most people know, in Arkansas and Louisiana. In Arkansas, in the 1965-66 school year, administrators at a Little Rock high school agreed with the wishes of their biology teachers to use a text setting forth evolutionary ideas, even though a never-enforced state law forbade any teaching of evolution. Susan Epperson, one of those biology teachers, agreed to be named in the suit and, after a two-hour trial, a judge ruled the Arkansas law unconstitutional. In 1967, the State Supreme Court reversed the ruling and an appeal for a hearing went to the U.S. Supreme Court, which agreed, late in 1968, that the lower court judge was correct and the act was unconstitutional. Then in 1981, State Senator James L. Holsted proposed a bill, later to be called Act 590, which was passed on March 17 and signed by Governor Frank White ten days later. The title of the bill indicates its purpose—"The Balanced Treatment for Creation-Science and Evolution-Science Act." After the American Civil Liberties Union filed suit to overturn the bill, Federal District Judge William Overton heard the case and found that the intent of the bill was unquestionably religious and, therefore, violated the Establishment Clause of the First Amendment.

A prolonged, if no more intelligent, attempt to enforce equal time for creationism alongside evolution, began with a Louisiana bill, which was rapidly signed by Governor David C. Treen, because in his words, "Academic freedom can scarcely be harmed by inclusion; it can be harmed by exlusion." After some legal maneuverings, the U.S. Supreme Court agreed to hear the case late in 1986, and announced its decision in June 1987. It's likely that few people were surprised that the Court struck down Louisiana's so-called balanced treatment law, but it is likely that some were surprised that the decision was a lopsided 7 to 2, with the newest justice, Antonin Scalia, providing a strong dissent. Pat Robertson called the decision "an outrage to every single American who believes he or she was created by God." He said, "The decision will accelerate the exodus of students from public schools to private schools." Presumably he was anxious to get his presidential campaign underway with some early political rhetoric.

The Controversy Rages On

Is it all over but the shouting (or the lamenting)? No. It's not over because the supporters of creationism do not recognize that, as reviewer George Levine claims, evolution has become a part of our cultural heritage. He said, "Despite the continuing rear-guard battles of religious fundamentalists, evolution is one of those scientific words that have been absorbed completely into our collective consciousness."[22]

No, creationism is not dead, nor should it be. It belongs in the public schools—not as part of a science course, but in a course in comparative religions (note the plural) in the junior or senior year when students are old enough to handle the topic without fear that they must protect their own religion at all costs. Unfortunately, some fundamentalist parents will not allow their children to take such a class. Those parents want their children indoctrinated into certainty, not educated about complexities and uncertainties. And, I fear, there would be temptations to both teachers and students to make it a compulsory course in Christianity, but obviously that should be resisted.

Creationism probably isn't even dead in science courses. Somewhere, somehow, some state legislator is saying to him- or herself, "Eureka! At last, a constitutional way to give equal time to creationism in science. It may not have worked in Arkansas or Louisiana, but this ought to play in our state." And, we're off and running once more.

Till that exciting event, teachers need to support their brethren in science, and librarians need to stock books and articles on all sides of the issue. They must be prepared to help students and parents alike find ammunition for either side. That's what education is all about, and that's what we're all about.

Notes

1. Carolyn Dougerty, "Teach Both Life Theories, Students Say," *USA Today*, Mar. 3, 1985, p. D-1.
2. Kathleen Stein, "Censoring Science," *Omni* 9, Feb. 1987, p. 96.
3. *Back to the Bible, or The New Protestantism*, 3rd ed. Review and Herald Publishing Co., 1920, p. 124.
4. Maynard Shipley, *The War on Modern Science: A Short History of the Fundamentalist Attacks on Evolution and Modernism*, Knopf, 1927, p. 176-177.
5. Willard B. Gatewood, *Preachers, Pedogogues, and Politicians*, University of North Carolina Pr., 1966, p. 229.
6. Shipley, p. 318.
7. Howard J. Beale, *Are American Teachers Free?* Scribner, 1936, p. 311.
8. Shipley, p. 173-174.
9. Beale, p. 226-227.
10. Henry M. Morris, *The Remarkable Birth of Planet Earth*, Creation-Life, 1974, p. 75.
11. Henry M. Morris, *The Troubled Waters of Evolution*, Creation-Life, 1974, p. 75.
12. Jeff Prugh, "Evolution Versus Creation," *Los Angeles Times*, Nov. 10, 1979, p. I-A-1.
13. Hyde Post, "Education Battle Evolving around Creation Theory," *Atlanta Journal*, July 16, 1979.
14. Gerald Skoog, "Topic of Evolution in Secondary School Biology Textbooks: 1900-1977," *Science Education* 63, Oct. 1979: 621-640. Skoog, "The Coverage of Evolution in High School Biology Textbooks Published in the 1980s." *Science Education* 68, April, 1984, p. 117-128.
15. John Harrigan, "Schools Cancel Yuma Play," *Arizona Republic*, Feb. 12, 1977, p. B-7.

16. Edna Goldberg, "Hartford Schools May Ban Play Based on Tennessee 'Monkey Trial'," *Baltimore Sun*, Jan. 6, 1982.
17. Russell Chandler, "Evolutionists Take on Creationists." *Los Angeles Times*, May 10, 1982, p. 1-19.
18. Francis J. Flaherty, "The Creation Controversy; The Social Stakes," *Commonweal* 109, Oct. 22, 1982, p. 555-561.
19. Stephen Jay Gould, "Evolution as Fact and Theory," *Discover* 2, May 1981, p. 34-35.
20. *New York Times.* April 18, 1977, p. 21.
21. Bill Honig, "Better Books for Better Schools," *Los Angeles Times*, Oct. 6, 1985, p. IV-5.
22. George Levine, "Darwin and the Evolution of Fiction," *New York Times Book Review*, Oct. 5, 1986, p. 60.

Bibliography

The History of Evolution/Creationism

Allen, Harbor. "The Anti-Evolution Campaign in America," *Current History* 24 (Sept. 1926): 893-897.
Bailey, Kenneth K. "The Enactment of Tennessee's Antievolution Law," *Journal of Southern History* 16 (Nov. 1950): 477-490.
Bruce, Robert V. *The Launching of Modern American Science.* Knopf, 1987.
Clark, Ronald W. *The Survival of Charles Darwin: A Biography of a Man and an Idea.* Random House, 1984.
Darwin, Charles. *On the Origin of Species.* John Murray, 1859.
_____. *The Descent of Man, and Selection in Relation to Sex* (2 vols.) John Murray, 1871.
Eiseley, Loren. *Darwin's Century: Evolution and the Men Who Discovered It.* Doubleday, 1958.
Hull, David L., *Darwin and His Critics: The Reception of Darwin's Theory of Evolution by the Scientific Community.* Harvard Univ. Pr., 1973.
Irwin, William. *Apes, Angels, and Victorians: The Story of Darwin, Huxley, and Evolution.* McGraw-Hill, 1955.
Keynes, Richard Darwin, ed. *The Beagle Record: Selections from the Original Pictorial Records and Written Accounts of the Voyage of H.M.S. Beagle.* M.I.T. Pr., 1979.
Larson, Edward A., *Trial and Error: The American Controversy over Creation and Evolution.* Oxford Univ. Pr., 1985. (The most readable and comprehensive book on the topic.)
Levine, George. "Darwin and the Evolution of Fiction," *New York Times Book Review*, (Oct. 5, 1986): 1; 60-61.
Loewenberg, Bert James. "Darwinism Comes to America, 1859-1900," *Mississippi Valley Historical Review* 28 (Dec. 1941): 339-368.
Miller, Jonathan & Borin Van Loon. *Darwin for Beginners.* Pantheon, 1982. (A fascinating book, both for its comic book format and the many ideas presented.)
Muller, H. J. "One Hundred Years without Darwinism Are Enough," *School Science and Mathematics* 59 (April 1959): 304-316.
Riley, Woodbridge. "The Fight against Evolution," *Bookman* 65 (May 1927): 282-289.

Evolution—Arguments Against

Fairhurst, Alfred. *Atheism in Our Universities.* Standard Publishing Co., 1923.
_____. *Theistic Evolution.* Standard Publishing Co., 1919. (Fairhurst was a professor of natural science at the University of Kentucky.)
Howard, Donald R. *Rebirth of Our Nation: The Decline of the West, 1970's, The Christian Educational Reform, 1980's.* Accelerated Christian Education, 1979.
Martin, T. T. *Hell and the High Schools: Christ or Evolution—Which?*, Western Baptist Publishing Co., 1923. (The most enjoyable of all those early rabble-rousing indictments of the awfulness of evolution.)

McCann, Alfred W. *God—or Gorilla; How the Monkey Theory of Evolution Exposes Its Own Methods, Refutes Its Own Principles, Denies Its Own Inferences, Disproves Its Own Case.* Porter, J. W. *Evolution—A Menace.* Sunday School Board, Southern Baptist Convention, 1922.
Price, George McCready. *Back to the Bible, or The New Protestantism*, 3rd ed. Review and Herald Publishing Co., 1920.
————. *The Predicament of Evolution.* Southern Publishing Assn., 1925.
Sims, J. J. "Why a Christian Rejects Evolution," *Bryan Broadcaster* 1 (Nov. 1925): 12-13.
Straton, John Roach. *The Famous New York Fundamentalist-Modernist Debate: The Orthodox Side.* Doran, 1925.

Arguments for Creationism

Bird, Wendell. "Freedom of Religion and Science Instruction in Public Schools," *Yale Law Journal* 87 (Jan. 1970): 515-570. (A legal justification for equal time for creation science alongside evolution in the schools.)
Clark, Robert T. & James D. Bales. *Why Scientists Accept Creation*, Presbyterian and Reformed Publishing Co., 1966.
Gish, Duane T. "Creation, Evolution and the Historical Evidence," *American Biology Teacher* 35 (Mar. 1973): 132-140.
————. *Evidence against Evolution.* Tyndale House Publications, 1972.
————. *Evolution—The Fossils Say No!*, Creation-Life Publishers, 1973.
Hahn, George. "Creation-Science and Education," *Phi Delta Kappan* 63 (Apr. 1982): 553-555.
Lammerts, Walter E., ed. *Special Studies in Special Creation*, Presbyterian and Reformed Publishing Co., 1971. (Selected Articles from the *Creation Research Society Quarterly*, Vols. I through V, 1964-1968.)
————. *Why Not Creation?* (Selected Articles from the *Creation Research Society Quarterly*, Vols. I through IV, 1964-1968.) Baker Book House, 1970.
LaHaye, Tim & John D. Morris. *The Ark on Ararat.* Creation-Life. 1976.
Moore, John N. & Harold S. Slusher. *Biology: A Search for Order in Complexity.* Zondervan, 1970. (A high school creationist text.)
Moore, John N. "Evolution, Creation, and the Scientific Method," *American Biology Teacher* 35 (Jan. 1973): 23-26; 34.
Morris, Henry M. *Evolution and the Modern Christian.* Baker Book House, 1978.
————. *Education for the Real World.* Creation-Life, 1977.
————. *History of Modern Creationism.* Creation-Life, 1984.
————. *The Remarkable Birth of Planet Earth.* Institute for Creation Research, 1972.
————. *The Scientific Case for Creation.* Creation-Life, 1977. (Probably the best book to begin with to understand the field and the believers.)
————. *Scientific Creationism*, general ed. Creation-Life, 1974. (Long bibliography at the end of procreationist materials.)
————. *The Troubled Waters of Evolution.* Creation-Life, 1974. (See especially the introduction by Tim LaHaye.)
————. *What Is Creation Science?* Creation-Life, 1982.
Morris, Henry & Donald Rohrer, eds. *The Decades of Creation*, Creation-Life, 1981.
Morris, Henry M., et al. *A Symposium on Creation.* Baker Book House, 1968.
Rice, Charles E. "Evolution Is a Religion," *New American* 3 (Aug. 3, 1987): 48-49 (The John Birch publication.) *Twenty-One Scientists Who Believe in Creation.* Creation-Life, 1977.
Viviano, Frank. "The Crucifixion of Evolution," *Mother Jones* 6 (Sept./Oct. 1982): 22-30; 56-59. (Investigative reporting of creationism with interviews at two creation-science think tanks.)
Whitcomb, John C., Jr. & Henry M. Morris. *The Genesis Flood: The Biblical Record and Its Scientific Implications.* Presbyterian and Reformed Publishing Co., 1961.
Young, David A., *Christianity and the Age of the Earth.* Zondervan, 1982.

Arguments for Evolution

Asimov, Isaac, "The 'Threat' of Creationism," *New York Times Magazine*, June 14, 1981, pp. 90+.

Berman, Sanford, "In the Beginning: The Creationists' Agenda," *Library Journal* 110 (Oct. 15, 1985): 31-34.

Brush, Stephen G. "Creationism/Evolution: The Case against 'Equal Time'," *Science Teacher* 48 (April 1981): 29-33.

Callaghan, Catherine A. "Evolution and Creationist Arguments," *American Biology Teacher* 42 (Oct. 1980): 422-425; 427. (One of the best brief presentations of the arguments against creationism.)

Dawkins, Richard. *The Blind Watchmaker: Why the Evidence of Evolution Reveals a Universe without Design.* Norton, 1986.

Eldredge, Niles. *The Monkey Business: A Scientist Looks at Creationism.* Washington Square Pr., 1982. (A handy paperback presenting the case against creationism, and the place to start your reading.)

Futuyma, Douglas J. "Is Darwinism Dead?" *Science Teacher* 52 (Jan. 1985): 16-21.

———. *Science on Trial: The Case for Evolution.* Pantheon, 1983.

Gatzke, Ken W. "Creationism as Sci-ence: What Every Teacher-Scientist Should Know," *Science Education* 69 (July 1985): 549-555.

Godfrey, Laurie R., ed. *Scientists Confront Creationism.* Norton, 1983.

Gorman, James. "Scientist of the Year: Stephen Jay Gould," *Discover* 3 (Jan. 1982): 57-63.

Gould, Stephen Jay. "Creationism Genesis vs. Geology," *Atlantic* 250 (Sept. 1982): 10+.

———. "Darwinism Defined: The Difference between Fact and Theory," *Discover* 8 (Jan. 1987): 64-70. (Witty and lucid, as is virtually anything Gould writes.)

———. *Ever Since Darwin: Reflections in Natural History.* Norton, 1977.

———. "Evolution as Fact and Theory," *Discover* 2 (May 1981): 34-37. (The best essay on the topic that I know, written after the Segraves' trial in California and the Arkansas legislature had passed the equal-time bill. See also Duane Gish's response in *Discover* 2 (April 1981): 6 and Gould's response to Gish's response, *Discover* 2 (Oct. 1981): 10-11.)

———. "In Praise of Charles Darwin," *Discover* 3 (Feb. 1982): 20-25.

———. *The Panda's Thumb.* Norton, 1984.

Kenkel, Father Leonard A. "A Case against Scientific Creationism: A Look at Content Issues," *Science Education* 69 (Jan. 1985): 59-68. (A readable and most helpful article.)

Kitcher, Philip. *Abusing Science: The Case against Creationism.* M.I.T. Pr., 1982. (A basic book.)

Koballa, Thomas R. & Earl J. Montague. "Creationism and Doublespeak" *Science Teacher* 52 (Jan. 1985): 28-30.

Mayr, Ernst. *The Growth of Biological Thought: Diversity, Evolution, and Inheritance.* Harvard University Pr., 1982.

McGowan, Chris, *In the Beginning . . . A Scientist Shows Why the Creationists Are Wrong.* Prometheus Pr., 1987.

Milne, David H. "How to Debate with Creationists—and 'Win'," *American Biology Teacher* 43 (May 1981): 235-245; 266. (Helpful, if a bit unscientifically cocky.)

Montagu Ashley, ed. *Science and Creationism.* Oxford University Pr., 1984.

Newell, Norman D. *Creation and Evolution: Myth or Reality?* Columbia University Pr., 1982.

Ruse, Michael, *Darwinism Defended: A Guide to the Evolution Controversies.* Addison-Wesley, 1982.

Simpson, George Gaylord. *This View of Life: The World of an Evolutionist* Harcourt, 1964.

Skow, John. "The Genesis of Equal Time," *Science* 218 (Dec. 1981): 54; 57-60.

Staley, Steven M. *The New Evolutionary Timetable: Fossils, Genes and the Origin of Species.* Basic Books, 1981.

Stein, Kathleen. "Censoring Science," *Omni* 9 (Feb. 1987): 42+. (Often amusing and always effective in dismantling creationists' arguments.)

Strahler, Arthur. *Science and Earth History: The Evolution/Creation Controversy*. Prometheus Books, 1987.

Strike, Kenneth A. "The Status of Creation-Science," *Phi Delta Kappan* 63 (April 1982): 555-557. (Brilliant attack.)

Wilson, David B., ed. *Did the Devil Make Darwin Do It? Modern Perspectives on the Creation-Evolution Controversies*. Iowa State University Pr., 1983.

Evolution in High Schools

Beale, Howard K. *Are American Teachers Free? An Analysis of Restraints upon the Freedom of Teaching in American Schools*. Scribner, 1936.

_____. *A History of Freedom of Teaching in American Schools*. Scribner, 1941.

Bergman, Jerry. *Teaching about the Creation Evolution Controversy*. Phi Delta Kappan, 1979.

Gould, Stephen Jay. "The Verdict on Creationism," *New York Times Magazine*, July 19, 1987, pp. 32; 34.

Grover, Herbert J. "Evolving State Policy on Creationism," *Education Leadership* 42 (Dec. 1984/Jan. 1985): 69-71.

Moore, John A. "On Giving Equal Time to the Teaching of Evolution and Creation," *Perspectives in Biology and Medicine* 18 (Spring 1975): 405-417.

Moyer, Wayne A. "How Texas Rewrote Your Textbooks," *Science Teacher* 52 (Jan. 1985): 23-27.

_____. *Young Earth Creationism and Biology Textbooks*. National Association of Biology Teachers, 1982.

_____. "Q: Whatever Happened to Creationism? A: It's Still Alive," *Educational Week* 3 (Mar. 21, 1984): 19; 24.

Nelkin, Dorothy. *The Creation Controversy: Science or Scripture in the Schools*. Norton, 1982.

_____. "Science, Rationality, and the Creation Evolution Dispute," *Social Education* 46 (Apr. 1982): 263-266.

_____. *Science Textbook Controversies and the Politics of Equal Time*. M.I.T. Press, 1977.

_____. "The Science-Textbook Controversy," *Scientific American* 234 (Apr. 1976): 33-39.

Raber, Oran L. "Evolution in the High School," *School Science and Mathematics* 14 (Apr. 1914): 323-326.

Skoog, Gerald. "The Coverage of Evolution in High School Biology Textbooks Published in the 1980s," *Science Education* 68 (Apr. 1984): 117-128.

_____. "Topic of Evolution in Secondary School Biology Textbooks: 1900-1977," *Science Education* 63 (Oct. 1979): 621-640.

Woodward, Arthur and David L. Elliott. "Evolution and Creationism in High School Textbooks," *American Biology Teacher* 49 (Mar. 1987): 164-170.

Zetterberg, J. Peter, ed. *Evolution Versus Creationism: The Public Education Controversy*. Oryx Pr., 1983.

A HAVEN FOR THE HOMELESS

Pat Woodrum

An old man paces outside my window, oblivious to the traffic and the bustling city life around him. For the last two months he has walked the sidewalks of a two-block area around the Central Library from early morning until dusk. Dressed in the same sport shirt, slacks, and old felt hat, shoulders stooped, he traverses from corner to corner. He stops at each crack or change in the texture of the sidewalk and stands imprisoned, sometimes for hours, unable to cross over. One foot crosses the crack but the other won't allow him to move even though he continues to try. As people pass, he appears to freeze until they are gone.

I wonder what monsters inhabit the mind of this poor man, another of the many who live on the streets. Once I might have viewed him sympathetically but as a stranger. Now I see him as one of the street people whose welfare has become closely entwined with our downtown library.

Public libraries have always been havens for the homeless, and the Tulsa downtown library has had its share of vagrants over the years. The first Tulsa public librarian referred to the problem as early as 1914 in an annual report. But the situation had always been manageable—until recently.

Almost overnight, the number of homeless spending their days in the downtown library grew to epidemic proportions. The chain of events that created this problem actually began in the early 1980s when the recession hit major industrial areas of the country. During that period, Tulsa remained in an enviable economic position with the lowest unemployment rate in the nation and many believed the city would continue to remain relatively untouched. Oil flowed freely and there were many more jobs than people to fill them. People from every part of the country made their way to Tulsa, seeking a mecca in their time of despair.

At the same time, local evangelist Oral Roberts built the City of Faith, a 25-story medical center and hospital. On his weekly television broadcasts Brother Roberts encouraged members of his TV audience to come to his place of healing. And they came. They came from all over the country,

"A Haven for the Homeless" by Pat Woodrum in *Library Journal* Vol. 113 (January 1988), pp. 55-57; reprinted with permission from Reed Publishing, USA, copyright © Reed Publishing, USA.

adding to those looking for work.

Unfortunately, many of those searching for jobs were unskilled workers not qualified for the openings that existed. Many seeking help from Oral Roberts had only enough savings for a one-way ticket to Tulsa and no money to get back home. Suddenly Tulsa was confronted with a tremendous influx of people. Some lived in tent cities formed on the outskirts of town; those were the fortunate ones. Others were forced to live in their cars or under bridges. Almost 1,300 people were on the streets.

Then Tulsa's economy changed for the worse. Oil prices dropped, banks closed, companies retrenched or moved out of town, and unemployment rose drastically. A new group joined the street people—Tulsa residents evicted from their homes because they were unable to pay rent or make their mortgage payments.

The Salvation Army and similar groups provided overnight sleeping accommodations and churches set up feeding programs. But there was no place for the homeless to go during the day to pass the time and to get out of inclement weather. No place except the downtown library!

As winter approached and the temperature dipped below freezing, street people began moving into the Central Library—in large numbers. They brought in their bedrolls and bags of personal belongings. Some were bathing in the library's rest rooms, others napped at study tables and in lounge areas. For the first time building rules had to be adopted and posted—rules prohibiting loitering, public intoxication, sleeping, etc.

Paper towel dispensers in the rest rooms were replaced with blow dryers. (The paper towel bill had increased considerably.) Then most of our upholstered furniture (many pieces needing to be cleaned or reupholstered) was placed in storage. On one particularly cold day, almost every seat in the six-story building was occupied by a street person. Patrons began to complain and a potentially inflammatory situation developed.

Finally, in the spring of 1985, in frustration, I called together a group of people, consisting of county, city, and library commissioners, and representatives from the Police Department, Chamber of Commerce, and Community Service Council. I told them we had tried everything within our means to control the situation but it was really a community problem and we needed their help. After several meetings it was decided that additional security guards should be hired. The Police Department cooperated fully by patrolling the building on a regular basis for a three-week period, supplementing our security force.

But still the problem persisted. So I went to the Community Service Council director and asked that he call together another group of concerned citizens. Thirty people, representing local churches, community agencies, and others who had learned of the problem through the media, attended that first meeting. Before we left it was agreed that working together we would attack the problem and attempt to achieve a long-term, positive solution. The first step was to learn how other communities were dealing with the people living on the streets.

We found that our situation was not unique. It is estimated that there are 2.2 million homeless people in this country and the number is growing.

We heard of some surprising "solutions." A city council member in Florida suggested spraying all trash receptacles with kerosene or rat poison to discourage foraging. He reasoned that the way to get rid of vermin was to cut off their food supply. An Arizona city shut down all shelters or soup kitchens or dispersed them to the outer edges of town. It passed a law making sleeping on city property a misdemeanor and claimed that all trash was the property of the city. Anyone caught taking trash could be arrested for stealing public property.

Then we learned of a project in Denver that had been highly successful; a day shelter for the homeless. After numerous phone calls, written inquiries, and a visit, it was decided that a similar shelter for our homeless could solve many of the library's, and the city's, problems. We needed a shelter located in the heart of the city, close to the Salvation Army and the library; a shelter that would meet the needs of the street people as well as provide a place other than the library to go to during the day.

Some in the downtown community preferred that the shelter be placed on the edge of town, but we felt the shelter would work only if it was where the people were. A proposal was written for the establishment of a day shelter and the Tulsa Metropolitan Ministry was asked to take over the project. A task force chaired by Clarence Knippa, a well-known retired Lutheran minister, was formed to oversee the project.

The news media fully supported the idea. A member of our library commission, Phil Dessauer, chaired the fundraising committee under the leadership of Henry Zarrow, a Tulsa businessman known for his philanthropic contributions to the community. The fundraising proved to be remarkably easy; $300,000 for a two-year budget was acquired from the United Way, foundations, churches, private and corporate contributions.

The task force found a one-story vacant building that could be leased and renovated, within walking distance of the library in the heart of the downtown area, and across the street from the Salvation Army. A zoning hearing was held and even though neighbors voiced their concerns about security, a variance was approved.

Marcia Sharp, an individual dedicated to helping the homeless, was hired as the director. Her background included a master's degree in corrections and extensive experience with social services programs. Sharp stated that "they set out to create a center that would have a nonjudgmental atmosphere like that found in the library."

Less than a year after I first called on the community for help, a day shelter for the homeless opened its doors. Last January, the shelter celebrated its first anniversary. During that first year it logged 87,000 visits by street people, 9,000 showers, 7,000 shaves, and 400 haircuts. In addition to providing shelter from the elements and a safe place during the day, the center offers mail and phone service, free clothing, laundry facilities, a children's area, health and employment counseling, snacks, showers, and recreation including a depository library that we provide. It is open seven days a week and is staffed by four people at all times, supplemented by volunteers.

Recently a nicely dressed man in his mid-thirties stopped by my office. He introduced himself and said he just wanted me to know how much he appreciated the Tulsa library and how much it had meant to him for a number of years. I invited him to sit down. In the following 30 minutes he related the most incredible story.

He was a member of a local, prominent, well-to-do family and had graduated from a private high school. He earned a bachelor's degree from an internationally recognized university. Just when his future looked bright, he became hooked on cocaine. In the next few years, he became deeply enmeshed in the drug scene and the bottle became his best friend. His family disowned him and he ended up on the streets for five years, spending his night in the alleys or under bridges and his days in the library.

It was hard for me to believe that the clear-eyed, articulate, well-groomed man in front of me had been one of Tulsa's homeless. He finished his story by saying he finally "cracked" and had been sent to a treatment center out of state, where he had been rehabilitated. He is trying to recapture those lost years, has applied for admittance to a seminary, and wants to enter the priesthood. He later hopes to work with street people. He stood, firmly shook my hand, and said, "Please thank all of the great people in this library for being so kind to me when I was down and out."

Unfortunately there are few success stories like this one of reentry into the mainstream. The homeless will continue to haunt public libraries. Yet, the number of street people in Tulsa's downtown library has diminished. The upholstered furniture has been moved out of storage and back into the library. All because of a group of caring citizens—citizens concerned for the homeless, concerned for the library, and concerned about their quality of life in our community. We found in Tulsa a ready public response to a serious human need.

TWILIGHT AND EVENING BELL: A MEDITATION UPON AGING AND THE ELDERLY IN AMERICAN SOCIETY

Joe Morehead

INTRODUCTION

Optimism, that eupeptic belief raised to a pseudophilosophy by Leibnitz and ridiculed by Voltaire, is alive and well when we as a nation contemplate our aging and aged citizens. We cite as examples a few allegedly vigorous septuagenarians and even octogenarians in high offices. Do they not assay their administrative tasks with the same vitality exhibited by their junior colleagues? Are they not still capable of rendering wise decisions in their juridical roles? Do they not evince élan in pursuing their legislative duties? One who peruses journals, documents, reports, and other instruments of government might well agree with Yeats: "There is indeed a confluence of wisdom and time, and ineluctable consanguinity." [1]

In the lacquered ads on television and in glossy magazines we are increasingly given a picture of carefree, attractive senior citizens in affluent settings, gamboling on leisure's greensward. But these seductive images belie the inevitable descent into senility, darkness and death and present a distorted vision of America's aged. While a handful of venerable triathletes merits our admiration, there exists another confederacy of older persons. If we look carefully, this multitude presents a somber and disquieting aspect of aging. As their numbers rise, they pose a crisis of calamitous proportions to a government that scarcely looks beyond the next election. There is little long-range, systematic planning for the growing phenomenon that has been euphemistically called the "graying of America."

Ultimately, the problems of the aged are *our* problems. For those who have reached a great age, decrepitude is permanent, irreversibly beyond the fullness of time. It is almost impossible for the young to form

"Twilight and Evening Bell: A Meditation Upon Aging and the Elderly in American Society" by Joe Morehead in *The Serials Librarian* Vol. 13, no. 4 (December 1987), pp. 5-19; reprinted with permission from Haworth Press, Inc.

an idea of death, but the thought of it lies in wait for us in the most unlikely ambuscades.

SUNSET AND EVENING STAR

Jejune statistics often reveal poignant realities. The elderly population increased more rapidly from 1950 to 1980 than the population of the United States as a whole. Data show that the population 75 years of age or over increased more rapidly than the population 65-74 years of age. Moreover, figures disclose that the population 75 years of age or over are "at high risk" of chronic disease, disability, and institutionalization in a nursing home.[2] These data and the information that follows are extracted from reliable federal government serials.

Long-Term Care

There is no question that the "graying of America" will accelerate. Projections indicate that in the decades 1990-2000 and 2000-2010, the 85 years of age or over group will increase three to four times as fast as the general population. Figures suggest that 29 percent of the long-term care population reside in an "institutional setting," for example, nursing homes. The other 71 percent are in the community. While residents of institutions are generally more disabled than dependent elderly in the community, for every person 65 years of age and older residing in a nursing home, there are *twice* as many persons living in the community who require similar levels of care.[3]

A Place to Lie Down

According to research disseminated by the government, there is a great deal of interstate variation in the number of nursing home beds per 1,000 elderly, ranging from a low of 22 per 1,000 in Florida to a high of 94 per 1,000 in Wisconsin. Moreover, federal and private sector inadequacies are indicated in this indictment: "Neither Medicare . . . nor insurance payments . . . are significant sources for nursing home care. Currently, Medicare and Medicaid expenditure for noninstitutional long-term care are small relative to those for institutional care."[4] The very old are also very proud. Many resist being institutionalized (the very word carries a pejorative and degrading connotation). But the collusion among hospitals, governments, and social service agencies engenders a callous process that often denies dignity to those already humiliated by their own impuissance and by the ostensible indifference of the bureaucratic machinery, with its bewildering forms and plethoric documentations. No matter how supportive and compassionate are the *individuals* who work within the health-care establishment, the collective *process* is dispiriting.

Thin Gruel

Writing in the quarterly federal periodical *Health Care Financing Review,* Doty et al. proffered suggestions. "In light of the escalating expenditures for long-term care, which are expected to continue in the next 20 years because of the aging of the U.S. population, many proposals have been made for reforming the long-term care financing system. Most of these options are designed to control government costs or to increase the use of noninstitutional long-term care services. Proposals to increase private-sector financing include development of private long-term care insurance, life-care communities, and home-equity conversion. Proposals to increase public financing include public long-term care insurance. Other options include terminating the open-ended entitlement to Medicaid services and substitute a closed-end block grant." [5]

Many of these measures are band-aids on a festering wound, an abscess that will metastasize. Society faces a problem that will, in the next thirty years, consume our social resources unless imaginative, far-reaching programs are affected. And this cannot be accomplished without the full resources of the federal government. The catastrophic illness insurance proposal advanced by the Secretary of Health and Human Services is a small step in the right direction. Reform of the monster that is Medicare is urgent. The One-Hundredth Congress will pass some measure before it adjourns *sine die* in the autumn of 1988. There can be no ethical compromise. As the Psalmist said, "Cast me not off in the time of old age; forsake me not when my strength faileth." [6]

AN ISLAND SURROUNDED BY DEATH

While the federal government does not shirk from discussion of the ailments that aged flesh is heir to, neither does it fully address the consequences of the aging process. However unpleasant, specific problems must be articulated through the legislative process. Too often government and commercial writings convey the impression that the nation is filled with "young old" seniors enjoying the best years of their lives. While this salutary aspect of the dialectic is worthy of kudos, the baneful side of the quietus commands equal attention.

Montalvo has written that "Old age is an island surrounded by death." [7] To walk down the corridors of a nursing facility, as I have done for the last eight years, is to experience the despair of things impermanent, of the mystery that is life and death. This is a facility in which, for $110 *per day,* the old and infirm sleep away the hours of their slowly ebbing life. There is no adequate way to describe one's feelings in visiting those once young and vibrant men and women, many of them now mere empty husks. Not tethered to life-support machinery, they exist in a twilight state that is, perhaps, worse than death. What cobwebbed thoughts, I have wondered, are filtered through the interstices of their diminished minds? Those who visit nursing facilities on a regular basis cannot help but harbor a pellucid vision of their own future, perhaps lying in those very beds now occupied, oblivious of the last bootless hours, day upon day.

GOVERNMENT INFORMATION ON PROBLEMS OF THE AGING

There is no shortage of published information generated by or for the federal government on the sundry problems accompanying the aging process. Merely to keep up with the specialized vocabulary in the field requires, for the layperson, a dictionary of terms. Such a useful source has been issued by the National Institute on Aging. Entitled *Age Words: A Glossary on Health and Aging*, it provides concise definitions of terms like "functionally dependent elderly," "hospice," "gerontology" (as distinguished from "geriatrics"), and many medical words. Equipped with an adequate index, *Age Words* is a useful reference book.[8]

Through *CIS/Index* one finds abstracts of hearings, reports, and other congressional documents on the variegated problems of the elderly. The House Select Committee on Aging and the Senate Special Committee on Aging issue a number of useful publications. Titles include *Blindness and the Elderly, Caring for America's Alzheimer's Victims, Nursing Home Care: The Unfinished Agenda, Rights of America's Institutionalized Aged: Lost in Confinement, Dying with Dignity: Difficult Times, Different Choices.* One report issued by the Senate Special Committee on Aging expressed concern over the impact of the Balanced Budget and Emergency Deficit Control Act of 1985 (known as the notorious "Gramm-Rudman-Hollings" law, or G-R-H) on programs affecting the elderly. Under the first sequestration (automatic budgetary reductions) that took place on March 1, 1986, non-exempt domestic programs were sliced 4.3 percent, thus reducing expenditures by $4.9 billion. If there are further sequestrations in future fiscal years, the Senate report noted that these mandated reductions under the G-R-H formula would have an adverse impact on the elderly. "Many of these programs [Medicare, community health centers, etc.] provide important services to senior citizens, such as housing, low-income energy assistance, older Americans programs, social services, transportation, health research into Alzheimer's and other diseases, block grants, and home weatherization projects."[9]

Federal Periodicals

While *Aging* is probably the best known of the United States government periodicals, a number of other federal periodicals contain articles about aspects of the topic. The *Index to U.S. Government Periodicals* always cites many articles under the headings AGE and AGED. Subdivisions of the latter include Alcoholism, Community Service, Day Care, Education, Employment, Federal Aid, Finances, Housing, Independent Living, Institutional Care, Medical Services, Nutrition, Physical Changes and Disorders, Recreation, Social Services, and Transportation. A selected sampling of periodical titles where articles on some aspect of aging and the aged have been published includes *Postal Life, Social Security Bulletin, Public Health Reports, Health Care Financing Review* (mentioned *supra*), *Airman, American Rehabilitation, Sharing, Family Economics Review, Programs for the Handicapped, Monthly Labor Review, Alcohol Health and Research World, Food and Nutrition, U.S. Navy Medicine, ADAMHA News, Black News Digest, Women & Work, New Perspectives, Medical Bulletin, Research Resources Reporter, Psychopharmacology Bulletin,* and *Trends.*

Aging, the Periodical

Formerly issued bimonthly, *Aging* is now issued quarterly by the National Clearinghouse on Aging, Department of Health and Human Services. Available to depository libraries (HE 23,3110; item 444-A), as of 1987 it was sold by the Superintendent of Documents for the bargain-basement price of $5 a year.[10] First issued in 1951, its growth as a useful federal serial was traced by the author in a previous column.[11] According to Gilligan and Hajdas, it is indexed in *Hospital Literature Index, Index to U.S. Government Periodicals, Magazine Index, PAIS Bulletin,* and *Readers' Guide.*[12] The brief annotation that accompanies its listing in *Price List 36* describes *Aging* as a "medium for sharing information about programs and activities among interested individuals, agencies, and organizations in the field of geriatrics."[13]

Its frequency of publication has fluctuated in recent years. Following the August-September 1984 issue (Number 346), the periodical ceased indicating the months covered and began providing only the issue number and year. Beginning with issue Number 347 (1984), this change was effected because of the magazine's "difficulty [in] adhering to a strict bimonthly schedule due to production problems."[14] Number 355 marked its last issue as a bimonthly, and with issue Number 356 (Spring 1987) it became a quarterly. Budgetary constraints, the confluence of Reaganomics and G-R-H casuistry, conspired to diminish the currency of this valuable source of information.

Although a mix of articles on various topics is a typical feature of *Aging,* its contents are not infrequently devoted to a single theme. For example, recent years have seen issues like "Ageism in America" August-September 1984 (Number 346), "Special Issue on Rehabilitation" (Number 350, 1985), and "Special Issue on Independence" (Number 349, 1985).

Recurring features in *Aging* include "Experience Exchange," which provides accounts of workshops and seminars on topics such as the relationship between stress and caregiving; "News Notes," brief items on current activities and projects emanating from the Administration on Aging (AOA) and private-sector initiatives; "The Numbers Game," which presents facts and figures about older Americans in an informative and easy-to-read style; "State and Community News," accounts of innovative and interesting projects funded or encouraged by state offices of programs for the elderly; and "Publications," annotated announcements of monographs (directories, resource guides, bibliographies, sourcebooks, etc.) issued by federal, state, and local agencies and private-sector institutions.

The signed articles, written by agency staffers and authorities in universities and professional associations, adequately cover the range of complex issues arising from the aging of our nation's population. No brief commentary can do justice to the scope and importance of these articles. What follows is an attempt to describe a few topics articulated in the pages of *Aging*, other federal periodicals, and accounts from the serial publications of nongovernmental entities.

TOPICAL CONCERNS

There are so many difficulties attendant upon the very old that they engender a sadness thick as forest shadows. In one article, "Bereavement and the Elderly," the author captures the poignancy of this universal human condition:

> Although people of all ages may experience the death of someone they love, for old people losses occur much more frequently. Now that many people live into their 80s and 90s, it is no longer unusual to outlive one's children in addition to one's peers. For the institutionalized elderly in hospitals or long-term care facilities, death is all around. Although the people who die may not have been particularly close friends, their deaths do not go unnoticed. At the very least, they are constant reminders of one's own mortality.

The writer goes on to describe basic approaches to helping the bereaved, methods like mutual support, psychotherapy, and medication, which can be used alone "or in conjunction with one another." There is no easy palliative to bereavement; it usually "triggers a long and painful process in which one's emotional, social, and psychological functioning may be substantially altered for more than a year." [15]

The deinstitutionalization of the elderly who are also mentally ill is a particularly vexing social problem. Community placement is frequently feared and resisted by healthy members of a city, town, or village. "Deinstitutionalization has enabled thousands of patients to return successfully to the community. But it has also resulted in the 'dumping' of thousands of impaired older people into boarding and nursing homes, with few or no community services to help them cope with daily living." One major problem "in providing assistance to elderly mentally ill people is a shortage of workers. Even more devastating is that those willing to work with this population often have no special training in dealing with the mentally ill or elderly." The writer of this article goes on to describe a Missouri program called Project LIFE, an initiative that has met with some success.[16]

"When Someone Dies in the Hospital" discusses the impact on survivors of "their experience in hospitals as a relative's life draws to a close." Figures indicate that the majority of Americans (63 percent of the total) "end their lives in hospitals." The article suggests that many hospitals are not sufficiently responsive to the patients' needs in their last hours of life or to the relatives who wish to be there at the end. When my father took ill, he was rushed from his nursing home residency to a nearby hospital; he had been dead for an hour before I was notified by the hospital. The author of this article makes a trenchant observation: "Over the long term, medical educators need to give attention to the impact on very sick patients and their next-of-kin of indifferent, insensitive and hostile behavior on the part of medical personnel at all levels."[17]

When a son or daughter must place a parent in a nursing facility, guilt is a universal emotion. Often children of ailing parents have given all they possibly can in time and attention, but when the only recourse is institutionalization, anger, sadness, even shame, and especially guilt, fill the mind and cause additional stress in an already stressful situation. In an article "The Hardest Decision," a set of suggestions is proffered to minimize the agony attendant upon the fateful judgment.[18]

In an article in the excellent government journal *Federal Probation*, the problems of treatment and needs of elderly prisoners are considered. A topic like this is, I would suggest, not one that occupies the thoughts of a vast majority of people; yet it is of legitimate concern. Research suggests that "the number of elderly offenders are increasing" and, eventually, "elderly offenders can become elderly inmates." The authors identify five categories of problems and special needs of elderly inmates: adjustment to imprisonment, vulnerability to victimization, adaptation to physical conditions, lack of suitable programs, and diversity of the elderly inmate population. Their commentary and analysis are insightful. After all, they conclude, "Corrections, like other social institutions in society, must be prepared for the 'greying of America.'"[19]

OTHER ISSUES

There are so many problems that they tend to overwhelm the understanding. The care of those suffering from the dreaded and hideous Alzheimer's disease, a form of progressive dementia first described in 1906 by German neurologist Alois Alzheimer, is almost too unbearable to contemplate or discuss. There are stories of spouses or relatives of persons afflicted with Alzheimer's, whose heroism over days, months, and years exceed in steadfast courage and endurance all the recorded bravery on all the battlefields in all the wars in the history of this wretched planet. Not less heroic, perhaps, are those who provide hospice care for the incurably ill. The term "hospice" derives from a medieval word for a wayside shelter for travelers on difficult journeys, a "house of rest" for pilgrims, the destitute, or the gravely ill. According to the National Hospice Organization in Arlington, Virginia, the word denotes "a program of palliative and supportive services which provides physical, psychological, social and spiritual care for dying persons and their families." [20] According to the *Age Words* glossary, hospice care "can be given in the home, a special hospice facility, or a combination of both." [21] When my wife's mother was in the last month of a losing battle with cancer, a hospice team was there to lend succor and try to alleviate her appalling pain and agony. To be there for another in the darkest hours of impending death is an act of transcendent devotion. For no matter what combination of good genes, good habits, and good luck preserves the vitality of the very old, the endgame cannot be postponed indefinitely. Job's anger at an inscrutable Yahweh provoked this eloquent plaint: "He removeth away the speech of the trusty and taketh away the understanding of the aged." [22]

The list of adversities continues. The House Select Committee on Aging heard testimony that "nearly one out of every six Americans age 65 or older is blind or severely visually impaired—a group totaling approximately 4.5 million (National Eye Institute, 1985). . . . According to the National Society to Prevent Blindness, it is estimated that 47,000 individuals become blind each year in the United States. Of the five major causes of blindness . . . four are age related." [23]

Between 700,000 and 1 million of the nation's elderly are chronically abused or neglected by members of their own family. A profile of the "typical victim is female, average age 75 years. She may be ailing, perhaps with one or more medical problems. Her money and other possessions may be taken, her medication, food and other basic personal needs withheld. She may be locked in her room, denied visitors, forbidden phone calls. She may be subjected to a continuing barrage of threats. At worst, she may be beaten, even sexually assaulted. Who would inflict such treatment on a defenseless person? In this case, the perpetrator is most likely a member of the victim's own family." [24] While the aged of both sexes suffer indignities few young people would tolerate, the apothegm attributed to Ninon de L'Enclos characterizes the plight of the elderly woman in this country as in other lands: *"La vieilesse est l'enfer des femmes."*

The catalog of contumelies may be subsumed in the practice of "ageism," a word first coined in 1967 by Robert N. Butler, former director of the National Institute on Aging. Butler defined *ageism* as a "process of systematic stereotyping of and discrimination against people because they are old, just as racism and sexism accomplish this with skin color and gender. Old people are categorized as senile, rigid in thought and manner, old-fashioned in morality and skills. . . . Ageism allows the younger generations to see old people as different from themselves; thus they subtly cease to identify with their elders as human beings." Writing about ageism in *Aging*, one author opines that the "scarcity of positive words in the English language referring to old age is probably merely a reflection of society's fear of growing old." [25] The aged have enough problems without the added burden of the pernicious effects of ageist language.

THE OTHER SIDE OF EASY STREET

I have deliberately dwelled upon the crepuscular facets of the aging process, if for no other reason than to balance a view of senior citizens that is becoming recklessly fashionable. We hear authoritative gerontologists proclaim the existence of an *au courant* version of the Fountain of Youth. We read that greater numbers of the elderly are "postponing their slide into infirmity," and "the population as a whole is moving toward . . . a prolongation of healthy life, followed by relatively short, sharp drop-off into illness and death." [26] Of course this is the way we all would like the script to be written: exuberant vitality to the very end, followed by a short and painless demise. One suspects more wishful thinking than science is displayed in these pronouncements.

The Leibnitzian view of philosophical optimism applied to the elderly finds its most bizarre and asinine expression in sociologist Lynnette Milner's trivialized crystal ball:

> Shopping malls in the year 2000 won't be jammed with yuppies or teenagers but with an aging brand of savvy consumers [called] "Senior Independent Pioneers" or SIPPIES. Sippies are today's baby boomers in granny shoes. This generation will mature into a group of aged, active consumers who will bring their own kind of clout to the marketplace. At the turn of the century, 30.6 million Americans will be over age 56. Sippies will be 55- to 80-year-olds, mostly women. . . . They will have more time and money to burn than today's seniors. [27]

There seem to be differences of opinion as to how the elderly are faring in this society. A study commissioned by Congress and prepared by the non-profit Villers Foundation indicated that "42 percent of people over 65 are living near or below the poverty line." Titled *On the Other Side of Easy Street*, the report challenges the prevailing view that most senior citizens enjoy the high life, that the elderly are largely rich, leisure class, pampered by the government, placing an onerous burden on younger generations through an indulgent, overly generous Social Security Administration. Out of a total senior citizen population of 27.3 million, the report said, 3.5 to 4.2 million are living below the federal government's poverty line and another 8 million are considered as "economically vulnerable," earning less than $10,312, which is twice the official poverty level of $5,156 for a single person. Moreover, poverty is "exceptionally high" among elderly women; and nearly three-quarters of the nation's black elderly (71 percent) are either poor or economically vulnerable by federal standards.[28]

Other data on disability and the need for services suggest that there are roughly three distinct age groups of elderly with differing degrees of support needs. There are the "young old," age 65 to 74, which comprise about 60 percent of the aged population. "The majority of the young old are relatively fit and active." The next largest group consists of the "moderately old," age 75 to 84. "Persons in this group, comprising 30 percent of the elderly, have increasing rates of illness and disability, and yet half of them have no limitations in their ability to carry out [most of] the activities of daily living." The oldest group, those 85 and older, are the most vulnerable and in need of assistance. Although they comprise only 9 percent of the elderly, the majority in this group "either are limited in the kind or amount of major activity they can undertake, or are totally unable to carry out the major activities of daily living. This group requires the most extensive support, which often includes personal care such as washing, bathing, and supervision of medical regimes."[29]

A compassionate nation will not forsake that 9 percent. Those in government who would advise benign neglect give but lip service to the noble tenets of the Judeo-Christian tradition.[30] Failing moral suasion, the elderly have a leverage that even the most cynical politician understands. The American Association of Retired Persons (AARP) enjoys a clout unequaled by any other lobby group save possibly the ineffable National Rifle Association. When AARP speaks, legislators listen. The membership of this body has the time and will to make its needs perfectly clear. And it votes! Data released by AARP in 1987 indicate that an astonishing 92 percent of its members voted in the November 6, 1986 election.[31] Politicians might find that figure more impressive than all the ethical teachings from Moses to Elie Wiesel.

THE COUNTERFEIT GENERATIONAL ISSUE

This senior citizen power plus some dubious reporting in the news media has given the impression that there is an acerbic generational donnybrook taking place around the idea of "intergenerational inequity." Older people, the argument goes, are battening on youthful workers and their families, the former prospering as the latter slide into penury. In fact, as Elliot Carlson points out, "the conflict isn't one in which the young people themselves are engaging." Polls taken by the respected Yankelovich consultants "indicate that Social Security taxes are either about right or too low (67 percent) and that they are fair (70 percent)."[32]

Fueling this spurious controversy is the shameful fact that the "poverty rate for children has soared in recent years (reaching 21 percent in 1985), while that for older persons has declined (leveling off at 12.6 percent)." But certain media personages illogically link the worsening plight of children with the increasing proportion of federal spending allocated to older Americans. Even proponents of "generational equity" cannot stomach this reasoning. Senator David Durenberger (R-Minnesota), no champion of senior citizen causes, decries that species of sophistry. "That's like saying that government spends a lot on the elderly and nothing to control acid rain, so old folks must be the cause of acid rain. That's a *non sequitur.* It just doesn't follow." Adds Mary Bourdette of the Children's Defense Fund, "Programs for the elderly led the way in showing how poverty could be eliminated for one group. Now we need to make the same commitment to wipe out poverty among the young."[33]

A CONCLUDING EPIPHANY

The Bourdette statement quoted above is not wholly accurate. Both the aged and the young still suffer poverty. Millions of older Americans are infirm, lonely, neglected, and in the grip of irremediable diseases. Caring relatives and volunteers can work wonders, but the quality of their nurture is offset by the limited number of merciful ministrants. Governments have been of help, but they can do much more. Even those who have fared least badly in the inexorable senescence realize the premonitory intimations of life's end, like the sudden draft from a casement window.

For those who die in torment or those fortunate few who die in gentle surcease, there must come a prior *acceptance,* a state of being that is neither resignation nor surrender. It is the knowledge, finally, of things that matter, even as memory and desire wane. It is a perspective the young rarely achieve, absorbed as they are in the passionate pursuit of glittering prizes. This acceptance, this reconciliation of self with the world, may be likened to a journey. Somewhere in this journey, our life comes round a turn. The crisis can be hastened by a serious illness, by the loss of a loved one, or simply by the final, bitter admission that we can never again retrace the steps that led us to where we are. At this point we see, in the dim future, the unmistakable masque of death. From then on, we tend to be interested in, and remember, only that which is needed for the rest of the journey.

Notes

1. William Butler Yeats, "The Coming of Wisdom with Time."
2. Pamela Doty, et al., "An Overview of Long-Term Care," *Health Care Financing Review* 6: 69 (Spring 1985).
3. *Ibid.*, p. 70.
4. *Ibid.*, p. 79.
5. *Ibid.*
6. Old Testament, *The Book of Psalms*, 71: 9.
7. "Old age is an island surrounded by death," Juan Montalvo, *On Beauty.*
8. U.S. National Institute on Aging, *Age Words: A Glossary on Health and Aging* (NIH Publication No. 86-1849), January 1986.
9. *Developments in Aging: 1985, Volume 1* (S. Doc. 99-242), February 28, 1986, p. 386.
10. *Price List 36*, Edition 204 (Winter 1987), p. 1.
11. Joe Morehead, "Tattered Coat Upon a Stick: Aging, the Process and the Periodical," *The Serials Librarian* 4: 271-72 (Spring 1980).
12. Judith Gilligan and Susan Hajdas, "A Checklist of Indexed Federal Periodicals," *Government Publications Review* 13: 512 (1986).
13. *Supra*, note 10.
14. *Aging*, Number 347 (1984), p. 1.
15. Marian Osterweis, "Bereavement and the Elderly," *Aging*, Number 348 (1985), pp. 8, 12, 41.
16. Jaclyn A. Card, et al., "Learning to Do More," *Aging*, Number 352 (1986), pp. 14, 16-17.
17. Margaret Gold, "When Someone Dies in the Hospital," *Aging*, Number 345 (June-July 1984), pp. 18, 22.
18. Nancy Badgwell, "The Hardest Decision," *Modern Maturity* (December 1986-January 1987), pp. 82-86.
19. Gennaro F. Vito and Deborah G. Wilson, "Forgotten People: Elderly Inmates," *Federal Probation* (March 1985), pp. 18-19, 24.
20. Don Colburn, "Hospices Special Places for the Dying to Go on Living," *Washington Post*, republished in the *Albany* [New York] *Times Union*, November 27, 1986, p. H-10.
21. *Supra*, note 8, p. 50.
22. Old Testament, *The Book of Job*, 12:20.
23. U.S. House Select Committee on Aging. *Blindness and the Elderly*, Hearing, April 26, 1985 (Washington: Government Printing Office, 1985), p. 5.
24. Annette Winter, "The Shame of Elder Abuse," *Modern Maturity* (October-November 1986), p. 50.
25. Frank Nuessel, "Old Age Needs a New Name," *Aging*, Number 346 (August-September 1984), pp. 4, 6.
26. "Why We Age Differently," *Newsweek*, October 20, 1986, p. 60.
27. *Parade Magazine*, January 4, 1987, p. 13.
28. Thomas Hays, "Study Finds High Life Not Real Life of Elderly," *Albany* [New York] *Times Union*, January 22, 1987, p. A-9.
29. Marjorie H. Cantor, "Families: A Basic Source of Long-Term Care for the Elderly," *Aging*, Number 349 (1985), p. 9.
30. New Testament, *Matthew*, 25: 35-40.
31. "Capital Outlook," *Modern Maturity* (February-March 1987), p. 94.
32. Elliot Carlson, "The Phony War," *Modern Maturity* (February-March 1987), pp. 34-35.
33. *Ibid.*, pp. 36, 44.

ORAL CULTURE AND LIBRARIES

Raphaël Ndiaye

The Written Word and the Library:
A Fundamental Relationship

We may say that the relationship between the written word and libraries is innate. The written word is called upon to embody messages and deliberately to confer permanence on them, which depends both on the materials and the processes used.

The written word is also called upon to ensure that the messages it carries are securely established in space. There is thus a two-pronged movement toward spatial and temporal dominance.

It is for this reason that, down through the ages, man has sought to improve the materials used in the writing process: inks and various writing media (stone, clay, papyrus, wood, hide, cloth, paper, film . . .) as well as the ever wider possibilities for the reproduction and dissemination of the finished product.

It is quite natural that this chain of operations should have been extended by the aims of collection, preservation and dissemination which it is the library's role to carry out.

First of all collect, to have available real storehouses of written messages or knowledge; multiply those storehouses to make their contents available wherever possible; take all steps to see that these messages resist the passage of time; ensure their regular renewal using techniques for the reproduction of the written word: this could be, in outline, the vocation of the library.

This explains why these steps leading to the birth of libraries date from so far back in history. Indeed, libraries are almost as old as man's attempts to assemble a group of written texts in a given place.

The *innate* relationship between the written word and libraries is revealed also in their parallel history. Libraries have constantly adapted

"Oral Culture and Libraries" by Raphaël Ndiaye in *IFLA Journal* Vol. 14, no. 1 (1988), pp. 40-46; reprinted with permission from K. G. Saur Verlag, Munich, West Germany.

to the evolution of the written word, to be in harmony with the changes it has undergone throughout history. Recent decades have been particularly significant in this respect. . . .

Can African Libraries Be Based on the Written Word?

The same cannot be said of the relationship between oral culture and libraries. In fact, they seem to be mutually exclusive. The process of creation of the written word culminated in libraries—yet these represent to some extent, despite the parallel development already referred to, a stage *beyond* the written word.

Oral culture, in contrast, appears to be a stage *prior* to the invention of writing and therefore (in an even more striking way) of libraries.

Taking a linear view of history, based on numerous examples, it is thought that man goes from oral to written expression, and more broadly from oral culture to written culture. Man's efforts to conceive and create a representation of his thoughts and emotions and to communicate through media which render these adequately, have been long and arduous, and are seen as important stages in development.

Jean Derive, analyzing the work of Walter J. Ong, writes that the author "reminds us of the natural primacy of the oral tradition of language, which is dialect before grapholect", and emphasizes further on that "out of the thousands of languages which have existed or which still exist, only a few have attained the stage of writing: oral culture thus has primacy and is always present".[1]

Theophile Obenga, from the Congo, reminds us that "writing presupposes anatomical organs which have been identified as being located in the cortical layer of the two lobes of the brain". In this context, he refers to the work of the French scientist Paul Broca who studied the brain and language functions, and who, in 1861, was the first to determine "that the destruction of the base of the second frontal fold near the upper frontal lobe led not to paralysis of the arm but to incapacity to describe written characters".[2]

At the end of his analysis, Obenga determines that "the discovery of writing—the coordination of sound and its graphic representation—comes after a long process of intellectual trial and error generally lasting over several centuries."

This is why many peoples who have not received writing from other regions reach only with difficulty the threshold of *phonetic writing* (the alphabet stage).[3]

The oral tradition has always had a privileged position in Africa but it would be wrong to think that writing has not sprung up there from native roots. Such writing systems do indeed exist there, alongside those arising from contact with foreigners and from local adaptations (for example, arabic script adapted into *ajamis* and the various adaptations of the roman alphabet, to make both scripts conform to the phonology of African languages).

Examination of local writing systems reveals that they are situated at different stages in the evolution of writing. One may observe:

—what Obenga calls the *technical system*, a sort of *symbolic writing* with strings of cowries used by the Yoruba and called *arókó*. The author gives a detailed description of this system in the work already cited;[4]

— the *pictographic system* in which a thing is represented by a more or less accurate picture (cf. Egyptian hieroglyphs . . .);

— the *ideographic system* in which a word or idea is represented by an image, a genuine pictorial symbol;

— the *phonographic or phonetics* system which works on three levels—
  (a) to each word (sound) corresponds a sign (*system of verbal signs*)
  (b) to each syllable (sound) corresponds a sign (*syllabic writing*)
  (c) to each phoneme corresponds a sign or letter (*alphabetic writing*).

The length of the period of evolution which led to alphabetic writing can be explained in particular by the progressive divorce between the pictographic or ideographic symbols and the realities they once represented accurately. Symbols become stylized and come to refer increasingly to words of language, which leads to systems of *verbal* signs and hence to *syllabic* then *alphabetic systems*.

In order to illustrate the length of this evolutionary process, as far as the *Vai* script of Sierra Leone is concerned, Obenga notes that: "the *Vai* graphic system arrived at the *phonetic syllabic stage* (as revealed in 1849 to Europeans by Momolu Dawala Bukele) around 1800 and the pictographic stage around 800 AD",[5] that is, ten centuries before.

Besides the *Vai* script, there are other native African writing systems, among which may be listed:

—the *arókó* system of the Yoruba (Nigeria, symbolic writing);

— the *gicandi* system of the Kikuyu (Kenya, pictographic and then ideographic writing);

— the *nsibidi* system of the Efik (Nigeria, Calabar, pictographic and then ideographic writing);

— the *mende* system of the Mende (Sierra Leone, syllabic script);

— the *toma* or *loma* system of the Toma of Loma (Liberia, syllabic script);

— the *Vai* system of the Vai (Liberia, phonetic level, as this script has reached both the syllabic stage and—for its seven vowels—the alphabetic stage);

— the *mum* system of the Mum of Bamum (Cameroon; pictographic then ideographic; syllabic then alphabetic, which leads Obenga to say that this script was probably in use around 800 A.D., while it attained the last stage of its evolution with Njoya in 1895).

This brief outline of African systems of writing is both worrying and reassuring.

(a) We can see that despite their existence, oral culture prevailed to the extent that it caused them to be widely unknown and blocked their development. Nsougan Agblemagnon[6] calls this block the *non-use* of writing *in societies based on oral traditions*, and tries to explain this[7] by four hypotheses which we may summarize thus:

— the absence of pressure from development, which makes it necessary to find a more convenient system of signs;
— the shifting of writing systems by incompatible factors or social structures (for example esoteric groups such as priests . . .) as happened when the boatmen of the river Weser destroyed the first steam-powered boat built by Denis Papin in 1707;
— the level of sophistication reached by the system of oral communication, and the lack of need to develop another system which moreover would hardly be favorable to the secrecy so valued in African cultures;
— failure to overthrow magic signs, for whereas a system of writing evolves from the symbol of the thing to that of the word which designates the thing, then to signs representing the sounds of the word, the magic sign proceeds in the opposite way with the sacred or ritual word which becomes a symbol of the thing. Thus one can attack a person from afar by putting evil spells on his name pronounced in a ritual way.

(b) The existence of the systems described also shows (and this is reassuring) the reality of *traditions of African script* which are much more widely based when one takes into account what are called *ajamis* or systems of writing that adapt arabic script to the phonology of the languages of African peoples long since converted to Islam.

From the above considerations it is clear that the gulf between oral culture and writing in Africa or more broadly between oral culture and libraries can, indeed must, be narrowed in many respects from this point of view; libraries have an even stronger justification for anchoring themselves firmly in African oral cultures.

In making such a statement, we are denying neither the individuality of the former or the latter, nor the efforts that each needs to make to adapt to the other.

Oral Culture

We must look beyond the usual typologies which divide up oral traditions into individual genres, most often according to criteria of content and form (stories, proverbs, historical narratives, poetic genealogy . . .), and broaden our view of oral culture, seeing it not as a mere medium of communication but as a genuine *model of social interaction* and as an eminently cultural reality.

Professor Honorat Aguessy of Benin tries in his paper "Oral Tradition and Cultural Model"[8] to make us see the breadth of this field which covers the following five areas:

— the area of stories, proverbs, sayings, songs, parables, sketches, legends, family mottoes, family and village histories;
— the area of place names and personal names. Family litanies may be linked to this category. Here we witness oral tradition being firmly attached to the naming of places, persons, and family groups whose history is linked to the creation of particular places;
— the area of arts and crafts: dances, musical instruments, costumes, cooking, painting, theatre, basket-making, pottery, carving. These activities bear the marks of a certain social language;
— the area of herbal medicine and psychotherapy, in short the whole range of healing substances. Studies carried out among healers cannot but reveal the considerable wealth of knowledge in this area;
— the area essentially composed of myths and cultural elements contained in stories and religious rituals. The language of cultural drums, of ritual and of the priesthood must be analyzed with patience and thoroughness. This is the area of cultural elements with metaphysical and spiritual overtones.

Although exhaustive, this list could be extended even further. Working in the field of Sereer oral poetry (in Senegal) from a definition of the genres based on the classification developed by Sereer society itself, I have seen this poetry fall into 26 categories of sung poems perfectly identified according to criteria of form, content, musical instruments, setting and duration of performance, and the sex, age, social position and socio-professional category of those who take part in the performance by observing it.[9]

We should also remember that, as Walter Ong says (quoted by Jean Derive),[10] the utterances which form the heritage of oral culture must, in order to be memorized, have remarkable rhythmic, prosodic, melodic or syntactic properties, which means that in oral culture the poetic function, in the sense in which Jakobson understands it, is always active in the discourse of the oral heritage. This implies that the distinction which is frequently made in written cultures on "aesthetic" grounds between literary and non-literary utterances, is here relatively meaningless.

Orality as a cultural phenomenon is to be observed also in the structures it imposes on gestures, attitudes and behaviour, and through a certain philosophy of the existence of relationships to be woven between individuals. This is a culture where *hearing* takes precedence over *seeing*, where things are heard and identified from afar, in pitch darkness as in broad daylight—it is a particular relationship with the natural world, a certain perception of it, and a certain furnishing of the inhabited world.

This culture is also a special dimension bestowed on verbal exchange, the obligatory path of *recognition of the other* in the Hegelian sense: it is extremely subtle knowledge of the psychology of speech, and hence social sanctions through speech and notably through refusal to speak to a person, (which the Dogon people of Mali call *internalized speech*); it is also various therapies through speech; the creative power of speech whose negative aspects determine on the social level a whole series of different behaviour patterns and attitudes; it is the conditions of setting and duration under which speech may hold back or let out, etc, etc. All these elements define orality as a true culture and at the same time point up its distinctiveness. This needs to be clearly understood.

Oral Culture and Libraries

Thus orality can allocate inhabited space to people according to age and sex. On this basis, I was reproached, some years ago, with having spent a whole day in a room with a book. I should have been in the village square with the men, the house being reserved for the women and therefore soiled with femininity. Now, in the village square you do not shut yourself away to read—you speak!

There is a real conflict between the many attitudes required for the traditional operation of libraries and the behaviour which is stressed in oral cultures. The librarian's job is to try to gain in-depth knowledge of orality in order to mark out the areas where there is a conflict and those where orality and libraries are really compatible. The needs of both must be brought into harmony. The effectiveness of libraries is at stake in all the regions where books are today being introduced, and where the population is acutely aware of their value and necessity.

I have tried to put forward some tentative answers to this question, in the public library area, with an article entitled "The Role of Orality in a Public Library".[11]

Let us recall a few points from that article, noting that the public library in particular, but also libraries of all types in the context of oral cultures, should, as far as possible, be attentive to the possessors and content of orality:

— its possessors are men and women knowledgeable about a multitude of things and highly cultivated, who have a high idea of, and scru-

pulous respect for knowledge, and on whom, when they reach a
certain age, is traditionally bestowed the task of teaching. They
will be in a position to lead groups of library users and this will
allow them to identify themselves with the library and feel it to be
their own;
— its content—meaning all knowledge passed down by tradition which
proclaims that it is valid and must be adhered to, which nurtures
its essential verbal expression, that is to say its very substance, *as
words to be stored up* (as the Dogon phrase has it). All knowledge
accumulated down the centuries, the fruit of a rich and varied experience, of our links with nature, of our meditation upon existence
and its problems, etc., must be able to find a place in the library
beside books bearing modern knowledge, as seems to be happening
currently with rural audio libraries in Mali. This is how a dialogue
could be created between tradition and modernity, how our writers,
artists, craftsmen and men of science could be enabled to take
responsibility for our daily existence to try and develop adequate
responses to our daily experiences and our questions.

This was certainly the context of the meeting of writers and researchers
which, in January 1983, pondered on "the oral tradition as a source of
contemporary literature in Africa". This approach can and must be taken
up for almost all fields of knowledge:

— its *instructional processes,* as yet inadequately questioned and
mastered, a knowledge of which will help make libraries more
effective while at the same time encouraging a certain continuity
between the library and its social milieu;
— its audiences: our traditions always identify the audiences with
which they seek to communicate. By correctly understanding this
process, the library will fit without difficulty into its milieu and will
be able to plan its activities as precisely as possible;
— its setting and duration requirements, since tradition defines places
where people may meet and share knowledge and defines a time-
frame for these meetings;
— its tangible aids which can be interpreted as elements of culture
embodied in matter which allow audiences to visualize what they
hear, and to relive their own history.

Whereas all those actions aim to make the library more effective and
to adapt it better to the oral culture in which it bathes, another aspect
of its role is to help in collecting and preserving elements of oral culture.

The library, the memory of the written word today, has the capability to
be the memory of the spoken word, and to aid in the creation of organizations whose role will be to collect and preserve oral traditions, for several

reasons:

1) Oral cultures are an integral part of man's heritage and it would be criminal to let them disappear. It would be as if one burned the archive libraries of the West. In consequence, we must create national centres for oral traditions, veritable national libraries of oral history. These centres do exist in some countries but they suffer from a severe lack of resources.

2) The progress of technology which allows us to record sounds and images make such an operation very simple.

3) The West itself has become aware that beside its culture of the written word, there still exist cultures of the spoken word called "folklore", which people are today taking the trouble to collect and preserve as testimony to ways of life and areas of knowledge, etc. (cf. the Paris Centre for Popular Arts and Traditions, in the Bois de Boulogne and in Bondy.)

4) The bearers of the *national culture or of ethnic cultures* in our countries are still, in their vast majority, those who adhere to the oral tradition and not our modern writers. It is an injustice to ignore this reality; just as prizes are created to reward writers, so others should be created to encourage the *masters of the spoken word.*

5) There is, finally, an important choice to be made: do we want to create a written culture and break with oral culture? Do we want to create a synthesis of the two—and is such a synthesis possible? In the final analysis, this is a choice of *way of life, communication and social interaction.*

Although the force of events is causing us to tilt more and more toward written culture, there is value in asking ourselves such a question and in reflecting on it.

Assuredly, our answer will influence not only our way of life, but more specifically the type of libraries that we wish to create now in our countries.

References

1. Ong, Walter J. "Orality and Literacy: The Technologizing of the World". *Coll. New Accents.* London, New York: Methuen, 1982. (review by J. Derive).
2. Obenga, Theophile. "L'Afrique dans l'antiquite. Egypte pharaonique-Afrique Noire". Paris: Presence Afraicaine, 1973, p. 355.
3. *Ibid.* p. 358.
4. *Ibid.* p. 361-379.
5. *Ibid.* p. 413.
6. Agblemagnon, F. Nsougan. "Sociologie des societes orales d'Afrique Noire". Les Eve du Sud Togo-Paris-La Haye: Mouton, 1969, p. 32.
7. *Ibid.* p. 32.

8. Aguessy, Honorat, "La tradition orale source de la litterature contemporaine en Afrique". International Colloquium organized by the ICA (Institut Culturel Africain) and the Pen Club International with the support of the PNUD and Unesco, in Dakar (Senegal), 24-29 January 1983. Dakar: NEA, 1985.

9. Ndiaye, R. "Literature orale et structuration sociopolitique en pays sereer". *Ethiopiques, revue trimestrielle de culture négro-africaine*, nouvelle série, 3e trimestre 1985, vol. III, no. 3, pp. 65-87.

10. Ong, *op. cit.*

11. Ndiaye, A. Raphaël. "La place de l'oralite dans une bibliothéque publique". *Construction et aménagement des bibliothéques* (Mèlanges Jean Bleton), Paris: Ed. du Cercle de la Librairie, 1986, pp. 65-78.

PART III:
PROFESSIONAL PROBLEMS

"GOING PLATING" STEALING MAPS FROM LIBRARIES

Harold Otness

Introduction to Library Larceny

For several years in the 1970s, Tulane University English Professor Andrew Antippas stole maps from libraries. A highly regarded scholar, he was known and recognized in research collections throughout the country. While attending a reception at the Newberry Library, he simply wandered into a restricted area of the stacks and helped himself to early folded travel maps. He was finally caught in 1978 when a dealer offered Yale University some of its own rare maps, and identified Antippas as the seller.[1]

Recently the University of Georgia has become aware of over $1,000,000 worth of missing publications from its special collections. Included are a great number of Civil War maps and a very rare 1776 British atlas, one of only three copies held in the United States. The thief has been identified as Robert Willingham, Jr., a former library employee, described as a "gentleman, churchgoer, and respected member of the community."[2]

In April of 1987, Lawrence Pawlaczyk stole ten late nineteenth century Pacific Northwest maps from the Southern Oregon State College Library. These maps had been encapsulated and backed, but left out in the public access map cases. Pawlaczyk simply slit the tape and slipped the maps out and into a notebook. He also cut some plates from a nineteenth century set of bird books and sold them, along with the maps, to local antique dealers.

Pawlaczyk is a convicted library thief who has worked his way up and down the West Coast for the last ten years. Perhaps he has visited your libraries, and stolen material from you. And you may not even be aware of the loss.

I can make these statements because Pawlaczyk was caught, soon

"'Going Plating' Stealing Maps from Libraries" by Harold Otness in *Western Association of Map Libraries Information Bulletin* Vol. 19, no. 4 (August 1988), pp. 206-210; reprinted with permission from the *Western Association of Map Libraries Information Bulletin*.

after he hit our library. He stole a manuscript overland diary from the Oregon State Library in Salem, and was apprehended when he tried to cash the check he had received for it from a suspicious Salem bookdealer. With the cooperation of dealers in our area and the Ashland Police Department, we were able to implicate Pawlaczyk. He was brought to Jackson County (Oregon) to face several felony theft charges. Because our charges were relatively minor ones, he plea-bargained here, and was later convicted in Marion County (Oregon). Other charges from the Washington Historical Society in Tacoma are pending. The wheels of justice turn slowly, but not necessarily surely.

As a part of Pawlaczyk's plea-bargain, he was brought to Southern Oregon State College in handcuffs to tell us what he stole, and how he did it. This he did openly, articulately, and with no apparent sense of remorse. In fact, he was visibly proud of his knowledge of library operation, and his knowledge of the market for historical materials, including maps.

A high percentage of library thefts (there are no accurate figures but I have seen 80% bantered about) are committed by insiders. Willingham was an employee; Antippas a faculty member and scholar. Both Stanford and the University of California at Berkeley have been hard hit by graduate students using their collections for research and being tempted by the wealth of materials available and the lack of meaningful security. Pawlaczyk is a confessed and convicted library thief. According to police, he steals from libraries because he has found it the easiest way to support his lifestyle. He was caught because he needed money quickly, causing him to sell his loot locally: police told us that he ordinarily had sent what he stole to his brother in New York State to sell in that part of the country (his brother has been caught and convicted, and is presently out of commission). The wonder is not that Pawlaczyk had gotten away with his crimes for so long, but rather that he got caught. He may well return to this activity in the future. He has already completed his sentence in Oregon.

There is a growing literature on library security, and a publication devoted to it—*The Journal of Library and Archival Security*—and no shortage of good advice on how to reduce risks.

I will confine my remarks to the specific problem of maps, weaving into it our unfortunate experience with Pawlaczyk. Remarkably little has been published on map security, in spite of the fact that some of the recent major library losses have included maps. Maps are among the most tempting treasures in our libraries.

Reasons for Maps being Targets of the Thief

I see two trends in our society which are making maps more vulnerable to theft from library collections. One is the increasing attention given to pictorial representations, perhaps at the expense of the text or written word, in our culture. Everyone likes, and appears to understand, pictorial images. The walls of our homes and offices are covered with them. How many framing shops have come into your neighborhood in the last few years? While people may be reading less, there is no decline in the sales of objects that can be hung on walls—paintings, posters, all kinds of strange collages, and yes, maps.

The second trend is an increasing appreciation for historical artifacts —for things that remind us of the past. Old-fashioned maps, especially those with hand-colored borders and quaint mythological beasts, graceful hand lettering, and mountains that look like fuzzy caterpillars, are prime examples. But these maps need not be of great age. Our sense of history is compressing in this era of frantic change. World War II is ancient history to many college students of today, who, after all, were babes in arms during the Vietnam War, and perhaps not yet even conceived. The important thing is that these maps not look like those maps produced and commonly used today—no machine lettering, no high-gloss coated paper, no satellite imagery. A map only fifty years old looks positively ancient to many people today. As map librarians we must adjust our thinking as to what is old and valuable because the market has changed dramatically. The maps we lost at SOSC were $5 and $10 items in the 1960s and at that time it didn't make sense to put them in a secure area. Thus they were out and available to the thief. The fact that they were encapsulated was no deterrent. If you look in dealers' catalogs today, you are likely to find many maps listed at $50 and above that are in our open collections and essentially unprotected.

Plates in Atlases and Books are just as Vulnerable

In talking with Pawlaczyk, several things became clear to me. Map librarians tend to think first in terms of loose sheets, but many valuable maps appear as plates in books, or folded and in pockets in the backs of books. The problem of loose sheets for thieves is their size. They have to be folded or rolled to be stolen. It is awkward, although certainly not impossible, to steal a large sheet map. And these maps are too big, or too expensive, to frame. Thus they are less desirable on the market. Also, they are more likely to have property stamps. These can be obliterated, but this is troublesome. Individual maps in books are often not marked in any way. Smaller maps in books are simply easier to steal, and easier to sell.

I asked Pawlaczyk what kinds of maps are most marketable. He specializes in Americana and he has a network of dealers who have bought this kind of map from him over the years, without question. These are the kinds of maps most readily available and for which the demand is the greatest. And they need not be very old. City plans, railroad maps, maps showing gold and other mineral deposits, maps of trails and journeys of discovery, Indian reservations, battles, and track charts of voyages are particularly desirable. These kinds of maps are frequently found in the older U.S. government documents, and they are easy to remove. How many dealers' catalogs have you seen listing these kinds of maps, apparently removed from various government reports? Where do you think these maps have come from? I have come to look at some of these dealers' offerings in a new light.

"Going Plating"

Pawlaczyk has been primarily a plater, and he talked about "going plating" in libraries. His first stop was the card catalog to see what the library held in his areas of interest. He had specific works which he knows have good maps and plates which he could readily sell. He is enthusiastic about the new online catalogs where he can simply call up a subject and get a print-out of what the library holds. Computers in libraries have made his work easier.

As for detection systems, Pawlaczyk knows that sheet maps are seldom "bugged," nor are individual plates in books. When he wanted an entire book that circulates, he checked it out with a false ID when possible. He has also used a false ID to gain access to special collection materials. Librarians are very trusting and generally don't look carefully at IDs. In fact, we are often embarrassed to even ask for it. He has used a lead-foil to wrap around books he must pass through detection systems, but he has also passed material under and around exit gates. We all know how easy that is to do. He also knows how to remove Tattletape from books without making a mess. When cutting plates out of books, he used restrooms for privacy. He also has used standard master keys, plastic cards, and knives to get into locked cases. He said most library locked cases are common ones that are easy to get into, but he has been able to find so much of value on the open shelves that often he didn't have to bother with special collections and locks. He has observed that in libraries one key often fits many locks, and that a number of library employees will have ready access to the pass-key.

Pawlaczyk was able to draw us an accurate floorplan of our library, including the locations of our more valuable materials, four months after having left our area. He was aware of our valuable Shakespeare collection and had considered stealing from it, but his specialty is Americana and he found enough of that to satisfy his needs. He said he favored mid-size libraries which are large enough to have tempting older materials, but not large enough to have special staffing and facilities to protect rare materials. And he prefered libraries in less built-up areas because there is an informality and trust in the way we operate, and access is very easy. Big libraries in urban areas are more security conscious, and they have had some experience in dealing with thieves. Small and mid-size academic libraries are choice targets.

Prevention Measures

So, what can be done to deter the library thief?

There are guidelines issued by the American College and Research Libraries' Rare Book and Manuscripts Division which have appeared in *C & RL News*, including:

"Guidelines for the Security of Rare Books, Manuscript, and Other Special Collections." March, 1982. pp. 90-93.

"Guidelines on the Selection of General Collection Material for Transfer to Special Collections." July/August, 1985. pp. 349-352.

"Guidelines Regarding Thefts in Libraries." November, 1986. pp. 646-649.

The Association of Research Libraries, Office of Management Studies' SPEC Kit number 100 is on "Collection Security in ARL Libraries" (Jan. 1984).[3]

The American Antiquarian Booksellers Association (ABAA) has issued a number of statements on the subject which can be found in *AB Bookman's Weekly*. They also have BAMBAM, a hotline reporting missing materials from libraries. This is an acronym for "Bookline Alert: Missing Books and Manuscripts." Here I must interject that our thief finds this listing "a joke" because he had his stolen items sold long before they ever, if ever, got listed in BAMBAM. There is still considerable reluctance among library administrators to report losses and, in any event, losses are often not known until long after the event. My own observation here is that ABAA members, and many non-member bookdealers as well, are highly ethical and very cooperative with libraries reporting losses. In fact their tips led to the apprehension of our thief. But some of the "antique" and print dealers live by different ethical standards. At least three local dealers bought from our thief, even though they admitted later that the circumstances seemed suspicious. Needless to say, they were not joyful about giving up their ill-acquired maps, although they did in the presence of the police. I doubt that you can count on many of these kinds of dealers to make a serious effort to determine if maps offered to them at a low price have been stolen from libraries. Too many of them simply don't want to know. And should you report your losses to them, I wouldn't expect much cooperation from them without police presence. It is quick and easy to move stolen items through the trade and out of the area. We told our librarians to keep an eye out for our missing maps in the local stores, but if they spotted any to not confront the dealer, but rather notify me. I called the detective assigned to the case and we went together to recover the material. If you can identify the material and produce the records to prove that it belongs to your library, the dealer must surrender it. But expect that material to be held by the police as evidence until the case is cleared. In any event, don't try to make the recovery yourself.

Campus security services vary from institution to institution. At Southern Oregon State College they are primarily report-takers: the solving of crimes is referred to the Ashland Police Department. Yet it is important on our campus that all communication with the local police be directed through our security office. This is an extra step, but to bypass it would offend people and perhaps result in lessened cooperation in the future. We had excellent cooperation from the Ashland Police, who seemed to enjoy having, for once, a fairly clear-cut case, and a rather novel one at that. But in this era of violent heinous crimes, one can't expect the police to devote too much time and resources to the apprehending of library thieves. And one cannot expect convicted library thieves to be incarcerated for long, regardless of how many convictions. There is a huge and growing gap between sentences meted out by the courts, and time actually spent under lock and key, especially in Oregon with its crowded prisons.

Prevention Steps to be Taken

I will end this presentation with a summary of steps that we should take to protect our increasingly more valuable older maps. These steps are often given in the literature, but too often ignored because of the pressures of time or other considerations:

1. Identify valuable and irreplaceable maps on open shelves, both in map collections and in general library collections, especially in government document collections. Most librarians have little knowledge of maps in books, serials, and reports, nor an understanding of their value. Educate them on the existence of these maps and their value.

2. Transfer these items to secure areas.

3. Improve their bibliographic description, especially on the shelflist so that they can be identified as library property in the event of loss. Especially note such copy-specific features as defects and marginalia.

4. Mark each item with property stamps. This is a touchy subject to many librarians and archivists, but if you can't identify the item as yours, you cannot legally recover it. There are a wide variety of ways in which to mark maps, including some which are not readily visible.

5. Identify the users of your valuable maps. Photo-ID is preferable, and check each item carefully as it is returned; even if the user is your trusted colleague and best friend. Remember that a higth percentage

of library thieves are insiders. Some of your best friends can do the most damage.

6. Conduct regular inventories of valuable maps. If you have the time and resources to add valuable maps to your collection, you should make the time and resources available to periodically see that they are still with you.

7. Report all thefts promptly and publicly, to both your campus security and to your city police. And report your missing items to area map and antique dealers. This will at least make them aware of the problem, and make them aware of their risks in purchasing stolen property. Too many library thefts go unreported, and for the wrong reasons. Don't be embarrassed to admit that people have stolen from your collections. You are in good company, along with librarians at Harvard, the Library of Congress, Yale, & the Newberry.

8. If you have a theft, keep a detailed chronological record of all events that develop concerning it. This will be very helpful to the police in prosecution, and to the library profession in general. We need more documentation of these events.[4]

9. Work to make library thefts the felonies that they are, rather than just a misdemeanor and an event to make light of. Encourage stronger sentences for library thieves.

Conclusions

In reading off this pedantic list, I am reminded of Oscar Wilde's famous line: "the best thing to do with good advice is to pass it on." Librarians are torn between the commitment to the promotion of the use of their collections, and the commitment for preserving materials for future generations. Our commitment to service runs strong in this day, and it makes our collections vulnerable to theft. How can we possibly encourage use while at the same time protect our materials? We are in a professional dilemma that is not always well understood by the people we must report to. That which society pays us to maintain custody over is not simply paper and words and images, but our irreplaceable cultural and intellectual heritage. It is a great responsibility, and it should weigh heavily upon us all. If we can't take good care of it, we must face the question of whether we should have it in the first place.

Platers like Pawlaczyk are active now. Of that you can be almost certain. And the older maps you hold, in both sheet and book format, will become ever greater temptations to them as time goes on.

References

1. Mary Wyly, "Special Collections security; problems, trends, and consciousness." *Library Trends* 36 (Summer 1987) 241-256. (An excellent summary article on recent library security matters.)
2. "Scandal at University of Georgia over theft of rare items." *Library Journal* (April 1, 1987) 15.
3. David S. Zeidberg, *"We have met the enemy* . . . Collection security in libraries." *Rare Books & Manuscripts Librarianship* 12 (Spring 1987) 19-26.
4. Notes on the Pawlaczyk theft are from a file maintained by the Southern Oregon State College Library.

VIRUSES, TROJAN HORSES, AND OTHER BADWARE: INFORMATION AND IMPLICATIONS FOR ONLINE SEARCHERS

Steve Clancy

PART I . . . THE PROBLEM

Gotcha!

One afternoon last year after a long day of online searching, I dialed into a local bulletin board system and downloaded a likely looking program called MOUNTAIN.EXE. The program, which had been "uploaded" to the BBS by another user, was described as a "utility for hard disk statistics and diagnostics." No documentation accompanied the program, so after logging off, I ran the program to see how it worked.

The screen blanked, and I watched the hard drive run for several seconds without any apparent results. After nearly a minute had passed, I finally broke out of the program using the CONTROL-BREAK keys, and attempted to display a directory of files. Many of the filenames contained random characters. With mounting trepidation, I attempted to load and run another program. The system responded with Bad command or filename. Another directory listing produced even more corrupted filenames. Finally, using a floppy-based DOS diskette, I ran the CHKDSK program to check the hard disk. My worst fears were confirmed as I realized that most of my hard disk had been erased or corrupted, including all my stored searches. I was the victim of a "Trojan horse."

In actuality, things were not quite as bad as they seemed at first. Long experience with buggy software had taught me to back up my hard disk

"Viruses, Trojan Horses, and Other Badware: Information and Implications for Online Searchers" by Steve Clancy in *Database* Vol. 11 (August 1988), pp. 37-44; reprinted with permission from Online, Inc.

before running untested programs, so I was able to restore most of my files
with little loss.

An International Headache

Many computer users have heard the tale, no doubt somewhat apocryphal,
of the bored or disgruntled programmer who loosed the first computer
"worm" in a large mainframe system. As the story goes, the program was
designed to create endless copies of itself until it finally occupied virtually
all unused storage in the computer. The cure took the form of an "anti-
worm" program designed to seek and destroy all copies of the troublesome code. The reality is even more terrifying.

Dr. Fred Cohen, now of the University of Cincinnati, is credited with
the creation of the first computer "virus," a computer program capable of
"infecting" a computer system and destroying data, as an experiment on
November 3, 1983. (5) The experiments grew out of his thesis written at
the University of Southern California.

Since then, Trojan horses, computer viruses, and other such "badware"
have received a fair amount of publicity over the past couple of years. To
the general public, and to many computer users, they evoke a certain
sense of mystery akin to international espionage. Though this type of
destructive programming may have begun in larger computer systems, it
also may infect smaller personal computers. Incidents and rumors of computer sabotage are appearing in the popular and professional press with
increasing frequency. Both the *New York Times* and the *Los Angeles
Times* have recently published articles on the growing problem of computer sabotage specifically from computer "infection."

In Israel, a virus program, suspected to have been planted by a political saboteur, threatened to destroy data in Hebrew University computers
when a May 13, 1988 trigger date was reached. (9) The virus was detected
early enough to allow development of "vaccine" programs to fight the
"infection."

The "Christmas tree virus" which was introduced into IBM's electronic
mail network on December 11, 1987 by a source "outside of IBM in West
Germany," was not designed to destroy data, but to display a Christmas
tree and holiday message. (6) The program accessed routing lists each
time it was run by an unsuspecting user, and used these lists to proliferate
throughout the system, eventually slowing response time.

Also in 1987 at Lehigh University in Pennsylvania, a virus was found
to have infected hard disks in the microcomputer laboratory and program
diskettes loaned to students. (6) By the time it was discovered, the virus
program had disabled "several hundred" of the diskettes used by students,
as well as "several" hard disks in the laboratory. The virus modified the
COMMAND.COM system file in order to replicate itself on other disks,

erased data, and destroyed important system areas of disks.

Trojan Horses, Logic Bombs, Viruses, and Worms

What exactly are these vicious programs, and where do they come from? What implications, if any, do they have for online searchers?

Computer programs designed to create mischief within a computer system have been given a variety of names such as worm, virus, Trojan horse, logic bomb, etc. Definitions are not always clear-cut, or agreed upon by all.

Much of this badware is more common to the larger computer environment. Eric Newhouse, who maintains a list of known destructive and pirated microcomputer programs entitled "The Dirty Dozen" on his BBS, has described the two types which are most commonly created for microcomputers, the virus and the Trojan horse.

The Virus

Viruses, act in a manner analogous to their biological namesake. They infect a system slowly, attaching themselves to other programs, and proliferating throughout the host system each time the program is run. Viruses also move from system to system, often using floppy disks as "carriers." There seem to be strains for almost every system size from mainframe to microcomputer. Much recent publicity has been given to viruses which have infected Macintosh, Amiga, and IBM microcomputers.

The virus often modifies the part of a computer's operating system that contains the "boot-up" instructions, the commands that instruct and initialize the computer each time it is turned on or "booted." Most viruses modify the instructions which reside on certain areas of the floppy or hard disk, and allow the virus to replicate itself on other disks as they are used by the now infected machine. In IBM systems, COMMAND.COM is the most commonly modified file, and IBMBIO.COM and IBMSYS.COM (two hidden system files) are less frequent targets.

The Trojan Horse

Like the famous wooden horse of antiquity, an innocent-appearing program may harbor an unfriendly visitor. Trojan horses describe programs which claim to be something other than what they are. Many such as MOUNTAIN.EXE, described above, purport to be utility programs, but they are just as likely to be disguised as games, graphic displays, music programs, etc. In some cases, they may actually perform a legitimate function, while merrily deleting files. Eric Newhouse notes that "they almost always will shoot to disable hard disks. . . ." One favorite target of Trojan horse authors are well-known programs. They may give their creation the same name as one of these popular programs, and claim that it is an updated version. The program I ran into carried the same name as a bonafide hard disk utility. Other programmers may corrupt harmless programs, giving them a new, and deadly function!

"Trojan horse" can also describe a type of program which can be used, mainly on larger systems, to mimic logon sequences or other innocent programs, in order to gather user passwords and create illegal user accounts for the program's author.

Where Do They Come From?

It does not take a high level of skill to construct a computer program to erase data or format a disk. Many thousands of individuals with even a rudimentary knowledge of programming could construct a Trojan horse program. On our library bulletin board system I have encountered at least one Trojan horse which took the form of a DOS batch file and was painfully obvious to anyone with enough knowledge to display it on the screen! On the other hand, some viruses are very sophisticated, mimic well-written programs, and come complete with documentation. They may perform their devilish function quietly, with little fanfare, unnoticed until it is too late. A virus may take a bit more skill to create, but even a poorly written one could cause considerable headaches.

Unfortunately, the authors of these programs often remain anonymous. The old story of the bored programmer, may not be too far from the truth, since the creation of such a program can be an enticing test of computer knowledge and programming creativity. Some may be motivated by the "thrill" of destroying another's system, and the release of a virus or Trojan horse marks such persons as vandals and saboteurs. Whatever the original motive, the final effect is the same. Most computer users and programmers look upon this type of activity with disdain.

How Do They Enter a System?

The proliferation of microcomputers into many facets of our personal and professional lives increases the threat of damage from one of these programs, and obligates users to be at least aware of the potential for a problem. Unless one completely isolates a system, the possibility of sabotage always exists.

Software is constantly traded among microcomputer users, either directly or through bulletin boards and other online systems. Trojan horse programs may easily be uploaded by one user to a bulletin board, and downloaded by the next. The more insidious virus program may have infected a disk that one user gives to another, thereby spreading the infection. Avoiding BBSs and public domain software or shareware, does not guarantee immunity, however. There have been several instances of a virus or other destructive program which were distributed with a commercial program! Some software producers developed (or considered developing) virus-type programs as a form of copy-protection to ensure that illegal copies of their product could not be used. In 1984, Vault Corporation reportedly revealed a scheme using a "file-destroying worm" to destroy data files if protected software was run from other than the original disk. (10)

In October, 1985, Microsoft Corporation acknowledged that some early copies of its ACCESS communications program contained a copy of a "logic bomb . . . planted by a low level programmer". (7) The bomb, when triggered, supposedly gave the message "The weed of crime bears bitter fruit. Now trashing your program disk" to anyone attempting to make an illegal copy.

Another software producer has recently been accused of distributing a Trojan "unprotect" program which claims to remove the company's protection scheme. Users of the program, attempting to unprotect or backup an original protected disk, are informed that they have violated their license agreement while the program, dubbed SUG.COM, destroys data on all drives it can reach.

Is The Threat For Real?

Many experts consider stories of virus-caused destruction to be merely "urban legends," exaggerations of isolated incidents with perhaps a "grain of truth" in them. Judging from my own experience, published reports, and from user comments on many systems, I feel that there has been real damage caused by these programs. It behooves all computer users to be aware of how such programs could find their way into their personal system.

In my two-and-a-half years of operating an IBM PC-based library bulletin board system, I have encountered only two or three programs out of several hundred uploaded by users which could be classified as a Trojan horse or computer virus. In only two cases the program was not discovered before it was made available to other users (this was two cases too many!). Users of other microcomputer systems have not fared as well, however.

Recently, a "harmless" logic bomb was developed and released into Macintosh computer software. The *New York Times* reported that the program was developed by programmers in Montreal, Canada "associated with *MacMag*, a computer hobbyist magazine" for the Macintosh microcomputer. (8) The program was initially distributed with a graphics package called FREEHAND published by Aldus. The bomb was programmed to display a message on March 2, 1988 (the first anniversary of the Macintosh II's introduction), and was not intended to be destructive. However, at least one user claims that the program caused him to lose data. Users of the MACPRO forum on CompuServe have been carrying on a lively discussion of this virus. Many are quite angry that it was developed and released by a publisher of a hobbyist magazine.

A virus which targeted the Commodore Amiga microcomputer was released by a group from Europe named the Swiss Cracking Association some time in late 1987, or early 1988. The virus found its way, either accidently or purposely, onto copies of a floppy-disk-based magazine named AMnews (vol. 2, no. 1). Approximately 300 pre-release versions of the diskettes were released at the 1988 AMIGA-EXPO in Los Angeles, California, before the virus was discovered. This particular virus had the ability to infect a user's machine when booted with an infected disk. The virus, now in the computer's memory, could then infect another bootable disk when the computer was put through a "warm" boot (restart of the computer without shutting off power).

A newer virus, also targeting the Amiga, has the ability to infect any disk which has merely been inserted into the disk drive of an infected machine. The presence of the virus in the "boot block" of a certain disk containing commercial programs, renders the disk unusable. This particular virus has evidently been very prolific. Messages and discussion on various online systems indicate that it is running rampant nationwide. Though not confirmed, one user claimed to have found that the virus had infected commercial diskettes from retail computer stores!

In the wake of these attacks, many anti-virus or "vaccine" programs have been written by concerned users. An annotated list of some of these is contained in Part II . . . "Some Solutions," towards the end of this article.

Early Warning Systems

The most current information about current strains of viruses or Trojan horses is online in the on-going discussions on many BBSs and large online information systems such as CompuServe. CompuServe offers mini-bulletin boards or "SIGs" (special interest groups) for many types of microcomputers. If a virus is on the loose, it will most likely be reported on a CompuServe SIG. Much of the information may be second-hand, or gleaned from other online sources, and there is no substitute for first-hand reports of those that have been "bitten." In addition, the experts who dissect these little monsters, and develop vaccines, will often report their findings online as well as post the cure.

Many university computing centers now operate message boards, which are good sources for this information. Local computer user groups may also be good sources of current information on local viruses.

"The Dirty Dozen—An Uploaded Program Alert List" is one of the best and most comprehensive lists of "badware" or "bogusware" currently available. The list was begun in 1985 by Tom Neff, and is now maintained and updated by Eric Newhouse of Los Angeles, California. The list, which is limited to those programs which infect the IBM PC/MS-DOS systems, is available from Mr. Newhouse's own BBS (The Crest RBBS at 213/471-2518) in Los Angeles, California, or from my own Wellspring RBBS (714/856-7996), or many other bulletin board systems around the country. The "Dirty Dozen" details many of these destructive programs, and also lists known "pirated" or illegal copies of commercial programs which may be circulating.

Occasionally, a program accused of harboring a virus or other destructive function, will be found simply to be a poorly-written, "buggy" program. Not every system, or hard-disk crash is due to a Trojan horse. Eric Newhouse, in the "Dirty Dozen" offers sound advice and notes that users ". . . can be sure of only one thing about hard disks, and that is that they will crash. Often times a user will blame a program for a hard disk failure when in fact his problem lies in his/her hardware. Remember, a Trojan rumor is much easier to START than to STOP."

Searchers Beware?

It is tempting to say that online searchers are immune from this type of nastiness. The bibliographic and textual databases that we access by their nature do not currently contain executable programs (unless a program's source code appeared in a full-text database) that can be captured and run. However, searchers could still be affected in two different ways.

It is possible that one of the databanks or communications networks used by online searchers could fall victim to a viral attack or some other form of sabotage. Online systems such as BRS Information Technologies and Dialog Information Services have taken extensive precautions against such an eventuality by isolating the main system from dial-in access, and developing audit and quality control checks on all input. Though these types of precautions make tampering unlikely, it is still not outside the realm of possibility. Such violations of system integrity, if they happen, could have far-reaching consequences. Though for users of commercial online services, this would only disrupt service and not damage personal systems.

The other way in which a searcher's computer may be damaged is through software that is acquired by purchase or otherwise. As described above, many dangerous programs can be disguised as, or infect legitimate software. Many computer users after initial training on the standard commercial software begin to expand their collection of software through user groups, copies from friends, bulletin board systems, etc. This may include public domain software, shareware, and "pirated" copies of commercial software. Eventually, it is possible to acquire a destructive program.

How To Protect Your System

There are several precautions computer users can take to safeguard their systems against these types of programs, while still enjoying the wide variety of software available. Though these suggestions are not foolproof, they can provide a good first line of defense.

1. One of the best hedges against trouble is a recently backed-up disk. Regular backup of your hard (and floppy) disks will enable you to restore much, if not all, of what was lost. This is a wise practice in any event. There are several relatively inexpensive programs on the market for IBM-compatible systems which will back up a hard disk to floppy diskettes in much less time than the DOS-based BACKUP command. While a recent backup may allow a relatively painless recovery from a Trojan horse attack, a virus may have infected backups as well, compounding the problem.

2. If possible, never run untested public domain or shareware programs on a hard disk the first time, but instead test your new software on a floppy drive. Many, though not all, of these programs prefer to attack the data on a hard disk, due to the amount of information available for destruction. If the program is sophisticated enough, it may still be able to locate your hard disk, even when it is run from a floppy drive.

3. Many programs exist which allow a user to view the contents of a program before running it. One excellent program, CHK4BOMB.EXE, for IBM and MS-DOS systems, dumps the entire contents of a program to the screen, including any text it might find. Many authors of Trojan horses and viruses like to brag, and may insert a message such as ARF, ARF! GOTCHA! in the program. CHK4BOMB will also look for any destructive functions the program might contain. It is not foolproof, however.

4. Other programs exist which will temporarily lock or otherwise protect a hard disk from being written to or formatted, and provide a relatively safe environment in which to test new software. Most are either public domain software or shareware, though some are being developed commercially. Again, these are not foolproof. Many legitimate programs often have a need to write to the disk.

5. DON'T use pirated copies of software. Authors of Trojan horses and viruses often seem to play on the inherent greed in all of us. It is almost an axiom among microcomputer users that "there is no such thing as one copy of a program." Despite copyright laws, copy protection, and licensing agreements, users continue to distribute pirated software via bulletin boards, and to "close friends." This is an excellent avenue for distribution of a virus.

6. DON'T share DOS. Recently, certain computer viruses, such as the Lehigh University virus, attach themselves to system files or sectors on a diskette. On the IBM system the target is the COMMAND.COM program, and on Macintosh systems, the "System Folder." Microcomputer users

often give a friend a copy of a program on a "bootable" diskette, i.e., one which has the necessary instructions, including a COMMAND.COM file, to start the computer. If this diskette should contain a virus, the "friend's" system and disks run the risk of being infected as well. This is one of the ways the dreaded SCA and similar Amiga system viruses have been spread.

7. If you are a user of bulletin board systems, be especially wary of files that you download. While many system operators are conscientious, and check all software before it is posted, many don't. Even among those who do review their software, the occasional bad program may slip through. Be especially careful of downloading from the UPLOAD directory, where users contribute files to the system. If you should discover such a program on a BBS, please let the SysOp know.

8. Do check any published lists of "badware" such as the "Dirty Dozen" that you might come across. SysOps and other users are beginning to band together to get the word out on bad programs.

If You Fall Victim

So what do you do if you start up your computer one day and see the gloating message ARF, ARF! GOTCHA! as the last three years of your tax records disappear? The answer to this depends somewhat on the type of microcomputer you own, and what exactly has happened. The damage done, and the steps taken to repair it will vary from system to system.

"The Dirty Dozen" describes several steps a victim can take to assess damage to the system, and to attempt repair. The first point of advice is to calm down and diagnose the damage. Were all, or only some of your files erased? Was the hard disk formatted? Has the file allocation table (FAT), or hard drive's boot sector been affected (erased, formatted, scrambled)?

At this point, you may want to consult an expert to help you recover your data if possible. Any remedies beyond a simple restore from a backup, will probably require more than a nodding acquaintance with disk editing.

Some commercial utilities for IBM systems may allow you to recover partially or completely. The "Dirty Dozen" recommends three:

PC-TOOLS ($79—Central Point Software, 9700 S.W. Capitol Hwy., Portland, Oregon 97210, 503/244-5728)

MACE UTILITIES ($99—Paul Mace Software, Inc., 400 Williamson Way, Ashland, Oregon 97520, 800/523-0258, 503/488-0224)

NORTON UTILITIES ADVANCED ($150—Peter Norton Computing Inc., 2210 Wilshire Blvd., #186, Santa Monica, CA 90403, 800/451-0303)

A virus program may not only have caused damage, but may continue to infect portions of your hard or floppy disks and certain system files. Several programs have been developed for the Amiga which allow users to check for this, and to "kill" the virus. Others have been written which not only protect, but test the integrity of certain IBM system files.

Computer A.I.D.S.

Unfortunately, the battle continues between those who would build and those who would tear down. As a new cure is created for one virus, a more virulent strain is released. It is perhaps ironic that computer infection should become so prevalent at a time when the AIDS epidemic is also in the forefront of our consciousness. Just as AIDS threatens to destroy personal relationships and communication, the specter of electronic infection serves to make microcomputer users wary of sharing programs and information among their systems. The reputation of many fine public domain and shareware programs have been tainted by Trojan horse "versions." Software companies have likewise suffered when viruses have been found contaminating their own software products.

By taking a few precautions, however, you can still enjoy the wide variety of software that is available.

PART II . . . SOME SOLUTIONS

Protection Programs

(Computer Vaccines)

I have personally been able to test only those vaccines and anti-Trojan horse programs written for the IBM PC and compatibles, but this list includes programs for Amigas and Macintoshes as well.

Many of these programs are memory-resident. Once run, they remain active in memory to intercept destructive actions by a program. They are often used only to test a program, since they may also stop legitimate attempts by a program to create or update a file.

The programs listed are either public-domain or shareware (unless otherwise noted) and may be freely copied and distributed. Some request a small donation or registration fee. All of the IBM-related programs are available for download from my U.C. Irvine Wellspring RBBS (they may be also found on many other BBSs).

I will provide copies of the IBM programs on a limited basis by return mail. Requesters MUST suply one FORMATTED 5¼", double-sided, double-density, IBM-compatible floppy diskette accompanied by a postage-paid/stamped self-addressed diskette mailer. PLEASE be sure to include the diskette AND sufficient return postage.

Online Sources of Protection Programs and News

Wellspring RBBS, University of California, Irvine
Biomedical Library
Steve Clancy, SysOp
714/856-7996; 5pm-8am P.T. Mon-Fri, 24 hrs. weekends.
300-9600 baud; N,8,1
IBM & compatibles

Crest RBBS, Los Angeles, California (The Dirty Dozen)
Eric Newhouse, SysOp
213/471-2518; 24 hrs.
1200-2400 baud; N,8,1
IBM & compatibles

BXR INFO Corner BBS, Falls Church, Virginia
Ginny Loiacona and Marianne Crockford, SysOps
703/756-6109; 24 hrs.
300-2400 baud; N,8,1
IBM & compatibles

Amiga Inn BBS, Anaheim Hills, California
Steve Snyder, SysOp
714/283-3202; 24 hrs.
300-2400 baud; N,8,1
AMIGA microcomputers

CompuServe Information Service
5000 Arlington Centre Blvd.
Columbus, Ohio 43220
800/848-8199 (voice)
614/457-0802 (voice)

Amiga Forum (GO AMIGAFORUM)
Macintosh Personal Productivity Forum (GO MACPRO)
Macintosh Business Forum (GO MACBIZ)

IBM PC

1. BOMBSQAD.COM and **CHK4BOMB.EXE** are written by Andy Hopkins, Swathmore Software Systems, Swathmore, PA 19081. The current version is available from Bob Klahn's FIDO BBS, 302/764-7522.

BOMBSQAD will check for read, write, and format actions by a program depending on how it is initially installed. The program will halt execution with warning messages, and allow the user to continue the program or abort it. BOMBSQAD can be used to protect both floppy and hard drives.

CHK4BOMB reads and displays a "dump" of a program on the screen including any ASCII or text strings it may find. This allows the user to heck for suspicious messages like "NOW ERASING ALL YOUR FILES!" CHK4BOMB also attempts to spot any potentially dangerous capabilities that the program may have such as writing to absolute sectors or formatting a disk, in which case it will sound an alarm. It is not foolproof, and it is possible for a perfectly legitimate program to trigger a CHK4BOMB warning.

2. DPROTECT. COM is written by Gee M. Wong, Gee Wiz Software Company, East Brunswick, NJ 08816.

DPROTECT will "write-protect" one or more diskettes and all fixed disk drives from destructive acts. Once a drive is protected, DPROTECT will warn if any program attempts a disk write or format, and initiate a cold boot of the system.

3. FLUSHOT3.COM is written by Ross M. Greenberg, Software Concepts Design, New York, NY 10016, and the current version is available from a 24-hrs, BBS at 212/889-6438.

Early copies of this program were accused of *being* a Trojan horse. Versions 1 and 2 apparently contained a bug that caused erasure of programs under certain conditions. FLUSHOT version 3 works well. FLUSHOT will halt any attempt to modify the COMMAND.COM system file, as well as other destructive actions. It will warn the user and allow the option to continue or abort.

4. HDSENTRY.COM is written by Andrew M. Fried, Titusville, FL. HDSENTRY allows the testing of any program on a floppy disk, while preventing any destructive calls to the fixed disk.

5. VACCINE.EXE will verify that the size and date of the COMMAND.COM system file has not changed. Some viruses may modify this file and change its size and/or date. When installed properly, VACCINE will verify the current size and date against the original and inform the user if there is a discrepency.

6. MACE VACCINE is available commercially from Paul Mace Software, Inc. It is a supplement to the MACE UTILITIES, and is available for $19.95. MACE VACCINE allows the same protection as many of the above programs, and has several levels of protection.

AMIGA

I do not have extensive information about these programs. Most are currently available from the Amiga Inn BBS, as well as other AMIGA BBSs. Many Amiga users suggest that *all* disks be checked for a virus *before* they are used.

PROTECTOR and PROTECT provide virus detection and protection. They are created and distributed by the SCA to destroy their own virus on an infected diskette.

VCHECK12 and VCHECK19 check for virus. Some newer viruses may not be detectable. Both programs may be needed to identify a particular virus.

Other Amiga protection programs include: VDISK, by Bill Koester, which checks for virus on disk; VMEM, by Craig Bowen, that checks for virus in memory; VIEWBOOT, which is a boot block viewer and virus checker; VIRUSTEST, which detects the new "LSD" virus; and VIRUSX, which tests all drives for viruses from Workbench.

APPLE MACINTOSH

VACCIN.CDV from CE Software is the only vaccine program I know of for Macintosh computers. There may be others. It is available in the MACPRO forum on CompuServe.

References and Further Reading

1. Clancy, Steve, " 'Vet Med' for the Trojan Horse." *OCLC Micro.* October 1986, 2(5):18-19.
2. Colby, Wendelin, "The Insidious Infection." *Infosystems.* May 1985, 32(5):94-96.
3. Dvorak, John C. "Virus Wars: A Serious Warning." *PC Magazine.* 29 February, 1988, 7(4):71.
4. Edersheim, P. "Arf! Arf!" *Wall Street Journal.* 15 August 1985, 206(33):29.
5. Finke, Nikki. "A University Professor's 'Startling' Experiments Began it All." *Los Angeles Times.* 31 January 1988, part 6:1,7.
6. Finke, Nikki. "Does Your Computer Have A Virus? Experts Debate Whether Electronic Attacks Are Urban Mythology or Threat to Security." *Los Angeles Times.* 31 January 1988, part 6:1,8.
7. Glossbrenner, Alfred. "Trojan-Horse Programs Invade the Public Domain." *Lotus.* July 1986, 2(7):13-4.
8. Markoff, John, "A 'Virus' Gives Business a Chill: 'Bug' in Software Can Destroy Data." *New York Times.* 17 March 1988, sect. 4:27,37.
9. McLellan, Vin. "Computer Systems under Siege: 'Virus' Programs That Can Elude Most Barriers Have Begun To Infect Computers Around The World." *New York Times.* 31 January 1988, sect. 3:F1,F8.

10. McLellan, Vin. "Gnawing Insecurities: Satellite Jamming and Software Destruction Threaten Corporate Data Processing Sites." *Digital Review.* March 1986, 3(6):25-6.
11. McWilliams, Peter. "Of Worms And Viruses And The End Of Winter: Computer Bugs Aren't A Big Worry For Most Users." *Los Angeles Times.* 27 March 1988, part 4:3,5.
12. Nieburg, Hal. "Virus Hobgoblins and Trojan Horses." *Computer Shopper.* March 1988, 8(3):266-8,72.
13. "Warning! (Programs Available on Computer Bulletin Boards Sometimes Destroy Data)." *PC* (The Independent Guide to IBM Personal Computers). 13 July 1985, 4(15):33.
14. "Worries over Computer 'Viruses' Lead Campuses to Issue Guidelines." *The Chronicle of Higher Education.* 2 March 1988, 34(25):A15.

BOOKS AS DISEASE CARRIERS, 1880-1920

Gerald S. Greenberg

Introduction

When Andrew McClary addressed the issue of books as carriers of disease in the fall 1985 *Journal of Library History* ("Beware the Deadly Books: A Forgotten Episode in Library History" [20/4]), he revived a subject that had apparently passed into obscurity. Indeed, *Library Literature* used the subject heading "Books as carriers of diseases" only three times in the past forty years and has apparently discontinued its use entirely, electing to index McClary's article under "Books."

Approaching the issue basically from a medical/scientific viewpoint, McClary established that medical doctors were divided on the danger posed by infected books, while research scientists proved the presence of microbes but could do no more than theorize about how they were transmitted to readers. While insisting library books were not dangerous, librarians undertook burdensome disinfection of books and detailed record-keeping procedures to insure circulation safety. Drawing on previous research concerning America's cleanliness fetish, McClary theorized on causes for the fear of infected books, questioning whether actual disinfection of books by libraries did not fuel the panic.

The following paper, while substantiating much of McClary's medical/scientific findings, answers no to the above question. A more comprehensive, detailed look at what actually happened during the height of the book scare leads one to believe that the extraordinary actions taken by libraries (burdensome as they undoubtedly were) very likely helped maintain and/or restore public confidence in book safety. Of crucial importance were the social forces that gave rise to the public health movement in Britain and America—a movement that virtually paralleled the rise of public libraries.

"Books As Disease Carriers 1880–1920" by Gerald S. Greenberg in *Libraries & Culture* Vol. 23, no. 3 (Summer 1988), pp. 281-292; reprinted from *Libraries & Culture* with permission from the University of Texas Press.

By effectively calling on the legislatures to mandate healthful practices and procedures, public health legislation—of national dimension in Britain —was passed. These laws (specifically inclusive of public libraries) and their subsequent enforcement helped bring about the decline of infectious disease and the accompanying public panic.

In practical terms it is evident that public health officials and legislators as well as librarians in both Britain and America deserve credit for the control and eventual resolution of the great book scare.

Libraries and Disease: 1880-1900

The question of whether infectious disease is likely to be transmitted by books circulated among the populace has had a long and enduring life. Greatest concern, however, was given to the problem by British and American librarians and public health personnel in the two decades before and after the turn of the century as evidenced by the amount of literature on the subject. This was a time when epidemics—tuberculosis, smallpox, and scarlet fever in particular—took a fearful toll in urban areas. With the germ theory generally accepted as fact, quarantines were enforced in order to protect the healthy from the diseased. Could not books, as fomites, transmit disease as effectively as any other inanimate object?

When W. F. Poole, Chicago public librarian, reported hearing the previous question raised at a library directors' meeting in 1879, the subject was a new one. Not only could no one present offer an answer, but hardly anyone had ever before heard the questions posed. Consequently, Poole wrote to America's foremost medical authorities as well as librarians in the nation's largest circulating libraries and asked the same question. Of the nineteen responses received, only Surgeon General Dr. John S. Billings had ever heard of a disease supposedly transmitted by a book (he believed the case occurred in London). The consensus of opinion among the other respondents was that infection from such a source was possible but unlikely. Several doctors recommended that books not be loaned to houses sheltering infected individuals. Dr. Henry Lyman, however, professor at Chicago's Rush Medical College, expressed his belief in the futility of extraordinary and unnecessary health measures by sarcastically advocating hiring of 15,000 sanitary policemen to bar everyone from infected homes, deliver children to school in glass cages, and sterilize all U.S. mail![1]

By 1888 we hear of the first in a series of technological responses to the theoretical problem of disease transmission by books. Sheffield, England, employed a disinfection technique using carbolic acid crystals heated in an oven. The resulting vapor apparently both disinfected and cleaned the books exposed to such treatment.[2]

Great Britain was suffering from a smallpox epidemic in 1888, and even precautions such as those described in Sheffield could not restore confidence in the safety of circulating books. In Bradford the library was furnished with a list of all infected persons by the medical authorities. The library compared the list to its own register of borrowers, thereby identifying all possible infected book holders. Books held by such borrowers were seized by the medical authorities and transferred to the local hospital for use by patients there. (Previously such books had been destroyed.) If the infected borrower was holding no books, he was informed he would not be permitted to borrow any until his house was certified disease-free.[3]

During this same period, Britain's library journal, the *Library*, was criticized for ignoring the danger posed by infected library books. Its editors responded by asserting that any intelligent physician would promptly order the disinfection and return of public library books found in the possession of a patient and report the disease to both library and public health authorities (as required by law).[4]

In America W. F. Poole had continued to investigate the subject, uncovering nine more doctors who knew of diseases transmitted by books. These included Dr. H. W. Baker, who reported scarlet fever spread by both book and letter, Dr. J. D. Plunkett, president of the Tennessee Board of Health, and Dr. C. F. Folsom, secretary of the Massachusetts Board of Health, who cited cases of smallpox spread by books. Professor Joseph E. Winters of the City University of New York's Medical College advocated providing infected patients with books that might be destroyed after use without great loss to the collection. Winters also recommended sulphurous acid gas and live steam as disinfectants. Poole also reported that a prominent bacteriologist favored sulphur, live steam, and dry heat (up to 120 degrees F.) as disinfecting processes—in that order.[5]

In 1895 the *Library Journal* reported the death of one Miss Jessie Allan of tuberculosis widely believed to have been contracted from a contaminated book. Stating only that Miss Allan was associated with a "delicate organization" that did "much good work in a good cause," *LJ* sought to assure the library community (many of whom knew Miss Allan) that the real danger in such sad news lies in overestimating actual health risks posed by circulating books. The article pointed to the fact that life expectancy of city-dwellers compared favorably to that of country inhabitants, proving that heavily populated areas are not in and of themselves unhealthy.[6]

In Britain the editorial staffs of the *Library* and *Science Siftings* began a running debate over the likelihood of contracting infectious illness through books. The editor of *Science Siftings* apparently fired the opening salvo when he was reported by the library as declaring he believed that "the bulk of disease among educated classes is spread in this way." The *Library* challenged the editor to prove the veracity of his bold assertion, adding that its own poll of medical officers failed to uncover a single case of infectious disease traced to a book (though admitting later in the publication that tests at Dresden revealed that soiled book pages rubbed with wet fingers yielded many microbes). Retort from *Science Siftings* was not long in coming. Pronouncing the *Library* editorship to be out of its element, *Siftings* advised *Library* to restrict its opinions to weighty matters such as literature or "the ethics of logrolling." The *Library's* editor retaliated by citing a bizarre experiment he conducted three years earlier involving monkeys at the Brown Institute that were fed milk served on fragments of filthy books previously handled by infected readers. No illness in the primates resulted. In summation, the *Library* angrily declared that no danger exists to the ordinary library user, but (citing the Dresden study) that anyone who moistens fingers to turn book pages might well be infected —and deservedly so! The *Library's* wrath was founded in the belief that semiscientific overstatements were fueling the fires of opponents of the public library movement still in its infancy. Not to be deterred, *Siftings* seized upon *Library's* acknowledgment of the Dresden study's findings to claim victory in the debate.[7]

News of further scientific investigation reached American library literature in 1896 when the *Lancet* reported on the experiments of Drs. du Cazal and Catrin of France. Books used in hospital wards were soaked in bouillon, added to various culture media, and inoculated into animals. Streptococcus, pneumococcus, and diphtheria bacillus were effectively transmitted in this manner, while typhoid fever bacillus and Koch's tuberculosis bacillus were not. Disinfection with "formic aldehyde" or by autoclave was recommended, but difficulty of application of the former and damage to book bindings with the latter were acknowledged.[8]

Dr. Elmer Grant Horton of the University of Pennsylvania successfully employed vaporized formalin (a formaldehyde solution) to disinfect contaminated books. Findings indicated 1 cc of formalin to 300 cc of air required no more than fifteen miniutes to achieve the desired effect. Books were undamaged by the procedure.[9] In Britain the *Library*, apparently losing patience with spirited dialogue, advocated outright destruction of books in the possession of infected borrowers, thus obviating any further rejoinders on the subject.[10]

It appears that public libraries were unable to put to rest the question of contagion via book circulation. The medical community continually asserted that such disease transmission was possible—though not necessarily probable—and the fear resulting from such reports only added to the dread already felt by the citizens at risk. It began to appear as if destruction of suspected books was the only sure way to assuage the incipient panic and preserve the public library movement. Accordingly, news of such drastic action became more frequent in the library literature. In London it became common practice for library books in infected homes to be returned directly to public health authorities for destruction, though such procedures required an amendment to the Public Health (London) Act of 1891.[11] In the United States the Western Massachusetts Library Club felt

THE NEW YORK PUBLIC LIBRARY
CIRCULATION DEPARTMENT
ST. GABRIEL'S PARK BRANCH, 303 EAST 36th STREET

New York, _____ *19* ____

The Board of Health has notified this Library that contagious disease exists at your home. Kindly let us know immediately what books, belonging to the Library, you have at present in your household, and the date on which each was borrowed. The accompanying card may be used for the purpose. Keep all books in your possession until the Board of Health has fumigated your premises.

☞ WHEN BOOKS ARE RETURNED PLEASE BRING THIS CARD WITH YOU ☜

Branch Librarian

This Board of Health notification card and the N.Y. State Assembly Act #1125 shown on the following pages are reproduced courtesy of The New York Public Library Archives—The New York Public Library—Astor, Lenox and Tilden Foundations.

State of New York.

No. 1125.   Int. 1052.

In Assembly,

March 2, 1914.

Introduced by Mr. KARPEN — read once and referred to the Committee on Public Health.

AN ACT

To amend the public health law, in relation to the disinfection of books in public libraries.

The People of the State of New York, represented in Senate and Assembly, do enact as follows:

1 Section 1. Chapter forty-nine of the laws of nineteen hundred

2 and nine, entitled "An act in relation to the public health, con-

3 stituting chapter forty-five of the consolidated laws," is hereby

4 amended by adding thereto after section three hundred and thirty-

5 two, a new section, to be section three hundred and thirty-two-a, to

6 read as follows:

7 § 332-a. *Disinfection of public library books. It shall be the*

8 *duty of the governing board or body or officer having the charge and*

9 *control of every public library, and the authorities having charge*

10 *and control of every school library, to provide for the sufficient*

EXPLANATION — Matter in *italics* is new; matter in brackets [ ] is old law to be omitted.

1 *disinfection of each book circulated, immediately upon its return,*

2 *and before it is again taken from such library. The members of*

3 *any such board or body, or any of such authorities, or any librarian*

4 *or other person in charge of any such library, permitting a book to*

5 *be taken which has been previously circulated without causing the*

6 *same to be disinfected in compliance with the provisions of this*

7 *section, shall be subjected to a penalty, hereby imposed, of fifty*

8 *dollars for each violation.*

9 § 2. This act shall take effect immediately.

books that had been exposed to scarlet fever, diphtheria, or smallpox (and possibly tuberculosis and typhoid) should be burned.[12]

The Infectious Diseases (Notification) Act of 1889 had empowered local authorities in Britain to gather pertinent information on all cases of infectious disease in their districts. Employing such information received from the medical officials, libraries established an efficient reporting system in which both the public health department and the ill borrower received notices. The borrower was instructed to turn over books in his possession to the health authorities. The Health Department was told which of the infected citizens were in possession of library books and was empowered to dispose of said books as it saw fit.[13]

The public library movement saw its worst fears realized in January 1900 when the health department in Scranton, Pennsylvania, terminated library circulation in the city in order to preclude possible spread of scarlet fever. Public libraries had long since voluntarily adopted the policy of refusing to loan books to infected borrowers, and the scarlet fever outbreak in Scranton did not appear especially severe. Nevertheless, the city's public health officials felt compelled to take drastic action because they were suffering substantial criticism for their inability to prevent the spread of the most recent epidemic, which came on the heels of a similar outbreak of diphtheria. Book circulation remained suspended for about three weeks, during which time all returning books were treated with formalin vapor for thirty-six hours before being returned to the collection.[14]

In Britain it was suggested that all library books be routinely treated with heated vapor of formalin before being reshelved.[15] Though, to this point, libraries and public health boards were sharing the responsibility of insuring that books did not transmit disease, it is interesting to note that London's Public Health act of 1891, Section 68, allowed for fines up to five pounds for anyone suffering from a contagious disease who willingly loaned a book to another.[16] In addition, localities such as Croyden sought to shift the burden to the reader by assessing fines against anyone who returned to the library any book known to have been exposed to infection.[17]

The Public Health Movement

Paralleling the rise of the free circulating library in England and America was the development of the public health movement. Before the 1880s disease was widely believed to be caused by dirt, and the embryonic public health movement was almost solely concerned with public hygiene. The term "public health" appears to have been used for the first time in Britain's Public Health Act of 1848. In both this and the Public Health Act of 1858, focus was on punishment of offenders, who were perceived as those who lived in the dirtiest conditions—the poor. Improvements in Britain's public health policies grew as the franchise was extended.[18]

England's Public Health Act of 1875 represented landmark legislation. It consolidated existing laws and directed public attention to preventive medicine. It also was to become the model for future public health policy on both sides of the Atlantic. Section 126 sought to preempt epidemics:

Any person who—

(1) while suffering from any dangerous infectious disorder wilfully exposes himself without proper precautions against spreading the said disorder in any street, public place, shop, inn or public conveyance without previously notifying to the owner, conductor or driver thereof that he is so suffering; or

(2) Being in charge of any person so suffering, so exposes such sufferer, or

(3) Gives, lends, sells, transmits or exposes without previous disinfection, any bedding clothing, rags or other things which have been exposed to infections from such disorder, shall be liable to a penalty not exceeding five pounds. . . .[19]

Section 68 of London's Public Health Act (1891) is a virtual restatement of the above, and it was apparent that books would easily qualify as one of the "things" proscribed from circulation after exposure to infection. Section 59 of Britain's Public Health Acts Amendments Act of 1907 spoke directly to the issue of infected library books:

Provisions as to library books—

(1) If any person knows that he is suffering from an infectious disease he shall not take any book or use or cause any book to be taken for his use from any public or circulating library.

(2) A person shall not permit any book which has been taken from a public or circulating library, and is under his control, to be used by any person whom he knows to be suffering from an infectious disease.

(3) A person shall not return to any public or circulating library any book which he knows to have been exposed to infection from any infectious disease or permit any such book which is under his control to be so returned, but shall give notice to the local authority that the book has been so exposed to infection, and the local authority shall cause the book to be disinfected and returned to the library, or to be destroyed.

(4) The local authority shall pay to the proprietor of the library from which the book is procured the value of any book destroyed under the power given by this section.

(5) If any person acts in contravention of or fails to comply with this section, he shall be liable in respect of each offence to a penalty not exceeding forty shillings.[20]

Not only is the circulation of a potentially infected book dealt with in great depth and detail, but compensation to the library for destroyed books is provided for.

In America one finds no comparable national effort to address such public health problems. According to the Constitution, such efforts are reserved for state and local authorities to address. While states possess power to limit individual freedom and/or seize property to protect the public welfare, they have usually delegated health enforcement to cities and towns.[21] Without national leadership on the issue, progressive local leaders often had to battle disinterested and/or corrupt political organizations that were well entrenched and determined not to surrender any of their power. New York City serves as a case in point.

In 1857 New York had the highest death rate of any large city in the world (36.8/1,000 as compared to London and Berlin's 25/1,000). Boss Tweed's Tammany Hall political machine consistently defeated public health bills placed before the state legislature. It was not until a cholera epidemic wreaked its havoc in 1866 that such a bill was pushed through the state body by Dorman B. Eaton and Stephen Smith (who later went on to establish the American Public Health Association). Based on England's sanitary system, a Metropolitan Board of Health was instituted, empowered to act within New York City.[22] In the 1870s the Board actively attacked public health problems by instituting and enforcing sanitary codes dealing with problems ranging from quarantine of smallpox and typhoid to citations for faulty plumbing. In 1885 the New York State Legislature enacted legislation equivalent to England's 1875 Public Health Act requiring areas that were not already doing so (New York City, Brooklyn, Yonkers, Albany, and Buffalo were excepted) to institute proper methods of inspection and control of persons and "things" in order to guard against spread of infection.[23]

Libraries and Disease after 1900

Vapor of formalin remained the disinfectant of choice for those seriously concerned about the threat posed by contaminated books after the turn of the century. Dr. Andrew F. Currier, trustee of the Mt. Vernon (N.Y.) Public Library, presented a paper testifying to the efficacy of such treatment.[24]

The British took note of the Miguel method employed in France and publicized in a paper read before the Académie de Médecine in Paris. A disinfectant solution of two parts formaldehyde to one part calcium chloride was found somewhat effective.[25] The French are also credited by the American library community with introducing a series of suggestions intended to prevent book contamination. In a 1907 dispatch from Paris, Drs. Jose Badia and Nicholas V. Greco advocated introducing wash bowls at the entrance and exists of library reading rooms for patrons usage; scrubbing of floor and furniture with antiseptic; employing "sterilizable moisteners" for readers addicted to finger wetting to turn book pages; and distributing glass plates to be placed over book pages while reading, thereby preventing book contagion through sneezing or coughing.[26]

Formaldehyde advocates received a blow from an article appearing in the *American Journal of Public Hygiene* in 1908 touting steam as a more efficient disinfectant due to its penetrating power.[27] Steam, however, might injure books. W. L. Beebe announced a solution to this dilemma in 1911, advocating the use of 2% carbolic acid in gasoline as a disinfectant solution. Books were soaked and dried without injury. The author recommended use of peppermint, wintergreen, or cinnamon oil for those who objected to the gasoline odor.[28] Unfortunately, L. B. Nice of Harvard Medical School could not replicate Beebe's excellent results. Nice theorized that Beebe did not permit the contaminating culture to dry on the book pages adequately before soaking in the solution. Nice preferred moist hot air as a disinfectant agent.[29]

While the anxiety over handling germ-laden library books remained a constant concern, by 1910 there did not appear to be any significant impetus to the fear. One might say the panic seemed to be losing momentum. Certainly there was no noticeable increase in serious illnesses being reported among library workers or patrons. Nor did it appear that epidemic-related death rates were higher among these groups of people. Some began wondering why handling library books should represent any more of a health hazard than handling paper currency. Of course libraries still routinely routed books in the possession of contagious borrowers to public health agencies (the New York Public Library adopted this procedure as well in 1908), but the issue appeared under control. The worst was over.

It had to be all the more disheartening, therefore, when an alarmist article by William R. Reinick appeared in the *American Journal of Pharmacy* exceeding all predecessors in fantastic claims and bizarre investigations.[31] Cases recounted by Reinick included smallpox contracted from a book; a fatal blood poisoning episode that occurred when a translator transferred mold from a Turkish manuscript to an open facial cut (a Hungarian physician diagnosed the tragedy but was unable to save the unfortunate victim); several incidents of gonorrhea traced to books; and severe colds suffered from inhaling book dust. The author also warned of the possibility of readers contracting cancer by coming in contact with malignant tissue expectorated upon the pages by patients. To emphasize the danger, Reinick reported the death of forty guinea pigs inoculated with dirty book paper.

Such esoteric accounts could only serve to obscure the fact that outbreaks of disease were not being traced to libraries. Librarians themselves were becoming more confident of their own health—so much so that we encounter the first report of books in the possession of scarlet fever patients being returned to the shelves without treatment.[32] No further cases resulted.

Still, in 1914 the New York Public Library was continuing to receive a daily list of persons infected with contagious diseases from the Board of Health. The Library identified borrowers from the list and notified them not to return books to the collection. When such borrowers notified the Library of books in their possession, it transmitted the information to the Board of Health, which subsequently collected and destroyed them. If a patient's books were returned to the Library before the Board of Health could act, New York's branch librarians routinely tossed them into the furnace rather than accumulating them for later pickup by the Health Board.[33] Such behavior speaks of a lingering fear very much alive among library personnel. Perhaps the libraries were doing a better job in dismissing the public's fears than they were in dispelling their own.

The New York Public Library had good reason to review its policies regarding treatment of books in the possession of contagious patrons. Early in March 1914 a Brooklyn Assemblyman named Karpen introduced a bill before the New York State Legislature in Albany requiring disinfection of every book returned to public and school libraries in the state before recirculation. Edwin Anderson, director of the New York Public Library, declared that "the enactment of such a law would put all public libraries out of business at once."[34] Anderson turned to Dr. John S. Billings, who was now both director of the Bureau of Infectious Diseases and medical officer of the New York Public Library. Responding upon request in his first capacity, Dr. Billings declared the proposed disinfection of books to be unnecessary (because formites rarely transmit infection), ineffective (because formaldehyde did not penetrate book leaves), and harmful (because moisture necessary to the process damaged bindings and illustrations).[35] Brandishing Billings's letter, Anderson announced his readiness to mount a citywide protest of Karpen's bill, if necessary.[36] But by 14 March William Watson of the New York State Education Department was able to report that the Public Health Committee had unanimously rejected the proposal.[37]

Once again, public librarians and public health authorities had acted quickly and responsibly to protect library service—this time from a panicky, overzealous legislator.

In Britain Henry R. Kenwood, professor of hygiene at the University of London, concluded the risk of contracting tuberculosis from books to be very slight even under the worst possible circumstances (heavily soiled books) after conducting a series of experiments.[38]

By 1916 we read of doctors assuring the library community that exposure to sunlight provides all the disinfection that books require for safe usage.[39] Dr. Walter Brown of the Massachusetts Department of Health reported that the chances of books transmitting disease were almost nonexistent.[40] In 1920 the Advisory Committee of the National Tuberculosis

Association consisting of national authorities on the disease could state:

> The common use of recreation rooms, library facilities, and occupational
> aid facilities by tuberculous and non-tuberculous patients is without
> hazard to the non-tuberculous in any general hospital where ordinary
> sanitary precautions are instituted and efficiently enforced. The same
> principles would govern the use of the library and other recreational
> facilities of a hospital as are usually applied to public libraries and public
> places of amusement from none of which ambulatory tuberculous patients
> are excluded.[41]

Sanitary common sense was deemed sufficient in dealing with the health
threat posed by circulating libraries.

Yet the question would not die. After all, bacteria were indisputably
present in books. Though they are unlikely to be present in sufficient
quantity to pose a serious health threat, investigations by the medical
community continued throughout the 1930s and 1940s in Britain, America,
and even Japan. Public health agencies also continued to address the
issue. Summarizing the medical problem for the library community in 1950,
William Hill, a British hospital librarian, indicated the jury was still out
on the actual threat posed by infected books.[42] Anxiety had subsided
because risk was nil, but in theory, at least, the possibility remained.

The drastic decline of the very diseases that gave rise to the panic
makes it unlikely that contagion by books will ever again become a crucial
issue.[43] Indeed, greater attention is given today to the future existence of
the book as a communication vehicle than to the public health threat
posed by the print media. Nevertheless, the contagion issue was one that
activated the library, legal, and medical communities in opposition to what
was perceived as a genuine threat—one that could have ended the public
library movement almost before it had begun. Libraries in Britain and
America demonstrated proper concern and instituted practical procedures
and safeguards aimed at countering the apparent threat of contagion. As
a result, public confidence in the libraries was maintained and the future
growth of the movement made possible.

Notes

1. W. F. Poole, "The Spread of Contagious Diseases by Circulating Libraries," *Library Journal* 4 (July-August 1879): 258-262.
2. *Library Journal* 13 (March-April 1888): 105-106.
3. Butler Wood, "Infectious Diseases and Circulating Libraries," *Library Chronicle* 5 (1888): 24.
4. *Library* 1 (1889): 171.
5. *Library Journal* 16 (March 1891): 80.
6. *Library Journal* 20 (October 1895): 338.
7. The point and counterpoint of this debate are to be found in *Library* 7 (1895): 221-222, 290, 330, 336-337.

8. *Library Journal* 21 (April 1896): 150-151.
9. *Library Journal* 22 (August 1897): 388.
10. *Library* 9 (1897): 34.
11. *Library Association Record* 1 (June 1899): 385.
12. *Library Journal* 24 (December 1899): 684-685.
13. William J. Willcock, "Notification of Infectious Disease and the Public Library," *Library World* 2 (1899): 89-91.
14. Henry J. Carr, "Disinfection by Formalin at Scranton Public Library," *Library Journal* 25 (1900): 71-72.
15. *Library Association Record* 2 (May 1900): 249.
16. Thomas Aldred, public librarian at St. George-the-Martyr, quoted the relevant section in correspondence to *Library World* 2 (1900): 198.
17. L. Stanley Jast, " 'Infected' Books," *Library World* 3 (1900): 146.
18. See Harley Williams, *A Century of Public Health in Britain* (London: A. and C. Black, 1932), pp. 10-23.
19. Public Health Act, 1875, 38 and 39 Vict., C. 55.
20. Public Health Acts Amendment Act, 1907, 7 Edw. 7, C. 53.
21. See Lloyd Ackerman, *Health and Hygiene* (Lancaster: Jaques Cattell Press, 1943), pp. 297-298.
22. See Wilson G. Smilie, *Public Health* (New York: Macmillan Company, 1955), pp. 288-293.
23. *Laws of the State of New York* (Albany: Banks and Brothers, 1885), ch. 270d.
24. Andrew F. Currier, "The Sterilization of Books by Vapor of Formalin," *Library Journal* 27 (October 1902): 881-883.
25. *Library Association Record* 9 (February 1907): 92.
26. *Library Journal* 32 (October 1907): 442.
27. Burt R. Rickards, "The Disinfection of Books," *American Journal of Public Hygiene* 18 (1908): 325-328.
28. W. L. Beebe, "Carbo Gasoline Method for the Disinfection of Books," *Journal of the American Public Health Association*, 3rd ser., 1 (1911): 54-60.
29. L. B. Nice, "Experiments in Book Disinfection," *Journal of the American Public Health Association*, 3rd ser., 1 (1911): 775-777.
30. *New York Times*, 8 March 1908, sec. 6, p. 61, col. 6.
31. William R. Reinick, "Books as a Source of Disease," *American Journal of Pharmacy and the Sciences Supporting Public Health* 86: 13-25.
32. *Library Journal* 38 (January 1913): 27-28.
33. Secretary to Chief of Circulation Department, 10 March 1914, Record Group 6, Director's Office, New York Public Library Archives.
34. Edwin H. Anderson to William R. Watson, 13 March 1914, Record Group 6, Director's Office, New York Public Library Archives.
35. Billings to Anderson, 10 March 1914, Record Group 6, Director's Office, New York Public Library Archives.
36. Anderson to Billings, 14 March 1914, Record Group 6, Director's Office, New York Public Library Archives.
37. Watson to Anderson, 14 March 1914, Record Group 6, Director's Office, New York Public Library Archives.
38. *Library Association Record* 17 (September 1915): 415.
39. *Wisconsin Library Bulletin* 12 (November 1916): 390-391.
40. *Library Occurrent* 4 (April 1917): 178.
41. Elizabeth Koehler, "Are You A Phthisiophobist?" *Special Libraries* 11 (June 1920): 149.
42. William Hill, "Books and Infectious Diseases," *Library Association Record*, 4th ser., 17 (May 1950): 146.
43. Andrew McClary, "Beware the Deadly Books: A Forgotten Episode in Library History," *Journal of Library History* 20/4 (Fall 1985): 431-432.

ARE YOU *SURE* THAT BOOK WON THE CALDECOTT MEDAL? VARIANT PRINTINGS AND EDITIONS OF THREE CALDECOTT MEDAL BOOKS

Kathleen T. Horning

It is quite easy to find a copy of virtually any book that has ever won the Caldecott Medal. They are readily available in libraries and bookstores. The title that won forty-nine years ago is just as easy to find as the title that won this year. Maybe easier. Indeed, winning the Caldecott Medal assures a book of a very long life. Currently only one of the fifty Caldecott Award-winning titles is out of print.[1]

It is *not* easy to find a first edition of a Caldecott Medal book. Because these titles are highly visible and heavily used, they frequently wear out. They are easily replaced. But because they stay in print for so long and because times change, so, too, do the books. It could be that the copy of a decades-old Caldecott Medal book that you purchased last week looks slightly different from the book that was actually awarded the medal. Or it could be that it looks *very* different. If you don't have a copy of the first edition handy for comparison (and chances are you don't), you'll never know. But you may wonder why the book you're holding won the Caldecott Medal.

The answer is—it didn't.

In this article I will describe, as examples, three Caldecott Medal books that have changed over the years—one slightly, one moderately, and one drastically—and I will briefly discuss the implications that these changes have for those who are concerned with children's literature.

In 1938 Dorothy Lathrop won the first Caldecott Medal for *Animals of the Bible* (Stokes), and it was discovered later that the child pictured in the final double-page spread had two left feet. This was corrected in

"Are You Sure That Book Won the Caldecott Medal? Variant Printings and Editions of Three Caldecott Medal Books" by Kathleen T. Horning in *Journal of Youth Services in Libraries* Vol. 1, no. 2 (Winter 1988), pp. 173-176; reprinted with permission from the American Library Association, copyright © 1988 by ALA.

subsequent printings. While it makes for an interesting bit of book lore, and perhaps tells us a little bit about either the impercipience or the generosity of the 1938 Newbery-Caldecott Committee, no one with a corrected edition is likely to question the absence of two left feet. You may, however, question the absence of clarity in the black-and-white lithographs appearing in, say, the sixteenth printing of *Animals of the Bible*. Oh, but if you could *see* the subtle gradation of light and dark in the softly textured illustrations appearing in the first edition, you would award the medal yourself! These are the illustrations that won the Caldecott. Those appearing in the sixteenth printing are a pale imitation.

In 1966 two stereotypical illustrations of a black child were deleted from Maud and Miska Petersham's *The Rooster Crows: A Book of American Rhymes and Jingles* (Macmillan), which won the Caldecott Medal in 1946. Since it is impossible to remove just two pages from a book, Macmillan opted to replace the offensive illustrations with a drawing of Little Jack Horner and six additional rhymes from Mother Goose. In the revision the order of the pages in the third signature has also been completely changed, so that no individual double-page spread is the same as it was in the original edition. There was a subtle but logical organization of material in the book that won the Caldecott Medal. The rhymes and illustrations appearing on opposing pages were often related. Verses about food, for example, made up one double-page spread, as did rhymes about the weather. Some of the careful organization used in designing the book has been lost in the revised edition. Ironically, the illustration for the rhyme that gave the book its title now appears opposite "Little Miss Muffet" and "The Rooster Crows" next to a red sky at night.

The most dramatic change in a Caldecott Award-winning book, however, occurs with Edgar and Ingri Parin d'Aulaire's *Abraham Lincoln*, originally published by Doubleday in 1939. Much has been written about the d'Aulaires' pioneering work, using stone lithography, to bring a wide range of color into children's picture books.[2] The arduous process involved in printing from stone ultimately serves, according to the d'Aulaires themselves, to "give the finished work a handdrawn look."[3] Anyone lucky enough to possess a copy of the first edition of *Abraham Lincoln* will see that this is true, but first editions are hard to find. If you look, what you are likely to find is the completely redrawn edition that Doubleday first published in 1957. Handling and storing the stones from which the Caldecott Medal book was printed proved to be too great a burden: the d'Aulaires were asked to redraw the illustrations on acetate. Edgar Parin d'Aulaire said,

> We tried to keep the drawings as close as possible to the originals, though we made a point of making at least one small change in each picture, which brightened the tediousness of the mechanical work. Instead of stone lithography we had to use acetates for the new Lincoln. With a

heavy heart we had to give up our beloved stones, not because our backs broke but because the offset printers hate to handle them. We try to work on acetates just like the stones, but you cannot get as much life out of dead material.[4]

The small changes to which the artist refers consist of several visual jokes and minor adjustments in posture. A small vase set on a bureau in the original edition, for example, lies on the floor in pieces in the 1957 edition. The blade of the axe Lincoln holds in many of the illustrations always points towards his body in the 1939 edition and away from it in the revision. The big changes are more difficult to describe, but they stand out immediately when you compare the redrawn illustrations with the originals. The characters' faces have undergone remarkable changes: Lincoln looks like a completely different person in the 1957 edition. The color in the 1939 edition is softer, as there is a more subtle variation in tone. In the revision there is less variation, and the colors look harsh and flat. Gone is any trace of a "handdrawn look."

We do not need to make judgments, however, as to which edition has better illustrations in order to question whether or not it is appropriate for the Caldecott Medal to appear on the jacket of the 1957 edition. It is clear that the illustrations appearing in the 1939 edition of *Abraham Lincoln* were chosen by the 1940 Newbery-Caldecott Committee and that the illustrations appearing in the 1957 edition were not.

What implications do all of these have for those concerned with children's literature? Librarians who work directly with children and want to provide them with the best in picture books may wish to consider how they define *the best*. It could be that the revised edition of *The Rooster Crows*, even with its loss of order, is best for contemporary children, since hurtful stereotypical images have also been lost. Page order in the third gathering is a small price to pay for progress. As for the loss of clarity and fine quality in both *Animals of the Bible* and *Abraham Lincoln*, certainly children lose a little when they are denied the artwork at its best, particularly when the gold medal on the jacket tells them that the art inside the book is considered to be the most distinguished.

Members of the Association of Library Service to Children entrusted with administering the medal may want to keep a closer eye on the current state of past award winners. Should ALSC allow Doubleday to continue printing the Caldecott Medal on the jacket of a book that was never awarded the medal? Does ALSC have the power to insist that subsequent printings and editions of any book bearing the medal be a close approximation to the original? Who is responsible for quality control?

Finally, I appeal to children's literature specialists engaged in studies of the award-winning books. As representatives of *the best* in twentieth-century American children's books, Newbery and Caldecott Award-winning titles are frequently singled out for research. Since it is apparent that these particular titles are selected for study *only* because they won the award, it is imperative that scholars study the books that were actually selected. The only way to ensure this is to use first printings in research or to verify that there is no variation between the first printing and the one being used in the study. Overall, there is a need for more careful attention to bibliographic detail in the field of children's literature. There's no time like the present.

Bibliography

Caldecott Medal Books Examined for This Study

d'Aulaire, Edgar, and Ingri Parin d'Aulaire. *Abraham Lincoln*. Garden City, N.Y.: Doubleday, 1939. 1st ed.; 1st printing.
_____. *Abraham Lincoln*. Garden City, N.Y.: Doubleday, 1957. 2d ed.; printing undetermined.
Lathrop, Dorothy P. *Animals of the Bible*. New York: Stokes, 1937. 1st ed.; 1st printing.
_____. *Animals of the Bible*. New York: Lippincott, 1937. 1st ed.; 16th printing.
Petersham, Maud, and Miska Petersham. *The Rooster Crows: A Book of American Rhymes and Jingles*. New York: Macmillan, 1945. 1st ed.; 1st printing.
_____. *The Rooster Crows: A Book of American Rhymes and Jingles*. New York: Macmillan, 1966. [Rev. ed.]; 15th printing.

References and Notes

1. With the exception of *White Snow, Bright Snow* (Lothrop, 1947), all Caldecott Medal books appear in *Children's Books in Print, 1986-87.*
2. See, for example, a discussion of the d'Aulaires' work in Barbara Bader's *American Picturebooks From Noah's Ark to the Beast Within*. (New York: Macmillan, 1976), p. 42-46.
3. Ibid., p. 44.
4. *Illustrators of Children's Books, 1957-1966*. Comp. by Lee Kingman, Joanna Foster, and Ruth Giles Lontoft. (Boston: Horn Book, 1968), p. 98.

PART IV:
ISSUES IN EVALUATION

TRADE-OFFS: QUANTIFYING QUALITY IN LIBRARY TECHNICAL SERVICES

Carol A. Mandel

Seemingly endless and often paralyzing debates over the appropriate balance of quality versus quantity are common in library technical services. Trade-offs haunt our daily work. We are faced with an overwhelming array of retrospective conversion options, automation alternatives, and processing methodologies. We have been given the opportunity—in the form of the online catalog—to rethink bibliographic control and cataloging. We have been given the mandate—in the form of reduced budgets, growing backlogs, and an increasingly impatient clientele—to rethink all of our practices. These are economic issues in library technical services, and economists provide some tools to help address them.

Cost-Benefit Analysis

The obvious economic tool to aid library technical services is cost-benefit analysis. Very simply stated, there are five steps to performing a cost-benefit analysis:

1. The actions or policies to be analyzed are identified.
2. *All* costs and *all* benefits, present and future, are determined.
3. Monetary values are assigned to all costs and benefits.
4. Net benefits (total benefits minus total costs) are calculated.
5. A choice is made.

It is important to note that step 5 does not dictate which choice is made. Cost-benefit analysis should be viewed as a decision aid, not as the triumph of the balance sheet over good judgment.

Although cost-benefit analysis is a standard technique in public policy decision making, it has had a somewhat checkered history in the library

"Trade-Offs: Quantifying Quality in Library Technical Services" by Carol A. Mandel in *Journal of Academic Librarianship* Vol. 14, no. 4 (September 1988), pp. 214-220; reprinted with permission from the *Journal of Academic Librarianship*.

field. The now notorious University of Pittsburgh study gave cost-benefit analysis a bad name in the library press.[1] Purported in its title to analyze the cost-benefit of "some critical library operations," the 1978 study made the fatal mistake of defining research library benefits solely in terms of circulation. It also sidestepped step 3 and did not assign a monetary value to library use. Thus, although the Pittsburgh study stacked up the costs of library operations in admirable detail, its management implications were dubious and its title a misnomer. In fact, there are any number of published studies lurking in the library literature ("A Cost-Benefit Analysis of . . .") which are, at best, simply cost studies adorned with the jargon of cost-benefit analysis.

Cost-Effectiveness Analysis

Analysis of cost effectiveness is a related technique that has been applied far more successfully, although not often enough, to library operations. Cost-effectiveness analysis allows the study of benefits and costs without the need to assign monetary values to benefits. This analysis can only be used, however, to study one side of the equation. That is, either the costs of two or more alternatives are assumed to be the same and one is seeking best value or greatest productivity for the dollar, or the benefits of two or more alternatives are the same and one is seeking to determine which will incur the least cost.

Cost-effectiveness analysis does not relieve the analyst of the difficult tasks of accurate costing or of the even more challenging work of defining and measuring benefits. But it does avoid the often controversial practice of describing benefits in terms of dollars. Both types of analysis necessitate finding answers to tough, revealing questions. What result is desired? How can we evaluate whether this result has been achieved? What are we willing to pay for this result? Can we get more of what we want for our money? Unlike choices presented as the allegorical battle between Quantity and Quality, these questions are answerable through measurement and analysis.

Measuring Costs

In contrast to the available information on benefits, there is ample literature on costs and costing in libraries. The successful, sometimes even profitable, operations of utilities, vendors, and contractors providing library technical services indicate that it must be possible to define and record the costs attributable to specific processing functions. Whether costs are derived by modeling specific projects or operations, or by determining appropriate percentages of fixed and variable expenditures, it should be possible for any technical services manager to maintain a cost list (as opposed to a price list) for each of the outputs produced in his or her departments.

Art and science. This is not to say that costing is simple or even precise. In fact, for such a dollars-and-cents activity, it can be as much an art as a science. The identification of relevant costs and the selection of costs to attribute to an activity rely on considerable judgment. Costs must be defined and selected in relation to a particular analysis being undertaken. Cost data for management decisions should approximate incremental costs defined to fit the particular resource allocation or pricing decision.[2] For example, a cost-effectiveness analysis comparing an in-house retrospective conversion effort with a quote from an off-site contractor should include the library's overhead for space. On the other hand, figuring the costs of space and other overhead into a comparison of two procedures that would both be performed by the same library staff members is a wasted exercise.

Hidden costs. The major pitfall of costing for a comparative analysis, especially comparisons of project and automation alternatives, is the hidden cost. Economists have conceptualized and found ways of calculating costs not ordinarily considered, such as lost opportunity costs (which are benefits that could have been derived if money had been spent another way). They also take into account the difference between a dollar spent now and a dollar spent tomorrow by allowing both for inflation and discount rates.

Other examples of hidden costs are the costs of recruitments, downtime, and the failure of a project. This last factor, a very real consideration in today's world of library automation, can be calculated by multiplying the probability of failure by the expected cost of the loss. Calculating the probability of a failure requires knowledge of past performance, future trends, and statistics on failures, and expert judgment. Depending on one's purposes, cost analysis can be straightforward, extremely complex, or even subjective.

Quantifying Performance

If a function as seemingly straightforward as cost measurement requires considerable judgment, it is easy to understand why so many librarians are daunted by the problem of quantifying performance. (Some may even feel morally indignant at the very idea of placing a dollar value on certain kinds of benefits.) But it is possible—in fact, necessary—to make sensible use of such measures and to keep their use in perspective. Fortunately, some very useful research and practical development has been done in the area of quantifying and measuring library effectiveness. This is not to suggest that librarians have perfected the art of performance measurement, but rather that there are sensible measures available. The automated operations of technical services and the online catalog lend themselves to such scrutiny.

Useful considerations. F. W. Lancaster, in his well-known, fundamental work on measuring and evaluating library services, suggests consideration of the following factors in evaluating the effectiveness of an information service:

- coverage,
- response time,
- presentation,
- degree of user effort,
- precision, and
- recall.[3]

Because evaluations of these kinds of factors have proved useful when applied to a particular service or information project, they have been used in the analysis of specialized information services. They have been applied less frequently, however, to the analysis of other library operations. But if we take a micro-level look at a specific technical service process, it is frequently possible to define a measure that reflects the objectives of the operation. For example, response time, or more characteristically, turn-around time, is certainly a reasonable measure for a rush cataloging service. Coverage, defined as actual holdings of serials issues as a percent of all the issues that should have been received, is an appropriate measure of effectiveness of a serials check-in and claiming operation.

Two measures have most commonly been employed to define the overall effectiveness of libraries: use and availability. As the furor over the Pittsburgh study indicated, book use and circulation can be very controversial measures of library service. Availability is a much sounder concept for characterizing library effectiveness, and it is also a useful concept for technical services, since technical services operations play a significant role in the availability of library materials.

Availability. Paul Kantor suggests analyzing availability by breaking it down into five components.

- Acquisitions (Did the library acquire the book?)
- Catalog (Could the user find the book in the catalog?)
- Circulation (Was the book available in the library rather than out circulating?)
- Library Inventory Control (Was the book on the shelf and in the right place?)
- Users (Could the user locate the book even when the library had done everything right?)[4]

Bibliographic access. For the purposes of technical services, the most relevant element of the availability equation is bibliographic access—the ability of users to locate an owned item in the library's catalog. Because so many technical services processes and expenditures are devoted to providing bibliographic access, we must be committed to finding ways to measure its effectiveness. It is important to think of the catalog as an access tool and measure its success in terms of successful user searches or "hits." The number of hits may not alone be a sufficient criterion for evaluating the results of, for example, a particular rare book cataloging effort, but the majority of technical services processes can and should be evaluated in terms of that access.

Monetizing Benefits

Responsible management requires that librarians think of the services they perform in terms of their dollar value, and, concomitantly, that they relate library effectiveness to implicit and explicit costs. As noted earlier, a pure cost-benefit analysis includes the articulation of all costs and all benefits, and the translation of both into the same medium for comparison. That medium is money. The idea of translating intrinsically valuable activities and conditions such as research, scholarship, or literacy into dollars and cents is distasteful or ridiculous to many librarians. But economists argue that when alternative courses of action are known and subjectively evaluated, every action has a cost. The act of making a decision will quantify a host of intangibles, because in the real world decisions result in actions taken, time spent, and costs incurred.

Public policies. Frequently, public policy decisions are made in terms of cost-benefit determinations. For example, the Flood Control Act of 1926 explicitly stated that only those projects for which benefits exceeded costs could be submitted for Congressional action.[5] But the cost-benefit analyses behind many decisions are less obvious. According to a television news report, Daylight Savings Time began three weeks early in 1987 in part because the backyard barbecue industry was able to translate the extra hours of sunlight into an increase in leisure activity and, thus, increased profits.

A recent study of regulatory policies indicates that public policy makers are valuing a human life at about $2 million.[6] That is, policies such as clean air regulations or waste clean-up requirements are not likely to be implemented if analyses show that implementation will cost more than $2 million per death avoided. In theory, if we can put a dollar value on human life, we certainly ought to be able to monetize the benefits of maintaining a controlled vocabulary.

Assessing the Value of Libraries

A review of the literature indicates that three approaches have been used in trying to assess the value of libraries. Library services have been viewed in terms of their benefits (1) to society, (2) to individual library users, and (3) to the operations of the library itself.

Societal benefits. The first approach places library decisions into the realm of public policy. For example, one could try to define the benefits of a university library in terms of the benefits of the research it supports. This, in turn, leaves another seemingly intangible benefit to define. Is research valued simply in terms of the monies expended on it, or in terms of the benefits it has brought to society? In the Pittsburgh study, Cohen suggested monetizing the value of book use by looking at the human capital of students—that is, how much more would be earned in a lifetime by a student with an academic degree.[7] But this does not seem to meet the criterion of articulating *all* the benefits of research performed in the library.

User benefits. A second cost-benefit approach suggests viewing library services as possessing the characteristic of a common good.[8] That is, for purposes of evaluating a library service, one can assume that the service benefits society in general; societal benefits need not be quantified. Instead, the cost-benefit analysis looks only at the direct users of the library service as the primary beneficiaries, and at the value of benefits in relation to these library users. If the service requires a user fee, then the service can be valued at the market price, assuming tests have confirmed the fee to be the highest price the market will bear. For the most part, however, librarians have not been able to use such readily quantifiable approaches and have had to approximate the monetary value of the services they provide. Attempts at approximation described in the literature include:

- valuing the time a user saves by using the service,
- looking at the price of alternative services when these are commercially available,
- looking simply at the market value of the book or information acquired by the user, and
- asking users to estimate the value of the service provided.

Library benefits. A third way of looking at the monetization of the benefits of library services, particularly library technical services, is to consider the library itself as beneficiary. (That is, if one assumes that the library is a public good *and* one assumes that the library is already offering the right public services to its users.) The benefits of a proposed technical service alternative may be viewed in terms of the value provided to the library itself, or, in other words, in terms of the amount that the library would be willing to pay or might otherwise have to pay for the service. For example, internal transfer charges for technical services would allow public services librarians to indicate the dollar value they would assign to various technical processing activities. An obvious example of the kind of benefit that can be defined in terms of value to the library itself is cost savings. A limited cost-benefit analysis that simply looks at potential expenditures and likely cost savings is straightforward, and most of us use it frequently. Another example of benefits that can be monetized are results for which the library would be willing to pay an external vendor. For example, we could argue for many years about the value of authority control to library users. On the other hand, there are aspects of authority control that actually have a market value. Librarians have demonstrated that they believe there is a dollar value for consistent forms of headings in their online catalogs by paying for those processed headings. We can view this price as the minimum dollar value of authority control. Another benefit is increased output for a particular activity deemed desirable by the library. One could put a dollar value on increased output by looking at the unit costs currently expended by the library to provide the output, and multiplying those costs by the increased increment expected.

Complex Determinants

If we take this narrower, library-oriented approach to defining benefits— and such an approach is reasonable when looking at technical services—a cost-benefit analysis can be seen to be a practical and more straightforward decision aid than it has been portrayed to be in the library press. Many situations which appear at first glance to require a cost-effectiveness analysis—e.g., comparative costs of vendors that provide the same service— are, in fact, cost-benefit analyses. Under scrutiny, the benefits side of the equation almost always seems to vary among alternatives. Most workflow and productivity analyses are not simply assessments of how to produce more of the same output. In most cases, alternative workflows and procedures create somewhat different outputs, and we are left with the task of assessing the different benefits of each.

In reporting on Paul Kantor's recent study of research library processing costs, Martin Cummings noted that for every activity examined one or more of the research libraries studied had found a significantly lower cost processing method than the others in the group.[9] This finding immediately leads to speculation on why libraries have not been quicker to adopt each other's more productive practices. One reason is that the varying methods do not produce exactly the same results, and libraries have been stymied by an inability to analyze those differences in terms of equivalent effects.

In these cases, the challenge is to conceptualize the determinants of beneficial performance and then find a way to measure them.

A cost-benefit approach can be employed to assess the effectiveness and value of some of our existing practices in bibliographic access. The following section suggests several models that could be used to address pervasive questions in library bibliographic control. The tables for the models contain hypothetical (but obtainable) data.

Cataloging Time vs. Search Benefits

The first example is a hypothetical cost-effectivness analysis comparing the benefits of alternatives for full and minimal original cataloging. (See Table 1.) It may seem a very simple-minded model in that it measures benefits solely in terms of likely user searching. However, since this is normally the main objective of bibliographic access, it is a valid approach. The model assumes that all books in the particular group targeted for cataloging are of equal potential interest to users—i.e., any user is as likely to search for a cataloged item as for an uncataloged one. Its purpose is to quantify and compare the benefits of alternatives for a given expenditure of time on cataloging.

TABLE 1
Cataloging Alternatives Evaluated in Terms of Potential Searches Satisfied

Alternative	Number of Records Available After 1,000 Hours of Cataloging Time	Probability that Users Will Search on Access Points Provided	Potential Successful Search Score
Full cataloging	1,000	100%	1,000
Main entry and title	3,333	45%	1,500
Main entry, title, subjects	1,667	85%	1,417

Obtaining data. The model requires concrete information on time requirements for various types of cataloging and on the likelihood of a user searching for materials via the kinds of access points provided. Table 2 illustrates the information needed to fill in the blanks on the model. (Remember, all tabularized data are speculative.) The cataloging time breakdown should be easy for any library to gather from original catalogers and by trying some alternatives. This time assessment allows a library to gauge its relative productivity under each cataloging alternative—Table 1 indicates that 3,333 records with only main entries can be created in the time it takes to produce 1,000 full records.

The frequency of searches on different access points—that is, searches on subjects, titles, class numbers, or names—can be determined from online catalog use studies. Online catalog transaction logs provide a record of how often each kind of access point is searched, and more detailed sample studies could be undertaken to determine how often author searches retrieve names used as main entries versus those used as added entries. It should not be necessary for every library to perform its own studies; libraries with similar clienteles can share transaction log data and develop useful heuristic assumptions.

TABLE 2
Figures Used to Obtain Data in Table 1

Breakdown of Original Cataloging Time

Type of Cataloging Activity	Percent of Total Cataloging Time
Description (including main entry)	30%
Added entries	20%
Classification	20%
Subject headings	30%

Breakdown of Searches for Each Kind of Access Point

Access Point	Frequency of Use
Title	30%
Author (used as main entries)	15%
Author (added entries)	5%
Subject	40%
Class number	5%
Series	5%

The search score. The model suggests evaluating each cataloging alternative in terms of the likely potential user searches it *could* satisfy. That is, the model provides for the calculation of a "potential successful search score" in order to compare numerically the benefits of having limited access points for a larger group of records to the benefits of full cataloging for a smaller group of records.[10] The score is derived by multiplying the frequency that users search under the kinds of access points provided by the number of records created in 1,000 hours of the kind of cataloging necessary to produce the access points. The hypothetical figures in Table 1 indicate that more potential searches can be satisfied by creating 3,333 brief records than by producing 1,000 full records.

Strengthening the model. This quantitative measure is only valid, however, if there is no difference in the likely need for any particular title in this group; some titles might merit provision of all possible access points, even when cataloging resources are limited. This model could be further strengthened if it included a figure on the percent of searches satisfied through shelf browsing—a figure that cannot be derived from online catalog studies. Such a figure would be needed to gauge the true contribution of classification numbers to the "potential successful search" score.

Worksheet Revision vs. Access Points

Table 3 introduces a model that takes a slightly different view of successful searching. It is a hypothetical cost-effectiveness analysis of cataloging worksheet revision. In this analysis, the assumptions are that full cataloging is beneficial and that all standard access points are of equal value. The model's purpose is to quantify the benefits derived from the labor-intensive process of revising original cataloging worksheets in terms of the resultant useable access points. While this may not be an appropriate model for rare book cataloging, it is justifiable in terms of the cataloging done for most collections.

The data needed to perform the analysis in any particular library are easily obtained through sampling. The following questions should be answered.

- How much time does revision add to the cataloging process?
- How many errors that would have inhibited access are found through revision?
- What is the error rate even with revision?
- What is the number of access points per record?

The resultant model can then provide a relatively clear-cut means to determine whether or not the time invested in revision is cost-effective.

TABLE 3
Effectiveness of Worksheet Revision Evaluated in Terms of Useable Access Points Gained for a Given Expenditure of Catalogers' Time

Alternative	Records	Access Points	Percent Useable	Total Useable Access Points
With revision	1,000	5,000	95%	4,750
Without revision	1,250	6,250	75%	4,688

Assumptions: worksheet revision adds 25% to time spent by original catalogers; each record has average of 5 access points; revisor finds 20% errors that inhibit access; and there are 5% errors even after revision.

Revision vs. Errors and Access in a Shared Database

For most libraries, original cataloging should not be viewed only in terms of access in a single library catalog, but also in light of records contributed to a shared database. If the library that performed the hypothetical analysis decided to stop worksheet revision, what would be the costs and benefits for libraries using the same shared database?

The model shown in Table 4 is set up following a format illustrated by Griffiths and King.[11] Because this is a cost-benefit (rather than a cost-effectiveness) model, it requires that benefits be quantified in monetary terms. This model assumes that the cost of performing revisions can be determined by both the lowered productivity in Library A and the consequent higher costs for other libraries which must contribute additional original cataloging records to the shared database. On the other hand, the cost of *not* performing revisions can be found in increased errors. But how do you place a dollar value on the additional errors?

TABLE 4
Costs and Benefits of Revision by Library A When Contributing Original Records to OCLC

Levels of Measure	Revision	No Revision	Cost of Revision	Benefit of Revision
Records created by Library A	1,000	1,250	$12,500	
Number of errors	63	313		
Expenditure by 20 other libraries to correct errors (at $2 each)	$2,520	$12,520		$10,000
Cost of lost access in 10 other libraries that do not correct errors (at $2 each)	$1,260	$ 6,260		$ 5,000
Higher order effects				Increase in esteem, morale, clout in OCLC

Error correction costs. This model places a value on revising an error that is equal to the amount other libraries must spend to correct the error in the database. The model assigns an average dollar amount of $2 per corrected error. It assumes that libraries correcting the error are not using OCLC's "Enhance" and thus the correction would have to be done over more than once. It also assumes that some libraries will miss or not bother to correct the error, and that there is a cost in lost access in those libraries. How do you place a dollar value on lost access?

Lost access costs. In this case, the cost can be measured by the dollar value that at least some libraries are willing to pay to avoid lost access. Since we know that $2 probably does not characterize the full cost of the lost access point, one could also note the incommensurable benefits of fewer errors. Thus, Table 4 lists "higher order" benefits of revision in the benefits column (such as the staff satisfaction of creating high-quality records).

Putting it all together. Table 4 compares the costs of revision against those of no revision. Costs are attached to each of the levels of measure shown, except for those characterized as higher order effects. Differences between the two alternatives are shown in the third and fourth columns. Error rates are based on those in Table 3.

If Library A expends $50,000 in cataloging time (including revision), it will create only 1,000 records. The additional expense of that alternative will include the cost of 250 records that are either lost or that must be created by another library. This model shows that cost at $50 per record, or $12,500.

When Library A performs revision, 63 errors will remain for some libraries to correct; without revision there will be 313 errors. The costs and benefits must be measured for a defined universe of libraries. The universe examined in Table 4 is a hypothetical group of 30 libraries of which it is assumed that 20 will expend time to correct the errors and 10 will not. However, the "costs" to both groups are the same since an error is a "negative benefit" valued at $2. Incommensurable benefits of revision, such as improved staff morale when high-quality records are produced, are also listed but not quantified. The bottom line in this model shows that the costs and benefits of revision are close (although the numbers are illustrative only).

The approach used in Table 4 is but one illustration of the need to look at cataloging costs and benefits in a national, or even international, context. As long as machine-readable records are shared, the costs and benefits of creating and using these records are shared. Similar costs and benefit models can be used to compare different alternatives for sharing records.

LC-Based vs. Utility-Based Cataloging

A national project: NCCP. Eight libraries are currently participating in a two-year pilot coordinated cataloging project with the Library of Congress to create national-level bibliographic records that will be distributed and maintained by LC.[12] While libraries have been sharing records through bibliographic utilities for some time, this project, known as the National Coordinated Cataloging Project, or NCCP, is an effort to extend the body of records which bear the same benefits as LC-created records. These benefits include: national-level quality, central distribution to all utilities and others, and maintenance by LC. Other expected benefits of NCCP include more timely appearance of records in shared databases and greater sharing of records by both LC and cooperating libraries, which will free cataloging time for increased production of original cataloging. NCCP participants will contribute catalog records online to LC.

A model. The costs and benefits of the project will be enumerated and evaluated by participating libraries and sponsoring organizations during the course of the pilot. Table 5 illustrates an application of cost-benefit modeling to some of the factors being explored by NCCP. It is by no means the definitive or complete model for describing the effort, but simply an illustration of a quantitative approach to examining some of the benefits.

TABLE 5
Cost and Benefit Analysis of Library X Contributing 500 Records to LC-Based Cataloging Cooperative

Level of Measure	Contribute 500 Titles to LC	Contribute 500 Titles to Utility	Cost	Benefit
Expenditure by Library X	$ 45,000	$ 25,000	$20,000	
Expenditures by 50 libraries on OCLC to use the 500 records	$375,000	$625,000		$250,000
Expenditure by Library Y on RLIN to use/create the 500 records	$ 7,500	$ 25,000		$ 17,500
Expenditure by 20 libraries on RLIN to use the 500 records	$150,000	$250,000		$100,000
Savings by LC when using 250 of the records	$ 12,500	—0—		$ 12,500

Assumptions: Average library cataloging costs are: $50/title for original, $25/title for member, and $15/title for LC or Co-op Copy. Library X cataloging costs are: $50/title for original and $90/title for original contribution to LC. LC will use 50% of co-op records created, saving $50/title.

This model compares the contribution of 500 records to the national database through an LC-based cooperative to contribution directly through a bibliographic utility. The costs of the cooperative are assumed to be the added costs of cataloging. It will probably prove more expensive to add cataloging records via the LC-coordinated program and its standards than by contribution to OCLC or RLIN. The dollars suggested here—$50 locally and $90 via LC—are hypothetical, but the current pilot project should be able to ascertain real figures.

Cost savings. The benefits of the LC cooperative illustrated here are cost savings in three possible areas:

1. less expensive copy cataloging for libraries using records produced through the cooperative,
2. the avoidance of duplicative cataloging between OCLC and RLIN, and
3. savings by LC when it uses contributed records—savings that can be applied to increased LC cataloging production.

All three of these benefits can be quantified, measured, and costed. If there is a difference in the way libraries process LC records (and by future extension, NCCP records) from full-standard utility-member copy, then this can be analyzed and specified. If there is no difference, then this aspect of the project will not yield a significant benefit.

The information presented in Table 5 assumes a $10 per record difference in an average library's processing cost for LC versus member copy. The model also assumes that LC will use 50 percent of the cooperative records created in its own cataloging and will gain a savings of $50 each time it does so.

Limitations of model. For purposes of illustration, Table 5 looks at the costs and cost savings (benefits) of creating 500 NCCP records in terms of the costs and benefits to a small universe of libraries. The model considers 51 OCLC libraries (Library X plus 50 others) and 21 RLIN libraries (Library Y plus 20 others) which are cataloging all of the 500 titles in question. In reality the model would need to be more complex since the universe of interest might be larger, and since not all libraries in the defined universe would use each record.

Comparisons. The levels of measure compared between the alternatives are:

- original cataloging costs for Libraries X and Y,
- copy cataloging costs for all libraries but X (which is supplying 500 original records in all cases), and
- cost avoidance by LC.

In a more fully developed model, the savings to LC would, in turn, be translated into costs and benefits for the same universe of libraries that might use the additional LC records created.

The first column in Table 5 displays costs and savings when Library X, an OCLC member, contributes 500 records to NCCP. Under this alternative, 50 other OCLC libraries and all 21 RLIN libraries are able to use the

500 records for "LC-copy" cataloging. In additional, LC uses half of the records. The second column shows costs and savings when Library X performs its original cataloging directly on OCLC. In that scenario, the 50 OCLC libraries use the 500 records for member-copy cataloging, and the 500 records are also created originally on RLIN by one logical library (Library Y—which in operational reality could be several libraries each contributing some portion of the 500 records). The second column also illustrates that 20 RLIN libraries use the records created by Library Y for member-copy cataloging, and LC will not use the original records created. The costs and savings of creating the 500 NCCP records are shown in the last two columns of Table 5.

Some challenges. Table 5 shows that while Library X incurs significant costs, the benefits even to a small universe of 72 libraries could be considerable. This would still leave us with the challenges of determining whether costs could be reduced (e.g., by changes in cataloging procedures) and who should pay those costs. The answer to the former question will certainly be part of the management evaluation of the NCCP pilot. Participants will want to ensure that any added costs for coordinated work are those that contribute directly to the benefits of the enterprise. The latter question will require an examination of the costs and benefits to individual participants as well as to the larger universe of libraries using NCCP records.

A Model for a Smaller Universe

Table 6 illustrates the application of the same hypothetical costs and benefits shown in Table 5 to only the eight participating NCCP libraries. It looks at an aggregate of 500 records contributed by the group of eight libraries. For each record contributed to LC by one of the libraries, seven other libraries will perform "LC copy" cataloging to catalog the title (i.e., 500 titles at $15 a piece for each of the 7 libraries). As assumed in the previous example, LC will use half the records created at a savings to LC of $12,500.

Table 6 translates LC's savings into original cataloging savings for the participating libraries. Just for the sake of illustration, the example assumes that if LC were to use the $12,500 in savings to catalog 125 more books, and each library were to make use of the copy for half of those books (i.e., catalog 63 books at $15 per title) instead of cataloging them originally (i.e., 63 books at $50 per title), each would benefit by $2,205 from LC's savings.

For comparison, the second column in Table 6 lists the costs and benefits of the eight libraries' usual utility cataloging. For each record created by one library, one other library will perform duplicate original cataloging on another utility (500 records at $50 each). Six other libraries will perform member copy cataloging using the 500 records (500 titles at $25 each for 6 libraries). LC will not use the records. The costs and benefits of the contribution to LC are shown in the last two columns of Table 6.

TABLE 6
Cost and Benefit Analysis of Eight Libraries Contributing 500 Records to LC-Based Cataloging Cooperative

Level of Measure	Contribute 500 Titles to LC	Contribute 500 Titles to Utility	Cost	Benefit
Expenditure for original cataloging	$45,000	$25,000	$20,000	
Expenditure for copy cataloging	$52,500	$75,000		$22,500
Expenditure for duplicating original	—0—	$25,000		$25,000
Cataloging costs avoidance from LC savings	$17,640	—0—		$17,640

A positive indication. This hypothetical scenario indicates that net positive benefits would still accrue even within the small universe of participating libraries. (A result that will, of course, need to be carefully tested and measured by NCCP in their pilot project.) For each participant, the balance will be determined by how many records it contributes and how many records it uses. It is possible that the LC-based cooperative could cost participating libraries more than they will gain. Yet many, many other libraries could stand to reap cost savings. Results of the pilot study could indicate that some form of compensation for the participating libraries is in order.

Conclusion

Once again, it is important to emphasize that the models shown do not contain actual numbers. Even when one does have appropriate numbers to plug in, cost-benefit analysis is fraught with dangers and limitations— not the least of which is the danger of doing a very complicated analysis poorly.

Nevertheless, the study of library economics does begin to illuminate some of the shadowy corners that have unnecessarily confined our understanding of pressing technical services issues. It offers an analytical process to help formalize decision making when problems are too complex for managers to rely on common sense and intuition alone. And while politics and intangible factors may ultimately govern any decision, responsible managerial decision making should include an analysis and understanding of the numbers as well.

Here is a simplistic view of the current state of the economics of library technical services: we are all spending money; some of us know how much; fewer of us know what for. A formal and quantitative approach to analyzing questions of quality and productivity in technical services will result in a net benefit to library users.

References

1. Allen Kent, *A Cost Benefit Model of Some Critical Library Operations In Terms of Use of Materials* (Pittsburgh: University of Pittsburgh, 1978).
2. Gordon Schillinglaw, *Costing Methodologies and Applications* (Unpublished paper presented at the ALA Conference, July 1986).
3. F. W. Lancaster, *The Measurement and Evaluation of Library Services* (Washington, D.C.: Information Resources Press, 1977).
4. Paul Kantor, *Objective Performance Measures for Academic and Research Libraries* (Washington, D.C.: Association of Research Libraries, 1984).
5. J. Bentkover, "The Role of Benefits Assessment in Public Policy," in *Benefits Assessment: The State of the Art*, ed. J. Bentkover, V. Covello, and J. Mumpower (Boston: Reidel, 1986), p. 5.
6. C. C. Travis et al., "Cancer Risk Management," *Environmental Science and Technology* 21 (May 1987): 415-420.
7. Jacob Cohen, "Book Cost and Book Use: The Economics of a University Library," in *Library Resource Sharing: Proceedings of the 1976 Conference on Resource Sharing in Libraries*, ed. Allen Kent and Thomas Galvin (New York: Dekker, 1977), pp. 197-224.
8. Cheryl A. Casper, "Economic Pricing Models and their Application to Library Services," in *Information Services: Economics, Management, and Technology*, ed. Robert M. Mason and John E. Creps (Boulder, CO: Westview, 1981), pp. 129-145.
9. Martin M. Cummings, *The Economics of Research Libraries* (Washington, D.C.: Council on Library Resources, 1986), pp. 24-29.
10. This model does not attempt to predict the *actual* success of each search, but assumes that all have an equal chance of success or failure. Further refinement could incorporate varying success rates on each type of access point searching.
11. Jose-Marie Griffiths and Donald W. King, *Library Cost-Benefit Analysis: A Manual Prepared for the Library Cost Benefit Analysis Seminar Presented at the SUNY/OCLC Network Annual Directors' Day on February 17, 1983* (Rockville, MD: King Research, 1983), p. 20.
12. "National Coordinated Cataloging Program Pilot to Begin in 1988," *Library of Congress Information Bulletin* 46 (October 19, 1987): 449-450.

MATERIALS AVAILABILITY FILL RATES: ADDITIONAL DATA ADDRESSING THE QUESTION OF THE USEFULNESS OF THE MEASURES

George D'Elia

INTRODUCTION

Output Measures for Public Libraries[1] *(OMPL)* proposes the use of three measures of materials availability (title fill rate, subject and author fill rate, and browsers' fill rate) as indicators of library effectiveness. A recent paper by this author, however, demonstrated that, inasmuch as these fill rates are calculated from data obtained from surveys of patrons who report the outcomes of their searches for materials within libraries, the three fill rates do not measure library performance per se but rather measure patron success within libraries.[2] With the data collected from materials availability surveys conducted in the libraries of the Saint Paul Public Library (SPPL) system, Minnesota, this author calculated for each library in the system a mean patron title search success rate, a mean patron subject and author search success rate, as well as a title fill rate, a subject and author fill rate, and a browsers' fill rate as prescribed in the *OMPL* manual. The analyses of these data indicated that:

1. the observed differences among the patron title search success rates obtained for the libraries, as well as the observed differences among the patron subject and author search success rates, the title fill rates, the subject and author fill rates, and the browsers' fill rates obtained for the libraries were not due to meaningful differences among the libraries but rather were due to some as yet unknown differences among

"Materials Availability Fill Rates: Additional Data Addressing the Question of the Usefulness of the Measures" by George D'Elia in *Public Libraries* Vol. 27, no. 1 (Spring 1988), pp. 15-23; reprinted with permission from the American Library Association, copyright © 1988 by ALA.

the patrons, random error, or a combination of both; and

2. none of the patron search success rates and none of the fill rates were related to the resources available to the patrons within the libraries.

Since there were no meaningful differences either among the patron search success rates or the fill rates obtained for the libraries in the SPPL system and since the patron search success rates and the fill rates obtained for the SPPL libraries were not related to the varying amounts of resources available within those libraries, it was concluded that for the SPPL system either there were no differences in the performances of the libraries or, if there were, none of these patron search success rates or materials availability fill rates was a managerially useful indicator of library performance. Whether these results were unique to the SPPL system or whether they and their implications could be generalized to other library systems was open to question since the validity, reliability, and usefulness of the fill rates had never been demonstrated. This paper reports the results of materials availability surveys conducted in other library systems that corroborate the findings of the SPPL surveys and discusses the implications of these findings for the presumed validity, reliability, and usefulness of the fill rates as measures of library performance.

COMPARISONS AMONG BRANCH FILL RATES WITHIN OTHER LIBRARY SYSTEMS

Materials availability surveys of adult patrons were conducted in all of the libraries of the Fairfax County Public Library (FCPL) system, Virginia, in 1984 and again in 1985. The FCPL system comprises four regional libraries, ten community libraries, and six mini libraries. The resources available within these libraries differ considerably and they, as well as the patron uses of the libraries, have been reported elsewhere.[3] The results of these materials availability surveys were made available to this author and are presented in table 1. Each of the three fill rates obtained for the twenty libraries in 1984 was tested for differences among libraries by means of a chi-square analysis of the joint-frequency distribution of number of items found and number of items not found in each library. Each of the three fill rates for 1985 was similarly tested. The results of these analyses, reported in table 2, indicate that there was a statistically significant difference among the libraries for each of the three fill rates. However, for each chi-square analysis, the Cramer's V, an index that measures the degree of association between variables in a contingency table and that has values ranging from 0 (absolutely no association) to 1.0 (perfect association) indicates a very low degree of association between the libraries used by the patrons and the patrons' success in finding materials in those libraries. [See *Public Libraries* 24, no. 3:106-10 (Fall 1985) for further explanation.—Ed.] These results in turn indicate that the observed differences

TABLE 1
Materials Availability Fill Rates for FCPL

Library	1984 TFR	1985 TFR	1984 SAFR	1985 SAFR	1984 BFR	1985 BFR
1	47%	54%	62%	73%	84%	93%
2	61%	48%	67%	54%	91%	91%
3	53%	50%	50%	69%	86%	88%
4	59%	58%	68%	55%	86%	83%
5	38%	51%	62%	59%	84%	92%
6	56%	42%	57%	66%	92%	89%
7	53%	58%	73%	62%	93%	92%
8	55%	56%	58%	63%	86%	94%
9	54%	48%	62%	60%	90%	92%
10	51%	66%	68%	72%	95%	93%
11	46%	64%	58%	78%	89%	91%
12	63%	52%	76%	68%	87%	92%
13	61%	65%	70%	77%	93%	94%
14	63%	61%	71%	65%	91%	91%
15	53%	48%	59%	66%	89%	89%
16	53%	59%	44%	57%	92%	95%
17	37%	28%	54%	46%	88%	91%
18	49%	50%	67%	51%	98%	93%
19	57%	46%	52%	58%	96%	94%
20	58%	48%	82%	76%	95%	93%
System	54%	53%	63%	64%	90%	91%

TABLE 2
Chi-square Analyses of the Joint Frequency Distributions
of Number of Items Found/Not Found for Each of the
Fill Rates in Each Library of the FCPL System

	Chi-square	Cramer's V
1984 title fill rates	57.47*	.14
1985 title fill rates	86.05*	.16
1984 subject/author fill rates	73.32*	.17
1985 subject/author fill rates	83.91*	.17
1984 browsers' fill rates	56.06*	.13
1985 browsers' fill rates	31.71†	.09

*Statistically significant at $\alpha = .001$
†Statistically significant at $\alpha = .05$

among the libraries in the system for each of the materials availability fill rates were trivial or inconsequential differences that were found to be statistically significant only because of the extremely large samples used in the analyses. Test statistics, such as the chi-square statistic, are sensitive to large sample sizes. The larger the sample the more likely the test statistic will be statistically significant. Too often statistically significant relationships obtained with large samples are accepted at face value when in reality the relationship is trivial. Consequently, when working with large samples, an appropriate measure of association is calculated in order to determine whether the relationship has sufficient strength for use in decision making. The reader is referred to Hays[4] or McNemar[5] for a discussion of statistically significant but trivial relationships.

In a recently published paper, Van House[6] reported analyses of fill rate data obtained for nineteen libraries within the Baltimore County Public Library (BCPL) system, Maryland. The title fill rate data obtained for these libraries in 1983 were tested for differences among the libraries by means of chi-square analysis—as were the title fill rate data for 1984 and 1985, and the subject and author fill rate data for 1983, 1984, and 1985. Analyses of the browsers' fill rate data were not reported. The results of these analyses indicated that there was a statistically significant difference among each of these library fill rates for all years except for the 1984 subject and author fill rate. However, Van House also reported that the Cramer's V calculated for each of these chi-square analyses indicated a very low degree of association between the libraries used by the patrons and the patrons' success in finding materials in those libraries. (These data were made available to this author by BCPL and are included in the subsequent analyses reported later in this paper.)

The results of these analyses from both the FCPL and the BCPL systems corroborate the results previously reported for the SPPL system. In each of the three systems there were statistically significant but trivial differences among each of the fill rates obtained for the libraries within the systems.

COMPARISONS AMONG THE SPPL, BCPL, AND FCPL SYSTEM FILL RATES

The materials availability data collected by the SPPL, BCPL, and FCPL systems in 1984 (the only year in which materials availability surveys were conducted in all three systems) were aggregated, and a systemwide title fill rate, a systemwide subject and author fill rate, and a systemwide browsers' fill rate were calculated for each system. Each set of these fill rate data were then submitted to chi-square analyses to test for differences among the three systems and to test for differences between pairwise comparisons of systems. In making these comparisons it should be noted that there

TABLE 3
Chi-square Analyses of the Joint Frequency Distributions
of Number of Titles Found/Not Found in the
SPPL, BCPL, and FCPL Systems

	SPPL	BCPL	FCPL
Titles found	1,672	4,905	1,579
Titles not found	933	4,051	1,370
Titles sought	2,605	8,956	2,949
Fill rate	(64%)	(55%)	(54%)
	Chi-square	Measures of Association	
SPPL/BCPL/FCPL	83.38*	Cramer's V = .08	
SPPL/BCPL	72.96*	r = .08	
SPPL/FCPL	64.52*	r = .11	
BCPL/FCPL	1.34	r = .01	

*Statistically significant at α = .001

TABLE 4
Chi-square Analyses of the Joint Frequency Distributions
of Number of Subject and Authors Found/Not Found
in the SPPL, BCPL, and FCPL System

	SPPL	BCPL	FCPL
Subject/authors found	3,338	3,115	1,637
Subject/authors not found	1,102	1,297	949
Subject/authors sought	4,440	4,412	2,586
Fill rate	(75%)	(71%)	(63%)
	Chi-square	Measures of Association	
SPPL/BCPL/FCPL	111.42*	Cramer's V = .10	
SPPL/BCPL	23.47*	r = .05	
SPPL/FCPL	111.54*	r = .13	
BCPL/FCPL	39.87*	r = .08	

*Statistically significant at α = .001

TABLE 5
Chi-square Analyses of the Joint Frequency Distributions
of Number of Browsers' Successes/Failures in the
SPPL, BCPL, and FCPL Systems

	SPPL	BCPL	FCPL
Browsers' successes	3,451	5,782	3,036
Browsers' failures	507	877	330
Browsers' searches	3,958	6,659	3,366
Fill rate	(87%)	(87%)	(90%)

	Chi-square	Measures of Association
SPPL/BCPL/FCPL	25.12*	Cramer's $V = .04$
SPPL/BCPL	.28	$r = .00$
SPPL/FCPL	16.23*	$r = .05$
BCPL/FCPL	23.92*	$r = .05$

*Statistically significant at $\alpha = .001$

were differences in the data collection procedures employed by the three systems and that no attempt was made to weight each individual library's contribution to total system performance when the libraries' sample data were aggregated to estimate the system fill rates. The results of these analyses, reported in tables 3, 4, and 5, indicate the following:

1. There was a statistically significant difference among the observed title fill rates of the three systems; however, the index of association, Cramer's V, was only .08. Pairwise comparisons between the systems indicated that there were statistically significant differences between SPPL and BCPL and between SPPL and FCPL. However, the index of association, the fourfold point correlation coefficient (which is comparable to a Pearson correlation coefficient computed for two dichotomous variables) calculated for each pairwise comparison was only .08 and .11, respectively.
2. There was a statistically significant difference among the observed subject and author fill rates of the three systems; however, the index of association, Cramer's V, was only .10. Pairwise comparisons between the systems indicated that there were statistically significant differences between SPPL and BCPL, between SPPL and FCPL, and between BCPL and FCPL. Once again, however, the index of association, the fourfold point correlation coefficient, was only .05, .13, and .08, respectively.
3. There was a statistically significant difference among the observed browsers' fill rates of the three systems; however, the index of association, Cramer's V, was only .04. Pairwise comparisons between the

systems indicated that there were statistically significant differences between SPPL and FCPL and between BCPL and FCPL. Once again, however, the index of association, the fourfold point correlation coefficient, was only .05 and .05 respectively.

These results indicate extremely low degrees of association between the library systems used by the patrons and the patrons' success in finding materials in the different systems. It is reasonable to conclude, therefore, that the observed differences among the SPPL, BCPL, and FCPL system fill rates were trivial differences only found to be statistically significant because of the extremely large sample sizes.

DISCUSSION

The results of these data analyses indicate that regardless of the differences in resources available within these libraries and regardless of the possible differences among the patrons of these libraries, there were no meaningful differences among the library fill rates within the SPPL, BCPL, and FCPL systems or among the system fill rates of the three systems. Assuming that the fill rates are valid measures of library performance, Van House[7] has suggested two possible explanations for the failure of the fill rates to identify meaningful differences in the performances of the libraries within the systems: either (1) there were meaningful differences in the performances of the libraries but the fill rates, because of inadequate sample sizes, were not sensitive to these differences; or (2) there were no meaningful differences in the performances of libraries because patrons may have adjusted the demands that they made of the libraries based on their perception of the library's capability to satisfy their demands. It is also possible that the fill rates are not valid measures of library performance or, if they possess some adequate degree of validity, they do not possess adequate reliability. Before considering the validity and reliability of the fill rates it would be useful to discuss the two explanations suggested by Van House.

Sample Sizes and Fill Rates

In order to increase the sensitivity of the fill rates to potentially meaningful differences among libraries, Van House[8] suggested that sample sizes within libraries for each type of transaction should be increased from the recommended size of 100 in *OMPL* to about 400 to 500 transactions (i.e., 400-500 title searches, 400-500 subject/author searches, and 400-500 browser searches), which are the recommended sample sizes in the second edition of *OMPL* (*OMPL II*).[9] Larger sample sizes would decrease the sampling error associated with each fill rate estimate and thereby increase the precision of the estimate. For example, in 1985, library number two in the FCPL system had an estimated title fill rate of 48% with a margin of error of ±7% based on the results of a sample of 221 title searches. If the sample size for that library had been doubled to 442 title searches and if the estimated title fill rate were again about 48%, then the margin of error would have been reduced to ±5%. However, this improvement in the precision of the estimate, had it been accomplished for all of the libraries in the FCPL system, would not have affected the lack of meaningful differences among libraries, which is the problem at hand. If sample sizes for title searches within each of the FCPL libraries for 1985 had been doubled, and if the estimated title fill rates for the libraries were approximately the same the net result would have been a doubling of the chi-square statistic from 86.05 to about 172.10, but, since the sample size would also have been doubled, the measure of association, Cramer's V, would have remained about the same

$$(V = \frac{\sqrt{X^2}}{N} = .16).$$

It is apparent, therefore, that increases in sample sizes would have increased the precision of the estimates for each of the fill rates for each of the libraries in the system and would have increased the significance of the chi-square statistics generated by the cross-library comparisons but would not have changed the trivial degree of association between patron success and library used. Precision of estimate is a manifestation of the reliability of a measure. However, while reliability is a necessary condition for establishing the validity of a measure, reliability is not in and of itself a sufficient condition for establishing the validity of a measure. It is quite possible to have a reliable but invalid measure. Consequently, small sample sizes are not an adequate explanation of why, thus far, only trivial differences among libraries' fill rates have been identified. *Larger sample sizes, as recommended by* OMPL II, *will not make meaningful those differences among library fill rates that are trivial in nature.*

Patron Selection of Library and Fill Rates

Van House[10] has also suggested that there may, in fact, be no meaningful differences among the fill rates obtained for libraries within systems because patrons adjust their library use behavior to conform to system performance. Patrons may choose which library in the system to use based either on their past experiences with the performances of the various libraries or on their expectations of the performances the various libraries given their current set of needed items. Consequently, patrons would make lesser demands on weaker libraries and greater demands on stronger libraries with the result that comparable fill rates would be obtained for all libraries. Patrons could discriminate among libraries on the basis of the number of items sought, the type of items sought, or the subject matter of items sought. In the SPPL materials availability survey, the data were coded to indicate how many titles and how many subjects and authors were sought by each patron. (The data were not coded in a manner that enabled comparisons among libraries of the type or subject matter of items sought.) It is therefore possible to test for differences among the mean number of titles, as well as the mean number of subjects and authors, sought by the samples of patrons drawn from within each of the libraries in the SPPL system in order to determine if patrons discriminated among the libraries in terms of the number of items which they sought. These data were submitted to analyses of variance and the results of these analyses, reported in tables 6 and 7, indicate that:

1. the observed differences in the mean number of titles sought by the samples of patrons were statistically significant but trivial. Only 1% (eta^2) of the total observed variation in the number of titles sought by the patrons was explained by the libraries used by the patrons, while 99% of the total observed variation was due to unexplained variation among the patrons or random error; and
2. the observed differences in the mean number of subjects and authors sought by the samples of patrons were not statistically significant. The observed variation was not due to the libraries used by the patrons but rather was due to unexplained variation among the patrons or random error.

These analyses indicate that patrons within the SPPL system did not adjust their behavior by seeking different numbers of items from different libraries.

The possibility that patrons adjusted their behavior by selecting which library to use based on their expectations of which library would be more likely to have the type of material needed could not be tested with the data available from the SPPL survey. However, in a recent survey of patrons in the FCPL system, patrons were asked to indicate their reasons for using the library in which they were surveyed.[11] While this question did not measure the patrons' expectations of which library or libraries in the system would most likely have different types or subjects of materials, the question did measure the patrons' actual choice of which library to use for the reasons identified in the patrons' responses to the question. The analyses of these patron responses indicated that there were only trivial differences among the samples in their expectations of finding the needed materials in the library that they were using. The principal reasons cited by the patrons for using the library in which they were surveyed were "close to home" and "convenient parking." These analyses indicated that within the FCPL system either the patrons did not select which library to use on the basis of their expectations of successful searches, or, if they did, the patrons' expectations of success did not differ from library to library. Con-

TABLE 6

Comparisons of the Mean Number of Titles Sought by Patrons

Library	N	x̄	S.D.	.95 C.I.
1	68	1.74	1.25	1.43–2.04
2	59	1.37	.89	1.14–1.60
3	212	1.42	.86	1.31–1.54
4	300	1.50	1.06	1.38–1.61
5	216	1.46	.88	1.34–1.58
6	127	1.28	.56	1.18–1.37
7	99	1.45	.94	1.27–1.64
8	53	1.89	1.48	1.48–2.29
9	156	1.49	.91	1.35–1.64
10	332	1.47	.91	1.37–1.57
Main	138	1.57	.97	1.40–1.73
Total system	1,760	1.48	.95	1.44–1.53

Analysis of Variance Summary Table

Source of Variation	Sum of Squares	d.f.	Mean Square	F	∝	eta²
Between library samples	21.17	10	2.12	2.35	.01	.01
Within library samples	1,578.21	1749	.90			
Total	1,599.38	1759				

sequently, the proposition that patrons selection of library tends to equalize demand among libraries within a system does not appear to provide a viable explanation of the lack of meaningful differences among library fill rates in the FCPL system. An alternate explanation of why the fill rates failed to identify differences in performance among the libraries within the three systems and among the systems (assuming that there were differences in performance) is that the fill rates are not valid measures of library performance.

The Validity of the Fill Rates

In studying the availability of items within libraries as a possible measure of library performance, De Prospo and others[12] reported that (1) the probability of an item being available to a patron is equal to the joint probability that the library owns the item and that the item is on the shelf, and (2) the probability of availability is positively correlated with the size of the collection. It appears warranted to assume, therefore, that libraries that differed demonstrably either in size or mix of resources would differ in their capability to make available to patrons items which are sought. Con-

TABLE 7
Comparisons of the Mean Number of Subjects and Authors Sought
by Patrons

Library	N	x̄	S.D.	.95 C.I.
1	167	1.59	1.12	1.42–1.76
2	165	1.53	.89	1.40–1.67
3	258	1.48	.91	1.37–1.59
4	601	1.44	.82	1.37–1.50
5	371	1.46	.81	1.38–1.54
6	154	1.56	.89	1.42–1.71
7	141	1.54	.87	1.39–1.68
8	102	1.53	.85	1.36–1.70
9	156	1.55	.87	1.41–1.68
10	570	1.48	.76	1.41–1.54
Main	286	1.47	.86	1.37–1.57
Total system	2,980	1.49	.85	1.46–1.52

Analysis of Variance Summary Table

Source of Variation	Sum of Squares	d.f.	Mean Square	F	∝ eta²
Between library samples	6.21	10	.62	.85	n.s. —
Within library samples	2,166.42	2,969	.73		
Total	2,172.63	2,979			

sequently, a measure of the library's capability to make materials available to patrons would appear to be a valid measure of library performance. In considering the validity of the fill rates, however, it is important to recognize that the fill rates, as operationalized in *OMPL* and *OMPL II*, do not measure library performance per se but rather measure patron success within libraries. While these fill rates are obviously related to the library's capability to provide materials upon demand, they do not necessarily measure the library's capability to do so. The probability that a patron would be successful with a title search appears to be equal to the joint probability that the library owns the title, that the title is available for circulation, and that the patron can find the title. This last event, the patron's ability to find an available title, introduces a source of variation in the calculation of the title fill rate that confounds the fill rate as a measure of library performance. Recent studies of patron success in finding titles that were sought in academic libraries revealed that in one library 19% of the titles patrons claimed they could not find were actually available in the library at the time when the searches were conducted,[13] and in another library 51% of the failed searches reported by patrons involved titles that were actually available in the library at the time when the searches were conducted.[14] While there are obvious differences between academic and public libraries and their clientele, these studies demonstrate that (1) patron failure to find available titles could be a substantial factor included in the calculation of the title fill rate and (2) the patron failure rate differs from library to library and/or from sample of patrons to sample of patrons.

The probability that a patron would be successful with a subject and author search appears to be equal to the joint probability that the library owns the appropriate materials, that these materials are available, that the patron can find these materials, and that the patron judges these materials to be relevant to his needs. These last two events, the patron's ability to find materials and the patron's subsequent evaluation of the relevance of the materials, introduce two sources of variation in the calculation of the subject and author fill rate that confounds the subject and author fill rate as a measure of library performance. The probability that a patron would be successful with a browsing search appears to be primarily a function of the patron's subjective evaluation of the materials browsed in comparison to his need to be entertained or stimulated or perhaps something as ephemeral as his mood. Once again, this idiosyncratic process and subjective evaluation by the patron represents a considerable source of variation among patrons that is included in the calculation of the browsers' fill rate and that confounds the fill rate as a measure of library performance.

It appears reasonable to conclude, therefore, that to the extent that patron failure to find items introduces a source of uncontrolled systematic variation in the calculation of the fill rates, the fill rates are not valid measures of library performance. For example, if, using the procedures in *OMPL* and *OMPL II*, title fill rates were obtained for a group of academic libraries, it is clear that, given the extent of demonstrated patron failures within academic libraries, these fill rates would systematically underestimate library performance. Using the procedures developed by Kantor,[15] it would be possible for a library to develop an estimate of the availability of titles sought by patrons and an estimate of the proportions of failed searches that were due either to library failure or to patron failure. These data could possibly provide the bases for useful measures of library performance. While it would be possible to undertake similar analyses of failed patron subject and author searches, the procedural and methodological problems of intervening in failed searches and subsequently assessing the relevance of materials provided to the patrons by the staff would probably preclude the development of an easily used measure of library performance.

The Reliability of the Fill Rates

While the arguments presented above against assuming the validity of the fill rates are reasonable, they are nonetheless open to discussion. However,

even if we assume the validity of the fill rates, there is so much variation
in the measurement of the fill rates due to random error that the reliability
of each of the fill rates is seriously compromised. The detailed analyses
of the variations in patrons' search success rates within the SPPL libraries[16]
revealed that:

1. differences among the libraries could explain, at most, only 1.7% of
   the variation in the patrons' title search success rates, only 1% of the
   variation in the patrons' subject and author search success rates, and
   only 1.1% of the variation in patrons' browsing success; and
2. differences among patrons in terms of their sex, age, and educational
   level could explain, at most, only 3% of the variations in any of the
   patrons' search success rates.

Even when the combined effects of the libraries used and the demographic
characteristics of the patrons were taken into account, 95.6% of the variation in the patrons' title search success rates was due to unexplained variation among the patrons or random error, 98.4% of the variation in the
patrons' subject and author search success rates was due to unexplained
variation among the patrons or random error, and 96.6% of the variation
in the patrons' browsing success was due to unexplained variation among
patrons or random error. Given that the reliability of a measure is inversely
related to the amount of random error associated with the measure, it is
apparent that the reliability of each of the patron success rates and each
of the corresponding fill rates is very much open to question.

The first possible source of error variation in the fill rates is the
amount of unexplained variation among patrons—variation in the nature
of the materials that they seek, variation in their ability to negotiate bibliographic systems, variation in their ability to negotiate the shelving system,
variation in their motivation to succeed or to seek assistance, variation in
their evaluation of the materials that they do succeed in finding, variation
in their willingness to participate in the materials availability survey, variation in the amount of time and effort they are willing to expend in writing
the results of all or perhaps just a self-selected subset of searches undertaken, and variation in their ability or willingness either to write complete
and accurate titles or to differentiate clearly between titles and subject
areas. (Corresponding to this last source of variation among patrons is the
variation among the library personnel trying to code the sometimes cryptic
responses of the patrons.) In short, there are so many possible sources
of uncontrolled variation among patrons that could affect the estimation
of the fill rates for libraries and there are so many possible differences
in the compositions of the samples drawn from different communities of
patrons, that the fill rates are not reliable measures of library performance.

The second possible source of error variation among the fill rates is sampling error encountered when trying to estimate the theoretically true fill rates for any group of libraries based on random samples of patrons. The potential for sampling error is considerable and could be largely unappreciated by an uninformed user of the fill rates. A simple example may help to demonstrate the possible magnitude of sampling error in the estimation of the fill rates and the potential consequences of drawing untested inferences about the fill rates. The hypothetical title fill rates reported in table 8 for a fictious library system were generated from a table of random numbers. A table of random numbers models a distribution of the digits 0 through 9 in which these digits appear with equal frequency (i.e., the # of 1s = the # of 2s = . . . = the # of 9s). Consequently the number of even digits (0, 2, 4, 6, 8) in the distribution is theoretically equal to the number of odd digits (1, 3, 5, 7, 9). If we establish the rule that an odd digit represents a successful title search and an even digit represents an unsuccessful title search, then a table of random numbers models a distribution of title searches in which the proportion of successful searches is .50. The hyypothetical title fill rates for the library system reported in table 8 were each generated from a sample of digits drawn from a table of random numbers. This example was designed to model a library system in which the theoretically true title fill rate for each library in the system is 50%, that is to say, there are no differences among the true title fill rates (50%) for the libraries in the system. The observed differences reported in table 8 are the results of random sampling error. (An eleven-member system was selected in order to demonstrate to a group of librarians how the range of fill rates observed for the eleven libraries in the SPPL system could have occurred purely by chance.)

In this hypothetical library system the title fill rates obtained from a survey at time 1 range from a low of 43% to a high of 58%. Unsuspecting managers (assuming that low fill rates indicate inadequate performance) might try to determine why library #10 (TFR = 43%) performed so badly and why libraries #2 and #9 (TFR = 58%) performed so well. Based on a comparative analysis of the three libraries, the managers might then undertake a series of actions designed to improve the title fill rate in library #10. After passage of time, the system undertakes a second materials availability survey and obtains the title fill rates reported in column two. Once again, the theoretically true fill rate for each library in the system is 50%. The observed differences between each library from time 1 to time 2 and the observed differences among the eleven libraries at time 2 are due to random sampling error. Once again purely by chance, library #10 (TFR = 44%) obtained a very low title fill rate which would probably confirm the conclusion that library #10 is not performing adequately. At the same time, library #5 experienced a dramatic decline in its title fill rate from 55% to 42%. The unsuspecting managers might now try to determine what had happened in library #5 to cause such a decline in its title

TABLE 8
Hypothetical Title Fill Rates for a Library System
Generated from a Table of Random Numbers

Library	Time 1 ($n_j = 125$)	Time 2 ($n_j = 125$)
1	50%	44%
2	58%	52%
3	46%	51%
4	47%	51%
5	55%	42%
6	49%	46%
7	47%	45%
8	48%	48%
9	58%	54%
10	43%	44%
11	46%	50%
System	50%	48%

NOTE: The table of random numbers used to generate these hypothetical fill rates is contained within the required text for a statistics course that I teach (James T. McClave and P. George Benson, *Statistics for Business and Economics*, 3d ed. [San Francisco: Dellen Publ. Co., 1985], p. 955, 956.). The table is formatted in 14 columns with each column 5 digits wide. The first page of the table has 25 rows; thus each column on the first page contains 125 random digits. Columns 1 through 11 were selected to model the samples of title searches conducted within the 11 libraries in the hypothetical system at time 1. The second page of the table has 37 rows; thus each column has 185 random digits. Columns 1 through 11 were again selected to model the samples of title searches conducted within the 11 libraries.

TABLE 9
The Measures of Association Calculated for
Comparisons among the Libraries within the SPPL, FCPL,
and BCPL Systems and for Comparisons among the
Samples within the Hypothetical System

	SPPL Fill Rates	FCPL Fill Rates 1984	FCPL Fill Rates 1985	BCPL Fill Rates 1984	Random Fill Rates Time 1	Random Fill Rates Time 2
Title fill rate	.19	.14	.16	.12	.15	.12
Subject/author fill rate	.13	.17	.17	.10		
Browsers' fill rate	.14	.13	.09	.19		

fill rate. And, as at time 1, the managers would be responding to random differences among the fill rates that represent nothing more than illusional differences in performance. As these data demonstrate, random sampling error can be substantial and, by definition, unpredictable. It is important to remember that 97% or more of the observed variation among each set of fill rates obtained for the libraries in the SPPL system was due to unexplained variation among patrons or random error. Table 9 provides a comparison of the measures of association between the libraries used by the patrons and the fill rates obtained for the SPPL, FCPL, and BCPL systems and the measures of association between the samples of random numbers representing the hypothetical libraries and the fill rates obtained for each of these samples drawn from the table of random numbers. As is evident from table 9, the measures of association for the three systems and the hypothetical system are quite similar—another demonstration that the differences among the fill rates within the three systems were due to random error.

CORRELATES OF THE FILL RATES

In order for the fill rates to be useful for management decision making, it is necessary that (1) the fill rates be valid and reliable indicators of library performance, (2) the correlates of these fill rates be known, and (3) these correlates be amenable to manipulation by library management so that the fill rates can be influenced to fit the goals of the library. Unfortunately, the search for correlates of the materials availability fill rates is confounded by their questionable validity and reliability. However, given the necessity of identifying the correlates of the fill rates in order to establish their usefulness for management decision making and given the continuing professional interest in the fill rates, an attempt was made to investigate the correlates of the fill rates obtained for the SPPL, BCPL, and FCPL libraries. The reader is cautioned, however, that inclinations to draw conclusions from these analyses should be tempered by an awareness of the magnitude of random error associated with the measurement of each of the fill rates. The subsequent analyses, in effect, represent attempts to explain the observed trivial differences among each of the fill rates obtained for the libraries within the three systems.

The available data describing the fill rates, the amount of resources available, and the annual use statistics for each of the libraries in the SPPL, BCPL and FCPL systems were combined into one data set. Each of the three fill rates was then submitted to a series of correlation analyses with each of the measures of resources available and each of the use statistics in order to determine if any relationships were present in the data.

**Correlation Analyses Between the Fill Rates and
Measures of Library Resources**

The amounts of library resources available to patrons were measured by
size of collection, collection per capita, size of staff, staff per capita, and
hours of service. The per capita measures were included because they are
commonly used by the profession for descriptive purposes. In the context
of these analyses of materials availability for library patrons, however, the
possible relationships of the fill rates to the per capita measures would be
open to interpretation. Per capita measures are adjusted to reflect an
estimate of the population served and consequently reflect both patrons
and nonusers of the library. The potential relevance of the per capita
measures to materials availability for patrons depends on the proportion
of the community that actually uses the library (i.e., amount of resources
per number of patrons) and these proportions for the communities served
by the libraries in this study are unknown. The results of these analyses,
reported in table 10, indicate that there were no statistically significant
relationships between any of the fill rates and any of the measures of
resources available. Within the three systems studied, none of the fill rates
was related to the amount of resources, either actual or per capita, available to the patrons within the libraries.

**Correlation Analyses Between the Fill Rates and
Measures of Library Uses**

The extent to which patrons used the libraries' resources were measured by
annual circulation, circulation per capita, and collection turnover (annual

TABLE 10
Pearson Correlations between Measures of
Library Resources and Library Fill Rates (N = 49)

	Title Fill Rate	Subject/Author Fill Rate	Browsers' Fill Rate
Size of collection			
Actual	−.03	−.11	−.02
Per cpaita	−.10	−.06	−.05
Size of staff			
Actual	−.06	.07	−.07
Per capita	−.16	.04	.01
Hours of Service	−.17	−.06	−.06

r (.05; 47) = .28

circulation divided by size of collection). The results of these analyses, reported in table 11, indicate that:

1. there was no statistically significant relationship between the title fill rate and annual circulation, but there were statistically significant inverse relationships between the title fill rate and circulation per capita and collection turnover; and
2. there were no statistically significant relationships between the subject and author fill rate, the browsers' fill rate and any of the use statistics.

These results indicate that, within the three systems studied, neither the subject and author fill rate nor the browsers' fill rate was related to the uses made of the library but that the title fill rate was inversely related both to circulation per capita and collection turnover. It appears that, within the three systems, libraries with high circulation activity tended to have low title fill rates.

TABLE 11
Pearson Correlations between Annual Measures of Library Use and Library Fill Rates (N = 49)

	Title Fill Rate	Subject/Author Fill Rate	Browsers' Fill Rate
Annual circulation	−.08	.07	−.03
Circulation per capita	−.40*	−.02	.02
Collection turnover	−.42*	−.01	−.13

*Statistically significant at α = .05

Interpretation of the Results of the Correlation Analyses

Within the three systems, neither the subject and author fill rate nor the browsers' fill rate was related to any of the measures of size of resources and any of the measures of use of those resources. It appears, therefore, that within these three systems neither the subject and author fill rate nor the browsers' fill rate is a useful measure of library performance.

Given that within these three systems the title fill rate was not related to amount of resources available within the libraries and inversely related to circulation per capita and collection turnover (each of which is a proposed measure of library performance), it appears that the interpretation of the title fill rate and hence its usefulness as a measure of library performance is open to question. For example, it could be argued that either (1) low title fill rates and high rates of circulation per capita and collection turnover are indicative of good library performance (i.e., the success of the library in stimulating the use of its collections), while high title fill rates and low rates of circulation per capita and collection turnover are indicative of inadequate library performance (i.e., the failure of the library in stimulating the use of its collections), or (2) low title fill rates and high rates of circulation per capita and collection turnover are indicative of inadequate library performance (i.e., the failure of the collection to support adequately the demands of the patrons), which high title fill rates and low rates of circulation per capita and collection turnover are indicative of good library performance (i.e., the success of the collection in supporting adequately the demands of the patrons). Given the inverse nature of these relationships, each of these interpretations appears to be viable, and each of these interpretations would lead to very different administrative responses to these output data. For example, if alternative number one above is espoused by a given library system, then libraries with high fill rates could presumably try to implement strategies designed to increase circulation; if alternative number two above is espoused by a given library system, then libraries with low fill rates could presumably receive higher priorities for collection development. There are no doubt other interpretations of these relationships and other possible administrative actions that serve to underscore both the complexity of the construct, library performance, and the role of management value judgments in establishing the priorities among the various proposed indicators of performance.

Assuming that the validity and reliability of the title fill rate can be demonstrated, one implication of this inverse relationship between the title fill rate and intensity of circulation activity would be the need to determine the effect of collection size on the behavior of the title fill rate given that the fill rate appears to be primarily driven by circulation activity. In order to explore further the relationship between collection size and title fill rate, the title fill rates were correlated with the size of collection, actual and per capita, while controlling for differences among the libraries in circulation per capita and collection turnover. These analyses, in effect, were aimed at determining if among libraries experiencing similar amounts of circulation activity the libraries with larger collections had higher title fill rates. The results of these analyses, reported in table 12, indicate that there were no statistically significant relationships between the title fill rate and size of collection, actual and per capita, when circulation per capita was held constant, that there was no statistically significant relationship between the title fill rate and the actual size of the collection when collection turnover was held constant, and that there was a statistically significant inverse relationship between the title fill rate and size of collection per capita when collection turnover was held constant. These analyses indicate that within the three systems, after differences among

TABLE 12
Partial Correlation Coefficients between the
Title Fill Rate and Size of Collection Holding Circulation
Per Capita and Turnover Constant

	Holding Circulation Per Capita Constant
TFR with size of collection	.19
TFR with size of collection per capita	.11

	Holding Turnover Constant
TFR with size of collection	−.21
TFR with size of collection per capita	−.33*

*Statistically significant at $\alpha = .05$

libraries in circulation per capita were controlled, libraries with larger collections, either actual or per capita, did not have higher title fill rates. These analyses also indicate that within the three systems, after differences among the libraries in collection turnover were controlled, libraries with larger collections did not have higher title fill rates, but that libraries with larger collections per capita actually had lower title fill rates. This last relationship is difficult to understand. It may simply be an artifact of the data from these three systems or a manifestation of the invalidity and unreliability of the title fill rate or a demonstration of our limited understanding of the behavior of, and relationships among, the various indicators of performance that are currently being proposed and used. For example, it could be that the size of the entire collection is not as important as the size of that part of the collection that is in demand; or it could be that the actual number of individual patrons using the library, many of whom would be competing for the same titles, is the driving force behind the title fill rate.

Given the results of all these correlation analyses and recognizing that (1) these results are only known to hold for the three systems studied, (2) that the observed variations among the title fill rates obtained for the libraries within these three systems were demonstrated to be trivial in nature, and (3) that a library must obviously have some as yet undefined adequately sized collection for its community of patrons, it appears that some of the variations among the title fill rates within the three systems were due to variations in the circulation activity of the libraries rather than to variations in the sizes of the collections. If this last statement is corroborated with studies within and between other library systems, it would then appear that low title fill rates are a concomitant of high circulation activity while high title fill rates are a concomitant of low circulation activity.

SUMMARY OF THE DATA ANALYSES

Comparative analyses of fill rate data obtained from the SPPL, BCPL, and FCPL systems have indicated that:

1. within each system, the observed differences among the title fill rates obtained for the branch libraries were statistically significant but trivial. Similarly, within each system, the observed differences among the subject and author fill rates and the observed differences among the browsers' fill rates obtained for the branch libraries were statistically significant but trivial;
2. the observed differences among the systemwide title fill rates obtained for the SPPL, BCPL, and FCPL systems were statistically significant but trivial. Similarly, the observed differences among the systemwide subject and author fill rates and the observed differences among the systemwide browsers' fill rates obtained for the three systems were statistically significant but trivial; and
3. these observed variations among each of the fill rates both within and among the systems were due primarily to random error rather than to any diagnostically meaningful differences among the libraries.

Attempts to identify the correlates of the fill rates within the three systems indicated that:

1. none of the fill rates was related to the amount of resources made available within the libraries;
2. neither the subject and author nor the browsers' fill rates was related to the annual use statistics reported by the libraries; and
3. the title fill rate was inversely related to circulation per capita and collection turnover.

However, given the trivial nature of the differences observed among each of the fill rates and the magnitude of the random error obtained in the estimates of each of the fill rates, the results of the analyses aimed at identifying the correlates of the fill rates are very much open to question.

CONCLUSIONS

Given the results of these analyses, and in the absence of any evidence demonstrating the validity, reliability, and usefulness of the fill rates, it is reasonable to conclude the following:

1. The fill rates, as operationalized in *OMPL* and *OMPL II*, are not valid measures of a library's capability to make available to patrons items which are sought; rather, the fill rates appear to be measuring indirectly the patrons' successes in finding materials in a library;
2. while this construct of patron success within a library has appealing face validity as an indicator of library performance, the amount of variability inherent in patron behavior and reflected in the random error manifested in the measurement of the fill rates appears to render these fill rates unreliable indicators of library performance;
3. the use of the fill rates for analyzing the performance of a given library, or for comparing and analyzing the performances of libraries within systems, or for comparing the performances of systems of libraries cannot at this time be justified;
4. the promulgation of standards, or recommended levels, of performance for libraries based on the fill rates is without any empirical foundation and could place unwarranted onus on libraries with high circulation activity; and
5. library managers should evaluate carefully the various unsubstantiated claims about the usefulness of the fill rates and should consider the relative merits of using indicators of library performance that have been demonstrated to be error bound.

References

1. Douglas Zweizig and Eleanor Jo Rodger, *Output Measures for Public Libraries* (Chicago: American Library Assn., 1982).
2. George D'Elia, "Materials Availability Fill Rates—Useful Measures of Library Performance?" *Public Libraries* 24:106-10 (Fall 1985).
3. George D'Elia and Eleanor Jo Rodger, "Comparative Assessment of Patrons' Uses and Evaluations across Public Libraries Within a System: A Replication," *Library and Information Science Research* 9:5-20 (Jan.-Mar. 1987).
4. William Hays, *Statistics for the Social Sciences*, 2d ed. (New York: Holt, 1973), p. 413-17.
5. Quinn McNemar, *Psychological Statistics*, 4th ed. (New York: Wiley, 1969), p. 149.
6. Nancy A. Van House, "Public Library Effectiveness: Theory, Measures, and Determinants," *Library and Information Science Research* 8:261-83 (Oct. 1986).
7. Ibid., p. 271, 272.
8. Ibid., p. 272.
9. Nancy Van House, Mary Jo Lynch, Charles R. McClure, Douglas L. Zweizig, and Eleanor Jo Rodger, *Output Measures for Public Libraries* (Chicago: American Library Assn., 1987).
10. Van House, "Public Library Effectiveness," p. 275.
11. D'Elia and Rodger, "Comparative Assessment," p. 12-13.
12. Ernest R. De Prospo, Ellen Altman, and Kenneth E. Beasley, *Performance Measures for Public Libraries* (Chicago: American Library Assn., 1973).
13. Terry Ellen Ferl and Margaret G. Robinson, "Book Availability at the University of California, Santa Cruz," *College & Research Libraries* 47:501-8 (Sept. 1986).

14. Neil A. Radford, "Failure In the Library—A Case Study," Library Quarterly 53:328-39 (July 1983).
15. Paul B. Kantor, *Objective Performance Measures for Academic and Research Libraries* (Washington, D.C.: Assn. of Research Libraries, 1984).
16. D'Elia, "Materials Availability," p. 108-10.

THE RISE & FALL & RISE OF JUVENILE NONFICTION, 1961-1988

James Cross Giblin

Watching my friend, Russell Freedman, stride to the podium at the 1988 Newbery-Caldecott banquet to accept his Newbery Medal for *Lincoln: A Photobiography*, I experienced a tremendous surge of pride. I was proud that Russell's gifts as a writer had been recognized, and that we at Clarion had published his winning book. I was also proud to be a writer of nonfiction myself in this time when reviewers, librarians, parents, and children were responding to juvenile nonfiction with an enthusiasm that I could never remember seeing before.

As Russell got into his speech and recounted his start as a writer for children back in 1961, my thoughts inevitably focused on that year, too. For 1961 was the year that Russell and I met, and was my first full year as a children's book editor. How much had happened to each of us, and to the field of juvenile nonfiction, since then!

In 1961, after a year as publicist, I got the break I'd been looking for and assumed the duties of assistant editor at Criterion Books. Sidney Phillips was editor-in-chief and his then-wife, Gertrude, served as production manager. I knew next to nothing about editorial procedures, but I loved working with children's books and was willing to put in overtime to learn the job. Meanwhile, through a friend, I'd met Russell, who was writing his first book, *Teenagers Who Made History* (Holiday), and was seeking part-time work to pay the rent. We used freelancers to copy edit and proofread our manuscripts at Criterion, and after Russell assured me that he could do a respectable copy editing job, I gave him an assignment: to copy edit the heavily rewritten English translation of Aimee Sommerfelt's prize-winning Norwegian novel, *The Road to Agra*.

He did the job quickly, and as far as I could tell, carefully. I turned the manuscript over to Gertrude Phillips for design and production. That

"The Rise & Fall & Rise of Juvenile Nonfiction, 1961–1988" by James Cross Giblin in *School Library Journal* Vol. 35 (October 1988), pp. 27-31; reprinted with permission from Reed Publishing, USA, copyright © Reed Publishing, USA.

afternoon she summoned me into her office, and as soon as I saw the expression in her eyes I knew that something was wrong. "Just look," she said, pointing to a page in the manuscript. "Here 'splendor' is spelled in the American way. But here"—she riffled a few pages ahead—"it's spelled 'splendour.' Do you call this copy editing?"

I mumbled an apology, saying I'd go over the manuscript again, but that didn't satisfy Gertrude. Staring out the window, she groaned (more to herself than to me), "What am I going to do? First, I have to work with a kid who doesn't know anything about editing, and now I've got to deal with a copy editor who doesn't know his job, either!"

Russell's and my fortunes could only rise from that low point, and they did. *The Road to Agra* was published in the fall of 1961, no one found any copy editing errors, and the book went on to win the Child Study Association Award and several other honors. Russell's *Teenagers Who Made History* appeared in that same fall season, receivied excellent reviews, and launched Russell on the writing career that culminated in *Lincoln*.

Back at Criterion, I found myself spending much more time editing nonfiction than fiction. For this was the era of the National Defense Education Act enacted by Congress to provide funds for the purchase of science books by libraries to help counter the threat posed by Soviet scientific successes such as Sputnik. Publishers everywhere jumped on the science bandwagon, and the first government-supported boom in juvenile nonfiction was on.

From this period emerged such innovative programs as Crowell's "Let's Read and Find Out" series of science concept picture books, launched by the pioneering editor, Elizabeth M. Riley. This series was in many ways the nonfiction counterpart of Harper's "I Can Read" series, for it employed topflight writers like Roma Gans, Paul Showers, and Franklyn Branley, and their texts were assigned to illustrators like Paul Galdone and Ed Emberley. The result was a line of books that combined solid information with lively, colorful graphics, books that entertained young readers even as they educated them.

At Criterion, we were concentrating on a nonfiction series of British science books for older children that had its own unique problems. The information in the books was accurate and well-written, and they were illustrated with appropriate black-and-white photos, but the texts were filled with passages like the following from the original version of J. G. Crowther's *Radioastronomy and Radar*: "On some fair Sunday, maybe you can persuade your Mum and Dad to drive you down to Jodrell Bank for a first-hand look at the radar installations there."

The trick, of course, was to edit such passages for the American audience, and inject additional information about installations in the U.S. and Canada while maintaining the tone of the British original. We also had to locate photographs of American sites. This was no easy task. To perform it we hired freelance editors such as Iris Vinton and Edith Patterson Meyer (but not Russell, who no longer needed as much part-time work). In coordinating the freelancers' work as in-house editor, I learned a great deal about the basics of nonfiction that have stood me in good stead ever since: the need for liveliness, clarity, and sound organization in the text, as well as accuracy; the importance of the illustrations and the need to relate them as closely as possible to the text; the added importance of well-written captions to help the reader's understanding. In addition, there is a need for such aids as an index, a list of suggestions for further reading, and perhaps a glossary of unfamiliar terms. All of these fundamentals of juvenile nonfiction became ingrained in me as a result of my editing *Radioastronomy and Radar* and the other titles in that science series.

However, the graphic standards for nonfiction that prevailed in the early 1960s were very different from those that have characterized the best nonfiction of recent years. *Radioastronomy and Radar*, for example, was published in a trim size of 5½" x 8¼", which meant that the type had to be small and few of the photographs could be given large-scale treatment. Even so, it included more illustrations than most nonfiction titles of the day. Elizabeth Ripley's popular series of artists' biographies (Lippincott) contained a mere smattering of black-and-white illustrations, and they were poorly reproduced. Russell's *Teenagers Who Made History*, which included brief biographies of eight young people, from Toscanini to Galileo to Edna St. Vincent Millay—all of whom accomplished great things while still in their teens—featured only a single line drawing of each subject.

When I decided, in 1962, to move on from Criterion, my experience with nonfiction helped me to get my next editorial job at Lothrop, Lee and Shepard. As a tryout for the position, I was asked to do a detailed report on J. J. McCoy's *Animal Servants of Man*, a project that Lothrop's editor-in-chief Beatrice Creighton had contracted several years earlier, but had not had a chance to edit. I pointed out that the manuscript was basically solid but would benefit from revision, so after I was hired I was assigned *Animal Servants of Man* as my first Lothrop book.

Encouraged by Creighton, who believed that all children's books should be attractive, we did *Animal Servants of Man* in an oversize 8" x 10" format with black-and-white wash illustrations. The book generated considerable review and sales interest, and several years later Joe McCoy proposed that we do another natural history title about the years-long search for the nesting grounds of the whooping crane.

I was immediately attracted to the idea, but wondered if a straightforward account of the search would be the best approach. After Joe and I discussed the content, we decided that it would be more interesting to alternate fictionalized chapters about the life of the cranes on their remote nesting grounds in northern Canada, with straight nonfiction chapters describing the work of the scientists as they got closer and closer to the majestic but elusive birds. For the fictional chapters—which, by the way, were entirely accurate in their description of the cranes' behavior—we used line drawings as illustrations, while the straight nonfiction chapters were illustrated with photographs. The book had a generous 6 " x 9 " trim size.

Apparently we made the right choices with the material, for *The Hunt for the Whooping Cranes* was an Honor Book in *The New York Herald Tribune's* Spring Children's Book Festival, and was named a Notable Children's Book of 1966 by the Association for Library Services to Children (ALSC). Beyond these honors, working on *The Hunt for the Whooping Cranes* taught me an important lesson about nonfiction in general: namely, that a nonfiction author is telling a story the same as any other author. The only difference is that it's a true story. So there's nothing wrong with using fictional techniques of scene-setting and atmosphere-building to make factual material more interesting and involving for the reader. All the best authors do it, including Freedman in both *Indian Chiefs* (Holiday) and *Lincoln,* and I made considerable use of fictional techniques myself in the chapter "A Climbing Boy's Day" in my book, *Chimney Sweeps* (Crowell).

(A cautionary note: fictional techniques should never be confused by authors, editors, or book selectors with a distortion of the facts. Anthropomorphizing animals in natural history books should be avoided at all costs, and invented dialogue should never be put into the mouths of the figures in biographies; anachronisms and inaccuracies of any type do not belong in nonfiction books.)

By 1966, when *The Hunt for the Whooping Cranes* was published, the United States was in the midst of Lyndon Johnson's "Great Society" and funds for the purchase of children's trade books were pouring into school libraries. There was an even greater demand for nonfiction than in the NDEA years, and children's book publishers scurried to meet it by launching new series of informational books for every age group, in every conceivable subject area.

Duplication was rife. In one season, I remember, at least three different versions of the life cycle of the horseshoe crab appeared—and hack work abounded as some authors ground out book after book. But there were shining lights, too. Julius Lester's *To Be a Slave* (Dial, 1968) helped to redress the black experience, which had long been slighted in children's books. It was named a Newbery Honor Book. And, in 1969, Jean Fritz published *George Washington's Breakfast* (Coward), the first of a group of books in which she dealt with the idiosyncracies of America's early leaders, proving that juvenile biography could be fun as well as informative.

Although not everyone realized it at the time, 1969 marked the end of the boom in children's books. Richard Nixon was in the White House now and the nation, preoccupied with Vietnam, put aside goals of the Great Society. Juvenile nonfiction was one of the first victims of this changed mood as publishers cut back or closed down series they had begun with such confidence just a few years before.

Children's book publishing went on, however. The better writers continued to produce, promising new authors and illustrators made their debuts, and as far as nonfiction was concerned, there was still room for books that approached familiar material from a fresh viewpoint. That lesson was brought home to me sharply and clearly in 1970 when I edited *Lilies, Rabbits, and Painted Eggs* by Edna Barth (formerly a fellow editor at Lothrop). After I went to The Seabury Press as editor-in-chief of what eventually became Clarion Books, Edna submitted a proposal for a book about Easter. I liked the tone of her writing, but wondered if there was room for yet another book that simply recounted the Easter story. We made an appointment to discuss the idea, however, and from that conversation came a different approach to the project. Every morning, on my way to the office, I passed an elementary school, and before every major holiday during the school year I'd see the same construction paper symbols go up on the classroom windows that we'd pasted on our windows when I was in school —painted eggs and rabbits for Easter, witches and pumpkins for Halloween, pilgrims and turkeys for Thanksgiving. When I mentioned this to Edna, it sparked memories of her own days as a grade school teacher. Before our editorial meeting was over Edna had decided to focus her book on the symbols of Easter and on the role each played in the holiday.

The result, *Lilies, Rabbits, and Painted Eggs*, was so successful that Edna went on to write similar books for Clarion about five other holidays. In the process of editing them, I found myself constantly amazed that she could fulfill her responsibilites as editor-in-chief of Lothrop while doing the extensive research that her books required. But research was never a chore for Edna. Like all good nonfiction writers, she got great pleasure from delving into books and finding just the right fact or anecdote to bring life to whatever topic she was writing about. This kind of enthusiasm communicates itself to readers, and makes nonfiction books like Edna's as appealing to children today as when they were written. Edna's example also served as an inspiration to me when, in 1978, I began to do research for the first of my own nonfiction books.

Even though nonfiction in general seemed to be at a low ebb in the mid 1970s, there were a few signs that pointed to a revival of interest in the genre. Milton Meltzer's 1976 *Horn Book* article, "Where Do All the Prizes Go? The Case for Nonfiction," attracted considerable attention. And a new type of nonfiction book, the photo essay, made a tremendous impact when the first examples appeared on the scene in the late 1970s.

Actually, the concept of the photo essay was not new. *Life* magazine had pioneered the approach with its photo feature stories, and adult publishers had long employed it in art and travel books. It wasn't unknown in the children's field, either. At Lothrop, Beatrice Creighton had used carefully chosen photographs and spacious layouts in such classic non-fiction books of the 1940s as *One God: The Ways We Worship Him* by Florence Fitch and *Discovering Design* by Marion Downer. Closer in time, author Carla Stevens and photographer Leonard Stevens had collaborated on their sensitive study, *The Birth of Sunset's Kittens* (Young Scott, 1969). But it was really Norma Jean Sawicki, then editor of children's book at Crown, who established the photo essay as a genre unto itself with such titles as *Small Worlds Close Up* by Lisa Grillone and Joseph Gennaro, *The Hospital Book* by James Howe, and *Journey to the Planets* by Patricia Lauber. For each of these, and other photo essays she published, Norma Jean insisted on top quality photographs, reproduced in handsome formats on heavy, expensive paper. As a result of her efforts, the Crown photo essays made a major splash in both the institutional and retail markets, and other publishers soon imitated them.

The timing couldn't have been better for the photo essay approach. Accustomed to seeing a topic explored largely through visual images on television, youngsters were far more likely to respond to a photo essay than to a typical nonfiction book of the past with its large chunks of type, interrupted only by an occasional line drawing. The photo essay format not only suited the TV-acclimated attention span of these youngsters, but it fitted neatly into the fast pace of their lives.

Not everyone admired photo essays, however. Some critics felt that by emphasizing the visual and down-playing the verbal, the style pandered to youngsters' tastes instead of attempting to elevate them. Perhaps the term "photo essay" itself was partly to blame. Like all labels, it was often applied indiscriminately to everything from photographic picture books for the very young, to books for the middle grades where the text and the illustrations were in balance—the true photo essay—to heavily illustrated books for older children.

I disagreed then with the critics of photo essays, as I do now, both as an editor and as an author. Perhaps the strength of my feelings stems from the fact that the first book I wrote for children, *The Scarecrow Book*, was a photo essay, and it was edited by Norma Jean Sawicki. I often bristled when Norma Jean slashed through some of my favorite passages in the early drafts and scrawled in the margins, "Compress; this rambles too much," or "Cut; not necessary; the illustrations will convey this." But by the time the book reached the final stages of production, I realized she was right. The text hadn't lost anything by being tightened; instead, I could now see that it was stronger than before.

The Scarecrow Book certainly wasn't unique. In my opinion, all of the best photo essays and heavily illustrated nonfiction books of recent years display the same sort of tight, economical writing. It's a case where, as Mies van der Rohe claimed of modern architecture, less truly is more.

Led by the interest in photo essays, the juvenile nonfiction area made a quiet but steady comeback in the early 1980s. Unlike the era of the National Defense Education Act and, later, Lyndon Johnson's Great Society programs, this revival wasn't occasioned by any single government act but rather by a combination of circumstances. Educated young parents were eager to expose their children to challenging books, and these included nonfiction titles as well as fiction. Although national programs dwindled during the Reagan administration, school and public library budgets rose in many localities in the face of pressure from parents, and specialized children's bookstores sprang up across the country to cater to their needs and wants.

Perhaps most significant of all, children in school were still assigned to do book reports on whatever they were studying at the moment—the workings of the sanitation department, life in ancient Egypt, the American Civil War—but many of the standard nonfiction titles from the past had gone out of print in the lean years of the 1970s. Now there was room for good new books to replace them in all of the major subject areas, from natural history to history to pure science to biography.

Both new and experienced authors responded to the call for more nonfiction material. Aiming at the picture-book audience, author-illustrator Gail Gibbons covered a wide range of topics from locks and keys to the development of the modern highway system, and Betsy Maestro offered simple but not simplistic treatments of such complex subjects as the framing of the U.S. Constitution. For older children, Jean Fritz examined her Chinese roots; Brent Ashabranner confronted some of America's most pressing social problems; Dorothy Hinshaw Patent brought careful scholarship to a series of books about wild and domestic animals; Milton Meltzer pursued a variety of topics, from a biography of Winnie Mandela to a study of Gentile heroes of the Holocaust; Russell Freedman went from highly visual accounts of sharks and rattlesnakes to equally visual explorations of immigrant kids on city streets and children in the Old West; and I had great fun delving into such offbeat subjects as milk, defensive walls, and the history of eating utensils and table manners.

As nonfiction texts became livelier and more appealing, so did the appearance of the books. Editors and art directors started to give nonfiction books the same Tiffany treatment that had been reserved for picture books. Oversize formats were common and color photographs, once the exception, now seemed to be the rule for certain types of juvenile nonfiction.

It wasn't long before children's book award committees began to recognize the literary and graphic qualities of the new nonfiction. The Boston Globe-Horn Book Awards established a separate category for nonfiction as far back as 1976, and the Society of Children's Book Writers followed suit the next year with its Golden Kite Awards. The children's Book Guild of Washington initiated an annual award to a nonfiction author for his or her body of work in 1977.

Soon afterward, the Newbery Award committees of ALSC began to acknowledge the literary excellence of nonfiction in a more consistent way. Kathryn Lasky's and Christopher Knight's photo essay, *Sugaring Time* (Macmillan), was singled out as a Newbery Honor Book in 1983, as were Rhoda Blumberg's *Commodore Perry in the Land of the Shogun* (Lothrop) in 1986 and Patricia Lauber's *Volcano: The Eruption and Healing of Mt. St. Helens* (Bradbury) in 1987. Then, in 1988, Russell Freedman's *Lincoln: A Photobiography* received the highest literary honor ALSC can bestow— the John Newbery Medal. It was the first time the award had been given to a nonfiction book since 1956, when Jean Lee Latham's biography, *Carry On, Mr. Bowditch* (Houghton), copped the prize.

As Russell neared the end of his Newbery acceptance speech on that warm night in New Orleans, I found myself remembering how *Lincoln* had come about, and thinking of the way in which it not only crowned Russell's career but also reflected all of the main trends in the new nonfiction.

Ever since the 1920s, if not earlier, children's book editors and children's librarians have worked closely together. *Lincoln* was yet another example of this continuing association, although in this case, the librarian in question didn't know it. In the fall of 1983, I participated in a one-day conference on nonfiction at the University of Iowa. Ginny Moore Kruse, of the Cooperative Children's Book Center at the University of Wisconsin, was one of the other speakers at an afternoon workshop. When the subject of biography came up, I listened with special attention because we'd long wanted to publish a line of biographies at Clarion. A librarian in the audience asked Ginny if she could recommend some outstanding biographies of Presidents. After thinking for a moment, Ginny replied that the question wasn't as easy to answer as it might seem. Many of the older biographies had gone out of print and few of those that remained were truly outstanding. My thoughts wandered: maybe we should focus our biography line on the Presidents; but if we did, whom should we approach to write them . . .?

A few months later, in the spring of 1984, Russell Freedman delivered the manuscript and photographs of *Cowboys of the Wild West*. His editor, Ann Troy, and I took him to a celebration lunch, and over dessert, we discussed ideas for possible future books. We told Russell of our desire to do a group of biographies illustrated with photographs—specifically, biographies of the Presidents. Russell's eyes brightened immediately. "I like that," he said, "and Lincoln should definitely be the first. He was a fascinating man, and he was also the first President to be widely photographed."

Delighted by his enthusiasm, we offered Russell a contract then and there. He went on to write the book, and the rest is history, as they say.

Why did *Lincoln* make such an impact? For a combination of reasons, in my opinion. First, it offered—as did the Barth holiday books—a fresh approach to familiar material, demythologizing Lincoln without debunking him, as Mary Burns said in her introductory remarks at the Newbery/ Caldecott banquet. Second, like *The Hunt For the Whooping Cranes* and other noteworthy examples of juvenile nonfiction, it told a dramatic true story, recounting the life of one of the most compelling and contradictory figures in American history. And third, its emphasis on the visual, starting with the subtitle "A Photobiography," not only reflected Russell's skills as a photo researcher, but also carried forward and developed the best features of the photo essay approach to nonfiction.

The most significant factor in the book's success was, of course, Russell's accessible yet literate text. In just 74 manuscript pages, he offered a many-sided portrait of Lincoln, his family, his colleagues, and his times, proving—if any proof was still required—that the tight, compressed writing style so characteristic of the new nonfiction can result in a profoundly satisfying book. A book that, in the opinion of the Newbery committee, made the year's "most distinguished contribution to American literature for children."

While *Lincoln* is certainly a benchmark in juvenile nonfiction, it's by no means the last word—neither for Russell Freedman nor for anyone working in the field. From biography to history to science, the possibilities for entertaining and informative books have barely begun to be tapped. And, with the new emphasis on quality education, the desire of parents to help their children get a leg up on learning, and the increasing use of children's trade books in the classroom, there are thousands of teachers and librarians ready and eager to introduce nonfiction material to young people in stimulating and imaginative ways. All they need is the book.

As a publisher and as an author, I want to help provide these books in the years ahead. It promises to be an exciting time for everyone concerned.

WHY DO ACADEMIC LIBRARIES GET SUCH A BAD RAP?

Shirley T. Echelman

I have spent a good part of the past seven years attempting to represent the interests of the largest academic libraries in the United States to those who have influence in the making of educational policy and in the appropriation of funds for libraries. This has been an absorbing task but not, as I am sure you can imagine, an easy one.

The majority of people with whom I've had contact are highly educated and dedicated to the importance of education in our democracy. Given the slightest opportunity, most of them will launch into their favorite story about a formative experience with a book, a librarian, or a library. Hearing foundation officers, university presidents, and renowned scholars recount library stories is enough to bring tears to the eyes of a librarian. Time and again, I've come away from such encounters energized by pride in my profession and its ability to influence the lives of the young.

Why, then, are the roles of librarians and libraries in academic institutions so poorly understood? Why do scholars persist in regarding their university libraries as inert collections of books and journals rather than vital support centers staffed by expert colleagues who can assist them in their work of expanding on civilization's conversation with itself? Why do university presidents so persistently and depressingly view their libraries solely as mysterious black holes into which money endlessly disappears? Why are librarians so often viewed as being ancillary, rather than central, to the process of education and research that is the mission of the university?

Some Answers

There are, of course, no easy or definitive answers to these questions. However, some of the miscomprehension arises from three factors—age, complexity, and dissimilarity.

"Why Do Academic Libraries Get Such a Bad Rap?" by Shirley T. Echelman in *Library Journal* Vol. 113, no. 16 (October 1, 1988), pp. 39-41; reprinted with permission from Reed Publishing, USA, copyright © Reed Publishing, USA.

Age: Libraries are ancient institutions. They have appeared in most cultures shortly after the development of written language and an economic and cultural base of sufficient complexity to allow a society to differentiate among the tasks of providing food, securing the group against death by hostile enemies, and mastering the mysteries of the natural world. Libraries predated universities, even in their most primitive form, by many centuries. Indeed the oldest universities originated more or less as spontaneous gatherings of students around individual scholars who were willing to teach, and who either owned, or had access to, a collection of books.

These scholars were as valued, I suspect, for their familiarity with the contents of their libraries as for their pedagogy. This familiarity was nearly occult in an era in which only a few souls had the leisure to become literate, and even fewer were learned.

We find the scholar-librarian in the priestly function of ancient times. One of the most vivid evocations of this situation, albeit a dark and devilish one, may be found in Umberto Eco's novel *The Name of the Rose*. Here the library is laid out on a plan that is obscure to all but the librarian. The librarian alone moves with surety through the labyrinth of the library. He (in this text) alone is responsible for the safekeeping of the accumulated knowledge represented by the collection and knows how to find what is in his keeping. Only he knows what truths, falsehoods, and secrets are contained therein; he alone decides who may and who may not have access to those secrets. What power the librarian has in this situation.

Fiction as Paradigm

While *The Name of the Rose* is a work of fiction, the situation it depicts is a paradigm of historical reality. Is it any wonder—given the potentially dark power that control of such a resource implies—that, even in our day, many scholars insist that libraries are, in reality, simple? They swear it is the librarians who complicate and not the innate nature of libraries that is complicated. Even historians like Arthur Schlesinger subscribe with hope to the myth of simplicity. During the 1974 hearings in the U.S. Senate on the nomination of Daniel Boorstin for Librarian of Congress, Schlesinger testified that all the librarian needed to know about the operation of the world's largest research library could be learned in a few weeks. A few American universities, and many more abroad, still believe that. So still, apparently, do the president and Senate of the United States.

Not a Mere Collection

This leads me to the second factor—**complexity**. Libraries are inherently complex for the very reason that they are more than mere collections of books and journals. The output of published information has become so immense that librarians are weighted with the problems of the past at the very time when they need most to be free to consider and implement solutions for the future. Oscar Handlin characterized the situation in "Libraries and Learning" (*The American Scholar,* September 1987, p. 205-218):

> The volumes gathered in a research library . . . do not simply flow together as rivulets of rain accumulate in a pool. Apart from the budget conferences to cajole legislators, deans, provosts, chancellors, and presidents into making the required funds available, assembling the books and journals is only the beginning and not the end of problems. Collections require constant nurture; they must be cataloged, housed, preserved, pruned, and added to. There is no end to it.

Handlin, a noted scholar and an exception to my previous statement in that he has a thorough, indeed an exquisite understanding of the complexity of a university library, aptly delineates the mission of a library: to acquire, to organize, to preserve, and to make available. It is unfortunate but true that these activities tend to defeat one another. The more books, journals, manuscripts, and other materials a library acquires, the more difficult it becomes to organize them coherently for use. But coherent organization is essential if the vast, multiformatted inventory of the modern library (both its owned and its accessed inventory) is to be made available to its clients.

Thus we come to another complexity: enhancements in access exacerbate the difficulty of preserving materials for future use. Resolving these difficulties can easily seem impossible—a vicious cycle of acquisition, access, deterioration, and loss. Little wonder that universities seem to have a more and more difficult time successfully filling senior library management positions than they did in earlier and apparently simpler decades.

Nontraditional Access

Yet another complexity in modern libraries is in providing access to information in nontraditional formats through off-site central databases or campuswide local area networks. In addition to traditional library resources, online access is now available for full-text information traditionally available only in print, as well as information that was previously not available at all except to a few insiders.

One of our problems in encompassing these new complexities professionally is that of title and image. Although it has seemed in the past to be wasteful of time and energy, the topic of what librarians should be called in the new information environment is worthy of at least a modicum of consideration. We live in an age in which one's title is a symbol of one's empowerment. Much has been written about this topic, and there is little need for me to review the arguments for "librarian," "information manager," or "chief information officer."

Personally, I prefer to call myself a librarian, even though I haven't practiced professionally in nearly ten years. But that's because I'm a traditionalist at heart, and I like the idea of being a member of a profession whose roots are in the ancient priesthoods of the intellect. Nevertheless, I recognize the need for a modern definition of the profession that expresses what we do with more immediate recognition value. Robert Spinrad, in a recent essay on "The Electronic University" (in *Cohabiting with Computers*, edited by Joseph Traub, Wm. Kaufmann, 1985), offers the title of "information coordinator." His essay elegantly delineates the complexities of the university of the near future.

Not Like the Others Only More So

Let us turn to the third factor that contributes to the miscomprehensions about academic libraries and the role of academic librarians—dissimilarity. The library is basically unlike other parts of a modern university. Rather, it has many of the characteristics of a business organization. It is both capital and labor intensive, and its day-to-day operations require the ability to deal successfully with long- and short-range planning, personnel and labor relations, inventory control, complex purchasing arrangements, scheduling problems, marketing techniques, change and crisis management, budgetary and expense control, public relations, technology development and adaptation, and the provision of products and services that meet the needs of several levels of clientele.

These characteristics make it difficult for academics to understand what the librarians are doing, why they are doing it, or what it all has to do with the scholarly or pedagogical pursuit. In order to gain the understanding and sympathetic support of critical academic constituencies, librarians must engage in ongoing educational and public relations efforts.

Library/Computer Alliances

One source of support for such efforts might be the academic computing center. Although computer center directors and chief librarians often see themselves as rivals on campus for control of information service functions, there are striking similarities between the two organizations; and both are similarly dissimilar from the rest of the academic institution. Therefore, wisdom would dictate the forging of alliances rather than the fomenting of rivalries. After all, educational and scholarly processes are changing inexorably, and these changes are driven largely by revolutions in communications and information technologies. Who can better assist the university in accommodating to these changes than the librarians and the computer managers? The potential benefits of such a coalition of expertise and interest are self-evident.

I have attempted to explore some of the cultural factors that underlie the current difficulties that many academic librarians face. I have barely touched the structural difficulties engendered by aging buildings, brittle books, rising prices of serials, the costs of networking, or the many other problems that beset libraries.

Educational Reform and Libraries

During the past half-dozen years, there have been a number of studies of American education. Most of these have highlighted the historical and comparative inadequacies of our educational institutions, and have urged that substantial change is necessary. Among the most important of these are *A Nation at Risk* and *American Memory* (both resulting from studies undertaken by federal agencies) and Ernest Boyer's *College: The Undergraduate Experience in America*, sponsored by the Carnegie Foundation for the Advancement of Teaching. These studies deserve close attention, as much for what they leave out as for what they include.

Only Boyer considers the library at all, and his consideration is a troubled one. He deplores the state of academic libraries, the lack of even minimally adequate funding at many institutions, and the separation of the library from the undergraduate learning process. His 1984 survey of undergraduates showed that 27 percent of the students in colleges and universities spend no time at all in the library in a normal school week, and that only 15 percent spend more than ten hours a week there. These percentages do not differ widely between liberal arts colleges and research universities.

Furthermore, most students who do use the library use it only as a quiet study hall. More than half never consult special bibliographies or read a basic document referred to by an author. Teachers only infrequently refer to the library or encourage students to use it, and, when they do, it is usually in reference to the materials that they have put on reserve.

Higher education in the United States has had a strongly practical thrust since the establishment of the federally assisted land-grant universities just after the Civil War. Despite many recent reassessments and the vaunted return to the core curriculum, most Americans still view a university education as preparation for work rather than as preparation for life. Handlin says the primary function of the university has become the preparation of technicians.

> Increasingly geared to fill the need for skilled practitioners of medicine, law, government and business, American higher education can and should assure a flow of competent technicians to hospitals and courts, and keep engineers and politicians abreast of current knowledge in their fields. Insofar as the university can transmit those skills, it should. And the library serves a useful function in performing that task, housing as it does a huge database from which users can draw vast stores of information.

Yet the library is more than a database of information. It is also a source of inspiration, a serendipitous journey from question to wonderment. Once again from Handlin:

> The library is a place of learning as the school is not, a place where questions are not stifled in ready answers but provoke thought, and where one thought leads to another. The warfare between the established learning ensconced in the . . . lecture hall and the subversive learning hidden in the library is more acute and more vital than ever. The outcome will decisively influence our culture.

Two Faces: Past and Future

So here we librarians stand, Janus-like, guardians of the accumulated knowledge of the past and guides to the information upon which future knowledge will be built. Our responsibilities to present and future generations are immense, and our resources are so terribly limited. What must we do? We must recognize that the traditional knowledge base, consisting of printed materials maintained by labor-intensive management systems, is increasingly dysfunctional in the face of technologies that encompass personal computers and artificial intelligence. Without abrogating our responsibilities to our collections, we must harness the technical means both at hand and aborning to the search for knowledge. We need to rethink every aspect of our professional work in order to find where major reallocations of resources can be made. And we need to find new resources because, as Boorstin has pointed out, new technologies do not supplant older ones, they supplement them.

Reevaluate and Reorganize

Spinrad's information coordinator concept provides a clue to the exciting implications for library service of the convergence of computing, communications, and information. In order to realize this concept fully, some hard things need to be done. Zero-based evaluations of every function currently performed in libraries should be undertaken. The understanding should be that this evaluation will ask why as well as how, and will probably result in a major reoganization of resources, both financial and human. I suspect that fewer professional librarians will be employed after the evaluation is complete, and that many tasks now performed by librarians will be delegated to support staff, will be done by computers, or will not be done at all.

Professional education should be thoroughly revamped, and expectations of employers should be rethought as well. It does little good for practitioners to rail at library educators for inculcating students with first-job skills rather than preparing them for ever-changing careers when the advertisements for entry-level jobs still demand the skills being denigrated.

In order to improve both practice and preparation, librarians must actively support research in a way that they have not done at all, or have done only marginally in the past. I am not talking about more surveys of ARL libraries, either. I may not still be working at ARL, but I do still have pity for my friends and colleagues. What is needed is knowledge about information behavior; expert system capabilities for ordering and reordering information to individual needs; simulation methodologies—information studies rather than library studies.

Enthusiasm, If Not Unity

Warren J. Haas, president of the council on Library Resources, has conceptualized the new academic library as having the following components: materials owned, materials owned cooperatively, planned dependence, and purchase of access. The new academic librarian must be technically competent as a base, but must also be a skilled analyst, and imaginative planner, a resourceful cooperator and negotiator, a coordinator of available information resources, and an inventor of new methods of access.

How is this all to be accomplished, you ask? A good question, and one to which I do not have an answer. Indeed, I suggest that there are many questions to be addressed before we arrive at any answers: how to recruit the kinds of people we need; how to raise salaries to attract and keep those people; how to retrain and develop our present staffs; how to educate faculty and administrators to the new possibilities; how to think past our institution-based traditions; and what we must abandon both in terms of collections and services.

I have tried to present issues of interest; it is my hope that I have succeeded in arousing enthusiasm, if not unity. No matter how difficult the responsibilities that the future will bring, the task of explaining what libraries are and how they fit into the structure and functioning of the academic institutions of which they are a part remains an essential activity for senior academic library administrators. Political skills such as coalition building are essential. Valuable lessons may be learned from public librarians who are, in many cases, a good deal more sophisticated politically than their academic counterparts.

MISSING & WANTED:
BLACK WOMEN IN ENCYCLOPEDIAS

Henrietta M. Smith

An in-depth study of the achievements of women in American history would substantiate the fact that black women have made major, identifiable contributions in many fields of endeavor, including business and professional occupations and the arts. Many of their achievements predate the Civil War. For example, Elizabeth Keckley was a noted seamstress and designer who made dresses for Mrs. Abraham Lincoln among others. Born a slave in Virginia in 1818, Keckley bought her freedom, settled in Washington, D.C., and opened a shop that eventually employed 20 seamstresses. She is registered in the records of the prestigious Association of Fashion and Accessory Designers, Inc. Other outstanding black women include Charlotte Ray, Henrietta Duerte, Ma Rainey, and Zora Neale Thurston.

Although refused the *right* to practice, Charlotte Ray was the first black woman to graduate from a law school. She received her degree from Howard University in 1872, but had to earn her living as a teacher because of legal restrictions. In the January 15, 1927 *Tuskegee Messenger*, it was reported that throughout the United States at least 200 black women were qualified as undertakers. The pioneer in this field was Henrietta Duerte, who established her business in Philadelphia in 1896![1]

At the opening of the twentieth century, Ma Rainey (Georgia Pridgett) stirred the hearts and souls of both black and white audiences with her unique rendition of the blues. It is unfortunate that, from the early days of the Harlem Renaissance, literary critics have paid little attention to the works of Zora Neale Hurston; only a few may remember that she received a Guggenheim Fellowship. In one tribute, Hurston was called ". . . the most outstanding folklorist of her time . . . colorful and unorthodox."[2]

This problem of omission of notable black women may well have been the catalyst for a critical review of selected children's encyclopedias by Beryl Graham—"Treatment of Black American Women in Children's Encyclopedias," published in the *Negro History Bulletin* of May, 1976 (pp. 596-598). When working as a librarian in Boston's Plain High School, Graham was well aware of the students' dependency on encyclopedias as their first choice for fulfilling a research assignment. After an analytical review of eight children's encyclopedias, all dated prior to 1971, Graham found that factual material on black women was less than adequate. In summarizing her findings, Graham said:

> There remains a greater discrepancy in the treatment of black women in children's encyclopedias (than for women in general). The varied ways that children are affected by biographical information cannot be over-emphasized and models are most important to them. Most children tend to relate to heroes and heroines where they find them. Thus if a child discovers that an encyclopedia provides more information on certain racial groups or sexes, or that only certain professions are discussed, it is likely that the child will not be motivated to pursue certain careers or to form heroes and heroines from the under-represented group.[3]

Graham's review of these encyclopedias focused on the amount of information provided for 23 black women who had made contributions in such diverse areas as education, business, the arts, civil rights, and government. In addition, she checked the tenor of each entry and noted whether or not there were photographs accompanying any of the subjects. Graham, who summarized her findings in a chart (included in this article), expressed a need for more visual representation for the selected subjects, and made the following observations:

> • Encyclopedia editorial staffs show biases by the omission of women whom the black community consider heroic, but whose positions may not be acceptable to the non-black community, e.g., Fannie Lee Hamer and Rosa Parks.

> • Women whose ideology appears to be in conflict with traditional political ideology are often omitted from encyclopedias, e.g., Nina Simone, Angela Davis, and Odetta.

> • Women who have made inroads into "white-dominated" professions may be omitted also, e.g., Constance Baker Motley, Patricia Harris, and Shirley Chisholm.[4]

The Encyclopedias Revisited

After reading Graham's article published over ten years ago, I felt it would be appropriate and more than just an academic exercise to revisit these same encyclopedias to see what, if any, changes were evident. I examined the following: *Academic American Encyclopedia* (1987); *Britannica Junior Encyclopedia* (1984; o.p.); *Collier's Encyclopedia* (1986); *Compton's Encyclopedia* (1987); *Encyclopedia Americana* (1985); *Merit Students Encyclo-*

pedia (1983); *New Book of Knowledge* (1983); and *World Book Encyclopedia* (1987). Since *Encyclopedia International,* studied by Graham, is now out of print, it was replaced with *Academic American,* first published in 1970. The user level of this encyclopedia is from middle school to high school, and it is a leader in the development of computerizing encyclopedic information.

Before investigating each set of encyclopedias, I searched the library literature for current evaluations of the encyclopedias. In *Best Encyclopedias* (Oryx Press, 1986), Kenneth Kister gave high marks overall for every set. He did, however, also cite individual weaknesses in terms of writing style, typography, and quality of illustrations. Because one of Graham's concerns was the lack of illustrations for subjects examined, I paid close attention to the number of illustrations each encyclopedia was said to include, ranging from 11,000 in *Britannica Junior* to nearly 30,000 in *World Book.*

Among the other items analyzed were a statement of policy for reviewing and another describing the extent of updating and/or expansion of entries. According to William Katz in *Introduction to Reference Work* (McGraw Hill, 1987), an average 5 to 10 percent of material in an encyclopedia is revised and/or updated annually.

Recent Findings

In addition to the 24 subjects Graham examined, five women not included in her study were added for this current study. Each was selected on the

GRAHAM CHART								
	Compton's Encyclopedia	New Book of Knowledge	Britannica Junior	World Book	Merit Students Encyclopedia	Encyclopedia Americana	Collier's Encyclopedia	Encyclopedia International
Baker, Augusta								
Barnett, Ida W.								
Bethune, Mary M.	☆	☆ □	☆	☆	☆	☆		☆
Brooks, Gwendolyn	☆	□	□	☆ □		☆	□	☆ □
Brown, Charlotte				☆				
Chisholm, Shirley	□			☆ □	□			
Davis, Angela				□				
Dee, Ruby								
Dunham, Katherine	□			☆				☆
Hamer, Fannie	□	□				□		☆
Hansberry, Lorraine	□	□				□		☆
Harris, Patricia	□	□		☆				
Motley, Contance B.	□							
Odetta								
Parks, Rosa				□				
Price, Leontyne	□	□	□	☆		☆	□	
Simone, Nina	□							
Terrell, Mary				☆	□	☆		☆
Truth, Sojourner			□	☆		☆	□	☆
Tubman, Harriet	☆		□	☆	☆	☆	□	☆
Walker, Madam C.J.		Index						
Walker, Maggie								
Walker, Margaret								

☆ Entry under person's name   □ Entry under subheading in subject area premise that her major accomplishment was recognized after 1976, when the Graham article appeared.

After locating all entries, I discovered that the data on black women in encyclopedias is still limited; for the most part entries were not revised and/or updated in the ten-year interim. No deviation from the presentation of women traditionally given adequate coverage was found for Harriet Tubman, Phillis Wheatley, Mary McLeod Bethune, and Gwendolyn Brooks. But, although Brooks's literary prowess was well-covered, it was interesting to note that even in encyclopedias for children no mention is made of the poetry she wrote for children, particularly *Bronzeville Boys and Girls* (Harper, 1956).

Some encyclopedias made only minimal changes in the entires. For example.

• *New Book of Knowledge* contains a picture of Angela Davis identified only as "a black activist" along with males who were active in the civil rights struggle.

• *New Book of Knowledge* and *Merit Students Encyclopedia* contain two very brief entries for both Gwendolyn Brooks and Leontyne Price, and *Compton's* has included entries for Shirley Chisholm and Katherine Dunham.

• Nationally known storyteller Augusta Baker was listed in the original group of encyclopedias studied by Graham. A check of *World Book's* editorial board shows Baker listed among its members. Yet the only entry *World Book* has for this noted storyteller is that she compiled the stories in *The Talking Tree* (o.p., 1955) and that she, among others, was awarded the Regina Medal. Neither notation revealed her ethnic identity. In a bibliographic note under "Storytelling" in *Compton's*, the entry for Baker reads: "Baker, Augusta, *The Golden Lynx*; favorite tales from seven countries (1960) chosen by a well-known storyteller." There is no mention of her service as the first black coordinator of children's services in the New York Public Library system, her establishment of the James Weldon Johnson Collection of Children's Books on the Black Experience, or her bibliographies of books about the black experience for children, the first issue of which dates back to 1938.

• In *New Book of Knowledge*, actress Ruby Dee is cross-referenced to Ossie Davis, and in that context the entry only states that she is an actress who has had major roles in *A Raisin in the Sun* and *Purlie*. (Users would have to assume that these were plays with blacks as central characters since this fact is not stated.)

Of the five added subjects, only former Congresswoman Barbara Jordan was given what could be called *adequate* coverage, including a photograph in both *Academic American* and in *World Book*. Poet Nikki Giovanni earned an index notation in *Academic American*, but none of the collections she has compiled for children were listed in her bibliography.

No encyclopedia listed educator Marva Collins, who is often singled out for her innovative (if sometimes controversial) approach to education. Nor was there any mention of actress Cicely Tyson who won an Oscar nomination for her role in *Sounder* and a Grammy Award for her portrayal of the heroine in *The Autobiography of Miss Jane Pittman.* Tyson has given a new non-comedic dimension to roles for blacks in film and theater—knowledge of which would serve young readers well, if it were made available. Also omitted was Maya Angelou, whose writing, dramatic presentations, and personal strength in the face of adversity has gained nationwide prominence. It was interesting to note that although scant attention was paid to these positive images, *Encyclopedia Americana* found it expedient to provide information on Vanessa Williams, the first Black Miss America; and then include a brief account of her unfortunate dethronement. Indeed no one would change history nor deny the incident, but it seems that there could be a better balance between the Vanessa Williams negative kind of entry and the more-positive images reflected in the accomplishments of people like Collins, Tyson, and Angelou, all of whom were overlooked.

In this same vein, one might question why *Compton's* includes Leontyne Price in the "M" volume—not under music, but under "Famous people from Mississippi." This same list of famous Mississippians did not include the late Fannie Lou Hamer, a civil rights activist who was a native of that state. Was there editorial concern with the way in which Hamer gained national recognition—through her civil rights activities?

Finally, perhaps it is a time-worn cliche to say that a picture is worth a thousand words, yet numerous studies support the theory that minority children need the reinforcement of seeing *positive* role models to which they can relate. Based on the number of pictures, maps, diagrams, etc., ascribed to the various titles, the grand total would be upwards of 100,000. If each set had included even *one* picture of each of the 27 subjects of this study, the total would have been a mere 216 photos of black females. The actual count is a dismal 28 photos. (Yet for other subjects, some encyclopedias provided two pictures of one person under different subheadings, showing a serious lack of balance in treatment.)

Revisions Requested

Since encyclopedias are used in schools as primary sources, I enjoin editors to take a long and searching look at the contents to see what revisions are needed to better inform readers about the current status of all biographical subjects. My investigation of the treatment of black women of achievement reveals that such revisions are needed so that black children in particular can locate information about important personages in their cultural heritage. Such updating with factual, accurate information and

COMPARISON CHART

	World Book	Compton's Encyclopedia	New Book of Knowledge	Britannica Junior	Encyclopedia Americana	Collier's Encyclopedia	Merit Students Encyclopedia	Academic American
*Angelou, Maya Writer								
Baker, Augusta Storyteller	□	@						
Barnett, Ida W. Newspaper Editor		☆						
Bethune, Mary M. Educator	☆ #□	☆ #□	☆□	@	☆	☆	☆ #	☆
Brooks, Gwendolyn Poet	☆□	☆	☆	@	☆	☆	□	☆ #□
Brown, Charlotte Educator								
Chisholm, Shirley Politician	☆ #□	☆	☆	@	☆		□	☆ #□
*Collins, Marva Educator								
Davis, Angela Political Activist			□ #			#		
Dee, Ruby Actress	#		□					□
Dunham, Katherine Dancer	□	☆□	@	□	☆	□		☆
*Giovanni, Nikki Poet	□		@					☆
Hamer, Fannie Lou Civil Rights								
Hansberry, Lorraine Playwright	☆	□@	@	□@	□	□	□	□#
Harris, Patricia Government	☆ #□	□ #	□ # @	@				☆
*Jordan, Barbara Politician	☆ #		□@					☆ #
Motley, Constance Federal Judge		@	@ #□	@				
Odetta Folk Artist	□							
Parks, Rosa Civil Rights	☆ #□						□	□
Price, Leontyne Opera Singer	☆ #	□ #	□	☆ #□	☆ #□	□	☆ #□	☆
Simone, Nina Jazz Folk Singer								
Terrell, Mary Woman's Rights	☆.#□	@	@		☆		□	
Truth, Sojourner Abolitionist	☆ #	@□	□	☆ #□	☆ #□	☆□	☆□	☆ #
Tubman, Harriet Abolitionist	☆ @	☆ @	☆ @	☆ @	☆ @	☆ #@	☆	☆ #
*Tyson, Cicely Actress								
Walker, C. J. Cosmetologist		@	@					
Walker, Margaret Poet					@			☆

* Added to original subjects   # Photograph   □ Entry under subject heading   @ Index entry   ☆ Entry under person's name

the inclusion of good photographs will greatly assist all users looking for important, notable subjects to write about and discuss, not only during Black History Month but all year long, regardless of the user's ethnic background.

References

1. Barbara Reynolds. "History of Black Business and Professional Women" in *Dollars and Sense.* June/July, 1985. pp. 20; 27.
2. Jeanne Noble. *Beautiful, Also Are the Souls of My Black Sisters.* Prentice-Hall, 1978. p. 165; 217.
3. Beryl Graham. "Treatment of Black American Women in Children's Encyclopedias" in *Negro History Bulletin,* vol. 39, no. 5, May, 1976. p. 596.
4. *Ibid.* p. 598.

PART V:
TECHNOLOGICAL APPLICATIONS
IN LIBRARIES

TECHNOLOGICAL IMAGES AND THE CHILD READER

Kay E. Vandergrift

Children of the 1980s are immersed in a technological society. They live in a world where computers, robots, space walks, and satellites are commonplace. But they also live in a world of toxic waste, plutonium pollution, and mind control—a world in which a few seconds can turn an inspiring shuttle flight into a deadly ball of flames; in which laser-guided bombs are reported to destroy their targets with utmost precision. Young people watch television shows in which human characters play second fiddle to personified computerized cars or laser-equipped helicopters. They shoot down enemy robots in video arcades or on their home computer screens and, in general, play with the toys, talk the language—even wear the clothes—that glorify a high-tech society.

Now, obviously, this is not all bad. Technological characters of the mass media—from Voltron to Knight Rider—are, after all, this generation's "good guys" fighting the latest forces of evil. And we all enjoy the benefits —and the comforts—of our high-tech society, from microwave ovens and push-button TV to the latest marvels of medical technology. But there's still that nagging concern that children may not be getting a balanced view of what life and living is all about. What meanings do young people draw from encounters with these technological images? That balance may come from what John Naisbitt calls high-tech/high-touch, the notion that strong technological influences call forth counter-balancing human forces in a kind of backlash effect.[1] Thus, when our technological society seems to concentrate almost exclusively on facts and scientific ideas, human beings feel the need to turn to images and feelings. In a society that values the commodities of an objective reality, we embrace the subjective. When we are confused by the often senseless notions of a denotative or literal world, we make sense of this confusion by creating a connotative or literary world. Tired of explanations, we turn to narrative. We move from observation to insight, from concepts to percepts and from discourse to nondiscursive ways of perceiving and understanding our world. When logic seems lacking, we try inference. We reject the notion that the world is a puzzle with all its pieces precut to fit into their proper places and recognize the infinite possibilities of arranging those pieces of our personal realities into a multitude of ever-changing designs. When science and technology, even politics, concentrate on that which is verifiable but not quite believable to most of us, we seek the convincing believability of fiction. We turn from information to entertainment, from the mind to the imagination. The educated mind is essential for our survival, but the educated imagination is also a vital force for the continuance of society. One aim of literary education, perhaps the aim of all education, is to help the child reader see possibilities and imagine ways to make the best of those possibilities a reality. Those who have cultivated their educated imaginations are also much more likely to be tolerant of others, recognizing that their own beliefs are only a few of many possibilities. Such openness presents options for discussion and interaction with those who are, at least outwardly, very unlike themselves. This type of educated imagination is as essential for future scientists and politicians as it is for future artists and poets and librarians. Could anyone have more need of this kind of vision than those who control our scientific centers and the seats of government?

One of the things that technology does in this high-tech/high-touch society, therefore, is push us back to literature as a humanizing and socializing balance to the steely, cool images of that technology. But this presents a challenge to adults to make sure that children are exposed to the best literature available to them and to help them have the richest and fullest experience possible with that literature. The richest possible experience means that young people recognize the role of literature in increasing their power to make sense of all that surrounds them, to make their own meanings and to gain identity, control, and connections in this technological world.

Literature helps the young reader establish an *identity* as each one makes personal meanings from a shared symbol system. Thus, each reader is a unique maker of meaning, which is a way of being one's own self—not as a retreat from life or others but as a way to enter into life more fully—to confirm, illuminate, or extend one's own experiences. As individual readers share those private meanings with others in an interpretive community, they also participate in the making of a group identity and, it is hoped, learn to appreciate both the uniqueness and the commonalty of human beings.

Literature also helps a child gain control over the world. The mastery of decoding skills enabling a young reader to make sense of all those black marks on the printed page is a very powerful means of taking control of one's environment. Even more important, however, is the process of developing critical or literary abilities that enable the reader to become fully engaged with a literary work. This process of developing critical skills may be defined as learning to look sympathetically at what another is attempting to do or seeking out and demonstrating an appreciation of that which is considered the best of its kind. Criticism is a cumulative developmental process in which a reader makes judgments while engaged in discriminating among values. At first one's experience with a work of literature is personal and private and then there is a distancing from that experience as the reader attempts to make meaning that can be shared with others. This is the beginning of criticism. Moving from personal meanings to those shared through language in an interpretive community helps the young reader to gain a sense of control, first over the self and then in the context of the larger community.

At the same time, literature helps children gain a sense of connection to other people and to the world. In our high-speed technological age, there are more channels of communication than many of us knew as children; but there are also far more chances for disconnection, for crashing the system, for getting our wires crossed, or for short-circuiting relationships. Literature remains a means of reaching out to other times, places, and situations, perhaps to understand them better. Equally important, stories enable readers to enter situations vicariously, going into the minds and the hearts of characters similar to the people they encounter in their daily lives and, in this way, to increase their awareness of and sympathy toward the human beings with whom they share this world.

This very personal and idiosyncratic process of making meaning as a way of establishing a sense of identity, control, and connection in a complex world has intrigued me for some time, and I have been investigating how children actually do make meanings in the transaction between the individual child and the literary work. This article will explore some of the questions raised by technological images in various media as they contribute to the meaning-making powers of children and young people. It is part of a larger research project based on some of the theoretical work of Rosenblatt, Iser, and Fish, three of the most prominent of all those literary critics who have been shifting the emphasis of criticism from literary texts to the reader.[2] These critics view reading as a process of making meaning in which the reader assumes either an "efferent" or an "aesthetic" stance (Rosenblatt) fills in the "gaps" or areas of "indeterminacy" in the text (Iser) using "interpretative strategies" which are public and shared (Fish) to create that meaning. In discussing literary works with groups of subjects in this study, the interest in science fiction and the reference to technological images in other stories led me to look more closely at the kinds of questions such images raise in the minds of young readers.

In considering the transaction between young readers and technological images, it seemed appropriate to explore some aspects of science fiction as a genre and the relationship of that genre to the potential meanings derived by young readers. Much criticism looks at the characteristics of various genres, which is a very important ingredient in literary research. Unfortunately, adults working with young people and literature have too often assumed that the patterns or recurring images identified in these genres are "the meanings" and ask readers to "match" these meanings rather than to create their own meanings. If we accept that reading is a transaction between reader and work in which each contributes meaning, we must look more closely not just at these patterns and conventions of the genres but at how these aspects of the work influence the individual personal meanings.

The term *literature* will be used here in its generic sense—as a symbol system in which expression and form are as important as content—regardless of medium. Literature, therefore, includes television programs, motion pictures, computer games, etc. As adults we need to recognize that the predominant literature of this generation of children and young adults is not necessarily found in books; we need to exercise critical judgment in relation to all media. We must help young people recognize and appreciate the unique characteristics of each medium and learn to seek out the best of what is available in all media. The parallel act of reading then is that process in which one *brings* meaning to and *takes* meaning from any of these symbol systems.

"Knight Rider" and "Airwolf" are just two of many television programs in which there are various degrees of interaction between a human character and a computer-controlled machine. What kind of meanings do these shows using technological images evoke in young viewers? Who are the heroes of this technological age? The term *hero* is used deliberately because the male is almost always the major character with females present only in minor aspects of the stories. Although some females do demonstrate computer and/or technological competence, they seldom seem to achieve the status of a believable heroine. Might this suggest to young people that women will play only secondary roles in the highly technological society of our future? What do the contemporary literary images, both visual and verbal, convey about such modern phenomena as robotics, artificial intelligence, and genetic engineering, once purely science-fiction creations but now part of our everyday reality? And what meanings do young readers make from the reaction to and treatment of alien beings in fiction? Robotic images have changed from the early alien robots of *The Day the Earth Stood Still* to *Star Wars'* R2D2 to those robots that are indistinguishable from human beings. Even the continuing character of HAL changes from 2001 to 2010, as he becomes a more positive force and is responded to in a more human and humane fashion in the later film. Do any of these "characters" help children grasp the nuances of artificial intelligence that will undoubtedly play an important part in their world? The treatment of alien beings as portrayed in popular literature has also changed. Aliens have frequently been portrayed as threatening, as were the children in the film *Village of the Damned* and early science-fiction novels, but more recently we encountered E.T. and Yoda and the ectoplasms floating in space that were a part of *Cocoon* as well as the "lumpies" of H. M. Hoover's *The Lost Star.* Certainly these new characters offer the child a more positive and productive image of those unlike ourselves. E.T. and the "visitors" in *Close Encounters of the Third Kind* seem to have marked a major turning point in our perception of aliens and may help viewers to consider new meanings and more tolerant views of those who are "different," whether from this world or beyond. Some critics might even see *E.T.* as a reflection of that high-tech/high-touch mentality in the conflict between our technological, military-minded, fractured-family society and the need for fantasy demonstrated in the mother's acceptance of the young people's preoccupation with Dungeons and Dragons. Another critic might analyze the role of and the customs surrounding food and drink in our lives as revealed in this film. From the introduction of the human characters in the kitchen, to the family drama enacted around the table, to the many evidences of the reliance on fast foods, to the candy as the first means of reaching out and making contact with the extraterrestrial, there is much fodder for a hungry critic here. Does the child reader use this evidence in the text to foster a view of the importance of food and the rituals surrounding it in modern society? How does this view differ from Daniel Pinkwater's satirical look at those junk food addicts from outer space who first show up in *Lizard Music* and then have their own book, *Fat Men from Space?*

Let us now consider how literary patterns and techniques in science fiction have been shaping the process of meaning-making in young readers. For instance, did early science-fiction stories featuring gadgetry and gimmickry influence young people to perceive of science and technology as a means of developing elaborate devices to control or destroy the bug-eyed aliens who might someday arrive to disrupt our way of life? Or do the more introspective and socially and politically conscious novels read by science-fiction fans today encourage them to consider both the positive and the negative possibilities of scientific and technological knowledge? Some of the recurring patterns, conventions, and themes of science fiction indicate that this might be so.

One of the most common conventions in science fiction is the use of the "system break," a sudden and often cataclysmic event that causes major changes in society. The system break is most obvious in the postnuclear or other forms of technological disaster books such as John Christopher's The Prince Is Waiting trilogy or Robert C. O'Brien's *Z for Zachariah.*

The consideration of the possible annihilation of humankind is explored in a number of books and is even presented to picture book readers from its historical roots in *Hiroshima No Pika* by Toshi Maruki to Raymond Briggs' futuristic *When the Wind Blows*. But what meanings do young readers make in their transactions with such works? Do they consider more humane alternatives to the uses of science and technology or do these stories reinforce a nihilistic attitude as some critics believe? Fiona French's *Future Story*, one of the few true science-fiction stories in picture-book format, offers hope for the crew of its fictional spaceship when the warmth of the earth's sun overcomes the cold crystal from another world that would destroy them. Thus the meaning that readers may derive from some contemporary works is a sense of hope as well as a warning of dire consequences.

Computer dominance and artificial intelligence are concerns in many science-fiction stories as demonstrated so graphically in the film *War Games* and in Ben Bova's novel *Exiled from Earth* in which RAMO the computer betrays Lou Christopher, the young hero. In part, these types of stories cause readers to respond by considering their own views on machine importance, even superiority, in our technological society.

Concerns for the environment, including the availability of natural resources such as food, fuel, and energy, are certainly a part of the post-holocaust literature; but these concerns may also form the thrust of other novels such as Pamela Sargent's *Earthseed* and even O'Brien's *Mrs. Frisby and the Rats of NIMH*. Growth in population with its resulting pollution and the overtaxing of transportation and communication systems is forced into the reader's consciousness as we read these books. Sometimes the solution to such problems is in the creation of alternative environments and societies that go the whole range from quasi-medieval worlds (Christopher's *The Prince Is Waiting*) to exotic and romantic other planets (Anne McCaffrey's Pern) to a sterilized and regulated habitat either on Earth (Bova's *City of Darkness*) or in its domain in another world (Madeleine L'Engle's *A Wrinkle in Time*). These alternative worlds in some ways mirror Earth whether they exist only in the human mind or on other planets and distant worlds. Discussions with young readers indicate that they do seek out and pay attention to these new environments and that setting may be a key to their reactions and interpretations. As they consider the similarities and dissimilarities between these imagined worlds and our own, they raise critical questions about society's treatment of the environment. Science fiction has always dealt with that which is only temporarily impossible and, either through the shock of apocalyptic views or the hope of utopian ones, holds forth a vision of what might be.

Recent technological fiction deals with the social sciences and humanities as well as the hard sciences, exploring more of the meaning of life than some earlier examples of this genre. It is often difficult to distinguish between science fiction and fantasy because both use created creatures, transformations, and a mix of the ordinary and extraordinary to reflect upon the nature of our world. Shape-shifting (Voltron and other transformers) is often a part of science fiction as it has been traditionally a part of fantasy. Many aspects of historical fiction, especially medieval features, are present in the future worlds of technological fiction. John Christopher employs this technique in both his White Mountain stories and in the Prince Is Waiting series. Many such stories seem to represent an almost Luddite mind-set in which an anti-technological protagonist battles the latest examples of technological evil. On the other hand, the psychological and medical aspects of these stories, such as mind management and genetic engineering, sometimes make this literature difficult to distinguish from contemporary realism.

The concept of mental telepathic power is powerfully explored in Joan Vinge's *Psion* as well as in the works of Anne McCaffrey, most particularly in *The Ship Who Sang*. The responses to McCaffrey's work are especially interesting because some readers feel threatened by the child mind linked to a steel ship to form a replacement body for a physically deformed one. The power of this story seems to lie in the way a particular reader interacts with this concept of human-machine welding. Other science-fiction novels for young people cause them to consider the concept of mind control from very different perspectives. Pinkwater's *Alan Mendelsohn: The Boy from Mars* is, as one might expect, very humorous. Virginia Hamilton's Justice trilogy, on the other hand, has a much more realistic beginning and a more serious approach to telepathic powers and mind control as well as raising questions about individual differences, human rights, and family structures.

Cloning is another example of a topic of grave concern to thoughtful individuals that is also the subject of many science fiction novels. Those range from Margaret Cooper's *Solution: Escape* for young readers to adult books and motion pictures such as *The Boys from Brazil* that appeal to young adults. Such stories raise interesting ethical questions whether about medical ethics, genetic engineering, or the more traditional concern of whether or not the end justifies the means. This is demonstrated in the attempt to save Thorn Valley from Jones' company by reprogramming their computer in Jane L. Conly's continuation of her father's characters in *Rasco and the Rats of NIMH* or when Kira in Anne Mason's *The Stolen Law* is forced to decide how far she will go in upholding a law that is contrary to the dictates of her personal conscience. Richard Diem's study of children's attitudes toward new technology, specifically computers, warns us of the need to explore ethical behavior in the use of technology with students.[3] Science fiction is a form of imaginative literature that presents readers opportunities to explore the consequences of various ethical decisions.

Computer technology has also given rise to an alternative form of literature in which the conclusion is dependent upon the decision making of the reader. The "Choose Your Own Adventure" stories that really began with the Hi-Res computer adventures are extremely popular among young people and have spawned several magazines that continue some of these adventures. One might link these to some degree with the invasiveness of the Dungeons and Dragons cult in which young people are active participants in their stories.

Technological literature may be best understood as a form of modern myth,[4] not a displacement of traditional myth but rather as another mode of apprehension and an attempt to explain, either scientifically or metaphorically, certain aspects of human nature and of our world. What do young people take from this literature of technology? From conversations with them, it is clear that they accept certain things as given: other lifeforms, genetic engineering, telepathy, abortion, birth control, and intergalatic travel. Questions of mind control as revealed in William Sleator's *House of Stairs* and the use of telepathic powers in McCaffrey's *Get Off the Unicorn* and Pern stories are considered almost commonplace but are also of major concern to young readers. Both boys and girls are intrigued with androgynous characters and societies such as those of Ursula LeGuin's *Left Hand of Darkness* and are pleased to find women in more heroic roles in many science-fiction works today. The positing of something beyond our current world is stimulating to the imaginations and to the minds of young readers who might possibly encounter such future worlds; the values demonstrated by characters often push them to explore, and perhaps alter, their personal values.

The technological images that abound in science fiction and other contemporary literature for young people offer rich possibilities for the exploration of personal and social values necessary for the very survival of our society.[5] Speculative fiction, by its very nature, is one of the best means for developing that unique meaning-making talent of human beings in which each reader both brings to and takes from the literary work a personal vision of what might be. In this age of high technology, some might seek a technology of interpretation, a theoretical approach to solving the problem of literary analysis; but the problem of analysis and its alternative solutions are at the very core of the literary experience and of critical thought. A sense of mystery, that tension between what is known and what can never be known, is the very essence of the literary experience, and no theory of interpretation should deprive human beings of that mystery. What theory should do, in my mind at least, is to extend the appreciation and magnify the mystery and the magic of the composed world so that we might become absorbed in that world momentarily and return refreshed and renewed to our own world. Thus does literature contribute to that continual process of shaping and reshaping the world, of envisioning a more humane environment, and imposing that human vision on and maintaining it in an increasingly technological world.

References

1. John Naisbitt, *Megatrends* (New York: Warner Bks., 1982), p. 39-53.
2. Louise Rosenblatt, *The Reader, the Text, the Poem* (Carbondale: Southern Illinois Univ. Pr., 1978); Wolfgang Iser, *The Act of Reading* (Baltimore, Md.: Johns Hopkins Univ. Pr., 1978); Stanley Fish, *Is There a Text in This Class? The Authority of Interpretive Communities* (Cambridge, Mass.: Harvard Univ. Pr., 1980).
3. Richard A. Diem, "A Study of Children's Attitudes and Reactions to the New Technology," *Social Education* 49, no. 4:318-20 (Apr. 1985).
4. Janice Antczak, *Science Fiction: The Mythos of a New Romance* (New York: Neal-Schuman, 1985).
5. Linda Wicher, "Power and Progress: Themes in Fiction for a Technological Age," *English Journal* 74, no. 4:64-66 (Apr. 1985).

INTELLECTUAL PROBLEMS OF INDEXING PICTURE COLLECTIONS

Michael G. Krause

Intellectual problems in indexing are concerned with choosing headings or entries for media; they are not concerned with which indexing system should be used for a particular purpose, but with how it should be applied —how one defines subjects and decides which aspects of the item or of the subject are worth mentioning in the index.

These can be divided into hard or soft aspects. For example, in a picture collection hard indexing is concerned with description, what an indexer can see in the frame, what a picture is of; soft indexing relates to meaning, what an image is about, the personal reactions and feelings stimulated. Librarians sometimes say they stop at description, that they cannot and should not go any further. In fact, one can show that description often includes some comment on meaning, that description is not as simple a matter as some believe and that it is possible, and indeed desirable, to index the meaning of pictures.

Any series of pictures or any motion picture, especially when accompanied by a commentary, may contain the solution to some indexing problems as the intentions of the auteur may be made clear. The auteur of the piece can develop an idea, lead the audience and make the meaning of the images clear—or he can make it less clear, presenting the series of images and leaving the audience to react according to their own feelings, perhaps in the way originally intended, perhaps differently. However, I will concentrate on single, still pictures for two reasons. First, the problems related to description, interpretation and meaning are often increased. The meaning of one image is usually less well defined than that of a series of photographs or drawings where the pictures are arranged in a certain order, to provoke, to entertain, to describe, gradually to explain a message, be it technical or educational, social or political. Single items can perform the same function, but often do so less precisely, thus increasing both the

"Intellectual Problems of Indexing Picture Collections" by Michael G. Krause in *AudioVisual Librarian* Vol. 14, no. 2 (May 1988), pp. 73-81; reprinted with permission from *AudioVisual Librarian*; photographs with permission of Michael G. Krause.

difficulties of indexing comprehensively and the need to do so. Second, single pictures are easier to illustrate and this topic is best discussed with examples to consider. We know that pictures provoke reaction, stimulate ideas, rekindle memories. They are powerful instruments in story telling, teaching, propaganda and numerous other fields. Therefore, it is important that libraries provide access to images which illustrate ideas, even abstract ones like hunger, or the experience of hunger, which one may think is a feeling difficult to present pictorially. Yet who could doubt that shots of starving children in a barren African wasteland 'tell' the world what it is like to feel hungry. Photographs of malnourished Ethiopian refugees do convey this idea and this can be called the meaning of a picture, a personal reaction to it—in this case a clear one. It is these feelings which often prompt the use to which an image is put, and which are often very clear to any viewer or indexer. If we can index this aspect of the picture, we make it easily available to users requiring such an image; we make our collection more accessible.

Does the description of a picture also relate to meaning? Looking at examples of images which are not unusual but which illustrate that description, becomes an increasingly complex task. When more attention is paid to this, it will become clear that libraries do deal with meaning in some ways, without making a conscious effort to do so, and that indexing these soft aspects of pictures is possible, helpful and not necessarily difficult.

Semantics is not often regarded as important to indexing, but when one describes a picture in one word, or very few words, so that users will be able to retrieve it, the terminology chosen is important. The words one selects relate to the meaning of the image; in assigning certain titles, one may judge the picture in some way, suggest approval of its subjects or imply that the subjects are immoral, untrustworthy or shameful. Few picture librarians would claim to be passing judgement on the images they index, yet when they choose headings this is the result of their decisions.

Here are four terms, all with very similar definitions and all in common use, yet each has a different meaning in the public perception: *freedom fighter, guerrilla, partisan, terrorist*. 'Partisans' fight a heroic struggle against outsiders occupying their homeland; 'freedom fighters' fight unjust or corrupt, oppressive rulers; 'guerrillas' rightly or wrongly attack armies and police forces; 'terrorists' kill innocent civilians, with no thought for right or wrong. The first two are applauded and supported, the last meets with almost universal reproach. When an indexer encounters a picture of a guerrilla (to use the most neutral term) and chooses a heading for it, he or she makes a moral and political judgement—even if the same heading is used for all four categories. A library sponsored by the United States Government would index pictures of the 'Contras' in Nicaragua as 'Freedom fighters', one working for the Soviet Union as 'Terrorists'; any British

Government library which indexed photographs of the IRA as 'Freedom fighters' would be most unpopular. When do acts of terrorism begin to be indexed as pictures of a civil war?

Where should one locate the activities of M K Gandhi or Martin Luther King? Are they 'Civil disobedience', 'Civil disturbances', 'Demonstrations' or 'Direct action'? Or perhaps pictures of Indians taking part in a 'day of prayers and fasting' should be filed under 'General strikes'?

These choices which indexers have to make with images are often moral or political, but they are made none the less, regardless of librarians' claims that they are not. Consider pictures taken at Orgreave in 1984 during the coal dispute. *Should* one describe the setting as a 'Coal dispute', or as a 'Miners' strike'? The former suggests that it arose as a result of disagreements between the two sides of the industry, the latter that it was brought about by trade unionists opposing the National Coal Board's managers. Pictures of Orgreave could be indexed in more than one way. Should the 'Demonstrators' be called 'Pickets', 'Pickets—flying' or even 'Rioters'? The scenes of violence could be described as 'Police violence', 'Industrial violence', 'Civil disturbances' or 'Riots'. The choice of heading is a clear statement on the meaning of the picture and, as was hinted above, the decision is directly related to the library, its users, and what the librarians see as the way their users would approach the picture—in essence, what meaning the library staff attach to the image.

If one indexes pictures of fox hunting, hare coursing, grouse shooting or similar blood-thirsty activities as 'Sport', filing under 'Bloodsports' between 'Billiards' and 'Bobsleighing', or as individual activities, one gives them the same status, and therefore respectability, as other sports. If they are given a separate section or coupled with similar activities which are no longer accepted by society, such as bear baiting or cock fighting, they are clearly being seen as unsavoury, even immoral.

These problems can relate to the indexing of other materials, as well, but they can be stressed in picture collections, largely because these tend to be indexed by natural language which brings the decision into greater prominence. An entry in a subject index can be missed when someone retrieves a book from open shelves, a heading on a file cannot. Also, pictures prompt an immediate reaction and users can see an indexer's choice of heading at once, agreeing or disagreeing on the basis of a glance at and a response to an image, whereas books have less instant impact. (There may be some time between the sight of the indexer's heading and actually discovering what he or she thinks of the item.)

In these examples, the purely descriptive 'hard' indexing, providing access to what one sees in the picture, without devoting any conscious effort to defining meaning, has already told users something of the 'soft' aspects of the image. The indexer has made moral, political, intellectual decisions and informed users to some extent what the indexer believes the picture is about. I stated at the beginning that indexing description is not an easy matter. The descriptive indexing, as well as the terminology of the indexing, often involves some comment on meaning. This can be illustrated by considering the indexing of the accompanying photographs; in the main, they are not concerned with social or political issues, which are usually the most difficult semantically, but are pictures of buildings and town-scapes, the like of which could be found in most general picture collections. When indexing them, however, it is important to look closely in order to describe them accurately and fully. This exercise will show that indexing images is not an easy task and that, if it is done fully, it will frequently involve the meaning of the picture.

Figure 1 is a view of the Cathédrale Notre-Dame taken from the southeast and is perhaps an easy picture to begin with. Whether the library has chosen to file buildings under country, type, together under 'Buildings' or individually, this picture will not present difficulties; it can be headed 'France', 'Cathedrals', 'Churches', 'Buildings' or 'Notre-Dame'. But does this help users searching for Gothic churches or thirteenth-century cathedrals? To help answer such inquiries, picture libraries need either extra files containing duplicate copies of pictures of Gothic buildings, or cross-references in the form of notes on where these images can be found, or an index consisting of headings (here 'Gothic buildings') under which are listed reference or accession numbers. If the picture can have only one entry,

Fig. 1

the user will need to search under all the Gothic buildings which come to mind, and is almost bound to miss useful illustrations in the collection. What usually happens, of course, is that librarians decide how their users will try to retrieve pictures; if users are likely to require photographs of Gothic buildings, some access of this type will have to be provided. In a general collection this is unlikely to happen, but the result will be that using this collection will not be as easy as it could be in certain circumstances and that the best and fullest use of the collection cannot be made.

If this photograph was taken using a filter or non-standard lens some libraries' users may benefit from access to this information (should the library have it); therefore there should be the facility to retrieve photographs taken using certain techniques. Specialized collections may need to index more architectural features—flying buttresses or rose windows—although this picture is not likely to be the best illustration in a specialized library; when dealing with a closer photograph, these factors may be important.

This picture may have wider relevance for some people; it may represent a romantic holiday in Paris or the beginning of an interest in fine church architecture. These meanings are necessarily very personal and do not need to be indexed; if Notre-Dame does mean one of these things, access can be through other means, as the user knows exactly what is required. The difficult 'soft' aspects of picture indexing are illustrated by a particular theme which could be represented by more than one image; in the case of buildings, such themes could be changes of use, redevelopment of cities, restoration of buildings, inner-city problems or inner-city decay and illustrative examples of these topics are provided here.

Figure 2 is not a great building, but it does illustrate this pre-World War II style quite well. What is more noteworthy and more important for indexing is the use the building was put to; it is likely that this type of picture will be used as an example of usage rather than of an architectural style and this may cause slight problems for the indexer. If the building can only have one entry, what should it be? It was designed as a cinema, so this will probably be the choice of most indexers. It looks like a picture house built early this century and is quite representative of Northern cinemas; it is not typical of the genre but is a good example of part of this style while being adapted to fit the site. (The ground slopes steeply from the main road and there is little frontage.) But this is actually a photograph of a bingo hall—this was the function of the building when it was photographed—so perhaps it should be indexed as this. Clearly no single entry will enable this image to be retrieved by all users interested in one of these subjects, so at least two entries are required. However, perhaps the point of the picture is that a once thriving cinema is now in use as a bingo hall. The picture is of a cinema/bingo hall, but the meaning is concerned with the decline of the movies as a mass entertainment medium;

Fig. 2

surely there should be some way of making this photograph available to people who wish to illustrate this point, whether concerned with the history of the cinema or with more general changes in English life since the last war. To achieve this, one needs multiple entries for this picture, including one which deals with the meaning of the photograph and the use to which it may be put.

The next two pictures also show buildings which have changed in use. Figure 3 was built as a non-conformist chapel—it is by no means an exceptional example of a Victorian neo-classical construction. However, the distyle in antis arrangement of the facade is not common and it is possible that a user in an architectural library would wish to compare it to a Greek original, such as a Treasury at Delphi. So it may be necessary, in some libraries, to index it as a chapel, as a certain type of neo-classical building and as an Indian restaurant and a night club, its present roles. Figure 4 began life as a warehouse; it is now a vegetarian restaurant. As important as the uses of these two buildings are the 'softer' aspects of the pictures. The fact that Figure 3 is no longer a place of worship illustrates not that Bradford is a less godly place but that residential areas have moved away from the city centre. It might be helpful to index this image as an example of how unused city buildings can be put to good use, of the cosmopolitan nature of English society and English eating habits. Figure 4 is similar again; an area which has lost its industrial base finds new functions for buildings which are in danger of becoming derelict. As eating habits

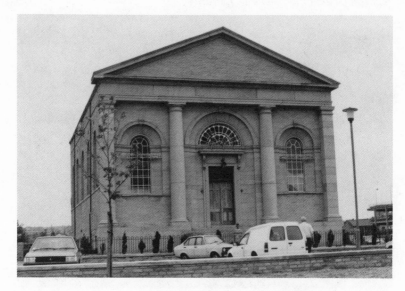

Fig. 3

Fig. 4

Fig. 5

Fig. 6

Fig. 7

Fig. 8

change, vegetarian restaurants become more common, and a modern trend takes the place of past industry. These two images could be used to illustrate these points and, if they are indexed so that access to these meanings can be provided, better use can be made of the pictures.

How many libraries would be able to locate pictures of buildings which have been imaginatively renovated? Figure 5 could be indexed as a theatre; its real value is to show how an Edwardian building can be made to look lively, modern and attractive, while still preserving the character of the original. It would not be difficult to keep an indexed list of such features in a picture collection, but most libraries do not. The renovation could well be considered as part of description, not meaning, and may be indexed; if it is possible to index this aspect of this picture, it is undoubtedly possible to index some of the less obvious but still important features of other photographs.

Figure 6 is not an outstanding view and many collections would include it with views of similar terraces of houses. But what it really represents is Victorian paternalism; the houses were built by Sir Titus Salt to house the workers who made him a rich man. Again, this is not an obscure interpretation, not a difficult aspect to index, but it does require the indexer to look deeply at the picture in order to make the most of it. Once indexers begin to look more deeply at what they are dealing with, they can come closer to the less obvious facets of description and the more obvious aspects of meaning, the indexing of which would make picture collections much more valuable to users.

Some libraries may be able to cope with Figure 7 as an illustration of industrial decay, including it in a section devoted to derelict or demolished buildings. Figure 8 is a picture of commercial office properties and will usually be indexed as such; however, this photograph is also about inner-city decay. The five 'to let' signs in such a small area indicate the lack of prosperity to be found in many British cities, the fact that many premises are empty and unproductive. These two photographs have similar meanings and picture libraries should be able to provide both of them for users interested in illustrations of inner-city problems.

A further point can be made about works of art. Paintings and drawings do not usually have any subject access provided, although it would help in many cases, and photographs often do not have any title or photographer entry in catalogues or indexes. Man Ray's 'Violon d'Ingres' (1924) is a photograph and a surrealist work of art. It would not be necessary or helpful to try to define the subject of this photograph; Man Ray did not see any difference between his paintings and photographs—they were all simply art. But when does a photograph become art? Harold Edgerton's famous 'Splash of milk' is a complex case. It should, perhaps, be indexed under 'Milk' for this is the subject, and under 'Fluid-dynamics' as it clearly illustrates the kinetics of this liquid. But this photograph is also seen as a work of art in itself and could be included in a library's collection of pictures of original works of art. In this case it is essential to index the subjects also, but no fixed dividing line can be drawn between pictures of 'things' and 'works of art'—the indexer must treat each case on its merits and should not be afraid to provide subject access to 'art' if it will be useful for those who use the picture collection, or to class a photograph as 'art' if it can be seen as such.

The earlier examples illustrate how it can be important to index the whole of a picture, not only to describe the most obvious features. This task of indexing the meaning of images, what they are about, improves the worth of a collection greatly. Users no longer have to search uncertainly under many headings in many parts of a collection to find pictures which illustrate the points they are interested in. This is done to some extent by conventional 'hard' indexing, especially semantically. The task of describing visual material is not a simple one; the deeper one looks at an image, the closer one gets to indexing meaning. This is not an easy exercise but the difficulties are not as great as some would suggest. More time spent by indexers in studying the picture and considering what uses it could be put to will give users the opportunity to retrieve the images they require much more quickly and will increase effectiveness, as users encounter pictures which suit their needs but which they could never have found under the headings otherwise assigned to them.

THE IAIMS PROJECT OF THE AMERICAN COLLEGE OF OBSTETRICIANS AND GYNECOLOGISTS: USING INFORMATION TECHNOLOGY TO IMPROVE THE HEALTH CARE OF WOMEN

Pamela Van Hine and Warren H. Pearse, M.D.

The American College of Obstetricians and Gynecologists (ACOG) is the national professional organization representing 27,000 practicing obstetrician-gynecologists. ACOG realized several years ago that, to accomplish its purposes, it must plan for the increasing role of information technology in the practice of obstetrics-gynecology. During 1982, ACOG appointed a task force on long-range planning for educational development whose purpose was to prepare a long-range plan for the educational programs of the college. In 1983 the task force released a long-range plan for an obstetric-gynecologic information system, to be put into use between 1987 and 1991. The plan includes a national electronic communications network; a fulltext ob-gyn database; a library-connected information system; educational programs for physicians and the general public; and office management, professional liability, and quality assurance programs. The plan was approved, and implementation began in 1984.

The first part of the plan to be implemented was the electronic network. Members of the executive board and key ACOG staff were given computers with modems and subscriptions to AMANET, which had an ACOG group conference in its electronic mail. Other early projects included

"The IAIMS Project of the American College of Obstetricians and Gynecologists: Using Information Technology to Improve the Health Care of Women" by Pamela Van Hine and Warren H. Pearse in *Bulletin of Medical Library Association* Vol. 76, no. 3 (July 1988), pp. 237-241; reprinted with permission from the Medical Library Association, copyright © Medical Library Association.

developing an ACOG database on CompuServe, which listed key ACOG services and publications and contained a feedback file for requests from users, and adding key ACOG publications fulltext to the CCML database on BRS Colleague.

In 1985, inspired by the Matheson-Cooper report recommendations and the long-range information plan prepared by the task force, ACOG applied for a planning phase IAIMS grant from the National Library of Medicine. In 1986, ACOG became the first national specialty society to receive an IAIMS grant.

The ACOG planning phase grant proposal contains other justifications for extending the IAIMS concept to national organizations in addition to those presented in the Matheson-Cooper report. A national society already has a strong communications network in place, is the authority source for information in that specialty, and reaches a far greater number of health care personnel than a medical school. A national specialty society can set up an information model for the subject area of its expertise, including incorporating its subject terminology into a unified medical language system. A society-based IAIMS project also tests and extends the IAIMS concept in different ways because it is national and subject specific.

STRATEGIC PLAN

All IAIMS planning phase projects must complete a strategic plan before continuing with the model phase. During the planning phase of the ACOG IAIMS project, ACOG staff, a national advisory committee, and a task force on computers completed the strategic plan for the ACOG IAIMS project.

ACOG IAIMS mission and goal statements. The overall mission of the ACOG project is to identify the core of knowledge necessary for the practice of obstetrics and gynecology, structure it and put it in electronic form, integrate it into a national ob-gyn information network, prepare fellows (ACOG members) to use it, and disseminate this core of knowledge to fellows in appropriate forms. The goal of ACOG IAIMS is that by 1992, all ACOG members will be able to communicate with and receive membership services via an electronic network.

Assumptions

Because the ACOG IAIMS project is significantly different from a medical school IAIMS project, assumptions about ACOG IAIMS were added to the strategic plan. These cover the nature of obstetric-gynecologic practice, the role of computers and knowledge in its practice, and the nature of the proposed ACOG IAIMS system. The assumptions stress the role of the college in setting standards for practice and the increasing importance of access to current and accurate information by practicing obstetricians and gynecologists. The emphasis of the ACOG IAIMS program is to support practitioners in their patient-care activities in the office setting. ACOG programs will use technology that is readily accessible by its members, and all programs will be easy to use and interactive.

Information Policy

The purpose of the ACOG IAIMS information policy is to ensure that ethical issues relating to ACOG information activities will be addressed and resolved, if possible. ACOG will also work closely with other organizations on policy issues and will develop models for information policy that can be modified and used by obstetrician-gynecologists at local, regional, and national levels.

The information policy covers: 1) personnel; 2) the general process of policy development; 3) a general policy principle emphasizing the potentially conflicting needs of users, producers, contributors, and others be identified and resolved prior to program implementation; 4) general ethical considerations concerning program development; and 5) specific ethical considerations, e.g., ownership, access, fees, quality control, security, and research. The policy emphasizes the possible ethical issues that may arise with a national medical information system. The policy is deliberately and necessarily open-ended and flexible. It has been reviewed by the ACOG Committee on Ethics, the National Advisory Committee, and the Task Force on Computers. Additional specific policies will be developed by staff when needed.

Needs Assessment

As ACOG is a national membership organization, the information and automation needs of its members were the subject of the ACOG IAIMS needs assessment survey. The needs assessment survey covered both the equipment and software that ACOG members are using, and the computer and information services that members want. The questionnaire on services was sent to 1000 randomly selected members and the software use questionnaire was distributed to interested members.

The primary findings indicated that more than 50% of ACOG members are using or plan to use computers. More than 80% of members currently using computers are using microcomputers, and more than 70% of the microcomputers are IBM PC or compatible computers. Members want to automate high-risk patient management, have access to national databases, patient appointment recall systems, clinical protocols and performances indicators, and patient recall by diagnosis. Of the twenty-five potential ACOG programs listed on the questionnaire, members chose fourteen programs for high priority development. These programs fall into four categories: coding systems and protocols, including uniform terminology and national statistics; electronic access to bibliographic and fulltext materials and ACOG library services; educational programs; and a clearinghouse of information on software for obstetrics and gynecology.

IMPLEMENTATION PLAN

The ACOG IAIMS implementation plan, based on the results of the needs assessment survey, incorporates guidelines contained in the information policy and list of assumptions.

The planning phase proposal contained three objectives for the project: educational programs, integration of ACOG IAIMS activities with other organizations, and specific program development.

Project Objective I: Assist health care practitioners and their staff to become information and computer literate by 1992 in order to access the proposed network. ACOG proposes four strategies to assist obstetrician-gynecologists in becoming information and computer literate. First, ACOG will provide courses and publications on the basic concepts of computer use and the application of computers in patient care, office management, and telecommunications. Computer Applications in Obstetrics and Gynecology, an introductory hands-on workshop on basic computer concepts and office automation, has now been taught eight times. Because the course can only be taught to twenty physicians at a time and is expensive to produce, its primary purpose is to serve as a model for testing programs that can be incorporated into other educational activities designed to reach a wider audience. The first by-product of the course is a stand-alone manual that has already been sold to over 400 physicians.

ACOG also publishes a separate newsletter, *On Target,* that contains items about ACOG IAIMS activities and computer and information tips. This newsletter is published quarterly beginning in 1988 and is distributed to all members of ACOG and the 20,000 members of the Nurses' Association of the American College of Obstetricians and Gynecologists (NAACOG), as well as other IAIMS institutions and interested groups.

The second strategy is to create a computer teaching center to provide small-group, laboratory, hands-on computer experience to members. This center will serve as a testing center for new courses and teaching techniques, which can be tried, reviewed, and used elsewhere when perfected. It can also serve as a place for training instructors, who can then teach courses at their own institutions and meetings.

To meet members' needs for information on software and automation, ACOG established a clearinghouse for information on computer applications, information resources, and office automation.

The fourth strategy is to design and introduce an educational program for teaching information management skills. Methods for implementing this program will be similar to those used for teaching computer skills, e.g., courses, stand-alone manuals, articles in *On Target* and the ACOG newsletter, and demonstrations.

Project Objective II: Define an integrated database, incorporating relationships between elements of medical knowledge, which will assist health care practitioners in providing the best and most current methods for patient care, and which also will provide the framework for lifelong medical education. This second objective is the heart of the model phase ACOG IAIMS project. ACOG proposes five strategies to accomplish the second objective. ACOG will define the boundaries and content of obstetrics-gynecology by creating integrated learning objectives which span undergraduate, graduate, and continuing medical education. These objectives are being developed in cooperation with the Council on Resident Education in Obstetrics and Gynecology (CREOG) and the Association of Professors of Gynecology and Obstetrics (APGO) and will be used to decide upon teaching objectives for all levels of education in obstetrics and gynecology.

Relying on expert judgement, ACOG will identify questions practitioners are likely to ask of an ob-gyn knowledge base, and how information transfer will lead to knowledge management. This information will be helpful in preparing the structure and contents of the knowledge base. ACOG staff will review data gathered from the needs assessment surveys; use of ACOG materials in the Comprehensive Core Medical Library (CCML), the fulltext database on BRS Colleague; and the published literature on information needs of health care professionals.

The college also proposes two additional studies of the information needs of obstetrician-gynecologists. ACOG Resource Center (library) staff are analyzing a sample of 1000 requests from members to determine the subjects queried; the type of response provided (e.g., online search, ACOG publications); and specific aspect of request (e.g., complications, diagnosis, and therapy). Preliminary analysis indicates that more than half of the requests relate to pregnancy (51.8%); that a high percentage are answered with existing ACOG publications (54.5%); that many requests concern complications (11.4%), therapy (12.6%), and indications (16.9%); but that few requests are for diagnosis (3.5%). Staff plan to review additional requests to refine the data and also study the information needs of practicing obstetrician-gynecologists. If the results of the additional review and study support the initial data, it would appear that obstetrician-gynecologists do not need a knowledge base that is diagnosis-based.

With the assistance of a special task force, ACOG will define a database structure (template) for diagnoses and problems that includes those elements necessary to answer expected questions. ACOG will assemble the knowledge base by identifying the many unique and extant ACOG resources that will comprise the knowledge core; by identifying the external databases that are applicable to the ob-gyn knowledge base and gateway mechanisms to them; by using the knowledge base "templates" to determine a knowledge elicitation strategy; and by completing the template for five representative ob-gyn diagnoses and five management problems as a pilot. ACOG will evolve access to the knowledge base which is both user-friendly and available through multiple formats.

Project Objective III: Create an integrated, interactive system that enables the health care professional to communicate electronically with ACOG and NAACOG to obtain membership services. Objective three involves automated access to ACOG and NAACOG services, and its implementation requires the automation of selected ACOG and NAACOG departments as well as national electronic access to the ACOG/NAACOG office. Eight strategies are proposed for the third objective.

The first strategy, providing a national electronic bulletin board system with direct access to ACOG/NAACOG services, has already been successfully achieved through ACOGNET, the national private bulletin board system for ACOG and NAACOG members. ACOG IAIMS staff designed and implemented ACOGNET using RBBS software running on an IBM AT with 40 megabyte hard disk and three modems and incoming telephone lines. ACOGNET contains electronic mail and conference services, fulltext ACOG publications, and data and program files useful to members. Staff plan to add gateways to the library and other networks as well as other features. The only charge to use the system is the cost of the telephone call, and ACOG has requested funds for a toll-free telephone line test for the model phase of the project. A quick reference card describing the features of the system is available to users. Strategies for providing communication, messages, networks, and conference services for members and other ob-gyn organizations are being implemented through ACOGNET.

Another strategy is to identify and automate appropriate membership services, including the resource center, ordering procedures, online registration for educational activities, and access to legislative and medicolegal support. Educating ACOG and NAACOG staff to prepare staff to use the new technology is a complementary strategy. Strategies for the automation of specific programs include developing a computer-based version of *Prolog*, the ACOG self-assessment program, and assisting pilot sites to integrate clinical outcome indicators developed by the ACOG Task Force on Quality Assurance. Finally, ACOG will continue to work with outside groups and corporations that are developing software for education, case records, and other programs relevant to obstetrician-gynecologists.

Project Objective IV: Serve as a model for medical information integration at a medical specialty organization level. ACOG proposes accomplishing the fourth objective through three strategies. The first is to establish mechanisms for sharing information with other organizations working toward common goals relating to medical informatics. Information will be shared through distribution of *On Target*, the ACOG IAIMS newsletter; dissemination of results through written and oral presentations to the medical, computer, and library community; and continued cooperative efforts with other organizations interested in medical informatics. ACOG also proposes to contribute to the development of a preferred obstetric-gynecologic terminology and cooperate in studies of unified medical language systems. The college has a strong history of involvement with obstetric-gynecologic terminology. ACOG has had several task forces on terminology, which have provided guidance on obstetric-gynecologic terminology for Current Procedural Terminology (CPT) codes, the International Classification of Diseases (ICD), and an obstetric-gynecologic dictionary. The Resource Center has already mapped more than 3000 obstetric-gynecologic terms and abbreviations to MeSH headings as part of the automation of the library. The proposed ACOG knowledge base will include mapping of alternative terms, ICD codes, CPT codes, and MeSH terms and tree numbers to preferred obstetric-gynecologic terms.

SIGNIFICANCE OF ACOG IAIMS

The ACOG IAIMS project is a model for the role of a national specialty society in meeting the future information needs of its members and the integration of national specialty IAIMS programs with locally-developed programs. During the model phase of the ACOG IAIMS project, ACOG will test propositions from the planning phase application—that a medical society can develop an effective IAIMS program and that medical specialty programs are complementary to medical school IAIMS programs. A specialty society can provide a national program to a large number of health care providers and thoroughly cover the subjects in which it has expertise through the development of a knowledge base. The specialty society can also provide leadership in the development of preferred terminology and a unified medical language by being responsible for the terminology specific to that specialty and cooperating with the integration of their terminology with other specialties.

REFERENCES

1. Matheson NW, Cooper JAD. Academic information in the academic health sciences center: roles for the library in information management. J Med Educ 1982 Oct:57(10 pt 2).
2. American College of Obstetricians and Gynecologists. ACOG IAIMS planning phase project (IAIMS Grant 1 G08 LM 04533-01). Washington: ACOG, 1986.
3. American College of Obstetricians and Gynecologists. ACOG Integrated Academic Information Management Systems: Model Phase. Washington: ACOG, 1987.
4. Hughes EC, ed. Obstetric-gynecologic terminology with section on neonatology and glossary of congenital anomalies. Philadelphia: FA Davis, 1972.

This project was supported in part by NIH Grant No. 1 G08 LM 04533-01 from the National Library of Medicine.

WHY INDEXING FAILS THE RESEARCHER

Bella Hass Weinberg

Introduction

It is part of the conventional wisdom of information science that indexing is concerned with aboutness,[1,2] and that index terms which accurately represent what a document is about provide 'good indexing', which in turn permits 'good retrieval'.[3] Maron has suggested that, in addition to aboutness, factors such as comprehensibility, timeliness, and style contribute to users' relevance judgements.[4]

It is the purpose of this paper to demonstrate that indexing limited to the representation of aboutness, even with indication of document type and level, has little utility for the scholar or researcher, which may explain the underutilization of indexing and abstracting services by this category of information consumer,[5] as well as poor citation practices.[6] This thesis is not based on experimental research, but rather on the observations of the author, who has spent the last fifteen years studying, teaching and conducting research on indexing. Many of the examples are drawn from the author's experience as a user of indexes.

Information Needs

In catalog use studies it has been repeatedly demonstrated that the scholar/researcher makes little or no use of the subject catalog in libraries, requiring only the author-title catalog to determine the location of specific books, of whose existence the scholar already knows.[7] Most researchers do not, however, claim that they have complete control of all the periodical articles in their fields; studies of information needs have shown that re-

"Why Indexing Fails the Researcher" by Bella Hass Weinberg in *The Indexer* Vol. 16, no. 1 (April 1988), pp. 3-6; reprinted with permission from *The Indexer*. Revised version of a paper presented at the 50th Annual Meeting of the American Society for Information Science, Boston, Massachusetts, October 1987, and published in its Proceedings ASIS '87. Vol. 24. Printed with permission of Learned Information, Inc.

searchers feel that some relevant literature is passing them by and 'experience instances of late detection'.[8] And yet, most do not use indexes to help identify these papers. Why?

Topic and Comment

Whereas the student or layman is looking for literature on or about a topic, the scholar/researcher's information need is, in most cases, substantially different. This group of users deals in ideas and theories, and wants to know whether specific ideas have previously been expressed in the literature. For example, a historian may have a new explanation for the cause of the Civil War, and going to this heading in a subject catalog or periodical index is not likely to answer precisely the question 'Has anyone ever expressed this theory in print before?'

One may then suggest that the use of subheadings such as 'Causes' or 'Theories' will minimize the length of the file that the researcher must scan. This is true, but it still requires an excessive amount of reading to determine whether the particular idea has been expressed.

Whereas the back-of-book indexes feature *coined modifications* which, in theory, precisely identify the aspect of a topic being treated,[9] the predetermined lists of subdivision in subject catalogs and periodical indexes do not permit exact specification of the aspect or point-of-view of the topic. I can illustrate this idea by describing the literature search for my first published paper, 'Transliteration in Documentation'.[10] I was questioning the use of transliteration as opposed to original script in catalogs and bibliographies. No index I consulted featured any subheading for the term *transliteration*, let alone 'negative views'; thus the principles of transliteration and the descriptions of particular schemes were lumped together. I had to read all papers about the topic to determine that the idea I was presenting had never been expressed in the literature.

The Special Interest Group on Classification Research of the American Society for Information Science and the Classification Research Group in England are concerned with both classification and indexing, which are viewed by some theorists as the same process. The classification scheme with the most highly developed list of auxiliary tables, including points of view-the Universal Decimal Classification-does not, however, have a subdivision for the concept 'negative point of view'. It is interesting in contrast, that co-citation analysis is purported to be able, in some cases, automatically to distinguish papers by the proponents and opponents of a theory.[11]

Classic subject headings, such as those of the Library of Congress, tend to group these under the subdivision 'Controversial Aspects.' *Medical subject headings* does have subdivisions such as *adverse effects*, but Feinglos has indicated that the subheading *drug therapy* is assigned to papers reporting that a drug has *no* therapeutic value.[12]

A recent study has shown that the subheadings in MeSH are under-utilized by end-users,[13] thus, even where relatively sophisticated treatment of aspects exists in an indexing system, its complexity may militate against its use by searchers.

The essence of the problem is that indexes focus on *aboutness* while neglecting *aspect*; the linguistic analogs of these notations are *topic* and *comment* respectively. In a particularly felicitous explanation of these terms. Lyons defines topic as the 'subject of discourse' and *comment* as 'that part of the utterance which adds something new (and thus communicates information . . .)'.[14] It is contended that the scholar/researcher is primarily interested in comment, and an index limited to identifying the literature about a topic, with only broad subcatergorization, is next to useless for the scholar's purposes.

Hutchins, in a linguistic analysis of aboutness, uses the terms *theme* and *rheme* for 'topic' and 'comment' respectively.[15] The distinction he draws is that the novice is interested in documents *about* a topic, while the scholar is interested in those that provide *new* information on a topic, with the basics of which she/he is already familiar. This is a perceptive observation, but it is felt to be useful primarily for selective dissemination of information as opposed to retrospective searching of the published literature for a highly specific research topic.

Specificity

It may be suggested that increased specificity in indexing is what the researcher needs. The discussions of this concept in the literature of library-information science tend to focus on specificity in naming the topic, however—e.g., *Roses vs. Flowers*—not the aspect.

Moreover, the true scholar in a discipline tends to be concerned with a relatively general topic. For example, the luminaries of our own discipline frequently write on theories of information or indexing. Their works are differentiated by the points-of-view they bring to the topic, e.g. that human indexing is unnecessary in an age of fulltext databases. Without classifying myself as a 'luminary', I would like to note that the main topic of *this* paper is quite general, but the highly specific aspect is not likely to be enumerated in the standard information science indexes.

Post-coordination

As more periodical indexes become available online, the use of subdivision in indexing is decreasing because of the possiblities of post-coordination. Schuyler, in her review of Lancaster's new manual on thesaurus construction,[16] notes that the topic of subheadings is not treated at all.[17] Subdivision is being abandoned by A&I services, even where the same indexing data appears in a printed tool, which requires pre-coordination.[18] While post-coordination works for a set of concrete topics such as 'Libraries in Boston', it does not work for theories and aspects of a general topic that are not easily named in distinctive terms.

Exhaustivity

The researcher would often like to know whether an idea that may *not* represent the major focus of his/her paper has previously been expressed in the literature. It may be suggested that this is a problem related to the *exhaustivity* of indexing, or depth of analysis. Whereas exhaustive indexing is not considered practical in printed indexes, fulltext databases are touted as offering the solution to this problem. These are useful for locating highly specific terms or jargon that has not been incorporated into thesauri, but very poor for searching an idea or aspect of a topic that may readily be paraphrased in numerous ways.

Exhaustivity is closely related to the concept of *indexable matter*. In books, indexable matter is generally considered text germane to the main theme of the book, but I tend to recall the digressions and seek these unsuccessfully in indexes. (In my personal library, I have annotated the indexes of my books for points I consider worthy of recalling.) In journals, indexable matter generally includes articles, reviews, and perhaps editorials, but I tend to recall the quotations sprinkled in between these (especially in *The Indexer*), which are unindexed. To give two examples, I have often wanted to cite the sources of the following ideas: (1) we all die of a lack of information [on how to cure disease], and (2) those who look down on the profession of indexing probably do not have the intelligence to compile a good index. I have despaired of the possibility of identifying these through indexes; my only hope is a knowledgeable colleague—the preferred information source of the researcher.

Non-use of A&I Services

A variety of reasons has been given for the non-use of databases by researchers. Probably the oldest one is Mooer's Law, which essentially states that an information system will not be used when it's more trouble than it's worth.[19] Motivation and complexity enter into Mooer's Law, but even a system that is easy to use will not be used if it identifies an excessive amount of literature on a topic for the researcher to scan, without zeroing in on the aspect of interest.

Butler explains non-use of indexes in terms of 'information avoidance'.[20] (I remember being afraid while a doctoral candidate to look at the contents pages of new issues of information science journals for fear of finding someone had already researched the same topic.) Researchers would not avoid databases, I feel, if they afforded fast answers to their questions.

The explanation of non-use of databases which comes closest to the one in this article is Breton's paper 'Why engineers don't use databases',[21] in which he explains that indexes in the field of engineering specify concrete topics, but not the concepts that are important to the practitioner, i.e., functions and attributes. Breton's ideas may be generalized to include humanities and social science scholars who do not find adequate indexing for their fields, as well as the researcher in the soft sciences, dealing with such slippery phenomena as information. Swift *et al.*[22] noted the limitations of indexing based on aboutness for the field of education and recommended a 'multi-modal' approach to indexing, which would record theoretical orientation and research method in addition to topic.

Probably the only scientists that are reasonably well served by indexes are those involved in experimental research examining the relationship between two concrete topics such as *smoking* and *lung cancer*; however, if such a scientist wants to know whether anyone has ever posited a particular theory *explaining* the relationship between the two phenomena, he encounters the same problem as his humanities counterpart.

Citation Practices

As a result of the non-use of indexes and bibliographic databases, we see many poorly documented papers, even in our own field, information science —where the researcher theoretically knows how to make effective use of such tools. There are no sanctions for the non-acknowledgement of prior ideas, however, except for outright plagiarism. Lack of citation of a journal referee's relevant papers may give a prospective author trouble, though!

Poor citation practices are explained in part by Garfield's *obliteration phenomenon*, i.e., that generally accepted ideas become part of the conventional wisdom of a discipline without formal citation to their originators.[23]

More often, however, I suspect that an author would like to acknowledge an intellectual debt, but does not recall where he first read an idea, and realizes that it would take too long to research it through indexes. An example of this may be found in Kochen's paper entitled 'How well do we acknowledge intellectual debts?'[24] (published after this one was submitted for review). The entire parenthetical anecdote is worth quoting here:

> There was a good article in the early days of the information retrieval discipline—perhaps in the early 1960s—that demonstrated how an error in a citation was propagated by uncritical, unchecked copying from one bibliography to another. My inability to recall or retrieve the citation to this article is an example of retrieval failure, even given strong clues.

Discussion and Conclusions

It is not the purpose of this paper to recommend radical changes in indexing methodology, but rather to explain some of the limitations of standard indexes to the serial literature and reasons for their non-use.

One could conceive of a variety of mechanisms to improve indexing for researchers, but in an age of fulltext databases and a decline of emphasis on content analysis at the input stage, this is probably futile. The analysis of aspect and the identification of new ideas within a document are time-consuming procedures. The history of information science shows that labor-intensive indexing procedures such as semantic factoring and the use of roles and links have been discarded because of excessive complexity.

One might argue that it is not the purpose of indexes to enumerate aspects of topics—that this is the task of abstracts and reviews—to explain in non-structured language the contribution made by a given paper to the literature on the topic. In my experience, these compactions or distillations of the literature often miss the key point or omit major points. There is undoubtedly a great deal of subjectivity involved in distilling the essentials of a research paper and in identifying the new ideas contained in it. But even in cases where all agree that an abstract is an accurate representation of a document, we are still dependent on indexes for providing access to them.

As it has been demonstrated that indexes fail the researcher because they do an inadequate job in representing the aspects of topics, we may conclude that for the researcher, there is no substitute for extensive reading and a prodigious memory. A personal documentation system[25] may serve as auxiliary memory, but the development of customized indexes entails prior reading to identify the points worth storing for future reference.

Epilogue

The thesis of this paper was supported in the process of its preparation—it took five times as long to retrieve the references to document the ideas that the author recalled having heard or read as it did to write the paper. Presumably, a search to determine whether any of the ideas believed to be new in this paper had ever been expressed before in the literature would take many years, requiring a sequential reading of the library-information science literature, rather than the consultation of indexes.

Acknowledgements

The author acknowledges the assistance of the members of her 'invisible college', too numerous to name, who were kind enough to discuss the ideas presented in this paper and to provide assistance with its documentation.

References

1. Wilson, Patrick. Some fundamental concepts of information retrieval. *Drexel library quarterly* 14(2) Apr. 1978, 10-24.
2. Beghtol, Clare. Bibliographic classification theory and text linguistics: aboutness analysis, intertextuality and the cognitive act of classifying documents. *Journal of documentation* 42(2) June 1986, 84-113.
3. O'Connor, John. Some remarks on mechanized indexing and some small-scale experimental results. In *Machine indexing: progress and problems.* Washington, DC: American University, 1961, 266-79.
4. Maron, M. E. On indexing, retrieval and the meaning of about. *Journal of the American Society for Information Science* 28(1) Jan. 1977, 38-43.
5. Ford, Geoffrey, ed. *User studies: an introductory guide and select bibliography.* Sheffield, Eng.: Center for Research on User Studies, 1977, 29.
6. Korennoi, A. A. Citation indexes: their uses in the science of science and informatics. *Nauchno-tekhnicheskaia informatsiia.* Series 2 1968, 3-6.
7. Tagliacozzo, R. and Kochen, M. Information-seeking behavior of catalog users. *Information storage and retrieval* 6 1970, 363-81.
8. Ford, 30.
9. Borko, Harold and Bernier, Charles L. *Indexing concepts and methods.* New York: Academic Press, 1978, 17.
10. Weinberg, Bella. Transliteration in documentation. *Journal of documentation* 30(1) 1974, 18-31.
11. Small, Henry. The lives of a scientific paper. In *Selectivity in information systems,* ed. Kenneth S. Warren, New York: Praeger, 1985, 83-97.
12. Feinglos, Susan J. *Medline: a basic guide to searching.* Chicago: Medical Library Association, 1985, 22.
13. Sewell, Winifred and Teitelbaum, Sandra. Observations of end-user online searching behavior over eleven years. *Journal of the American Society for Information Science* 37(4) July 1986, 234-45.
14. Lyons, John. *Introduction to theoretical linguistics.* Cambridge, [Eng.]: Cambridge University Press, 1968, 335.
15. Hutchins, W. J. The concept of aboutness in subject indexing. *Aslib Proceedings* 30(5) May 1978, 172-81.
16. Lancaster, F. W. *Vocabulary control for information retrieval.* 2d ed. Arlington, VA: Information Resources Press, 1986.
17. Schuyler, Peri. [Review of] Lancaster, F. W. *Vocabulary control for information retrieval.* 2d ed. *Bulletin of the Medical Library Association* 75(1) Jan. 1987, 43-4.
18. Milstead, Jessica L. *Subject access systems: alternatives in design.* New York: Academic Press, 1984, 31.
19. Mooers, Calvin N. Mooer's law, or why some retrieval systems are used and others are not. *American Documentation* 11(3) July 1960, ii.
20. Butler, Brett. Emotion in information: behavioral blocks in information processes. In *Education for information management: directions for the future.* Santa Barbara: International Academy, 1983, 102.
21. Breton, Ernest J. Why engineers don't use databases: indexing techniques fail to fit the needs of the profession. *Bulletin of the American Society for Information Science* 7(6) Aug. 1981, 20-3.
22. Swift, D. F., Winn, V. and Bramer, D. 'Aboutness' as a strategy for retrieval in the social sciences. *Aslib proceedings* 30(5) May 1978, 182-7.
23. Garfield, Eugene. The 'obliteration phenomenon' in science—and the advantage of being obliterated. *Current Contents* 51/52 Dec. 22, 1975, 5-7. Reprinted in his: *Essays of an information scientist* II. Philadelphia: ISI Press, 1977, 398.

24. Kochen, Manfred. How well do we acknowledge intellectual debts? *Journal of Documentation* 43(1) March 1987, 54-64.
25. Stibic, V. *Personal documentation for professionals: means and methods.* Amsterdam: North-Holland, 1980.

BACK TO THE FUTURE: MAKING AND INTERPRETING THE DATABASE INDUSTRY TIMELINE

Charles T. Meadow

How We Went About It

Our "thing," an industry or a discipline, depending on the role we individually play in it, is new, yet it is old enough to have a history. This short history, in the form of the timeline, and these notes, are being published in celebration of *DATABASE*'s tenth anniversary. Doing the necessary research has been a fascinating exercise. Most of the pioneers are still among us; many are still active in the industry. If only there were more time to get their full stories!

History is interpretation. Even in the history of one of the most modern of technologies there are questions as to exact dates, the exact sequence of developments, the exact degree of dependency of one development on another, and certainly on the importance of individual events. There has been a good bit of independent co-development in this industry, and it is often impossible to say who *really* developed the first whatsit.

In selecting entries for the timeline, I have used my own judgment, backed up by a good bit of personal recollection (I was doing data management in the early 1950's and information retrieval in the late 50's, with an online project in between). There was a lot of background reading, a mountain of letters to as many of the pioneers as I could find, and innumerable phone calls, but I must, of course, take the final responsibility for selection as well as non-selection of items.

In naming key individuals associated with any product or development, I have tried to be inclusive, but I also had to conserve space; hence I have generally named only a single person related to any project. This will, no doubt, slight those who played important roles but were omitted. It also

"Back to the Future: Making and Interpreting the Database Industry Timeline" by Charles T. Meadow in *Database* Vol. 11 (October 1988), pp. 14-31; reprinted with permission from Online, Inc.

would have been nice to list all the prominent databases, but there are too many, so I have had to hold the list only to those that seemed to set a new mark of some sort, in subject matter or content.

Where to Begin

One of the first "facts" (facts, anyway, as I saw them) that struck me was that there is no obvious point at which to begin this history. Does it date from 1972 when a cluster of online services were newly offered? Does it go back to the 1940's and early 1950's when serious scientists began to predict, design, and build information retrieval systems based on computers? Does it go back to the 17th century when giants like Napier, Pascal, and Leibnitz began to build calculating instruments, and these same people plus Isaac Newton began to develop modern mathematical calculation techniques? Or, do we go back to ancient times, and the development of the alphabet, the abacus, and the written record?

Writing, Books and Libraries

Libraries, of course are very old. Three thousand BCE* is a common estimate for their first appearance. That same approximate date is given for the appearance of writing, in pictograph form, in what we now call the Middle East. This suggests that it took little time for the database administrators of the day to decide that records worth writing were also worth keeping. The alphabet, more or less as we know it now, came from the same area around the 17th century BCE. Clay tablets (write-once, read-many) were the first major recording media. Papyrus, parchment, and paper occupy less space and weigh less than clay and, while basically still WORM media, allow some modification after the initial recording.

The movable-type printing press came to the Western world in the 15th century and, while it did not much change the nature of books, it did change the nature of the book market, leading in a surprisingly short time to a much more widespread use of these objects and contributing to the spread of learning. Some attribute the success of Martin Luther's reformation to his use of printed media to carry his message, a very familiar phenomenon to TV viewers of today. Dare we say that Gutenberg ushered in the era of the end-user?

Mathematics and Computation

We do not know when counting began, but it has become legend that ancient people used piles of small stones to represent cattle in a field, and kept track by setting up a correspondence between the pebbles and the

---

*BCE means "before the Common Era," and is a synonym for BC; CE means "of the Common Era," a synonym for AD.

cows. As a cow passed into a pasture a pebble was moved from one stack to another; the process was reversed as the herd returned. If any pebbles remained unmoved, then an animal was missing. This could be (and presumably was) done without having a *name* for the numbers, i.e., the primitive farmer did not know how to say *how many* cows were missing, but could note that *some* were. Notched bones, apparently used for this sort of application, have been dated as far back as 20,000 BCE. The abacus was (and is) a *recording* machine, not a calculator: the human operator does the calculations mentally, then stores the results. Clearly, it is of the "read-write" persuasion.

Numerals appeared at about the same time as writing, in the same part of the world. A form of decimal notation dates from *ca* 1000 BCE. The zero, as a distinct symbol, came into use around the 5th century CE. Our modern numeric notation scheme, based on Indo-Arabic numerals, and using place to indicate value, came into use in the neighborhood of 200 BCE. Our modern algebraic system of using letters for unknowns did not come about until around 1580.

Mathematics, of a sort, was known to the ancient Greeks, and refined by the Arabs about 1000 CE. But, it was not until the 17th century that we found great advances being made in computational mathematics. That was an era of Napier (logarithms and an early calculating instrument known as Napier's bones), Leibnitz (an early calculator and, simultaneously with but independent of Newton, calculus), and Pascal, (an early calculator). The slide rule, too, came from this period.

Stonehenge was a calculating device which, in modern terms, might have been called an expert or knowledge-based system, because it had expert knowledge of astronomical phenomena stored within it. It was a practical system. Astronomical data were needed for agricultural reasons. Of course, it didn't hurt the guy in charge that his machine *could* accurately predict events, giving us the invention of the "demo."

We generally credit Charles Babbage with invention of the computer, *ca* 1840, although he, himself, was never able to build a machine to his own designs. His friend, Ada Byron, Countess Lovelace, developed some of the modern concepts of computer programming. Alan Turing, a century later, developed a theory of computation, but it was not until the late stages of World War II that programmed computers, more or less as we know them today, came into being. The University of Pennsylvania is usually credited with the first, the ENIAC, developed for the U.S. Army. J. Presper Eckert and J. W. Mauchly were involved in ENIAC and later went on to build the first commercial general purpose computer, UNIVAC, delivered to the U.S. Census Bureau in 1951. The Census Bureau had also been the incubator for punched card systems, developed by Herman Hollerith who founded the company that evolved into IBM.

Information Systems

A computer is only one component of a complete information system. We do not know when humankind began assembling data and procedures for storage, retrieval, and analysis of data. Consider the Egyptian pyramids. Little, if anything, is known about how they kept managerial records in those days, but think of the vast numbers of personnel and material involved. Estimates are given that the pyramids at Giza required 700,000 dressed stones, weighing over two tons each and a workforce of 70,000 people. Spengler said that "old Egypt [was] a civilization that had for a thousand years thought of *nothing* but the organization of its economy." Wonder, if you will, how it could have been managed without some form of what we now call an information system.

Modern accounting systems date from the 15th century, although we may tend to think of their origins in Dickensian times and places, and to visualize sour-faced men perched on high stools, working with huge ledgers. Some people feel accounting systems were the first "information systems." If you doubt the intellectual magnitude of the design of an accounting system, Goethe called it "one of the finest discoveries of the human intellect," and Spengler said of Luca Pacioli, one of the developers, that he "ranked with his contemporaries, Columbus and Copernicus."

Databases

We know that our own online database industry developed out of bibliographic and legal files, and that these had their origins as early as the 17th century when scientific journals began, closely followed by subject-oriented library catalogs and related indexes.

Databases are not an entirely new concept, although the word seems to date only from the 1950's. The early computers of the 1600's to 1800's were largely concerned (as were the more modern ones of the 1940's and early 1950's) with mathematical tables: creating them, storing, and using them, or both. These, in today's jargon, are the ultra-modern numeric databases. Some of the bibliographic databases that are familiar to us today have been with us for a century; *Index Medicus* (1879), *Engineering Index* (1884), *Scientific Abstracts* (now INSPEC, 1898), and *Chemical Abstracts* (1907).

During the 20th century major scientific societies and government agencies began to produce indexes and abstract journals at a growing rate and these, in addition to those trail blazers listed above, became the early online databases. Then, we added business files, although in a sense when Thomas Edison improved the stock market ticker system in 1870, this telegraphic broadcast system might have been seen as the first online information system. Full-text files became possible only when computer memory permitted, in the early 1970's, first for legal materials (whose users were probably the only ones who could afford them in those days), and in the late 1970's for newspapers, as memory technology improved.

Modern Technology

We know we owe something to Jacquard, he of the pattern-weaving, punched card-driven loom; to Herman Hollerith, developer of the first punched card accounting systems; to Alexander Graham Bell and his company that became AT&T; to Eckert and Mauchly (whose intellectual feat in inventing the modern computer has been challenged, but whose commercial lead has not been) and their company that became Remington-Rand UNIVAC, producers of the first modern, commercially successful computer; to John McCarthy, Fernando Corbato et. al. at M.I.T. for inventing time-sharing on computers; to Robert Taylor and Lawrence Roberts for ARPANet, the first packet-switched telecommunications system for computers.

This series of inventions, at least those from the telephone forward to our times, were absolutely essential to the existence of online systems. I have experienced what even a slight slow-down of computers can trigger in the way of customer reaction at DIALOG—users have an intolerance for delay and extra cost once they become accustomed to high speeds and low costs. I find it staggering to imagine operating such a service without large, time-shared computers to search DIALOG's quarter-acre of disk drives, or for users to try to reach those computers without the inexpensive, reliable communications that packet-switching enables.

Searching the types of files we find on modern database systems, with the aid of a computer-like device, was described in the now famous Vannevar Bush article, "As we may think," published in a general periodical, *The Atlantic Monthly*, in 1945. Bush was President Roosevelt's science advisor during World War II, and as the war ended he became interested in salvaging what we could of the scientific developments of the war. Information was one of those developments. A hypothetical means of storing, retrieving, and annotating was Bush's own idea. The personalized annotations are still to come, but modern hypertext is pointing us that way. Incidentally, this was the same year in which Arthur Clarke, a science fiction writer, also writing in a popular medium, proposed the communications satellite.

Then, in the 1950's, came the real systems, still pre-online: Harley Tillet developed a retrieval system for the IBM 701 computer at the Naval Ordinance Test Center, China Lake California in 1954; James Perry and Allen Kent developed the Western Reserve University Searching Selector in 1958, working on a bibliographic database of metals information; Claude Walston of IBM built a batch retrieval system for the Strategic Air Command in 1959.

Also in the 50's we saw SAGE, an acronym for the U.S. Air Force's oddly named SemiAutomatic Ground Environment, a multi-computer, online, interactive air defense and intercept control system.

In the 1960's the computer industry experienced rapid and unstable growth. Companies came and went. If your employer did not go out of business or get swallowed by another, the employees moved about at whim. Corporate giants, one after another, challenged IBM's supremacy and fell by the wayside. RCA, General Electric, Sylvania, and Philco all tried, and today no longer exist as computer makers of consequence, or some of them even as independent companies. Time-shared computers went from laboratory developments to commercial reality, led by General Electric's Computer Department, which was quickly overtaken by IBM, UNIVAC, and the new upstart, Digital Equipment Corporation. The decade produced a remarkable series of machines and software which, collectively, constituted one of the key prerequisites to the online database industry, then still to come into its own.

The U.S. Government deserves much credit for fostering the computer and communications technologies we needed, and for directly nurturing the database industry. It sponsored many computer projects, database development projects, information usage studies, and combined computer-database development-usage projects. Some were hugely successful and their successors are still prominent today: DIALOG, MEDLINE, BRS, LEXIS, and the Chemical Abstracts Registry System are among them. There were countless others that left no lasting impression, but did train people and test ideas. The military departments and the National Science Foundation were prominent among the sponsors. Incidentally, this tradition of government sponsorship of scientific and technological development is neither new nor limited to the United States. Da Vinci, the navigators and navigational instrument makers of the 14th and 15th centuries, and Babbage were among the notables of the past who enjoyed government grants.

Also in the 1960's came the MEDLARS demand search service at the National Library of Medicine followed by several experimental online database systems: Carlos Cuadra's work with System Development Corporation, developing the Elhill software for NLM, used initially with an early NLM service called AIMTWIX, and eventually leading both to MEDLINE and ORBIT; Lockheed's similar work for NASA, and later the U.S. Office of Education, leading to the DIALOG software and service; Data Corporation's work, under Dick Gering, for the U.S. Air Force, and the Ohio Bar, leading eventually to LEXIS.

In this period Carl Overhage created the INTREX project at M.I.T., perhaps the first sizable project devoted to studying the use of online database systems. And, near the end of the decade came Lancaster's evaluation study of MEDLARS, the first of its type.

The 1970's brought us the telecommunications we needed. ARPANet, the first operational packet-switched digital communication network, actually began on a test basis in 1969. It was implemented by the U.S. Department of Defense (ARPA: Advanced Research Projects Agency). Commercial systems of the same type, such as Telenet, TYMNET, and GENet, soon followed. This was the last major piece of technology that had to be put into place. The world was ready for public, online database services. They came in 1972.

Finally, Online Databases!

There were three sequences of developments that had to come together to make our modern online database systems: computers, communications, and the databases, themselves. The final link in computer development was that of time-sharing, which, as we noted, came in the late 1960's. The communications link that could make remote database services economical and fast came with packet-switching in the early 1970's, immediately followed by the creation of our industry. The databases, again as we noted above, were evolving slowly in other forms, and then *after* online service began, we saw the real spurt in their growth.

The brief interval, 1971-1974, saw a remarkable series of developments: OCLC, DIALOG, ORBIT, MEDLINE, LEXIS, the New York Times Information Bank, Dow Jones News/Retrieval. The very earliest of them used leased telephone lines. True dial-up service required packet-switching and when that last link was put into place, our *industry* emerged out of a series of *experiments*.

The next leap forward came around 1980, when personal computers came into common use. Just plain terminals, while not very expensive, were also not routine office equipment. *Terminals* were for only a few people in any organization and their use carried no status, perhaps even denied it. *Computers*, however, quickly became status-enhancing and ubiquitous in the office and laboratory. Thus came about the era of the database *end-user*, an era we are still in, and I believe (and hope) we will never come out of. This phenomenon changed the thinking in the computer and database industry. Designers and marketers began to realize that the message "syntax error" did not win new customers to an online service.

The 1980's had still one more revolution for us, the CD-ROM. Introduced commercially to the database world only in 1985, it seems to have captured the imaginations of both producers and buyers; and has certainly captured all the prime space in the industry press. It is not yet clear what its economic impact will be. Already, a new announcement from Tandy Corporation hints of major changes: a read-write compact disk, in this decade. How will this affect the ROM's, and the investments in ROM's, and the online services? How many revolutions can one industry handle in two decades?

Acknowledgments

I talked and corresponded with so many people that it is difficult to list all of them. I hope I may be forgiven for mentioning the few who took an exceptional amount of time to help research this article: Robert Donati and Sophie Hudnut, Dialog Information Services; Frederick Kilgour, OCLC, Inc.; Maria Loranger, University of Toronto; W. V. Metanomski, Chemical Abstracts Service; and Margaret Y. Walshe, Canada Institute for Scientific and Technical Information.

ONLINE DATABASE INDUSTRY TIMELINE

1945
- Vannevar Bush's "memex" article, "As We May Think," in The *Atlantic Monthly*, postulates an online interactive information retrieval system
- Arthur C. Clarke's article, "Extra-Terrestrial Relays: Can Rocket Stations Give Worldwide Radio Coverage?", in *Wireless World*, proposed the communications satellite

1946
- ENIAC, first electronic computer, developed at University of Pennsylvania for U.S. Army

1948
- Transistor invented at Bell Laboratories by John Bardeen, Walter H. Brattain, and William S. Shockley

1951
- UNIVAC, first general purpose, commercial, electronic computer, developed by Eckert and Mauchly at Remington-Rand, delivered to U.S. Census Bureau
- Philip Bagley completes M.I.T. thesis, "Electronic Digital Machines For High-Speed Information Searching"
- Mortimer Taube delivered paper on "The Coordinate Indexing Of Scientific Fields" at American Chemical Society, Division of Chemical Literature

1953
- Uniterm indexing system proposed by Taube

1954
- First information retrieval system on a general purpose computer (IBM 701) by Harley Tillet, at U.S. Naval Ordnance Test Station, China Lake, California

1955 • Termatrex index searching machine, one of several pre-computer mechanical devices able to do simple Boolean searching, developed by Frederick Jonker

1956 • Atlantic telephone cable laid by American, British, Canadian consortium
• SAGE, first major online system, for air defense application, developed by academic-industrial group at M.I.T., for the U.S. Air Force

1957 • FORTRAN symbolic programming language and compiler, developed at IBM by John Backus
• The U.S. Patent Office begins experiments with computer patent searching on the National Bureau of Standards' SEAC computer

1958 • Western Reserve University Searching Selector developed by James Perry and Allen Kent to search Metals Abstract database
• Hans Peter Luhn, at IBM, produces an automatic document indexing program
• First communications satellites, SCORE and ECHO I

1959 • IBM produces operating information retrieval system for Strategic Air Command, designed by Claude Walston
• Second generation computers (transistorized) introduced by IBM

1960 • System Development Corporation demonstrates Protosynthex, an experimental online retrieval system for full text
• J.C.R. Licklider, of M.I.T., publishes "Man-Computer Symbiosis" defining the modern idea of an interactive computer system

1961 • Compatible Time Sharing System, CTSS, developed by McCarthy, Corbato, et. al. at M.I.T.
• System for the Mechanical Analysis and Retrieval of Text (SMART) begun by Gerard Salton at Harvard University
• Chemical Abstracts Service's Chemical Titles, becomes first regularly computer-produced publication in science-technology with a KWIC index

1962 • Telstar communication satellite becomes active
• John Horty at Health Law Center, University of Pittsburgh, develops a full-text legal information retrieval system, demonstrated at the American Bar Association

1964 • MEDLARS on-demand computer-based information retrieval service to the medical profession initiated
• Eugene Garfield's Institute for Scientific Information produces *Science Citation Index* as a print product, the first publicly available citation index for the sciences
• The U.S. Air Force produces the LITE (Legal Information through Electronics) system, based on Horty's work at University of Pittsburgh

1965
- Project INTREX (M.I.T.), 1963-72; Carl J. Overhage studies the use of information retrieval systems
- Third-generation computers, the 360 series, using integrated circuits, and called the largest private industrial development project ever, introduced by IBM
- Remote terminal online system (RECON) begun by Lockheed Palo Alto Research Lab under Roger Summit at NASA
- Original ORBIT software developed by Carlos Cuadra at SDC for U.S. Air Force
- Chemical Abstracts Service develops Chemical Registry System, with sponsorship by National Science Foundation, National Institutes of Health, and Department of Defense (NIH, DOD)

1967
- Data Corporation, under Dick Gering, awarded a contract by Ohio Bar to bring up Ohio statutes as a full-text file, work that led to the LEXIS system

1968
- Wolf Lancaster published his evaluation of the MEDLARS demand search service
- SUNY Biomedical Communication Network (SUNY BCN) was established, and used dedicated lines to offer the first online access to MEDLARS
- Carterfone decision by U.S. Supreme Court allowed noncarrier-provided terminal equipment on U.S. telephone lines
- Queens's University of Kingston, Ontario, and IBM form a project to investigate online, full-text, legal information retrieval
- Aspen Systems Corp, formed from the Horty project at Pittsburgh, announces the world's largest full-text, searchable database containing the statutes of all 50 states

1969
- Henriette Avram at Library of Congress produces MARC data interchange standard for catalog data
- ARPANet, first packet-switched data communications network, developed by Robert Taylor and Lawrence Roberts at Advanced Research Projects Agency, U.S. Department of Defense, begins test operation
- ERIC database of U.S. Office of Education brought online, for limited use, through DIALOG, an outgrowth of the earlier RECON system
- Data Resources Inc (DRI) becomes the first major numeric database service
- Canadian Institute for Scientific and Technical Information implements its CAN/SDI system
- European Space Agency initiates the first online information retrieval service in Europe, on an experimental basis, using NASA RECON software
- QUIC/LAW begins operation at Queen's University, under Hugh Lawford, with online, full-text legal information system

1970
- First overseas access to an online database, from Paris to DIALOG in Palo Alto
- Fourth generation computers, the 370 series, (large scale integration) introduced by IBM
- ELHILL software, developed by Carlos Cuadra at SDC, chosen to support National Library of Medicine's AIM-TWX experimental online database service

1971
- MEDLINE, the online version of MEDLARS, for the medical community, first major online dial-up service
- OCLC, under Frederick Kilgour, initiates first shared library cataloging system
- Pandex, the first commercial database, brought up on DIALOG for limited access
- Roger Summit, of DIALOG, and Richard Kollin, of Pandex, work out the basis for user charges for Pandex—by connect hour—which became the initial standard for the industry, at the ASIS meeting in New York

1972
- DIALOG offers first public, online commercial database service
- ORBIT, under Carlos Cuadra, offers its commercial database service

1973
- Dennis Auld and Greg Payne's ABI/INFORM, the first business-oriented, abstract database, goes online
- LEXIS, under Jerry Rubin, initiated by Mead Data Central

1974
- The New York Times Information Bank, under John Rothman, produces first public access online newspaper abstract and index service
- Dow Jones News/Retrieval initiated as a joint service of Dow Jones and Bunker-Ramo
- The Alto, an experimental personal computer, produced at Xerox Palo Alto Research Center
- IFI/Plenum Corp's CLAIMS/U.S. Patent files brought up on DIALOG, the first online files entirely devoted to patents

1975
- 300 online public access databases now available
- Richard Marcus and Franics Reintjes at M.I.T. begin experimental work with CONIT, a computer intermediary for online searching, based on a common command language

1976
- Radio Shack TRS-80 personal computer marketed
- Ron Quake, from the New York Division of Criminal Justice, and Janet Egeland, formerly of SUNY BCN, formed the new company, Bibliographic Retrieval Service (BRS)
- ISI's *Science Citation Index* brought online by DIALOG as SciSearch

1977
- CISTI creates first Canadian online science information service, CAN/OLE
- *ONLINE* magazine founded by Jeff and Jenny Pemberton
- *Online Review* magazine founded by Roger Bilboul
- First International Online Information Meeting held in U.K.
- Database Mapping Model, and experimental search front end developed at University of Illinois by Martha Williams
- First mention of "end-user" in an ERIC or LISA abstract: "Frequency And Impact Of Spelling Errors . . .," by Charles P. Bourne
- Apple II personal computer marketed

1978
- *DATABASE* magazine founded by the Pembertons
- The Globe and Mail database of the Toronto *Globe and Mail* becomes the world's first commercially available full-text newspaper database
- Information Access Corp.'s Magazine Index database goes online
- Hayes Microcomputer Products brings out its Micromodem II designed for the Apple II computer
- User Cordial Interface developed by Charles Goldstein as an experimental front end at National Library of Medicine

1979
- The Source and CompuServe, home-user-oriented online systems, initiated service
- ONLINE '79 conference held, first public meeting in U.S. devoted to online database searching
- 1200 baud service initiated by TYMNET
- PaperChase developed at Beth Israel Hospital, Boston, by Dr. Howard L. Bleich as an experimental system
- IIDA, an experimental computer intermediary for online searching, introduced at Drexel University by Charles Meadow and David Toliver
- Commonwealth Agricultural Bureaux announce a per-record user charge for retrieval from its database, CAB Abstracts, setting another trend in user billing

1980
- First mention of "end-user" in an article title in ERIC or LISA, "End-User Education . . .," by Art Elias
- First National Online Meeting held in the U.S.
- Information Access's Search Helper, developed by Richard Kollin, marketed; the first commercial front end for online searching, to search Magazine Index on DIALOG
- First commercial, multidatabase front end software packages marketed: User Link by Philip Williams at University of Manchester, and OL'SAM, by David Toliver at Franklin Institute Research Laboratory in Philadelphia
- 600 public access online databases now available
- Info Globe database offered with full public access
- Osborne I, the first portable personal computer introduced
- American Chemical Society brings up Journal of Medicinal Chemistry in a full-text, private file on BRS as an experiment

- BLEND, a project initiated by Brian Shakel at Loughborough University, U.K., establishes The Loughborough Information Network Community, producing first electronic journal, published only in online form

1981
- First newspaper newsroom devoted solely to producing online information created at Dow Jones
- IBM Personal Computer introduced
- ETHERNET, first commercial local area network system, introduced as a commercial product by Xerox
- DIALOG and BRS offer their simplified, reduced rate, after-hours services, Knowledge Index and BRS/After Dark

1982
- European Space Agency's Information Retrieval Service introduces the ZOOM command, enabling users to analyze retrieved sets
- Telecom Canada begins trials of its iNet 2000 online gateway system

1983
- STN begins as an international, commercial, distributed online database service
- 10 million computers in use in the U.S.
- Institute for Scientific Information's Sci-Mate and Menlo Corporation's In-Search end-user front end package marketed
- BIOSIS initiates the BITS "selective dissemination of information" service, providing output to users on a floppy disk

1984
- 2400 baud service for public access online databases made available by TYMNET and TELENET.
- PaperChase, from Beth Israel Hospital, Boston becomes a public system
- Dick Kollin, at Telebase Systems, brings out EasyNet, a combination front end and gateway to other database services; also the first service allowing users to charge a search to a credit card at time of search
- The Business Computer Network (BCN) begins operation as a gateway service devoted to providing users access to other, remote database services

1985
- The first commercial CD-ROM drives for personal computers became available, shortly followed by the first commercial CD-ROM databases, the Library Company's LC MARC and Grolier's Academic American Encyclopedia
- EasyNet offers its SOS service, allowing a user to call for online reference assistance during a search

1986
- 3000 public access databases now available
- Grateful Med designed by Davis McCarn for National Library of Medicine continues trend toward simplified end-user services
- Roger Summit reports that 80% of new DIALOG "sign-ups" (new accounts) are end-users

1987
- 9600 baud service for public access online databases made available by TYMNET
- HyperCard, hypertext software developed by Bill Atkinson, offered as a Macintosh software product

1988
- Image searching and retrieval (from TrademarkScan database) first offered on a commercial search service, DIALOG
- Tandy Corp announces a read-write compact disk for release in 1988-89, and Philips announces they are working on a prototype of one in Europe
- 3893 online databases were commercially available, from 1723 database producers, and 576 online services
- Dialog Information Services, Inc., sold by Lockheed Corp. to Knight-Ridder Inc. for $353 million

THE COMPUTER CATALOG: A DEMOCRATIC OR AUTHORITARIAN TECHNOLOGY?

Judith A. Adams

The electronic library is a reality. The supporting automated systems technologies are being embraced by small and large libraries at a rate that might shock even such visionaries as Alvin Toffler. The library and information professions are now beginning to step back from their "computer romantic" stance to publicly assess the nature of the contributions of computerization, its effects on organizational structure, and alterations in work roles.

Patrica Glass Schuman, in a recent article in *LJ*, confronts us with a recognition of the "myths" of computer networks. For at least a decade, these myths have not only been generally uncritically accepted but also loudly espoused as ideological bulwarks to support for library automation projects. She gives voice to the profession's rather reluctant admissions that computer networks have not saved money, have not decreased bureaucratic structures, and perhaps most significantly, have not moved the profession toward a philosophy of access.[1]

Critical Choices

We now face a critical juncture in our relationship with computer technology: we can allow it to shape the future role of libraries or we can pattern it to serve the chosen values of the profession. Librarians are now familiar with the technologies and have envisioned their possibilities. It is imperative, at this point, to look beyond the capabilities of the computer to increase productivity as well as efficiency and to question seriously the goals we want to actualize through computerization. The design and mode of implementation of computer systems will subtly but forcefully direct the mission, the social roles, the values of the library as an institution.

"The Computer Catalog: A Democratic or Authoritarian Technology?" by Judith A. Adams in *Library Journal* Vol. 113 (February 1, 1988), pp. 31-36; reprinted with permission from Reed Publishing, USA, copyright © Reed Publishing, USA.

This marvelous technology is a boon to libraries and the research process. It frees staff from repetitive and tedious tasks, enhances access to information, facilitates sharing of resources, and provides the capability for individually tailoring retrieval of information. But at the same time, reflection regarding its application, a more critical regard for systems design and compatibility, and a consensual awareness of the societal values we want it to serve are urgently needed.

Electronic technologies in libraries are still flexible and may be shaped by various factors before a more uniform or rigid structural form is established. Right now, but perhaps not for much longer, there is the possibility to institute design and implementation alternatives that will reflect and augment specific shared values. In order to effectively steer the future course of automation, we must articulate our visions—do we see "progress" narrowly in terms of increased productivity and managerial efficiency, or broadly as the augmentation of access to information?

Online Public Access Catalogs

The most obvious democratizing effect of the electronic library is the vast augmentation of access to information generally objectified by the online public access catalog (OPAC). It is possible not only to provide enhanced retrieval of materials from a library's own collection, but to offer the public entry to the collections of many additional libraries, including the nation's largest institutions. Libraries can also furnish remote access to bibliographic data and other information services through personal computers located at sites throughout a local area network thus freeing the user from the confines of the library walls.

Perhaps the computer catalog's most liberating asset is its potential to free the user from the codified, standardized Library of Congress Subject Headings and even from structured word order in titles. The "keyword" searching capability is a stunning blow for individual freedom, since it assists in releasing the individual mind from the shackles of a highly authoritative, perhaps even somewhat totalitarian classification system. The storage capacity of computer technology also gives individual libraries the ability to supply information from many collections where access has traditionally been severely limited, such as government publications and local history files. An OPAC also accommodates the tailoring and limiting of retrieval to suit individual needs.

Since the computer catalog, as well as other automated services, are used by the general public (e.g., all ages, all educational levels, all cultural backgrounds), it can perhaps be claimed that libraries provide the most democratic access to computer technology available in our society. Limited though this access may be, many people are experiencing their initial hands-on contact with sophisticated computer technologies within the library. The profession and the library as institution can take significant credit for dispelling fears, eliminating ignorance, and promoting a fascinated interest in a technology that dominates our culture.

A Rosy Democratic Aura

This is a rosy picture indeed, a portrait of the library bathed in a democratic aura as a provider of nearly unlimited information to the masses, thanks to the computer. In his article titled "Mythinformation," Langdon Winner warns against predictions resulting from "optimistic technophilia" which contend that ready access to information will dissolve distinctions between classes and offer major opportunities to disadvantaged groups. Obviously, the supply of information is useless until joined with "an educated ability to gain knowledge and act effectively." Winner is not fooled by the myth of information:

> If the solution to problems of illiteracy and poor education were a question of information supply alone, then the best policy might be to increase the number of well-stocked libraries. . . . Of course, that would do little good in itself unless people are sufficiently well educated to use those libraries to broaden their knowledge and understanding. Computer enthusiasts, however, are not noted for their calls to increase support of public libraries and schools. It is electronic information carried by networks they uphold as crucial. . . . While it is true that systems of computation and communications, intelligently structured and widely applied, might help a society raise its standards of literacy, education, and general knowledge-ability, to look to those instruments first while ignoring how to enlighten and invigorate a human mind is pure foolishness.[2]

We cannot sit back content that through computer technology we have, as a profession, greatheartedly furthered the cause of knowledge and democracy. Instead, since the computer catalog is usually the most overt representation to the public of the computerization of libraries, we must evaluate its performance as an information tool and consider what it may be revealing about the mission of the library. Lurking beneath the obvious democratic attributes of the computer catalog are some factors that contribute toward authoritarian tendencies, specifically lack of compatibility between systems, certain system design options, potential invasion of privacy, barriers to database access and manipulation, and the linking of user fees to computerization.

System Incompatibility

Our decided rush to replace thousands of Victorian, rather repressive wooden drawers and millions of 3 x 5 cards with sophisticated, image-enhancing computer terminals has resulted in a plethora of over 50 significantly distinct OPAC systems in libraries. As is particularly evident from such compilations as Joseph R. Matthews's *Public Access to Online Catalogs*, which provides specifications and sample screens for 48 OPACs,[3] there is presently woefully little similarity in system attributes, design, and protocols for accessing the databases. We must be willing to recognize that this state of affairs is a disservice to library users. No longer, as in the past, can an individual expect to go from library to library with an understanding of the procedures required to use the collection.

Suddenly we have presented a new barrier to access which dictates that each patron must become a local "initiate" through a time-consuming training process. If equal, unobstructed access to information is to remain a cherished value of libraries, then it is our responsibility to work toward some basic consensus regarding protocols and features of OPACs. Presumably, we do not wish libraries to be viewed as separate "kingdoms" where favoritism and success are based on proficiency in manipulating BOBCAT, CATNYP, LUIS, SCORPIO, MELVYL, or any other OPAC system. Computer keys should provide access, not lock out the uninitiated. Training programs are a trenchant means to mitigate the local situation, but they are not sufficient. It is time to also focus our energies on the development of standards and affinities in system protocols.

Easy or Best?

In our efforts and deliberations toward compatibility of systems, however, we must be wary of the equation of "easy" with "best." Linda Arret has published provocative findings from research conducted at the Library of Congress that indicate that users expect computer catalogs to be highly sophisticated systems. The still entrenched adage that "user friendly" or "user cordial," that is easy-to-learn, systems should be the overriding goal of systems designers may be a crucial error. Adherence to a strictly democratic ideal could be a hindrance. To design a system to accommodate the lowest common denominator may actually be a disservice.

Arret has determined that learning will not occur with simple systems. Users want to learn and master the system and feel in control of their searching. They do not want the computer to carry them step-by-step in an authoritarian, Big Brother manner. We should provide incentive for users to progress to more sophisticated searching—to use not only the full capacities of the system but also their own intellectual abilities. Arret confidently asserts that users "expect a dialogue with a computer, which is more than they expect from a card catalog; and they expect the computer to operate in terms of its own formal logic."[4]

System Design Options

Studies conducted in the early 1980s, primarily those sponsored by the Council on Library Resources (CLR), have alerted us to user-perceived deficiencies of computer catalog systems. This research reveals that systems are especially inadequate regarding inclusion of publications and materials other than books, as well as the provision of enhanced subject searching capabilities. To date, the profession has been laggard in addressing these needs. The CLR survey revealed that between 20 and 40 percent of patrons in all types of libraries request the inclusion of government publications, newspapers, journals, dissertations, and older books in the computer catalog. Despite this evidence, libraries generally have not yet been noticeably responsive to these pleas.[5]

Beyond financial considerations, the primary reason for our hesitancy in responding to public demands is really quite simple. The genesis of library computerization lies with the major network utilities where the systems have been developed to provide bibliographic data on discrete known items, with a major focus on monographs. The public computer catalog rides piggyback on this technology. In addition, we have given commercial vendors too free a hand in design and implementation of systems.

Margaret Beckman has recognized that we have not "always and naturally put the needs of library users first." Thus far the powers of the computer have been exploited for bibliographic record handling. Beckman identifies several system characteristics required by bibliographic networks and technical services librarians that may be at variance with the needs of the public, and that are, incidently, authoritarian in nature, e.g., "emphasis on standards, on structure, on authority files."

In contrast, Beckman contends the public wants access modes not necessarily similar to the capacities of the card catalog: rapid response time; inclusion of all library materials in one system; status information; and the ability to initiate interlibrary loan requests.[6] A system that satisfies both the information profession and those it serves may certainly be possible, but costs can become prohibitive. Choices regarding priorities are constantly being made and in the 1970s and early 1980s these choices have favored the bibliographic networks rather than the library patron. As a result, few OPACs include materials other than books and journals, while subject searching capabilities are often inadequate, simply mirroring the potentialities of the antiquated card catalog.

Selective Inclusion

The problems generated by selective inclusion of materials in the online catalog are exacerbated by the public's general assumption that if the catalog is a computer, then it must include *everything*. Thus, the information that many patrons retrieve may often be limited to that available in the OPAC. The situation further deteriorates because the OPAC "spoils" its users. The public (and librarians too) enjoy working with an OPAC while, in comparison, searching through paper indexes such as *Readers' Guide* or *Psychological Abstracts* is increasingly considered to be laborious and primitive. I have personally encountered patrons who are actually insulted when a librarian suggests they consult the old card catalog. Such "sophisticates" feel that antiquated resources are beneath their dignity and infringe on their valuable time. Are we unwittingly creating computer snobs who consider paper to be trash?

The major survey of use of online catalogs, which was sponsored by the CRL, clearly determined that increased subject searching capabilities are desired by a majority of users of OPACs in all types of libraries. Users want to search by keyword, view related words, and search by book contents or index.[7] In addition, Karen Markey points out that various research studies have indicated that 35 to 57.5 percent of subject searches initiated at the online catalog result in no retrievals.[8]

That about half of the searches people attempt by subject are totally unsuccessful is an appalling state of affairs. If libraries are to serve the information needs of the public, we must begin to reengineer our computerized facilities so that they are increasingly responsive to our clientele rather than to bibliographic network suppliers.

Privacy

Ben Shneiderman lists the invasion of privacy as one of the "Ten Plagues of the Information Age." Obviously, with "the concentration of information and powerful retrieval systems" the violation of privacy can be accomplished simply and efficiently. But, Shneiderman emphasizes, "well-designed computer systems have the potential of becoming more safe than paper systems if management is dedicated to privacy protection."[9] In the past few months, the library profession's awareness of privacy concerns generated by computerization has been heightened by the threats inherent in the "Poindexter Memorandum," rescinded by Frank Carlucci, then new Assistant to the President for National Security Affairs, now Secretary of Defense. The memorandum had authorized monitoring of the contents of commercial as well as federal databases in order to restrict the release of undefined "sensitive, but unclassified information."[10]

It is not only these headline issues that must concern us, however. Privacy issues surround the computer catalog. Patrons express concern that their research may be monitored through system transaction logs and, most obviously, the relatively large size of the computer monitor that broadcasts a patron's search to anyone who happens to be in the vicinity. In most libraries, OPAC terminals are in clusters and patrons waiting for an available terminal queue directly behind users. Libraries have effectively assured their clientele that OPAC transactions are not monitored in a manner that supports identification of individual users. However, a lack of vocal complaints to date has allowed librarians to largely ignore the drawbacks of the physical OPAC setting.

It is a relatively simple matter for library managers and public service personnel to provide a setting where patrons can feel secure regarding the privacy of their research. Clustered terminals have advantages in respect to support from fellow users, the provision of professional assistance, and a lessening of anxiety about the system itself. Thus, while we may not opt for total dispersal of terminals, we can easily provide somewhat isolated terminals for those who may desire privacy and design a computer catalog area that discourages those waiting for an available terminal from crowding users.

In regard to technical systems design, it is imperative, in order to maintain the trust of our patrons, that the electronic monitoring of terminals be minimal, especially in regard to terminals located outside the library where usage can be assigned to individuals. Transaction logs should not be retrievable except by authorized library personnel, and perhaps they should not be retained beyond a brief period.

Barriers to Access & Manipulation

That the computerization of libraries will assist in the breakdown of rigid divisions between public and technical services and lessen hierarchical administrative structures have been fervent hopes of many spokespersons in the profession. Michael Gorman, for example, contends that automated systems will allow librarians to be "ecumenical" and exercise skills over the full range of librarianship rather than be defined by restricted functions such as cataloging and reference.[11] However, a 1985 survey by the Association of Research Libraries indicates that little substantive reorganization of technical and public services is actually occurring in libraries beyond the utilization of technical services personnel at OPAC information/assistance stations.[12]

A concept of systems "ownership" continues to pervade most libraries. Technical services departments guard access and prohibit manipulation of the database in order to preserve its authority, consistency, efficiency, and reliability. Efforts to facilitate input by public services personnel in database content are generally viewed as "tampering." As a result, online catalogs remain quite similar to the standard card catalog lacking enhanced retrieval and non-standard access points.

A recent print symposium in *The Journal of Academic Librarianship* explored the issue of the role of the public service librarian vis-a-vis the actual online catalog database. Under consideration was whether the reference librarian should have the ability to manipulate the database, that is, add local subject headings, perhaps in natural language, edit errors, add notes, or add local files. While most participants agreed that public service personnel are the "key channels for user reaction" and thus should have input in the improvement of the database, they were exceedingly cautious about "giving them the authority to input and alter records."[13] Viewing "conformity to standards" as an ultimate criterion for the online catalog, Gail Persky is adamant that "a library's technical services staff should be solely responsible for creating and maintaining catalog records." However, she recognizes the insularity and the authoritative nature of her stance and thus recognizes the value of contributions from the reference staff:

> exercising quality control over [the online catalog] should be a participatory activity of all staff and hopefully of patrons as well. It is essential not to politicize the issue of who is in charge of taking care of the catalog.[14]

The issue of control of the online catalog formulates a clear-cut democratic vs. authoritarian dichotomy—our response and mode of resolution of this controversy will actualize our political philosophy. Simply by encouraging formalized interaction and establishing tasks related to the maintenance and improvement of the OPAC database that must be accomplished through an integration of technical and public service personnel, we can begin to eliminate an authoritative force within the library, stimulate democratic cooperation, and utilize all available expertise. How difficult or unwieldy would it be to have alterations in and additions to the OPAC explored and "decided" by an interdisciplinary group of technical and public service librarians rather than "ordained" by a specific department?

User Fees

The appearance of the computer catalog is equated in the minds of the public with the advent of the imposition of user fees by libraries. Fees for service represent the greatest and most obvious threat to democratic-liberal ideals resulting from computer technologies in libraries. There is little doubt that the computerization of libraries can be linked with the trend in our society toward the commercialization of information.

Trade database vendors and the federal government, especially in the Reagan years, have taken firm steps to limit access to information to those with the ability to pay. Information can now be readily merchandised since the computer so handily facilitates accurate determination of usage and accounting of costs. While the library profession is effectively attacking attempts by the government to privatize information agencies such as the National Technical Information Service (NTIS), we have been less vigilant against commercial practices within our own doors.

There is a perception among many in the library profession that since information is a valuable commodity, people should not expect to receive it free. The concept of fee-based services is also embraced by many librarians as a means of image augmentation. If our services are not free, but instead are at a premium, then we can escape the image of the lowly "public servant" and can become entrepreneurs or the powerful gatekeepers to the riches of the present information society.

The recent study sponsored by the National Commission on Libraries and Information Science, titled "The Role of Fees in Supporting Library Services in Public and Academic Libraries," rather revealingly lists as the *first* "pro-fee argument" that "charging fees increases recognition of the value and importance of library services." [15] While purporting to provide an objective overview of the fee issue, this study seems compromised since it has a distinct pro-fee bias and it assumes the equation of new technologies with the charging of fees. It is essential that we pause and thoughtfully consider whether we want the New York Public Library, for instance, to resemble a branch of Macy's or to remain a hall of learning accessible to all members of society regardless of income, race, educational level, or age.

Many libraries are now providing elite pay services aimed at lucrative clientele. For example, Drexel University Library's new Executive Library Service (ExelLS), designed for the business and research community, sets fees for specific informational requests and provides extended research by subject specialist librarians. The ExelLS coordinator has extolled the service: "Every attempt is made to operate as if it were our own business. Client satisfaction is a major objective. ExelLS will attempt to acquire the tools needed to provide better and more efficient delivery of materials and perform the most precise research." [16] While such aggressive ventures may provide the library with revenue, they represent a troubling transformation—*access* to information is replaced by *merchandising* of information. When the library becomes a business concern, it loses its role as neutral preserver and provider of information.

A major reason libraries have gravitated toward fee-for-service exploits is the high cost of automated systems technologies. In 1983, Rosemary Anderson estimated that the costs of an online catalog in "a small academic library of 500,000 unique titles, 1000 journal subscriptions, and 50 terminals" would be "$805,000 for the first year" and "$192,286 per year" to maintain the system. She points out that when such figures are compared to a library's annual budget, "these systems are taking a large share of the library's finances. Online catalogs are not money saving devices." [17]

Oscar Handlin expresses some indignation at the prevalent assumption in libraries that the computer would lower costs through network collaboration and increased efficiency. He bluntly contends that "neither course opened a road to salvation."

Imaginations leaped eagerly forward to visions of completely electronic libraries; and the states of Ohio and Washington, along with such universities as Stanford, Chicago, Penn State, and Northwestern launched ambitious and expensive schemes for mechanization . . . none significantly lowered costs.[18]

While we may not acquiesce to Hanlin's sweeping indictment of the shortcomings of research libraries, we must recognize that libraries are increasingly being viewed by the society they serve as another democratic institution in the midst of a transition to a commercial enterprise.

Brown University is currently one of several institutions well entrenched in the development of an electronic campus through its "Scholar's Workstation Project" in which students and faculty have access to information via their personal computers wired in a local area network. University librarian Merrily E. Taylor is concerned about the effects of computerization on the library's budget and the changing role of the library:

> Considerable thought is also being devoted to whether it will be possible to go on providing all library services without charging patrons. Currently, Brown charges students and faculty for online computer database searching, but at a subsidized rate. There is a great resistance on the part of most librarians to charging students directly for other library services, especially since it already costs approximately $15,000 a year to attend Brown. Their strong preference is to insure that all students have access to the information they need without regard to their ability to pay. Whether this resolve can be maintained at Brown has yet to be decided.[19]

That the fee issue is many faceted and generates decided opinions and emotions is demonstrated by the special theme issue of the journal *Collection Building*, titled *Fees for Library Service: Current Practice & Future Policy*. It presents a broad spectrum of response from academic and public librarians, library science educators, and association and industry executives. The range of opinion is equally diverse. Malcolm Getz, director of libraries at Vanderbilt University, sees the issue from a resource allocation point of view. He believes the provision of electronic databases for "all comers at no cost" is a waste. His reasoning reveals a narrow vision: "Low-income persons may concentrate their expenditures more heavily on food and shelter and spend less on libraries. Because food and shelter are more urgent needs of the poor, spending our social resources to provide enhanced library services that are little used by the poor seems not to serve the poor very well."[20]

In contrast, Louise Berry, director of the Darien Public Library (Ct.), is concerned that certain fees jeopardize the institutional mandate of the public library: "User fees which place a barrier between the citizen and the information he or she seeks from a public library violate the mission of the library." And furthermore, she contends, "the imposition of fees nearly always brings pressure to impose fees on other 'special' services, ranging from story hours for children to the lending of very popular books and best sellers."[21]

The Integrity of Knowledge

Carlton C. Rochell, dean of libraries at New York University, urges the profession to use its "information assets," including electronic networks, to protect and preserve information resources that are increasingly threatened by commercialization. He notes that even information collected at taxpayers' expense is now disseminated by commercial databases and therefore is no longer free to the public. In addition, private enterprise will preserve what is profitable and discard anything without immediate utility. With wisdom, Rochell advocates a position that protects the integrity of accumulated knowledge:

> What better use can be made of our profitable assets than to support the preservation of those with little commercial appeal. Surely we cannot allow the creation, dissemination, and preservation of knowledge to become a decision of the marketplace.[22]

Libraries, while at the center of the "informatization of society," must, as noncommercial, *public* institutions, strive to preserve our intellectual heritage and aggressively seize influence in the management of information sources to insure that they are maintained and made increasingly accessible to society at large. Charges for "specialized" services, computer searches, printouts at computer catalogs, etc., will not enrich the library, instead they may impoverish the institution.

The delineation of certain democratic and authoritarian tendencies of the computer catalog reveals that this technology certainly has a "political" nature. It is well within our purview to resolutely encourage and augment its democratic potentialities while deemphasizing and eliminating its authoritarian traits. By stimulating a political awareness of this one technology, it is hoped that a similar consideration of other aspects of the electronic library, such as management structure and the role of networks, will also receive scrutiny. Some words of wisdom from Lewis Mumford, which seem particularly apropos of the electronic library, provide a fitting conclusion:

> we had better map out a more positive course: namely, the reconstitution of both our science and our technics in such a fashion as to insert the rejected parts of the human personality at every stage in the process. This means gladly sacrificing mere quantity in order to restore qualitative choice, shifting the seat of authority from the mechanical collective to the human personality . . . favoring variety and ecological complexity, instead of stressing undue uniformity and standardization, above all, reducing the insensate drive to extend the system itself, instead of containing it within definite human limits.[23]

References

1. Schuman, Patricia Glass, "Library Networks: a Means, Not an End," *LJ*, Feb. 1, 1987, p. 33-37.
2. Winner, Langdon, "Mythinformation," in his *The Whale and the Reactor: a Search for Limits in an Age of High Technology.* Univ. of Chicago Pr., 1986, p. 109.
3. Matthews, Joseph R. *Public Access to Online Catalogs.* 2d ed. Neal-Schuman, 1985.
4. Arret, Linda, "Can Online Catalogs Be Too Easy?," *American Libraries*, Feb. 1985, p. 118-120.
5. Matthews, Joseph R., Gary S. Lawrence, & Douglas K. Ferguson. *Using Online Catalogs: a Nationwide Survey.* Neal-Schuman, 1983.
6. Beckman, Margaret M., "Online Catalogs and Library Users," *LJ*, Nov. 1, 1982, p. 2043-47.
7. Matthews, Lawrence, & Ferguson, p. 134.
8. Markey, Karen, "Users of the Online Catalog: Subject Access Problems," in Matthews, Joseph R., ed. *The Impact of Online Catalogs.* Neal-Schuman, 1986, p. 60.
9. Shneiderman, Ben. *Designing the User Interface: Strategies for Effective Human-Computer Interaction.* Addison-Wesley, 1987, p. 428.
10. "NSC, Pentagon Spin Web of Restricted Access," *American Libraries*, Feb. 1987, p. 109; and "'Poindexter Memorandum' Dumped After Forum," *American Libraries*, Apr. 1987, p. 238.
11. Gorman, Michael, "The Ecumenical Librarian," *Reference Librarian*, Fall/Winter 1983, p. 55-64.
12. Association of Research Libraries, Office of Management Studies. *Automation and Reorganization of Technical and Public Services.* Spec kit 112, ARL, 1985.
13. "Tampering with the Online Catalog: a Look at the Issues—a Symposium," *Journal of Academic Librarianship*, Jan. 1987, p. 340-349.
14. *Ibid.*, p. 344.
15. National Commission on Libraries and Information Science, "The Role of Fees in Supporting Library and Information Services in Public and Academic Libraries," *Collection Building*, No. 1, 1986, p. 9.
16. "Drexel Claims Success with Library Service for Pay," *LJ Hotline*, Mar. 30, 1987, p. 2.
17. Anderson, Rosemary, "The Online Catalog and the Library Manager," in Matthews, Joseph R., ed. *The Impact of Online Catalogs.* Neal-Schuman, 1986, p. 75-76.
18. Handlin, Oscar, "Libraries and Learning," *American Scholar*, Spring 1987, p. 209-210.
19. Moran, Barbara B., Thomas T. Suprenant, & Merrily E. Taylor, "The Electronic Campus: the Impact of the Scholar's Workstation Project on the Libraries at Brown," *College and Research Libraries*, Jan. 1987, p. 15.
20. Getz, Malcolm, "The Usefulness of Fees for Library Services," *Collection Building*, No. 1, 1986, p. 20.
21. Berry, Louise, "A Short-Term and Short-Sighted Solution = User Fees," *Collection Building*, No. 1, 1986, p. 25-26.
22. Rochell, Carlton C., "The Next Decade: Distributed Access to Information," *LJ*, Feb. 1, 1987, p. 48.
23. Mumford, Lewis, "Authoritarian and Democratic Technics," *Technology and Culture*, Winter 1964, p. 8.

THE TIME IS RIGHT TO AUTOMATE

Catherine Murphy

In 1988, automation of the card catalog has become a reality for many school library media centers. In 1985, when I was conducting research on the standardization of cataloging in microcomputer online public access catalogs (OPACS) in school library media centers, I found that only about 160 school sites with stand-alone circulation and catalog systems could be identified by vendors selling to this market in the United States and Canada.[1] The reasons for today's increased interest in automation can be attributed to technological developments that permit easier use of systems, expanded capabilities in searching and reporting, and interfaces between stand-alone microcomputers and distributed networks or compact disks. In addition to these improvements in the technology, vendors are providing services for retrospective conversion, providing options that are geared to different budgets in the school market.

It is barely 10 years since the Apple was introduced in 1978, presenting an alternative to automation that was affordable for small libraries. The big online circulation systems had been introduced into university and other large libraries in the early 1970's and several years later some of these systems had grown into online catalogs for the public, influenced by the growth of online Machine Readable Cataloging (MARC) databases available from bibliographic networks and utilities, e.g., the Online Computer Library Center, Inc. (OCLC).[2] But, almost exclusively, the OPACS were turnkey systems developed by vendors into complete packages of hardware, software, training, and support. The minicomputer systems were too powerful and expensive for most school library media centers or any small library to consider. By 1981, *Computer Cat* was developed by the Costas for an elementary media center in Mountain View, Colorado,[3] and soon after that, there were a number of scaled-down OPACS designed for the microcomputer.

The early software for microcomputer catalogs promised new directions for school library media centers via improved library management and enhanced services to clientele. Most of the systems were essentially replicas of the card catalog, with searching options limited to first word or letters of the author, title and subject, perhaps with other fields available in the non-public mode. Few of these stand-alone microcomputer OPACS offered key word or Boolean searching, processing was slow, and conversion of card records to electronic format was limited to manual data entry. In the last seven years, the technology has advanced, and the market has been tested enough by both vendors and school library media specialists, to have caused an increase in sales of both microcomputer stand-alone systems and distributed network systems.

Although it is difficult to get exact figures for these sales, a few microcomputer systems vendors estimate their numbers of users in the thousands, while a number of others report hundreds of sales. It is probable that at this time there are 10,000 automated circulation and/or catalog sites in schools.

School library media specialists must plan carefully for automation, considering global issues as well as specialized needs, not only to participate in the automation revolution but to take a leading role. As sales increase, the market is correspondingly anxious to meet those special needs.

PREPARING FOR AUTOMATION

The items which follow are a broad checklist of the considerations in planning for any automated system. Knowledge of these issues should be expanded by reading the literature, examining different systems at conferences, or perhaps through purchasing demo disks, and finally, when the selection process has narrowed the choice, those systems should be reviewed in greater detail at a school site using the program.

1. Standards. There is only one standard for bibliographic records, the *Anglo-American Cataloguing Rules,* 2nd Edition (AACR2), which includes the format for MARC records. School library media centers were not early subscribers to cataloging standards, evidenced in the research of Rogers and Truett and attributed to school library media specialists' lack of training in cataloging, lack of support staff in the building, and/or lack of endorsement by state supervisors.[4] The development of online catalogs in school library media centers which might be interfaced in multilibrary networks focused new attention on the school library media specialists' lack of awareness of mainstream standards. The fact that record conversion to electronic format in the pioneer days of microcomputer OPAC development was largely accomplished by keying in all data from shelf-list cards at the local site did not contribute favorably to adherence to standards. My doctoral research, mentioned earlier, confirmed that the lack of awareness of cataloging standards which existed in the card catalog era had been continued into the microcomputer online age; by contrast, those schools belonging to bibliographic utilities and networks were influenced to conform to cataloging standards.

All of this has changed in 1988. The microcomputer stand-alone systems, as well as the minicomputer systems, provide for storage of the full MARC record although vendors' claims for data storage should be verified. Automated system vendors as well as specialized data conversion vendors offer varied retrospective conversion options. There are still a few microcomputer software systems on the market which do not conform to the mainstream standard for bibliographic records and these programs should not even be considered for purchase.

2. Networking. Multi-library networking offers to members various cataloging and interlibrary loan services as well as union catalog products that are online, on microfiche or in CD-ROM format. School library media centers participate in many state and regional networks but only those which are automated provide direction, and sometimes financial support, in the development of local cataloging and OPACS. Examples of these automated database networks are Access Pennsylvania's LE PAC, Wisconsin's WISCAT, Minnesota's TIES, and the Western Library Network's LASER CAT. Just as critical is local area networking, the cabling of terminals in an onsite multi-user system, which has just come of age. (Recent technology allows several different stations to access the database simultaneously.) This development permits processing in one location and public access from several terminals in another area. It is also possible (though still in the experimental stage) to customize network software to access from the same menu both a MARC record online catalog database and a non-Marc record database of perhaps a film collection.

3. Hardware—Micro or Mini. The debate is between a system with terminals linked to a remote bibliographic database or a microcomputer stand-alone system (IBM, or more recently, Macintosh). There is usually a correlation between large school districts and extensive computer systems because of the greater cost of a distributed bibliographic network, but sometimes there are joint school and public library automation projects which favor the selection of an online system by a smaller school. The smaller library usually chooses a microcomputer system because both the start-up and maintenance programs are less expensive. The greatest advantage of the online system is that it has the most current database, but the distinctions between the two types of systems are blurring as the technology provides for off-line, more frequently updated databases on compact disks which can be interfaced with different computer systems.

4. Cost. Cost includes software and peripherals such as a bar wand or scanner, as well as hardware, but even more significantly, the retrospective conversion of the library's shelflist to machine readable cataloging. Once the decision is made between minicomputer and microcomputer systems, there are further variations in the price of single- and multi-user networks, software programs, and retrospective conversion options. There are also vendor charges for yearly maintenance and support. The budget for automation should be based on planned obsolescence of hardware (perhaps 20% replacement cost per year over a period of five years) and software updates (change is constant as the vendor receives input from users and also tries to be competitive). An important aspect of the budget should be a one-time retrospective conversion of records, which may be transferred to a different system as needs change (this incurs far less expense than re-entry of data). It should be remembered, however, that automation does not usually save money. The result of automation is an improvement in services. This improvement justifies any increase in costs.

5. *Order of conversion.* Many more circulation systems than public access catalogs have been sold, but this is changing. It was considered less costly and easier to begin automating by typing in a brief bibliographic record for a circulation system, than to develop full bibliographic records for a public access catalog. Because the program vendors, as well as companies dealing strictly with retrospective conversion, are providing more options, school library media centers are now just as likely to begin automating by developing a database of records which can be accessed for different functions in an integrated system. Automating circulation facilitates the handling and inventory of materials but also encourages use analysis for collection development. The automation of the catalog provides greater access to materials because of improved searching options and indexing. Circulation and catalog modules are the two major components of an integrated system but acquisitions, serials, and inventory modules may be added. Data is shared between modules where needed.

6. *Retrospective conversion.* The vendors can provide brief records for a circulation system or full MARC records for a catalog. Vendors can do all of the data entry from the library's shelflist or they can supply a software program which the school library media specialist uses to identify a title. The data entry disks are then forwarded to the vendor to be expanded into full MARC records. Alternatively, the school library media specialist can pull partial or full records into a circulation system or catalog by using a CD-ROM database of Library of Congress MARC records or a shared union catalog of MARC records, or they may use an online bibliographic utility. The cost of retrospective conversion will vary according to the method and how much data the vendor provides. Current records for new acquisitions may also be downloaded to the local database from a network terminal or compact disc, or they may be secured in the MicroLIF format provided on floppy disks by book suppliers (along with bar-coded books). The MicroLIF format was cooperatively developed by the micro-

computer circulation system vendors and a number of major book suppliers including Baker & Taylor, Brodart, and Follett.

When considering options for retrospective conversions, it is wise to plan for archival copies of the library's full MARC records to be stored on magnetic tapes or disks. The companies which specialize in retrospective conversion will hold those archival copies in-house; the vendors of circulation and catalog software may deliver the converted records but once these are loaded into the system, it is possible that they will be altered and will no longer be complete MARC records. The rule is to keep a separate set of archival tapes or disks somewhere outside of the system.

7. Non-print bibliographic records. Because school library media center collections have more audiovisual materials than most other kinds of libraries, the lack of MARC records for these materials has been a particular problem. This will change as more schools participate in statewide library systems which develop union catalogs. The records for audiovisual materials in these catalogs might be made available by an enterprising distributor. Several school districts in Maryland are sharing their audiovisual cataloging by sending floppy disks to their vendor, Library Corporation, Inc., who returns the combined cataloging to each site for downloading into the *Intelligent Catalog* system.[5]

8. Reputation of the vendor. There are continuous changes in the automation market and it is wise to select a system that has been on the market for a while. This ensures that there are a number of users and that the bugs in the program have been worked out. Some vendors have a nationwide, as well as international, network of users who may be contacted by beginning users. Most vendors distribute newsletters which also connect users. There should also be telephone support available from the vendor during the workday, via a toll-free number.

9. Integration of school library software with school management software. One of the newer developments in this area is the marketing of library management programs by some of the companies that offer school management software. This increases the likelihood that some school library media centers will be automated because school records are computerized (perhaps it will also work the other way). The two programs can be integrated to facilitate the exchange of student data or the collection of overdue fines, for example. It is also technically possible to interface two different hardware and software systems—a school management program from one company with a library management program from another company—if a link is programmed to enable the exchange of necessary data.

10. Subject Access. The real revolution in online catalogs must be in improved subject access for users; otherwise, the investment of resources in automation does little more than replicate the card catalog. Improved subject access means, to begin with, access to fields not conventionally indexed, such as call number, notes, and copyright as well as the author, title, and subject. Key word and Boolean searching options increase the retrieval of subject information. Online help menus, location maps, and audio tutors can guide the user from one step of the search to the next step.

Some vendors are providing online indexes which link to the MARC record to create even greater access. Authority files for author's names and subject heading are important and have been standard in the big online systems for some time. Tables of contents and first pages of documents might also be linked to the main record. Enhancements to the record itself include local additions in the notes field such as curriculum units and grade and reading levels. Some vendors are providing or are planning to implement a number of these enhancements in microcomputer OPACS.

THE MARKETPLACE

Table 1 indicates microcomputer stand-alone systems which school library media centers are purchasing. Follett Library Software Company is the leader in this field, followed by Winnebago, and there are several new entries and one merger.

Table 2 lists four online systems which have also gained some of the school market; although, according to this author's survey, it is a small share (this information is comparable to a report in a recent article about the library automation market place).[6] More companies marketing retrospective conversion services are also appealing to the microcomputer market, as Table 3 shows.

SURVEY

Media specialists and directors were contacted by telephone or at the American Library Association Conference in New Orleans, LA in July 1988 and asked what their school district automation status was at the time. They were also requested to define their task for the next several years. The respondents are in school districts of varying sizes and represent different approaches to automation, from development of a microcomputer stand-alone system to a minicomputer shared network. [See Table 4.]

SOME FINAL SUGGESTIONS

It is apparent that there are some universal suggestions which all school library media specialists wishing to automate circulation and/or the catalog may wish to consider: become informed about the market by reading and attending conferences; learn what is going on with automation at the state and regional level which may affect local decision-making; analyze the resources of the school district in terms of the budget, staff, expertise, and

TABLE 1
Microcomputer Integrated Systems

Vendor	Hardware	Modules/Price	Notes
Charles Clark Co., Inc. 170 Keyland Court Bohemia, NY 11716 (800) 247-7009; (516) 589-6643	IBM & compatibles	Molli Circ/Catalog $1500; Circulation only $750; Multi-User System $2495; Marc Utility $200	Vendor conversion options
Columbia Computing Services, 8101 E. Prentice Ave. Englewood, CO 80111 (303) 773-6440; (800) 663-0544	IBM & compatibles	Columbia Library System Circulation $1095; Catalog $1325; Acquisitions $1325; Serials $545; MARC Records Interface $545	Formerly *Ocelot*; school adm. programs also sold; conversion options
CASPR (Computer Advance Software (Products), 10311 S. De Anza Blvd., Cupertino, CA 95014 (408) 446-3075	Macintosh	Mac Library System $1695 single user, $4995 multi user plus $195 per terminal; MacCards (library card & label production system) $169	New; a few school users
COMpanion Consulting Corp., 10101 Bubb Rd. Cupertino, CA 95014 (408) 446-9779	Macintosh	Mac Book, Mac Book II, and Mac Book II Plus, $995 to $5995 depending on circulation, cataloging or catalog, single or multi-user options	New; several schools in CA; online bulletin board, almanac and support
Data Trek, Inc. 167 Saxony Road Encinitas, CA 92024 (619) 436-5055; (800) 876-5484	IBM & compatibles	Card Datalog Circulation $995; Card Datalog Catalog $995; Card Datalog Acquisitions $995; Card Datalog Serials $995; $2495 for 3 modules (special prices for schools; will change 12/31/88)	Databridge MARC Conversion & Ultimate Searching Module (very flexible)
Follett Library Software 4506 NW Highway Crystal Lake, IL 60014 (815) 455-4660; (800) 323-3397	IBM & compatibles (Apple-Cir Plus only)	Circ Plus $995; Cat Plus $795 until 12/31, $1295 thereafter; Textbook Plus $1695 (software only)	Vendor conversion options; enhanced bibliographic records, e.g. grade level
Library Automation Products, 875 Avenue of the Americas New York, NY 10001 (212) 967-7440	IBM & compatibles	The Assistant $6,270; Individual modules, single user $1800, multi user $2500 (Acq., Cat., Circ., & Serials)	Most libraries are corporate or special, a few schools.
Library Corp., Inc. One Research Park Inwood, WV 25428 (304) 229-0100; (800) 624-0559	Hardware Inc. with software for catalog; IBM & compatibles for circulation and catalog maintenance	Bibliofile Intelligent Catalog $2770; Bibliofile Circulation (w/o hardware) $3500 one time; Bibliofile Catalog Maintenance $975 one time	In-house conversion/ vendor updating; Enhanced Bibliofile for proc. centers

TABLE 1 (Continued)
Microcomputer Integrated Systems

Vendor	Hardware	Modules/Price	Notes
Media Flex, Inc. P.O. Box #1107 Champlain, NY 12919 (518) 298-2970	IBM & compatibles	Mandarin on-line circulation & catalog system $2500; Multi-user option $3000 per site	Very flexible database. Spindle dataconversion program; multi-lingual commands
Utlas Corp. 80 Bloor St. West Toronto, Ontario Canada M5S 2V1 (416) 923-0890	IBM & compatibles	MSeries 10 license fees are: Circulation $3375; Catalog $2700 for multi-users, plus other costs for software database set-up and maintenance, per site	Online cataloging and retrospective conversion services
Winnebago Software 121 So. Marshall Caledonia, MN 55921 (507) 724-5411	IBM & compatibles	Winnebago Circ. $995; Winnebago Cat. $995 (combined offer $1695 until 12/31/88)	Vendor conversion options

This is a representative list of vendors who exhibited at the 1988 conference of the American Library Association; other microcomputer programs used by school library media centers are also available. All prices quoted, current as of July 1988, are subject to change.

TABLE 2
Microcomputer Integrated Systems

Vendor	Notes
CLSI, Inc., 320 Nevada Street Newtonville, MA 02160 (800) 225-3076; (617) 965-6310	Carmel Clay, Indiana. (No information available about total number of installations in schools.)
Dynix, Inc., 151 East 1700 South Provo, UT 84601 (801) 375-2770	25 school district sites in a Dynix list of installations available by request; includes Provo Public Schools and Jefferson County (KY) Public Schools; others mostly in British Isles and Australia
INLEX, Inc., 1900 Garden Road, P.O. Box 1349, Monterey, CA 93942 (800) 553-1202	Response to telephone inquiry indicates about 5 school district installations.
NOTIS Systems, Inc., 1007 Church St., 2d fl., Evanston, IL 60201 (312) 866-0150	Wichita (KS) Public Schools. Response to telephone inquiry indicates that they are in a few districts.
UTLAS (see Table 1)	Stand-alone microcomputer system as well as other configurations

All systems have modules for other functions, including circulation and the catalog. Online cataloging is directly available from a shared network base and from a bibliographic utility link. The minimum startup costs for a school system, quoted by most vendors, ranged from $50,000 to $60,000, but, depending on the number of services and terminals required, the cost could be much higher.

TABLE 3
Retrospection Conversion Services

Vendor	Services
Amigos Bibliographic Council, Inc. 11300 North Central Expressway, Suite 321, Dallas, TX 75243 (214) 750-6130	Retrospective conversion on OCLC's MICROCON or on MicroSHARES for numeric searching.
Brodart Automation 500 Arch Street Williamsport, PA 17705 (800) 233-8467	Vendor shelflist and tape conversions, MicroCheck, MITINET and the Interactive Access System for ongoing cataloging.
The Computer Co. 1905 Westmoreland Street Richmond, VA 23230 (800) 446-2612; (804) 254-2357	Data integration, retrospective conversion online and with micros, magnetic tape upgrades, bar coding, microfiche and CD-ROM catalogs.
Automation Division Catalog Card Corp., P.O. Box 1276 Burnsville, MN 55337 (800) 328-2923	Retrospective conversion to MARC records with Library of Congress or Sears headings, circulation records. Complete conversions from shelflist and new acquisitions.
Information Transform 502 Leonard Street Madison, WI 53711 (608) 255-4800	MITINET software for retrospective conversions and ongoing cataloging
Marcive, Inc., P.O. Box 47508 San Antonio, TX 78265 (512) 646-6161	Conversions from shelflist, written lists and Cataloging Input System for IBM, Apple Skip or PC Skip software. Transmission of records online by modem, or by diskette or magnetic tape. Marcive/PAC microcomputer catalog available.

Retrospective conversion may be handled directly by the vendor of the automation system or bibliographic records may be transferred from an in-house CD-ROM database of MARC records or online from a shared bibliographic network. Per title costs will vary from 15¢ to more than $1, depending on the vendor's price and options.

TABLE 4
Schools Automating Circulation/Catalog

District/School	Respondent		Circulation	Catalog	Future Task
Brookline (MA) Public Schools	(9)	C. Markuson	Winnebago Circ. in high school (HS)	Winnebago Cat. in HS	Complete auto. other schools/ union catalog
Broward County (FL) Public Schools	(170)	J. Klasing	Book Trak in 48 schools	(Book Trak has category searching)	Complete auto. other schools/ union catalog
Carmel Clay (IN) Public Schools	(9)	K. Niemeyer	CLSI in HS	CLSI in HS/Public Library; OCLC for cataloging	Complete auto. other schools/ INTELNET for interlibrary loan
Concord (CA) Public Schools	(37)	R. Skapura	Circ Plus in two HS (one is the original test site for Circ Plus)	Card catalog	Complete development of Circ Plus
Glen Ellyn (IL) Public Schools	(5)	D. Adcock	Circ Plus in junior high school (JHS)	Card catalog	Circ Plus in 4 elem. schools

TABLE 4. *Continued*
Schools Automating Circulation/Catalog

District/School		Respondent	Circulation	Catalog	Future Task
Greensboro (NC) Public Schools	(38)	J. Davie	Circ Plus 10 secondary, 1 elementary	OCLC for cataloging and interlibrary loan	Consider Circ Plus for other schools; plan for Cat Plus
Henrico County (VA) Public Schools	(52)	E. Browning	Pueblo Library System in 7 HS (designed for Henrico)	Pueblo in HS/ Public Library	Complete auto. other schools
Madison (WI)	(32+)	C. Cain	Circ Plus in HS	Cat Plus in HS (was test site)	Circ Plus and Cat Plus in all HS/MS, then elem. schools
Provo (UT) Public Schools	(16)	K. Berner	Dynix 2 in HS, 2 in MS	Dynix 2 HS, 2 MS with Public Library; OCLC for cataloging	Extend Dynix to other schools, plan collection development
Robbinsdale (MN) Public Schools	(17)	B. Nemer	Winnebago Circ in 11 elementary schools	Bibliofile to get ready for conversion of catalogs in 6 HS	Complete auto. other schools/ union catalog
Sante Fe (NM) Indian School	(1)	A. McGrattan	Card circulation	Intelligent Catalog for Indian collection	Complete conversion of collection; auto. circ.
Shoreham/Wading River (NY) Public Schools	(5)	J. Bennett	Mandarin in HS; Utlas MSeries 10 in MS; Book Trak in MS; Utlas MSeries 10 in elem. schools	Same as circulation (database developed on Utlas)	Develop multiuser network, interface HS catalog and nonMARC CD-ROM ERIC, Info Trac, etc.
Stamford (CT) Public Schools	(17)	E. Kogan	Circ Plus in elem. schools	CLSI terminal access to public lib. from HS, pilot site for Project Amoeba (CT interlibrary loan database on CD-ROM)	Complete plan for automating schools
Tower Hill School, Wilmington (DE)	(1)	N. Minnich	Circ Plus in Upper and Lower Schools	Intelligent Catalog in Upper School, Bibliofile for conversion	Auto, based collection development for curriculum
Wichita (KS) Public Schools	(105)	J. Meyers	Card circulation	Notis at 51 schools, links in HS to Wichita State Univ. Notis catalog	Put other elementary schools online, auto. circ.

motivation necessary to implement an automated system; follow standards for retrospective conversion and new acquisitions of bibliographic records; and finally, form a committee in the school which involves all of the participants in planning for site automation. It is necessary to add that the technology is constantly changing and everyone must be aware of the inevitability that systems will become obsolete. On the other hand, this is an exciting time to automate because the technology, while costly, at last promises to deliver real improvements in the managing, indexing, and retrieval of library materials.

REFERENCES

1. Murphy, Catherine. *Microcomputer Stand-Alone Online Public Access Catalogs: Practices and Attitudes of School Library Media Specialists Toward Standardization.* Doctoral dissertation, Columbia University, 1987.
2. Seal, Alan, ed. *Introducing the Online Catalogue: Papers Based on Seminars Held in 1983.* Bath: University of Bath, 1984.
3. Costa, Betty and Marie Costa. "Microcomputer in Colorado—It's Elementary." *Wilson Library Bulletin* 58 (May 1981): 676-678+.
4. Rogers, JoAnn V. "Mainstreaming Media Center Materials: Adopting AACR2." *School Library Journal* 27 (April 1981): 31. Truett, Carol. "Is Cataloging a Passe Skill in Today's Technological Society?" *Library Resources & Technical Services* 28 (July/September 1984): 268-275.
5. "Networking a CD-ROM system: Bibliofile in Maryland," *Library Journal* (February 15, 1987): 96.
6. Walton, Robert A. and Frank R. Bridge. "Automated System Marketplace, 1987: Maturity and Competition." *Library Journal* 113 (April 1, 1988): 33-43.

PART VI:
LIBRARY PROFESSIONALS

COMPARABLE WORTH IN LIBRARIES: A LEGAL ANALYSIS

Nancy P. Johnson

I. Introduction

Despite opposition from corporate America, hostility from the Reagan administration, and the reluctance of the judiciary to embrace many of the legal arguments advanced by proponents, the comparable worth movement refuses to lie down and play dead. The chair of the United States Civil Rights Commission, Clarence Pendleton, made headlines in 1985 when he characterized comparable worth as "the looniest idea since Looney Tunes came on the screen."[1] The Reagan administration has warned that comparable worth could have disastrous budget implications, and some private employers dismiss it as a crude disruption of free-market mechanisms that will wreak havoc in the workplace.

On its face, the concept of comparable worth is a simple enough proposition: pay employees the same amount of money for jobs of comparable worth. *Power v. Barry County, Mich.* offers a succinct definition of the comparable worth concept:

> Although there are many definitions of comparable worth, the quintessential element common to all is that discrimination exists when workers of one sex in one job category are paid less than workers of the other sex in another job category and both categories are performing work that is not the same in content, but is of "comparable worth" to the employer in terms of value and necessity.[2]

As an example, while the job performed by a female city librarian is totally different from that performed by a male city planner, a comparable worth analysis might reveal that the work performed by the librarian was worth the same to the employer as the work performed by the city planner.

"Comparable Worth in Libraries: A Legal Analysis" by Nancy P. Johnson in *Law Library Journal* Vol. 79, no. 3 (1987), pp. 367-386; reprinted with permission from the *Law Library Journal*.

If the librarian received less pay than the city planner, a violation of the law would occur, and the librarian would be entitled to the difference between what her job was worth and the lower wage that she actually received. Hence, the comparable worth concept is not limited to a comparison of the work itself, but applies also to a comparison of the measures of worth.

Critics say the idea is conceptually flawed and utterly impractical. They contend that it is impossible to set up objective criteria that determine whether a librarian should be paid as much as a planner. One critic states, "In a complex economy, 'fairness' is a fictional ideal. Your pay reflects luck, skill, the supply and demand for different jobs, whether or not you work for a profitable firm or in a profitable industry, or whether you belong to a union. Fairness has little to do with it." [3]

This article focuses on the issue of comparable worth as it relates to librarianship. Librarianship, a profession that is 80 percent female, is a prime example of a sex-segregated occupation.[4] Low salaries are the rule for the library profession, and have been since the nineteenth century, when it was one of the few professions open to women. Librarians claim that they are paid less than other professions with the same or lower educational and skill requirements. Librarians also claim that since they are members of a female-dominated profession, they are paid less than the value of their work should dictate. Within the library profession, the positions of greater power and prestige are held predominantly by males.

These discriminatory factors have led to efforts to secure change through litigation and legislation. This article examines the factual patterns and legal theories of wage discrimination cases to determine their applicability to the library profession. Since the future of comparable worth is shifting to collective bargaining and state legislative actions, these activities are discussed in the final section.

II. Recognition of the Problem: The Wage Gap

The impetus behind comparable worth is grounded in at least one marketplace reality: women make less money than men. In 1955, according to a National Research Council study, women earned sixty-three cents for every dollar men earned.[5] The gap between women's and men's income increased during the 1970s, when women's average earnings dropped to 58 percent of men's.[6] The most recent government data shows that the average female full-time worker earns about sixty-four cents for every dollar earned by men, as calculated on an hourly basis.[7] This statistic remained the same as in 1983. Men working year round in 1985 had median earnings of $24,200, while the median for women was $15,620.[8]

Although these statistics show that women as a class earn lower wages than men as a class, the statistic alone cannot prove the existence of sex discrimination in wages. Therefore, in this article I examine the historical background of librarians as wage earners and the legitimate reasons for wage disparities (i.e., experience, skill, supervisory status, and educational requirements) to explain the reasons for pay inequities.

III. Economic Conditions of Librarianship

It has been 109 years since Justin Winsor, an early leader of the library profession, said at a librarian's conference in London that American libraries "set a high value on women's work. They soften our atmosphere, they lighten our labor, they are equal to our work, and for the money they cost . . . they are infinitely better than equivalent salaries will produce of the opposite sex."[9] In 1981, Jack Herrity, chairman of the Fairfax County, Virginia Board of Supervisors, put it a bit more bluntly when confronted with a charge of sex discrimination: "If you can buy librarians or anything else at a cheaper price, you're going to do it."[10]

Women were recruited into librarianship in the late nineteenth century. At that time it was one of the few professions that well-educated women could pursue. The cultural aspect of library work was supposed to compensate for the fact that women earned only half of what men in the profession earned. Melvil Dewey, the "father" of modern library science, recruited college women as a cheap source of literate labor for tangible and practical reasons.[11] In its early years, librarianship was called "Library Economy": library resources were scarce and the need for education was great. Operating under severe financial constraints, libraries sought ways to maximize their limited resources, and employing women was one way to do this. Librarianship, then, was open to women not because librarians had a progressive attutide toward affirmative action, but because libraries needed to keep costs down. The lower wages paid to women were not challenged in the nineteenth century, and lower salaries have stayed the rule. The average entry level position, a job that typically requires a master's degree, starts at less than $20,000 a year.[12] In 1985, the average beginning level salary of both men and women librarians was $19,753.[13] With the market for librarians expected to grow by only five percent between 1980 and 1990,[14] the possibility of substantially higher salaries seems slim. Women with valuable skills and graduate degrees cannot afford to stay in library work and are looking for higher paying fields.

In recent years, researchers have examined why some professions pay less than others.[15] It has been shown that the more an occupation is dominated by women, the less it pays. For example, for the year 1976, one study showed that the occupations of educators (including librarians), social workers, nurses, clerical, service, and private household workers were comprised of more than 70 percent women.[16] In 1983, the United States Department of Labor reported similar findings.[17] These studies indicate that many women workers continue to be concentrated in a smaller number of occupations; this is called "occupational crowding." Occupational crowding causes salaries to be driven down: employers pay lower salaries because the labor market will tolerate it.

Some sociologists claim that women voluntarily seek jobs that are less demanding, have a lower level of responsibility, and, hence, are lower paying.[18] Although women are committed to participating and staying in the labor force, they are even more committed to values and practices that center around marriage and family life. Researchers Bohen and Viveros-Long, who analyzed the responses of 700 workers in two federal agencies, concluded that "[a wage] disparity is due less to discrimination, in the views of our interviewees, than to the fact that they *chose* less demanding jobs because of their greater involvement in—and responsibility for—their children on a day-to-day basis."[19]

This study, whatever its value in explaining wage gap generally, cannot explain the depressed wage gap in librarianship. Most librarians work at least forty hours a week; librarians in academic positions have additional research and publication demands which require more than a forty hour work week. Librarianship has become progressively more complex. Librarians use sophisticated computerized data bases, have substantial administrative responsibilities, manage large budgets, and express independent judgment. Librarians are well-educated professionals. For example, in 1982 about 80 percent of the 135,000 full-time equivalent librarians employed in libraries had some type of library degree.[20] In 1981, in the specialized field of law librarianship, 56.2 percent of law librarians had advanced degrees (an M.A. or M.L.S.), with 17 percent having both an advanced library degree and a law degree.[21] Thus, librarianship is not representative of the less demanding, lower responsibility jobs women supposedly hold.

IV. Intraoccupational Intentional Discrimination

Intraoccupational intentional discrimination occurs in a field that is stratified, when positions of greater power and prestige are held predominantly by males. This is evident in librarianship, where the salaries for female librarians average only 75 percent of salaries for male librarians. In a 1981 survey of law librarianship, the average salary was $22,600.[22] Only 20.3 percent of the women that responded reported a salary of $25,000 or more.[23] Of the respondents who reported incomes under $12,000, 91.8 percent were women; of those reporting incomes over $50,000, 93.8 percent were men.[24] Men are disproportionately represented in the upper levels of the profession. In law libraries, a 1987 study indicates that 61 percent of head law school librarians were male.[25] Thus, librarianship is not only a sex-segregated occupation but also one within which segregation by positions and specialities occurs.

One might think that if more men entered a "woman's" profession the profession would be upgraded. This has not been the case in librarianship. In 1950 only about 11 percent of librarians were men; by 1970 the percentage had increased to about 18 percent.[26] But who has benefited by this change? Men have tended to move into the highest positions, ensuring the continuation of the earning gap within the occupation.[27] As more men were drawn into law librarianship, women held fewer positions in the American Association of Law Libraries and fewer top positions in law school libraries. In 1940 the numbers of women and men in top administrative positions in law school libraries were about equal.[28] Yet, as law school accreditation standards changed, so did the sex of head law librarians. In 1952, the AALS required the head law librarian to have "either a sound knowledge of the practical problems of a law school library or a legal education, or preferably both."[29] In the fifties, few women had law degrees.[30]

As recently as 1970, six years after the passage of the Civil Rights Act prohibiting sex discrimination, national journals advertised for men for library managers and for women for library assistants.[31] Intraoccupational sex discrimination in librarianship influences how compensation and promotion are granted to men and women employees. Intraoccupational discrimination and segregation among occupations must be considered together to prove "telltale sign[s] of purposeful discrimination."[32] It is these factors which, when viewed with the statistics, bring "cold numbers convincingly to life"[33] and strengthen the argument for comparable worth.

V. Comparison of Librarians to Other Professionals

Wage discrimination studies in California have shown a consistent pattern of underpayment—an average of 20 percent less pay—for librarian positions compared to positions of equivalent or less skill, effort, and responsibility.[34] In 1980 the Office of County Personnel in Fairfax County, Virginia, conducted a pay study of county librarians in comparisons with other county positions. At the entry level, where librarians are required to have a master's degree and to exercise supervisory responsibility, they were paid $18,000 per year.[35] This was at least $900 less than employees in the male-dominated occupations Planner I and Naturalist I, which required only an undergraduate degree and had no supervisory responsibilities. At each higher level, the responsibility of the librarian was greater and the pay less compared to other professionals. A Librarian III, who was required to have an M.L.S. and three years' experience, including one year as a supervisor and service as a branch manager, was paid only $21,622 a year. The positions of Planner III and Engineer III, for which a master's degree was not required, paid $7,000 more per year.

Several class actions have charged that librarians' salaries were depressed in relation to other employees whose jobs require similar educational qualifications and professional experience. For example, in 1978 a class action complaint was filed with the California Fair Employment Practices Commission charging that librarians in the university and state college systems were paid less than faculty or student affairs personnel, even though the educational and promotional requirements were the same.[36] Librarians at Temple University in Philadelphia filed a class action stating that librarians earned 31 to 39 percent less than comparable faculty in various other fields.[37]

Job evaluations are intended to measure the difficulty or value of jobs and to achieve some sort of internal or external equity in salaries: the job, not the worker, is evaluated.[38] At research facilities around the country, hundreds of management consultants and experts in matters of pay and salary scales use the concept of comparability in reevaluating existing job classification systems to see whether they betray sex discrimination. In *Corning Glass Works v. Brennan*, the United States Supreme Court observed that "most of American industry used formal, systematic job evaluation plans to establish equitable wage structures in their plants."[39]

Most job evaluation systems share a similar methodology.[40] The first step typically involves a careful description of each job within the unit being evaluated. Job descriptions form the basis for implementing a system of comparability. During the second step, each job is evaluated with respect to its worth to the organization, and all the jobs are hierarchically ranked. In evaluating jobs which have comparable worth, establishing the weight of compensable factors is often a subjective matter. The third step uses the results of the job evaluation in setting wage or salary rates.

Two management consulting firms, Hay Associates and Norman D. Willis and Associates, have been active in measuring job content according to compensable factors. The heart of the Hay and Willis job evaluation methods is to assign "worth points" to the various jobs, and then to group jobs of comparable worth together within several job grades.[41] An employee whose duties are routine, whose work is closely controlled, and who has a small impact on the organization will score lowest. By contrast, those in top management positions whose decisions have an organization-wide impact will score the highest. In one application, an Acquisitions Librarian (female) received 405 points and earned $952 per month; a Senior Planner (male) received 405 points and eanred $1,130 per month, or 18.7 percent more than a librarian.[42] This type of point system can show graphically the inequities of the wage disparities for female-dominated occupations.

Opinion is divided on whether job evaluation plans are bias-free. In general, opponents of comparable worth argue that they are not. Helen Remick, who was involved in the Washington state study, David Thompsen of the Compensation Institute, and Donald J. Treiman and Heidi I. Hartmann of the National Academy of Science find job evaluation plans both feasible and promising.[43] Remick notes, however, that factors such as male bias in language and job content and the tendency to rank physical work-ing conditions higher than mental working conditions are built into earlier systems and may create and perpetuate discrimination.[44] Often the abilities to work independently, under pressure, or with the public—characteristics common to library work—are undervalued.

VI. Leading Cases

In 1981, *County of Washington v. Gunther*[45] raised the issue of whether a sex-based wage discrimination claim can be brought under Title VII. Female jail guards challenged a county pay scheme in which they were paid only 70 percent of what male guards were paid, even though the county's job evaluation survey determined that the female positions were worth 95 percent of the male guard positions.[46] In a 5–4 decision, the Supreme Court ruled that persons bringing sex-based wage discrimination claims under Title VII are not required to satisfy the equal work standards of the Equal Pay Act.[47]

The *Gunther* case required the Supreme Court to discuss the relation-ship between two federal antidiscrimination statutes, the Equal Pay Act of 1963 and Title VII of the Civil Rights Act of 1964. The Equal Pay Act for-bids discriminatory compensation between employees of different gender who perform work of "equal skill, effort, and responsibility."[48] Congress intended Title VII of the Civil Rights Act, enacted just one year after the Equal Pay Act, to be a far-reaching, broad-based prohibition against dis-crimination in employment. Title VII makes it unlawful for an employer to "discriminate against any individual with respect to compensation, terms, conditions, or privileges of employment, because of such individual's race, color, religion, sex, or national origin."[49]

The legal issue resolved in *Gunther* was the narrow statutory question of whether the Bennett Amendment, found in the last sentence of sec. 703(h) of Title VII,[50] restricts Title VII's prohibition of sex-based compen-sation discrimination to claims of equal pay for equal work. The Bennett Amendment, added as a technical amendment to Title VII during the last two days before its passage[51] permits sex-based pay differentials if they are authorized by the Equal Pay Act.[52] Although recognizing that the language and legislative history of the Bennett Amendment "are not unambiguous,"[53] the Supreme Court concluded that the Bennett Amendment incorporates only the four affirmative defenses into Title VII, and not the equal work standard.[54] Thus, claims for sex-based wage discrimination can be brought under Title VII even though no member of the opposite sex holds an equal but higher paying job.

Therefore, *Gunther* answered one important question, but left open many others. The Court emphasized that the claim in *Gunther* was "not based on the controversial concept of 'comparable worth'."[55] Instead, the

Court characterized the claim as an attempt "to prove, by direct evidence, that their wages were depressed because of intentional sex discrimination, consisting of setting the wage scale for female guards, but not for male guards, at a level lower than its own survey of outside markets and the worth of the jobs warranted."[56]

As expected, proponents and opponents of comparable worth each view *Gunther* differently. Proponents laud the fact that the *Gunther* decision eliminated the major statutory obstacle to sex-based wage discrimination claims that do not allege equal work. Opponents of the decision decry any suggestion that the *Gunther* ruling removed all barriers to a comparable worth claim. Both views are correct, since *Gunther* represents only the first step in the process of developing a Title VII pay equity case.

Pay equity cases after *Gunther* have forced courts to address many of the issues left open by the Supreme Court. The first federal court opinion in which the plaintiffs prevailed in a comparable worth claim was *American Federation of State, County and Municipal Employees v. State of Washington*.[57] Library workers were included in the case. The plaintiffs were state employees in job positions that were seventy percent or more female, as represented by the American Federation of State, County, and Municipal Employees (AFSCME). Because the state reportedly perpetuated discrimination against women when determining salaries, the state's two civil service systems conducted a joint study of the salary schedules. The inquiry focused on the job descriptions of 121 classifications that were predominantly (70 percent or more) either male or female.[58] The 1974 report concluded that based on the job content of the classifications, women tended to be paid 20 percent less than men for comparable work.[59] In 1976, the study was updated to establish a method of implementation. Each job classification was valued on the basis of four criteria: knowledge and skills, mental demands, accountability, and working conditions.[60] Seven years after the wage study, however, the state had not appropriated the funds to eliminate the wage dissimilarities.[61]

The district court focused on whether the claim fell within Title VII, and, if it did, what burdens of proof the plaintiff and defendant had to carry. The court addressed the two traditional theories of discrimination: disparate treatment and adverse impact.[62] In setting forth the necessary elements of a Title VII disparate treatment case, the court used the allocation of burdens of proof in *Texas Department of Community Affairs v. Burdine*.[63] The court stated that to establish a prima facie case of adverse impact, the plaintiff must prove, by a preponderance of the evidence, that the defendant's wage compensation system has a significantly discriminatory impact. The plaintiff need not show discriminatory intent. The court then stated the question: Did the defendant's failure to pay the plaintiffs the amount of money that the comparable worth studies indicated was forthcoming constitute a violation of Title VII? Judge Tanner did in fact find wage discrimination under both the disparate treatment and disparate impact allegations. The court held that the defendant's implementation and perpetuation of the present system of compensation was intentional and resulted in unfavorable treatment of employees in predominantly female job classifications in violation of Title VII.[64] The defendant's system of compensation, while facially neutral, had the disparate impact of paying a 20 percent lower wage for predominantly female jobs than for predominantly male jobs. The defendant's presentation of evidence fell short of rebutting the plaintiff's prima facie case in both the disparate treatment and disparate impact analysis.

In 1985, however, the United States Court of Appeals for the Ninth Circuit set aside the *AFSCME* 1983 ruling.[65] The court declared that a state government's reliance on supply and demand and other market forces to set employee salaries is immune from challenge under the comparable worth theory.[66] The court warned that the concept of discriminatory intent or culpability would be undermined by a holding that payment of wages according to prevailing rates in the public and private sectors is an act which in itself supports the inference of a purpose to discriminate. Judge Kennedy reasoned that Title VII does not permit the federal court to interfere in the market-based system for setting employee compensation.[67] The court found nothing in the language of Title VII or its legislative history to indicate that Congress intended to abrogate fundamental economic principles.

"While the Washington legislature may have the discretion to enact a comparable worth plan . . ., Title VII does not obligate it to eliminate an economic inequality which it did not create."[68] Under the Ninth Circuit's approach, an employer who is following the prevailing market rates would violate Title VII only when convincing evidence shows that it adopted or maintained the market rate "'because of,' not merely 'in spite of,' its adverse effects" on women.[69] Therefore, the state and AFSCME had an option: either to face years of appeals and costly litigation or to reach a compromise that would produce a rapid improvement in wages for women workers. The legislature had appropriated funds to achieve pay equity if an out-of-court settlement could be reached by December 31, 1985. It was, and on that day AFSCME and Governor Booth Gardner announced that $41.4 million was available for pay adjustments, effective April 1, 1986. With annual pay adjustments, the total cost of the settlement would be $482.4 million.[70]

Although the court of appeals decision was viewed as a setback for comparable worth, the point was made to the legislature and governor of Washington that pay inequity was a problem that would not disappear. The specific legal questions which arose were not resolved, but state employees in specific job categories benefited from a salary increase of at least 2.5 percent.[71] Employees in specific classifications will receive $46.5

million between April 1986 and July 1987 and an additional $10 million each year thereafter through 1992.[72] Gerald W. McEntee, president of AFSCME, called the agreement "the latest in a solid string of successes on the pay equity front for 1985 in half a dozen states and several major municipalities. It establishes pay equity as a fact of life in state and local government." [73]

Women's rights advocates claim that their fight for pay equity is bolstered by a few recent judicial rulings. The Alaska State Commission for Human Rights determined in 1985 that the state of Alaska violated its equal pay statute by paying public health nurses, a predominantly female group, less than an all-male crew of physicians' assistants who perform work of comparable character.[74] The Commission held that the state violated a provision in Alaska's Title 18, requiring equal pay for members of each sex for "work of comparable character." [75] In its decision, the Commission pointed out that the state, as the largest employer in Alaska, has considerable influence in setting market wages in the private and public sectors.

On July 1, 1986, in *Bazemore v. Friday*, the Supreme Court ruled, in a case that did not deal directly with comparable worth, that employers who pay black employees less than white employees in the same jobs are violating federal civil rights laws.[76] The decision, which sends a North Carolina case back to lower courts for further proceedings, could mean that some black state employees will be able to collect years of back pay because they were paid less than whites with similar jobs. Marsha Levick of the National Organization for Women Legal Defense and Education Fund praised the ruling, saying, "In the same way blacks were historically discriminated against by employers in the setting of wages, . . . women were routinely discriminated against because of views [that] the man is the principal breadwinner." [77]

These two recent rulings are a solid affirmation of pay equity litigation. The rulings encourage persons to pursue litigation and lawyers to be more resolute about taking comparable worth cases.

VII. Establishing a Comparable Worth Claim for Librarians

Librarians and library workers have not been as involved in comparable worth litigation as nurses and members of other female-dominated professions. Litigation is extremely expensive, takes much time and energy, and, hence, is not the preferable route. However, in Virginia's Fairfax County, librarians have been seeking comparable pay since 1975.[78] Currently, Winn Newman is representing the Public Library Employees' Association in a complaint with the EEOC and, possibly, a federal court suit. Fairfax County has contended that it does not discriminate, but pays the "market rate." The Memo in Support of EEOC Charges states that Fairfax County does not pay anything that resembles a market rate for librarians.[79] Further,

Fairfax County's survey of the Washington metropolitan area deliberately excludes a selected group of its next-door neighbors, librarians working for the District of Columbia and the federal governments. As of 1987, the EEOC considers this complaint active; however, the librarians are not pursuing litigation at this time.

Librarians contemplating a comparable worth claim should be aware of the methods of proving sex-based wage discrimination. Although librarianship is a predominantly female profession that historically has been underpaid (which, in itself, constitutes a prima facie case of sex discrimination), a pure comparable worth claim has been rejected by the courts. In *Christensen v. State of Iowa*, a case involving women clerical workers of a university, the Eighth Circuit Court of Appeals rejected the notion that a prima facie case of sex discrimination was established "whenever employees of different sexes receive disparate compensation for work of differing skills that may, subjectively, be of equal value to the employer, but does not command an equal price in the labor market." [80] In *Lemons v. City and County of Denver*, a case involving nurses, the Tenth Circuit stated that "[t]he courts under existing authority cannot require the City within its employment to reassess the worth of services in each position in relation to all others, and to strike a new balance and relationship." [81] On June 17, 1985, the Equal Employment Opportunity Commission, in a case involving a public housing authority, also rejected the concept of pure comparable worth. The case claimed that 85 percent of the housing authority's administrative employees were female, while 88 percent of its maintenance employees were male. [82] "The mere predominance of individuals of one sex in a job classification is not sufficient to create an inference of sex discrimination in wage setting," the Commission stated. [83]

The issue, therefore, is what type of evidence will constitute a prima facie case of wage discrimination in the library context. Under Title VII, it is the plaintiff's burden to present sufficient evidence to create an inference that an employment decision was based on discriminatory criteria. [84] In *Gunther*, the Supreme Court referred to, but explicitly declined to determine, the elements of a prima facie case of sex discrimination compensation under Title VII. [85] Therefore, in answering how a plaintiff will prove and a defendant rebut sex discrimination in compensation, litigants must rely on the few Title VII wage discrimination cases already decided.

In a comparable worth case, the clearest case of sex-based wage discrimination is a disparate treatment situation involving direct proof that the employer has, at some point in the evaluation and wage-setting process, treated men and women differently. In *Wilkins v. University of Houston*, women in professional and administrative staff positions claimed that the University of Houston engaged in sex-based wage discrimination. [86] In 1975, the university had formulated a pay plan that was intended in part to cure the inequities between male and female professional and administrative employees. Plaintiffs introduced precise evidence that women were paid less than the minimum salary for the classification for their job.[87] On the basis of the evidence, which the court stated was somewhat similar to the facts alleged in *Gunther*, the Fifth Circuit held that the university had engaged in sex discrimination.[88]

To prove a sex-based wage discrimination claim, a plaintiff needs strong statistical evidence, usually consisting of a comparison of the wages paid to different employees.[89] Some courts are better equipped than others to deal with sophisticated statistical analysis. In *Craik v. Minnesota State University Board* the Eighth Circuit Court of Appeals was receptive toward the statistical analysis presented by female faculty members in the form of multiple-regression analyses that controlled such factors as rank, experience, and academic degree.[90] The court held that the statistical evidence, in light of other evidence showing sex discrimination with respect to appointments and promotions, demonstrated that salary differentials were the result of intentional discrimination.[91]

In *Melani v. Board of Higher Education of New York*, the plaintiff presented statistical analysis which included as many as ninety-eight independent variables, including age, years of service, academic degree, quality of degree, certificates and credentials, and time elapsed since completion of degree.[92] The court concluded that the City University of New York had engaged in sex-based wage discrimination.

To establish a prima facie case, librarians could compare librarians to student affairs officers. One such comparison took place at California State University and College System in 1978,[93] and showed that the two groups were directly comparable in educational qualifications, efforts, and responsibility, even though the positions had different duties. The librarians represented a female-dominated profession and the student affairs officers a male-dominated profession. The job evaluation methods were used to measure work value. In this situation, the differences in job content were quantifiable, and wage differentials could be computed with ease. If this case had been litigated, under a disparate treatment analysis, purposeful discrimination might have been proved because the imbalances in pay were not explained. The plaintiff, using a disparate impact approach, could have challenged the underlying fairness of the employer's plan and whether the plan devalued work performed by women because of cultural stereotypes. The above example represents the steps necessary in establishing a comparable worth claim for librarians. Although these steps are described succinctly in the example, each step can take years of planning and preparation.

VIII. Defenses

A. The Market System

The most common defense to a sex-based wage discrimination claim is that the disputed pay differential is based upon the marketplace: supply and demand are the ultimate determinants of what job should be accorded what wage. If there is a shortage of qualified personnel in a particular field, employers naturally pay more to attract workers under the theory of supply and demand. That this theory does not hold up can be seen in another female-dominated profession—nursing. There has been a shortage of nurses for the last fifteen to twenty years; yet, the marketplace has failed to provide nurses a fair and equitable wage.

The *Craik* case is particularly applicable to the field of librarianship. The court held that the university could pay higher salaries to professors in the fields of business, computer science, economics, and engineering than to professors in disciplines such as English and education, despite the fact that the former fields were occupied primarily by men and the latter primarily by women.[94] The court accepted the university's claim that the higher salaries were necessary to maintain a strong faculty in certain fields due to the market demand in those areas. When courts allow such a market defense, the judicial system not only acknowledges the marketplaces' inherent discrimination against female-dominated professions but also sanctions its use as a means to continue discrimination.

B. The Cost of Implementation

Employers may argue that comparable worth is too costly to implement. For example, the requested settlement in the *AFSCME* case, which included back pay, could have reached hundreds of millions of dollars.[95] However, an employer's complaint that comparable worth costs too much is not a defense that the courts recognize. The district court in *AFSCME* quickly discarded the state's contention that the economic burden would be prohibitive. The court stated that "where a legal injury is of an economic character, '[t]he general rule is, that when a wrong has been done, and the law gives a remedy, the compensation shall be equal to the injury.' "[96] The Supreme Court flatly ruled out any cost defense in *City of Los Angeles Dept. of Water & Power v. Manhart*, noting that Title VII did not contain "a cost-justification defense comparable to the affirmative defense available in a price discrimination suit."[97]

The University of Connecticut will serve as a model of the cost of pay equity in academic libraries. In July 1984, almost half of the library staff received an equity increase; other library staff were reclassified or promoted.[98] Most increases ranged between $1000 and $2500, although some were as high as $3500.

IX. Determining the Most Appropriate Action for Librarians

Recently, the focus of pay equity for librarians is away from the courts and toward state legislatures, city councils, and collective bargaining. Although the Seventh and Ninth Circuits have rejected comparable worth claims, and although the EEOC, the Justice Department, and the United States Commission on Civil Rights all are on the record as rejecting comparable worth as a basis for Title VII liability, the theory is still strong, as evidenced by recent litigation attempts, state legislation, job evaluation studies, and collective bargaining. Collective bargaining rights allow librarians and library staff to address their economic problems through private negotiation. The balance of pay equity activities will continue to shift to the state and local levels.

Comparable worth could enter the collective bargaining process either through state or federal legislation, judicial decisions, or demands made by employees. In the first U.S. comparable worth strike, library workers played a vital role. On July 5, 1981, members of the Municipal Employees Federation of San Jose went on strike against the City of San Jose.[99] A study done by the Hay Associates found that female-dominated job classifications were paid an average of 2 to 10 percent below the overall trend, whereas male-dominated job classifications were paid on the average of 8 percent above the overall trend. The strike ended on July 14, 1981, when union members ratified a two-year contract. The new contract contained provisions for the city to provide $1.5 million in extra compensation to help correct the inequities. The union agreed to $1.4 million in increases that narrowed, rather than closed, the gap between men's and women's wages. San Jose is an example of implementing comparable worth through collective bargaining. In 1985, according to Bob Farnquist, Director of Personnel for San Jose, the earnings gap still exists, but is improving: "Each year we move closer to the trend line through special pay-equity adjustments for female-dominated classes. I anticipate we will continue to move toward that line, if that's what the union chooses to negotiate."[100]

In May 1985 the City of Los Angeles and AFSCME, through the collective bargaining process, reached a precedent-setting agreement. The Los Angeles comparable worth case was unique because the union and the city worked through the traditional collective bargaining process to reach the agreement. The contract gave 10 to 15 percent increases to workers, male and female, in job categories where women hold seven or more out of every ten positions. For an individual librarian, the three-year contract would pay an extra $4,000 to $6,000 to compensate for what Mayor Tom Bradley termed the "iniquity . . . they have suffered."[101] Mayor Bradley and the city council decided against spending taxpayer dollars to hire outside consultants to do a job analysis or salary survey to substantiate discrimination and wage discrepancies for female-dominated classifications. Another strike over comparable worth occurred at Yale University. The comparable worth component centered on the union's publicizing that the average Yale clerical and technical employee earned $13,424 per year, while a Yale truck driver make $18,470 per year.[102]

The City of Chicago and AFSCME signed the city's first collective bargaining agreement covering librarians on December 13, 1985. The three-year contract covered 700 clerical, technical, paraprofessional, and professional employees at the Chicago Public Library. Several library employees had filed pay discrimination charges with the EEOC since 1979. As part of the settlement, the union dropped the charges. City negotiator Richard Laner stated that the city was "not embracing the concept of comparable worth," but rather that the agreement was simply a money- and time-saving procedure.[103]

Within the past two years, unions, women's organizations, and civil rights groups have lobbied state legislatures in support of equal pay for comparable work. The National Committee on Pay Equity, an organization comprised of unions and women's groups, has been very active in this regard.[104]

Twenty-six states have commissioned studies of pay equity among public employees (as of 1985), and several states have enacted equal worth legislation that is applicable to public employees.[105] Other states have enacted various pieces of legislation dealing with "similar work" or "comparable requirements." Idaho's comparable worth legislation is typical of those statutes that encompass all employers:

> No employer shall discriminate between or among employees in the same establishment on the basis of sex, by paying wages to any employee in any occupation in this state at a rate less than the rate at which he pays any employee of the opposite sex for comparable work on jobs which have comparable requirements relating to skill, effort and responsibility.[106]

In Illinois, a bill which endorsed a pay equity plan for the state was defeated in 1986; however, the bill won approval by a house committee in 1987.[107] This proposal would affect 140,000 employees of state government and state universities.[108] Minnesota has been successful in achieving pay equity and is often cited as an example for others to follow.[109] The Minnesota law states that "every political subdivision of this state shall establish equitable compensation relationships between female-dominated, male-dominated, and balanced classes of employees." [110]

Few comparable worth suits have been brought under state laws because the coverage of state laws is generally limited to employees not protected by Title VII. In the few cases that have been brought under existing state laws,[111] the state courts generally have applied traditional

Equal Pay Act standards and have refused to make value judgments about dissimilar jobs.[112]

Collective bargaining and the state legislatures provide only two forums for comparable worth activity. Another forum, one in which any librarian can become involved, is educational effort. Librarians have the skills to educate the public and policymakers about pay equity, as well as the responsibility to become involved on state and local task forces on pay equity and to write letters to members of the legislature, city council members, and governors. Although the passing of an ordinance or a resolution by a local or state governing body may seem unimportant, making comparable worth a more acceptable concept is a small victory in itself.

Professional library associations such as the American Library Association, the American Association of Law Libraries, and the Special Libraries Association lend their support to pay equity for library workers. In 1986 the American Library Association established a Council Committee on Pay Equity, charged with providing education, information, advice, and action on the pay equity issue as it affects librarians.[113] The American Library Association considers educating public officials and collective bargaining as preferable alternatives to litigation in establishing pay equity in libraries.[114]

The American Association of Law Libraries passed a pay equity resolution at its 79th Annual Meeting on July 9, 1986. The resolution calls for AALL to support the "national, state, and local legislative and legal efforts to achieve for law library workers wage comparability with other occupations requiring similar qualifications and training and which have comparable responsibilities" as well as those law library workers who are challenging discrimination in salaries.[115] At the AALL Annual Meeting, a "town hall meeting" on comparable worth provided an open forum for AALL members to debate and discuss the meaning of comparable worth as it applies to law librarianship.[116] AALL will join other professional groups in the battle against pay discrimination by informing professionals about the principles involved in pay equity and by lending support when applicable.

Comparable worth is one of the most fundamentally democratic issues to appear in the United States. It not only promises an end to low library wages, but expresses a new respect for the skilled and technical profession of librarianship. Without a doubt, proponents of comparable worth continue to face an uphill battle. However, the powerful sentiments that have carried pay equity for librarians this far will carry it into the next decade.

Footnotes

1. *New York Times*, Oct. 14, 1985, at A17.
2. Power v. Barry County, Mich., 539 F. Supp. 721, 722 (W.D. Mich. 1982).
3. Samuelson, "The Myths of Comparable Worth," *Newsweek*, Apr. 22, 1985, at 57.
4. See *Women, Work, and Wages: Equal Pay for Jobs of Equal Value* 52 (D. Treiman & H. Hartmann eds. 1981) [hereinafter *Women, Work and Wages*].
5. *Id.* at 16.
6. *Id*, at 15.
7. *U.S. Dept. of Commerce, Bureau of the Census, Money Income and Poverty Status of Families and Persons in the United States: 1985* (1986).
8. *Id.*
9. "Proceedings of the Conference of Librarians," 2 *Libr. J.* 245, 280 (1878), reprinted in *The Library and Its Workers 19*, 19 (J. McNiece ed. 1929).
10. "Quoted in *Nelson*, Dateline—Washington: A High Value on Women's Work," 58 *Wilson Libr. Bull.* 494 (1984).
11. Dewey, "Librarianship as a Profession for College-Bred Women," in *Melvil Dewey: His Enduring Presence in Librarianship 98*, 110 (S. Vann ed. 1978) (address delivered before the Association of Collegiate Alumnae, March 13, 1886).
12. Churchman, "Library Professionals: Fighting for Comparable Pay," *Christian Sci. Monitor*, Apr. 18, 1985, at 33, 33.
13. Learmont & Van Houten, "Placements and Salaries, 1985: Little Change," *Libr. J.*, Oct. 15, 1986, at 31, 31 (based on 1,493 known full-time professional salaries reported by 3,484 graduates of 58 library school programs).
14. *N. Roderer, Library Human Resources: A Study of Supply and Demand* iii (1983) (ERIC #ED 234799).
15. See, e.g., Beller, "Occupational Segregation and the Earnings Gap," in 1 *Comparable Worth: Issue for the 80's: A Consultation of the U.S. Commission on Civil Rights*, June 6-7, 1984, at 23.
16. *U.S. Dept. of Labor, Bureau of Labor Stats., U.S. Working Women: A Databook* 7-9 (1977).
17. *U.S. Dept. of Labor, Handbook of Labor Statistics* 49-53 (1985).
18. *Women, Work, and Wages*, supra note 4, at 53-54.
19. *H. Bohen & A. Viveros-Long, Balancing Jobs and Family Life* 212 (1981).
20. See *N. Roderer*, supra note 14, at 44.
21. Carrick, "Silk v. Corduroy: The Status of Men and Women in Law Librarianship," 78 *Law Libr. J.* 425, 429 (1986).
22. *Id.* at 430.
23. *Id.*
24. Percentages based on figures compiled from *id.* at 427, 431.
25. See M. Slinger, A Comprehensive Study of the Career Paths and Education of Current Academic Law Library Directors (1987).
26. See O'Brien, "The Recruitment of Men into Librarianship, Following World War II," in *The Status of Women in Librarianship* 51, 65 (K. Heim ed. 1983).
27. *Id.* at 61, 66.
28. Remarks of Jane Hammond at the program, "Status of Men and Women in Law Librarianship," Proceedings of the 75th Annual Meeting of the American Association of Law Libraries, Detroit, Michigan (June 14, 1982) 24, 35 (microfiche).
29. *See* "Report of the Special Committee on Revision of Library Standards," 1952 *A.A.L.S. Proc.* 171 app. A.
30. See Remarks of Jane Hammond, supra note 28, at 37.
31. Schiller, "Sex and Library Careers," in *Women in Librarianship: Melvil's Rib Symposium* 11, 17-18 (M. Myers & M. Scarborough eds. 1975).

32. International Brotherhood of Teamsters v. United States, 431 U.S. 324, 340 n.20 (1977).
33. *Id.* at 339.
34. Studies took place at California State University and College Libraries, Long Beach Public Library and Information Center, Los Angeles Public Library, St. Paul Public Library, San Diego Public Library, San Francisco Public Library, San Jose Public Library, Temple University, and University of California at Berkeley.
35. Memorandum in Support of EEOC Charges, Fairfax County Public Library 3 (1980) [hereinafter Memorandum].
36. J. Reynolds & J. Whitlach, Comparable Professions: Librarians and Student Affairs Officers, in *Pay Equity: Comparable Worth Action Guide*, apap. B (T.I.P. Kit –2, Nov. 1981) [hereinafter *Pay Equity*].
37. H. Josephine, Pay Equity Action Strategies and Case Summaries, in *id.* at 34. Librarians were compared to faculty positions where a Ph.D. was not required. *Id.*
38. See *D. Treiman, Job Evaluation: An Analytic Review* 1 (1979).
39. 417 U.S. 188, 199 (1974).
40. See Gasaway, "Comparable Worth, A Post Gunther Overview," 69 *Georgetown L.J.* 1123, 1155-65 (1981).
41. *D. Treiman*, supra note 38, at 21-23, 27.
42. *F. Hunter, Equal Pay for Comparable Worth* 65 (1986).
43. See *D. Treiman*, supra note 38, at 39-48; S. Stencel, Equal Pay Fight, in *Pay Equity*, supra note 36, app. D, at 225.
44. H. Remick, Comparable Worth Definitions, in *Pay Equity*, supra note 36, app. A, at 2.
45. 452 U.S. 161 (1981).
46. *Id.* at 180-81.
47. *Id.* at 181.
48. 29 U.S.C. § 206(d)(1) (1982).
49. 42 U.S.C. § 2000e-2(a)(i) (1982).
50. § 2000e-2(h).
51. The discussion on the floor comprised just a few short statements. See 452 U.S. at 173-74.
52. 42 U.S.C. § 2000e-2(h).
53. 452 U.S. at 168.
54. *Id.* at 176.
55. *Id.* at 166.
56. *Id.*
57. 578 F. Supp. 846 (W.D. Wash. 1983).
58. *Id.* at 860-61.
59. *Id.* at 861.
60. *Id.* at 861-62.
61. *Id.* at 863.
62. For a discussion of these terms, see *B. Schlei & P. Grossman, Employment Discrimination Law* 1286-90 (2d ed. 1983).
63. 450 U.S. 248 (1981).
64. 578 F. Supp. at 870-71.
65. Am. Fed. of S., C., & Mun. Emp. v. State of Washington, 770 F.2d 1401 (9th Cir. 1985).
66. *Id.* at 1408.
67. *Id.*
68. *Id.* at 1407.
69. *Id.* at 1405 (quoting Teamsters v. United States, 431 U.S. 324, 335 n.15 (1977)).
70. "Washington State Pay Equity Settlement Ratified by Legislature, Court Review Next," BNA Daily Lab. Rep., Feb. 6, 1986, at A-3.
71. 17 *Am. Lib.* 92 (1986).
72. Josephine, "The Fiscal Impact of Pay Equity," in *The Bottom Line* 18, 20 (1987).

73. Quoted in 17 *Am. Libr.*, supra note 71, at 92.
74. Alaska State Comm. for Human Rights v. State of Alaska, Case no. D-79-0724-188-E-E (Nov. 15, 1985).
75. *Id.*
76. 106 S. Ct. 3000, 3006 (1986).
77. United Press Int'l., July 1, 1986 (NEXIS, WIRES file).
78. 14 *Am. Libr.* 334 (1983).
79. See Memorandum, supra note 35, at 14.
80. 563 F.2d 353, 356 (8th Cir. 1977).
81. 620 F.2d 228, 229 (10th Cir. 1980).
82. "Decision of EEOC on Comparable Worth," BNA Daily Lab. Rep., June 18, 1985, at F-1.
83. *Id.* at F-2.
84. *B. Schlei & P. Grossman*, supra note 62, at 1286-87.
85. See 452 U.S. at 166 n.8, 178.
86. 654 F.2d 388 (5th Cir. 1981).
87. *Id.* at 401-05.
88. *Id.* at 410-11.
89. *D. Baldus & J. Cole, Statistical Proof of Discrimination* § 1.11 (1980).
90. 731 F.2d 465 (8th Cir. 1984).
91. *Id.* at 479.
92. 561 F. Supp. 769, 774 (S.D.N.Y. 1983).
93. J. Reynolds & J. Whitlach, supra note 36.
94. See 731 F.2d at 480.
95. *Pay Equity and Comparable Worth* 26 (1984).
96. *Id.* at 869 (quoting Wicker v. Hoppock, 73 U.S. (6 Wall.) 94, 99 (1867)).
97. 435 U.S. 702, 716-17 (1978).
98. Josephine, supra note 72, at 20.
99. Fischer, "Pay Equity and the San Jose Strike: An Interview with Patt Curia," 106 *Libr. J.* 2079, 2079 (1981).
100. Quoted in Lee, "Comparable Worth: The Saga Continues," *Training*, June 1985, at 33.
101. Quoted in L.A. Daily J., May 9, 1985, at 1, col. 2.
102. Hornblower, "Comparable-Worth" Issue Key to a Threatened Strike at Yale, *Wash. Post.*, Sept. 25, 1984, at A5.
103. Quoted in "Demise of Patronage," BNA Daily Lab. Rep., Dec. 19, 1985, at A-1.
104. Beyond "Equal Pay for Equal Work," *Bus. Wk.*, July 18, 1983, at 169, 169.
105. *L. Lorber, J. Kirk, S. Samuels & D. Spellman, Sex and Salary: A Legal and Personnel Analysis of "Comparable Worth"* 60-61 (1985).
106. *Idaho Code* § 44-1702(1) (1977).
107. "Panel Endorses Pay Equity Plan for State," *Chi. Daily Bull.*, Apr. 23, 1987. at 1.
108. *Id.*
109. Josephine, supra note 72, at 19.
110. *Minn. Stat. Ann.* § 471.992 (West Supp. 1987).
111. See, e.g., Tacoma-Pierce County Public Health Employees Ass'n v. Tacoma-Pierce County Health Dep't, 22 Wash. App. 1, 586 P.2d 1215 (1978).
112. Arthurs, "State Legislatures See Flood of Comparable Worth Proposals," *Legal Times*, Oct. 15, 1984, at 1, 8.
113. 17 *Am. Libr.* 720 (1986).
114. 15 *Am. Libr.* 498 (1984).
115. "Proceedings of the 79th Annual Meeting of the American Association of Law Libraries Held at Washington, D.C., Business Sessions, July 7-9, 1986," 78 *Law Libr. J.* 769, 781-82 (1986).
116. *Id.* at 785.

IS THE LIBRARIAN A DISTINCT PERSONALITY TYPE?

David P. Fisher

Alice Bryan(1) has generally been attributed with the dubious honour of having brought the personality of the librarian to the attention of psychology. Her classic study of the public librarian was one of the first pieces of work to suggest that there might be something distinctive (and not altogether attractive) about the librarian's personality. I shall endeavour to analyse the findings of psychological research conducted over the last 30 years, in order to see if any discernible personality profile common to librarians emerges. In the course of my investigations the very utility of psychological approaches to librarianship will necessarily be critically discussed. The question of whether or not psychology has anything constructive to say about the library as an organization will be addressed. For the personality profile approach to work, it is necessary to establish a consistent image and then to demonstrate what effect the librarian's personality has on the library organization.

Stereotypes

I shall look first at the notion of stereotypes and consider whether a particular image of librarians exists in society. The extent to which psychological approaches appear to be influenced by stereotypes will be an important element in the evaluation of such work.

'Observe the ass, . . . his character is about perfect, . . . yet see what ridicule has brought him to. Instead of feeling complimented when we are called an ass, we are left in doubt'.(2, p.xv) Being called a librarian can apparently create a similar 'doubt'. Penny Cowell(3, p. 167) has sketched what many might consider to be the typical librarian: 'a fussy old woman of either sex, myopic and repressed, brandishing or perhaps cowering behind a date-stamp and surrounded by an array of notices which forbid

"Is the Librarian a Distinct Personality Type?" by David P. Fisher in *Journal of Librarianship* Vol. 20, no. 1 (January 1988), pp. 36-47; reprinted with permission from the *Journal of Librarianship*.

virtually every human activity'.

Libraries are often portrayed as dull places, frequented only by the unfortunate: 'out-of-work men . . . and . . . elderly discoloured bachelor[s] who . . . study books on yachting by the hour'. (4, p. 226) Librarians are pitiable, introverted characters as a *Woman's Weekly* story testifies. The reader is told of the personality problems suffered by John Beckenham, the new senior librarian. 'His accursed shyness was the trouble . . . it afflicted him with a stammer which was the bane of his life'. (3, p. 168) Librarians are social outcasts, unable to find employment elsewhere. The depiction of a librarian, in the television series 'Sorry', as a 40-year-old bachelor who is afraid of his mother confirms this pathetic image. Even library schools recognize the force of such stereotypes. One prospectus adopts a defensive attitude, stressing that contrary to public opinion librarianship 'is not a calm haven for the over-shy or ill-adjusted'. (5, p. 4) The British Museum provides the backdrop for one of David Lodge's novels. He aptly describes the pedantic, austere and rather perverse nature of librarians.

> The room at the end of the corridor was an office, with a long, curving counter behind which sat two men, neat, self-possessed, expectant. A approached the nearer man, who immediately began writing on a piece of paper. . . .
> 'I wanttorenewmyReadingRoomTicket,' gabbled A.
> 'Over there'.
> 'But I've just been over there. He sent me to you.' Out of the corner of his eye, A saw the first man watching them intently. (6, p. 36)

The librarian does seem to occupy a singularly unenviable position in the popular imagination. Indeed, s/he is 'the most unpoetical of all God's creatures'. (7) One should note that the image is not without tension. The librarian is dubbed both diffident and severe. There is, then, a certain ambiguity as regards the overall portrayal. Yet the tension could be said to be more apparent than real since insecurity may underlie a severe attitude.

The Psychological Approach

How close is the foregoing image to the psychologist's photofit picture? To begin with one ought to try to define psychology.

> A psychological focus is necessary to understand the actions and feelings of people composing crowds. A sociological focus is necessary to understand the occurrence of mass phenomena . . . and the social conditions generally conducive to them. (8, p. 133)

While I think the above quotation is unfair to sociology, forcing it into a functionalist/behaviourist mould, we are rightly told that psychology is concerned with individuals. Even the most social of psychologies fail to have anything more than a shallow concern for the social world surrounding the individual. The psychological approach to librarianship will tend to centre upon the individual and regard the librarian as the most important element within the library organization. Such a method is justifiable only if one can prove that this is a (or the most) fruitful way of proceeding.

Psychological research has been concerned in the main with the issue of the librarian's personality. It is assumed by most authors reviewed here that there exists a consensus of opinion as to what personality is; it does not need to be defined. Black(9, p. 65) does at least recognize that 'personality is a subjective word'. The usual pattern, however, is for the researcher to state that something called personality exists and then to get on with analysing facets of this taken-for-granted entity. This lack of explanation of the very term *personality* casts a shadow on the whole enterprise. How can one be so sure that one is studying personality when it is not made clear exactly what it is? Agada(10) has arranged psychological approaches to the investigation of personality into four groups: the trait, social learning, psychoanalytic and phenomenological. Studies involving the librarian fall mostly into the trait group. In this version, as its name suggests, personality is divided up into elements called traits and attempts are made to predict a person's behaviour by measuring them. It is perhaps unfortunate that this theory should play such a significant role in psychological studies of librarianship because

> The personality factors found in a given study . . . have often depended on the type of data being analyzed (for example, self-ratings versus ratings of one person by another), and the specific factor analytic technique used. . . . The most critical limitation . . . is . . . trait theory's assumption of highly generalized behavioral consistencies across different times and situations. (10, p. 24)

Many shadows are now sweeping across the scene, making it quite depressingly dark.

'Trait' Studies

Bearing the aforementioned warnings in mind, let us now look at a few 'trait' approaches in some depth. Bryan(1) in her survey gave a personality test to 157 male and 1651 female librarians. She concluded that librarians score below average in terms of leadership and self-confidence, but average as regards masculinity of attitudes as opposed to femininity, lack of nervous tenseness/irritability and pressure for overt activity. In so far as librarians were found to be lacking in assertiveness and confidence, this fits in with the diffident side of the common stereotype of librarians. Contrary to the popular image, men and women fell within 'the normal range for their respective sexes on the masculinity factor', (1, p. 42) and were not found to be more fractious than others. A librarian reviewing the same material stated: 'Public librarians . . . were found to be insecure, suffered from inferiority complexes, were uncomfortable and inadequate in social situations and exhibited less dominant leadership characteristics than the average university student'. (9, p. 65)

Librarians seem to want to make things worse for themselves and confirm the stereotypes. It is surprising how more abnormal the picture becomes after a little medodramatic rewriting. A problem arises with Bryan's study, as with many others. What constitutes a normal score on the test? Black (9) states that a comparison was made with average university students. However, Bryan did not select the control group herself but used the results provided by the authors of the inventory. We do not know how large or representative the sample was. In any case, we can question the legitimacy and adequacy of generalizing from a sample of results provided by university students (or any other group) and using them as the norm. Furthermore, the GAMIN schedule employed by Bryan has long fallen into disuse and has been criticized on grounds of subjectivity. The literal nature of the questions makes it obvious to which personality trait they relate. Individual scores were spread across the scales and so a 'strongly marked profile was . . . hardly discernible'. (10, p. 31) There are two points to be made: first, Bryan's results have been exaggerated as I have shown, and second, those results may in any event be totally invalid.

Douglass (11) conducted the next study of note. He gave five different personality tests to 545 students in 17 library schools. It is important to underline the fact that although these were potential librarians, we do not know how many actually entered the profession. He found his respondents to be more orderly than people in general, but not compulsive. They appeared conscientious, but only showed a slight tendency towards submissiveness. The tests gave conflicting findings concerning librarians' sociability, but with one test giving normal, another subnormal and yet another above normal results, a positive conclusion can be drawn. Douglass (11) did not find his library students more anxious and less self-confident than people in general. Another study, conducted by Morrison, (12) in fact found librarians to be more sure of themselves than 'normal' people. This picture conflicts with that drawn by Bryan. (1) It is more positive in that the librarian appears to be quite confident and reasonably sociable (although there is confusion over exactly what Douglass tested, i.e. sociability or concern for social values). It is odd how commentators such as McDermoth (13) and Black (9) have attempted to hide the differences in results between studies. Black, (9, p. 66) for instance, says: 'The social inadequacies discovered by Bryan were evident in Douglass' results.' Some were and, more importantly, some were not. The fact that a couple of studies have shown the librarian not to be lacking in confidence does not necessarily confirm the tension apparent in the stereotype between diffidence and austerity. Rather, it could be said to challenge the stereotype because confidence need not imply severity of manner. Indeed, as suggested earlier, the opposite could be true—namely, a lack of confidence may produce a severe outlook.

Douglass(11) made a good deal of use of the Minnesota Multiphasic Personality Inventory (MMPI), which was designed for use in psychopathological testing and so may well be inadequate for understanding normal behaviour. Problems of what constitutes a normal response to the tests raised with Bryan's work apply equally here, as do the difficulties associated with self-rating techniques. The two studies do not present a consistent image, and cannot give a great deal of support to the picture of the stereotypical librarian. The results of both can in any case be regarded as defective because of numerous methodological problems. Furthermore, if a personality type cannot be established, psychology cannot say anything about its influence on the organizational structure of the library.

McMahon's(14) investigation of Tasmanian-Australian librarians is interesting in that it confirms the views of Douglass(11) on one particular issue. That is, the idea that the male librarian is more feminine in his interests than men in general. Such a contention is certainly in agreement with the popular picture of the librarian(3, 167) as 'a fussy old woman of either sex'. Is femininity, then, a trait common to librarians? First, we must remember that Bryan(1) found no such trait, merely that male and female scores were reasonably close together. Second, we have faulted the methodologies employed by Douglass and, since McMahon used the same MMPI schedule, similar doubts necessarily surface. However, studies carried out by Baillie(15,16) and Clayton(17,18) give support to McMahon's findings.

Consider some of the questions asked by the California Psychological Index (CPI) employed by both the above authors. In order to be regarded feminine, one should reply as indicated below, and in an opposite way to be regarded masculine.(19, 236)

> I thing I would like the work of a librarian (True)
>
> I want to be an important person in the community (False)
>
> I am somewhat afraid of the dark (True)
>
> The thought of being in an automobile accident is very frightening to me (True)

These questions are ideological and not a little farcical. The very job of being a librarian is thought to be a 'feminine' activity. The psychologist who created the scheme is guilty of blindly perpetuating gender stereotypes. All passive, weak qualities are viewed as feminine, while strong, aggressive attributes are said to be masculine. In addition, if females attain a high score on the masculinity scale they are described in pejorative terms, while males scoring similarly are described positively. Such schedules are blatantly sexist. Turner(19) thought he could do better, using the Bem-Sex-Role Inventory (BSRI). He claimed to find no significant difference between library students and the normative group in terms of masculinity-femininity orientations. However, the BSRI model is still ideological and sexist in as much as it defines 'assertiveness' as a masculine attribute and 'gullibility' as a feminine one. Males still need to score higher on masculinity and females higher on femininity to be considered normal. Whatever the outcome of studies measuring masculinity-femininity, the very ideological nature of such conceptions makes them extremely problematic. As Sharpe(20, p. 306) says:

> Although there is little evidence to show that girls and boys necessarily differ much in their abilities and characteristics the socialization of girls into 'femininity' and boys into 'masculinity' produces differences and perpetuates many myths about men and women.

Let us consider what we have discovered so far. There does seem to be an unattractive popular image of the librarian that some reviewers have regarded as replicated by psychological studies. We, on the other hand, have found a good deal of contradiction between the findings of different studies. The only traits surviving suggest the librarian may be very slightly less assertive than normal and more orderly and conscientious. Furthermore, if, as has been shown, some studies found the librarian to be more confident than 'normal', is this likely to engender submissiveness? This is the difficulty with artificially isolating variables; if they exist at all they exist not in isolation but in interaction with one another. A particular limitation is the assumption of behavioural consistencies regardless of the situation. The very presence of traits is questionable because of the methodological problems associated with the studies that produced them. It appears that the psychological approach to librarianship has very little to offer. Even accepting for a moment the existence of the above traits, what do they tell us about the library organization? Since the focus has been purely on the individual, to the exclusion of social contexts, it is difficult to make any sense of such findings in terms of the organization of the library as a whole.

There are, however, several writers who have attempted to use personality test findings in order to support their views about library organization. McDermoth(13) believes that the continuance of the rigid hierarchies found in libraries is aided by the personality type of the librarian. She is interested in the authoritarian potential of librarians, and is thus perhaps influenced by notions of austerity in the popular stereotype. She states that the personality traits discovered in librarians include above average intelligence, little tendency towards innovation, submissiveness, self-consciousness and feminine interest patterns. We have demonstrated the contradictory nature of the results regarding most of the above traits. Subtracting those, we are left with above average intelligence, little tendency towards innovation and, if we are generous, a degree of submissiveness. Many studies have found the first trait to exist, which is certainly a positive one. Douglass(11) did find his sample to be lacking in creativity, but then we discovered problems with his personality schedules.

Accepting the existence of the three traits for a moment, let us look at the basis of McDermoth's case. She attempts to fit the personality profile of the librarian into Adorno's notion of the authoritarian (fascist) personality. Conventionalism and submissiveness are the only elements which she finds are shared by librarians and Adorno's authoritarian personality. The most important characteristic—power and toughness—is missing. However, she has already allowed for this by noting at the outset that an authoritarian personality can be superior or subordinate. This is stretching the term a little too far. It is true that Adorno states that acquiescence to a ruling group's authority is a part of the authoritarian personality, but this alone would not make someone authoritarian. McDermoth(13) could at this point have called up the reserves, in the form of research by Busha.(21) He was one of the first to use the more reliable trait-situation interaction technique. Busha found a significant relationship between library student scores on censorship and fascist scales. As it turned out, Busha would not have been able to hold off the enemy for long because less than 10 per cent of his sample could be characterized as having authoritarian personalities. McDermoth does not in fact call for reinforcements; instead, wounded, out of ammunition and with counter-arguments getting nearer by the minute, she concludes that

> the librarian is often quite content in a subordinate position in a hierarchical structure. It is unlikely that he/she will make a concerted effort to achieve a position of power but, if awarded such a position, the librarian would probably exhibit . . . elements of authoritarianism. (13, p. 27)

Even forgetting the problems associated with the personality test findings she uses, McDermoth has not proved that the librarian is authoritarian, nor that the librarian's personality is a vital determinant of hierarchical organizational structures. She has been unable to furnish us with a tangible link between personality and social environment. She would need to demonstrate the role of personality variables in actual situations, and connect them with organizational structures. Her argument is based solely upon supposition and not very good supposition at that. Indeed, McDermoth(13, p. 27) says that her conclusions are nothing more than 'pure speculation'. Putting all the balls into the individual's court precludes anything but a cursory glance at the opposition in the form of societal and organizational power structures that often make it hard for the individual (whatever his/her personality) to win a game let alone the match.

The idea that librarians are poor leaders and resistant to change is a pervasive one. Morrison(12) found that librarians in his sample lacked good supervisory attributes. Fine,(22) Presthus(23) and Hamilton(24) have a common interest in the attitude of librarians to change. If it can be proved that librarians dislike innovation, then it may be possible to suggest that they constitute an important factor in the maintenance of existing organizational structures. Fine(22) is at least slightly more methodologically competent than most in as much as she looks at the interactions of several traits in an individual. However, the study gives poor support to those (e.g. McDermoth(13)) who view librarians as the main force behind the maintenance of the *status quo*. As Agada(10, p. 37) states: 'Little evidence was found to correlate . . . personality variables . . . with the resistance index.'

Hamilton(24) and Presthus,(23) as might by now be expected, found just the opposite: that librarians are bureaucratic and resistant to technological and social change. At first sight Sladen(25) seems to be giving added weight to these latter arguments. The results from his 16 Personality Factors Questionnaire, says Agada,(10, p. 35) 'strongly upheld the stereotypical image of librarians'. Or did they? In fact Sladen found that the scores from 25 librarians did not show any deviation from the norm on any of the traits measured, including assertiveness and imagination. Only when he cheats and reduces the sample to 8 and then 6 female librarians, does he obtain anything like the results he is looking for. this is definitely a case of the psychologist's sight being coloured by stereotypical images. Sladen(25) then gave the same test to 90 librarians at a conference and found that the scores matched those he manufactured from the 6 in his first sample. This showed, he said, that librarians are more introverted than the general population. His findings, of course, prove merely how ludicrous psychological research can become. Even adopting his own criteria, we can dismiss the results as redundant. He originally stated: 'since 25 library staff was too large a number and one was too small, a compromise was arranged [i.e. 8 respondents reduced to 6]'.(25, p. 118) Thus, the fact that 90 people supported his conclusions is irrelevant since, if 25 was too large a number, 90 certainly is. If we are more magnanimous than he deserves, and take the 'facts' as we find them (90 people confirmed his predictions, 25 did not), they hardly constitute conclusive proof one way or the other.

There do not appear to be overwhelming reasons why we should view the librarian as lacking in leadership qualities and resistant to change. Even Morrison(12) admits that he did not discover a consistent personality profile. Let us bring in the work of Lee and Hall(26) and dilute the picture even further. They used the same test as Sladen(25) in a comparative study of 45 female library science students and their non-library science colleagues. They found that the mean scores of library students on 13 of the 16 scales were within the average range and that scores for the other 3 were above average. Prospective librarians were found to be more intelligent, self-sufficient and experimental than the norm. In other words, according to this study librarians may well be more innovative than the rest of the population. One cannot say, then, with any conviction, that the personality of the librarian is mainly responsible for hierarchical structures, or for the suppression of new managerial ideas and/or new technology within libraries.

The Verdict

Basing one's answer upon the evidence reviewed, it is not possible to state that the librarian is a distinct personality type. The utility of the whole psychological approach to librarianship is also put in doubt. The studies discussed can be faulted on several levels. Each of the writers attempts to make generalizations from his or her findings, even though very small samples are often employed. The picture produced is so confused as to render it virtually useless. The only thing the results prove is that there are no conclusive results. The personality tests used by the studies have been shown to be largely inappropriate and inadequate (a severe limitation being the assumption of absolute, socially independent behavioural consistencies which underlies their static design). Therefore, even if the findings had not been conflicting, the notion of the librarian as having a distinct personality type would still have to be treated with suspicion. If we separate studies using library students from those employing librarians, a conflicting picture still emerges, as no consistent pattern of agreement or disagreement within or between the two groups can be discerned. No real attempts have been made to link the individual and the social, personality traits are mostly viewed as absolute, existing across all situations.

The Way Forward

Must we end with the pessimistic conclusion that psychology is of no use in the study of the social organization of libraries? To an extent the answer has to be yes, if psychology's track record is anything to go by. The 'trait' approach, to succeed, needs first to demonstrate that the librarian is a consistent personality type, and second, to show that the individual alone is the most important or only factor in shaping the organization. It has failed on both counts. One needs to recognize that the social world and the individual exist not in isolation but rather in interaction with each other. Some social psychologists, unlike those of the personality trait variety, have attempted to analyse such interaction but not in a library setting. (27) A couple of recent psychological studies of librarians have focused on memory as opposed to personality. It is too early to say whether any consistent and potentially useful results will emerge. (28,29)

In any event the search for consistent personality traits has proved so fruitless that I think it best abandoned. In fact, it might be as well to reject psychology altogether. Indeed, the following is as applicable to psychology's treatment of the librarian as it is to its approach to the arts: 'We all mistrust those so-called "psychological analyses" which reduce a work of art narrowly to some supposed and only half-proven complex or neurosis . . . existing mainly in the psychologist's own imagination'.(30, p. 237) Rather, a more sociological emphasis that recognizes the dynamic interaction between the individual and the social is needed. The structural properties of social systems are both the medium and the outcome of practices that constitute those systems. In other words, the individual influences and is influenced by the social. Merleau-Ponty well delineates the sociological enterprise: 'Sociological knowledge . . . requires that, while taking all objective indices as our guide, we recover the human attitude which makes up the spirit of a society'.(31, p. 90)

It is true that problems and difficulties will arise with whatever approach one adopts. Nevertheless, sociology is a more valid tool than psychology if one genuinely wants to increase one's knowledge of librarians and libraries and, more importantly, of the interaction of the two.

Popular myths concerning the librarian will continue to multiply as long as the media see fit to perpetuate them. The images created, though, are not always totally negative. In a recent episode of 'Taggart' (a television detective series), for example, a librarian was the only surviving victim of the 'bowman attacker'. The librarian confirmed the conventional stereotype to some extent, being slightly spinsterish in appearance, but she also showed herself to be a capable, sympathetic character. She was able to comfort a library user (supposedly worried about the attacker still being at large) by giving the user the benefit of her worldly wisdom. A second instance might be taken from the early days of 'Coronation Street'. Ken Barlow at one time had an affair with Marion Lund, a university librarian. The fictional librarian was cast in the role of the older woman (she was 33 and Barlow only 21). Ken finally ended the relationship after a few months because he felt their age differences were too great. Surely these events must have encouraged the growing number of 'Street' followers to view the librarian in a new, more interesting light.

The above, however, are really examples of exception proving the rule. Public conceptions of librarians tend not to be as dynamic and colourful as such rare instances suggest. Yet no matter what conventional stereotypes assert, we have not found any evidence to support the argument that the majority of librarians have a distinct personality type. The conflicting results, if accepted at all, would lead one to believe that libraries like other organizations are populated by staff with varied interests and attributes. Perhaps the last word should be left to a librarian. Talking about his colleagues, Skevington(32) says, 'most of them take part in activities which require extrovert and socially aggressive characteristics—there certainly aren't any quailing "violets" among them, male or female'.

References

1. Bryan, A. I. *The public librarian: a report of the public library inquiry.* Columbia University Press, 1952.
2. Twain, M. *Pudd'nbead Wilson.* Bantam Books, 1981.
3. Cowell, P. Not all in the mind: the virile profession. *Library Review,* 1980, 29, 167-75.
4. Orwell, G. *A clergyman's daughter.* Penguin Books, 1964.
5. Polytechnic of North London. *School of Librarianship and Information Studies prospectus.* PNL, 1985.
6. Lodge, D. *The British Museum is falling down.* Penguin Books, 1983.
7. Rettig, J. The reference librarian as 'the most unpoetical of all God's creatures'. *Reference Services Review,* 1984, 12(2), 9.
8. Gahagan, J. *Interpersonal and group behaviour.* Methuen, 1975.
9. Black, S M. Personality—librarians as communicators. *Canadian Library Journal,* April 1981, 65-71.
10. Agada, J. Studies of the personality of librarians. *Drexel Library Quarterly,* 1984, 20(2), 24-45.
11. Douglass, R R. *The personality of the librarian.* University of Chicago, 1957.
12. Morrison, P D. *The career of the academic librarian: a study of the social origins, educational attainments, vocational experience, and personality characteristics of a group of American academic librarians.* American Library Association, 1969.
13. McDermoth, M. Authoritarian potential in the personality of the librarian. *Argus,* January-February 1979, 22-7.
14. McMahon, A. *The personality of the librarian.* Libraries Board of South Australia, 1967.
15. Baillie, G S. *An investigation of objective admission variables as they relate to academic and job success in one graduate library education program.* Washington University, 1961.
16. Baillie, G S. *Library school and job success.* University of Denver, 1964.
17. Clayton, H. *An investigation of personality characteristics among library students in one midwestern university.* State University of New York, 1970.
18. Clayton, H. Femininity and job satisfaction among male library students at one midwestern university. *College and Research Libraries,* 1970, 31, 338-98.
19. Turner, R L. Femininity and the librarian—another test. *College and Research Libraries,* May 1980, 235-41.
20. Sharpe, S. *Just like a girl: how girls learn to be women.* Penguin Books, 1976.
21. Busha, C H. Student attitudes toward censorship and authoritarianism. *Journal of Education for Librarianship,* 1970, 11, 118-36.
22. Fine, S. *Resistance to technological innovation in libraries, final report.* Office of Education, 1979.
23. Presthus, R. *Technological change and occupational responses: a study of librarians.* Office of Education, 1970.
24. Hamilton, S S. Work motivation of Alabama librarians: a challenge for change. *Alabama Librarian,* 1975, 27, 4-7.
25. Sladen, D. The personality of the librarian: an investigation. *Library Association Record,* 1972, 74(7), 118-19.
26. Lee, D C, and Hall, J E. Female library science students and the occupational stereotype: fact or fiction? *College and Research Libraries,* 1973, 34(5), 265-7.
27. Pugh, D S, Hickson, D J, and Hinings, C R. *Writers on organizations,* 3rd edn. Penguin Books, 1983.
28. Neill, S D. The reference process and certain types of memory; semantic, episodic, and schematic. *RQ,* 1984, 23(4), 417-25.

29. Johnson, K A, and White, D M. The cognitive style of reference librarians. *RQ*, 1982, 21(3), 239-46.
30. Cooke, D. *The language of music.* Oxford University Press, 1959.
31. Merleau-Ponty, M. *Sense and non-sense.* Northwestern University Press, 1964.
32. Skevington, P W. Letters. *Library Association Record*, 1972, 74(9), 171.

LIBRARIANS' IMAGE AND USERS' ATTITUDES TO REFERENCE INTERVIEWS

Mary Land

Librarians have been fighting thoughtless characterizations of themselves for decades. "As early as 1909, a librarian used the word 'stereotype' in objecting to the portrayal of her profession in fiction. She complained that librarians were depicted in extremes, either as 'old fogy bookworms' or as unreasonably efficient and attractive young people" (McReynolds, 1985, p. 25). Unfortunately this librarian could raise the "fogy" objection to today's portrayals of librarians in the media just as she did about librarians in literature almost eighty years ago.

American Libraries' "image" column has been monitoring the popular vision of librarians through letters and other submissions since January 1985. The columns seem mostly to lament the "bun-and-chain" type with at least some mention of "unreasonably efficient and attractive young people." Judging by the contributions, readers do not seem able to find much neutral coverage of librarians or library activities in the non-library press. The inaugural column contained an angry letter from a cataloguer protesting a promotional piece in *TV Guide* about a character on a sitcom who "Stood Out . . . Like a Librarian at a Break-Dancers' Convention." The cataloguer complained, "Every time they need a stuffy image, the media drag out a librarian" ("Image." *American Libraries*, Jan., 1985, p. 7).

Dowdy, bespectacled, or frumpy women—with or without a bun—given to making "shushing" noises and generally being disapproving were found in television shows, cartoons, advertisements, and newspaper articles and noted in *American Libraries* in the February, March, May, June, July-August, September, and December 1985 "Image" columns and the January, May, and December 1986 columns. There was one mention of a "prim" male librarian (May, 1985).

The other extreme—"unreasonably efficient and attractive young people"—was highlighted in two columns (December 1985 and May 1986). The first column described the advertising of two U.S. department stores, contained in a Nordstrom catalogue and a Marshall Fields supplement to the *Chicago Tribune.* In the Nordstrom advertisement, a young female model is checking a card catalogue drawer and has "a modern haircut [that] complements her tailored suit, and . . . fashionable spectacles" ("Image." *American Libraries*, Dec., 1985, p. 759). In the Marshall Fields supplement, "a beautiful model . . . has just encountered a handsome young man with blond hair leaning against a row of shelves. She says to him, "You're kidding . . . I'm actually in the NBC library? And you're the librarian, right?" ("Image." *American Libraries*, Dec., 1985, p. 759). The second column described an article by *The Toronto Sun's* Christie Blatchford that dispelled the "bun-and-chain" stereotype but made librarians sound like a sisterhood of funky, bawdy, and ultra-hip stand-up comedians ("Image." *American Libraries*, May, 1986, p. 303; Blatchford, 1986).

These rather astounding extremes were balanced by at least three "Image" columns in which librarians were seen as managers trying to get on with their jobs. The April 1985 column summarized articles that appeared in the *New York Times* and *Time* magazine about overdue fines, difficulties of processing acquisitions in an academic library, and the use of computers in public libraries. A profile of the head of reference services at Arizona State University was also included.

In the February 1986 column there was a story from *Newsweek* about two highly successful librarians maintaining a long-distance marriage; articles from local publications about libraries changing their names by adding "information centre" and about the power of the computer to enhance librarians' status were also cited.

The July-August 1986 column profiled the Louisiana Library Association's spring conference entitled "Librarians: Images and Reflections" at which speakers disagreed over the seriousness of the image problem. Keynote speaker Pauline Wilson, author of *Stereotype and Status*, maintained that the "stereotype had become a preoccupation of the profession encouraged by too much press coverage." John Berry, *Library Journal* editor, agreed that energy spent in discussing image could be better used in management and service seminars.

Harmful Image Depicted

At the same convention, U.S. Representative Major Owens insisted that "a negative image *does* adversely affect the profession." He cited the downgrading of federal librarians in the civil service and urged librarians to use "constructive arrogance" in fighting for recognition in their field ("Image."

American Libraries, July-August, 1986, p. 502).

Karen Romanko, writing in *Publishers Weekly,* echoes Owens. "A few librarians themselves believe that we're doing our image more harm than good by complaining . . . I disagree. If it were just a matter of one or two of these 'funny' portrayals, we'd laugh it off. But this [fogy stereotype] seems to be the only image of librarians that the media depicts" (Romanko, 1986, p. 8).

Martha Merrill agrees that the "reality of librarianship has not been well publicized through the mass media" and remarks that U.S. television commercials for Pledge, Taco Bell, and Ruffles potato chips all feature a "60+ female—tall and emaciated, hair in a bun, wearing glasses and continuously making shushing noises" (Merrill, 1984, p. 17).

Canadian television commercials are not much better. There is the elderly ill-tempered man who brings his car into a muffler shop for repairs exclaiming, "I don't like noise!" while the mechanics announce fearfully, "It's the librarian." In another advertisement, a middle-aged female librarian working at the card catalogue, with the stacks visible in the background, vouches for the reliability of a product for incontinent adults.

There is evidence that "advertising stereotypes appear to have a negative impact on the career choices of young people" (Merrill, p. 17). If that is true, it seems obvious that teenagers would also associate negative images with certain careers because of demeaning advertising. Librarianship certainly would not fare well if that is the case.

The Toronto Star, in a caption with an article on pay equity, emphasized a "low skill" image of librarians by depicting them as having the same wage-earning power as caretakers: "Under pay equity, 1.7 million Ontario working women in female-dominated jobs like librarians may be paid the same as people in male-dominated jobs like caretakers" (Orwen, 1987, p. A4). Readers who bothered to skim the article would have found that library assistants were actually the ones discussed. However, a reader might be confused about whether or not a librarian and a library assistant are the same thing; to be an assistant, the article informs us, "requires . . . a high-school diploma, [the ability] to type and lift heavy library materials." It is hardly surprising then that the "general public does not know what librarians do, or that what they think they know is wrong. The impression is of individuals who[se] . . . activities . . . tend to be . . . clerical. Few people . . . understand why a master's degree is necessary for our profession" (White, Oct. 1, 1986, p. 66).

Given the predominant image of librarians in the media (sourpuss dictator, almost exclusive female), the patrons' ignorance should be excused. As demonstrated in the "Image" columns in *American Libraries,* very few items in the non-library media portray librarians as managers of information and experts in handling documents. Librarians are seen instead as caricatures of professionals—the prevalent stereotype being the tense, unimaginative guardian of the library with the basilisk stare, the other stereotype being the ravishing superhuman who could intimidate Dewey himself. Evidently, if these images, which in both cases discourage a user from approaching a librarian, are representative of community attitudes, then the value of librarians and "the potential of reference service is still not being told to the public" (Bourkoff and Woolridge, 1985-86, p. 62).

Clear Image Needed

The image of librarians presents an enigma to users. The "role of the librarian is undefined; people do not know what to expect . . . and communication problems arise" (Swope and Katzer, 1972, p. 161). In this climate of misunderstanding, the librarian's "tendency [is often] to treat users as problems, as sources of disorder rather than as sources of direction" (Martell, 1984, p. 378). Users are, however, offering us a direction: they seem to be saying that they don't know who librarians are or what reference work involves. Perhaps we should reconsider the generally accepted "notion that . . . the librarian need not make any conscious effort toward 'the creation of desired impressions'" (Katz, 1978, p. 67).

Indeed, it will be vital to make an effort in order to inspire users' trust. The "average client is . . . a bit wary" of reference librarians, and it is probably for this reason that Edward Kazlauskas found "the 'approachability' of the reference librarian by the user is by far the most important aspect of a satisfactory reference interview" (see Katz, pp. 62, 64).

This observation appears to be confirmed by other research. One study asked students why they did not request reference assistance. The responses included the remark that "they were suspicious of the librarian who was not likely to help them anyway" (see Katz, p. 11). Similarly, Ellis Mount found the "inquirer, either instinctively or through experience, dislikes the reference librarian and consequently avoids giving a true picture of his or her needs. This may be another way of saying the user lacks any real confidence in the ability of the librarian" (see Katz, p. 72).

Erving Goffman determined that if people are brave enough to ask their question they are often unwilling to volunteer the reason for needing the information (which would greatly aid the librarian's search). "Such reluctance [is] usually because the user (1) does not trust the librarian's reaction to . . . an embarrassing question; (2) does not trust the librarian's knowledge of the field" (see Katz, p. 72). Suspicion, lack of confidence, and lack of trust seem to mark the user's reaction to the reference librarian —a grim picture.

Other researchers have expressed the importance of the user's assessment of the librarian in more neutral terms. The user must decide, at some point, whether "(a) to ask an information specialist; or (b) to help himself. Most important in this decision is the inquirer's image of the personnel, their effectiveness" (Taylor, 1968, p. 182). Personal acquaintance also appears to affect the user's willingness to ask a reference question: "psychological barriers may be generated by the fact that users fail to get to know library personnel well, or at all" (Hatchard and Toy, 1986, p. 67). Maurice Line believes that improvement of the "inadequate use of reference material and library staff . . . demand[s] personal contact . . . between students and library staff" (Line, 1963, p. 116).

One step toward improved personal contact may be the abolition of the "anonymous professional-client encounter . . . [which] lowers the level of library service" (Durrance, 1983, p. 278) because users already unwilling to trust and have confidence in the librarian are not going to be bolstered by an inability to recognize exactly who is a librarian. As reference practice stands in public and academic libraries, "everyone behind a desk, from the lowest paid clerical to the head librarian, is perceived by the library user as 'the librarian' " (Durrance, p. 278), which certainly does not help librarians to increase their visibility or improve their image with the user.

Durrance examines and rejects four common arguments against the "identifiable" librarian, to which one more is added here: the "equality," "modesty," "sartorial," "harassment," and "popularity" arguments (Durrance, p. 279). The equality argument proposes that a neutrality is maintained by having an anonymous librarian and a nameless patron, although "why action *a*, not identifying ourselves, should result in action *b*, equal service to all, is not clear." Proponents of the modesty argument say that, if librarians are identified by name, every worker will have to be identified by name and rank, causing internecine strife. Durrance points out that many libraries already identify staff "*by rank* to their users, *but not by name.*"

Those using the sartorial argument are afraid "name tags will spoil blouses, dresses, and jackets" (Durrance, p. 279). Librarians who are bothered by problem patrons argue that wearing a name tag makes harassment a constant threat. Durrance replies that there are risks for anyone who presents himself or herself to the public by name and that these risks must be balanced against the probable benefits of being identifiable to patrons, adding that any librarian who cannot justify the risk can "choose a pseudonym."

The popularity argument (expressed in an "Issues in Librarianship" course at the University of Toronto's Faculty of Library and Information Science) states that, if users know reference librarians by name, they will make judgments about the competence of the staff and always ask for the best librarian, which will inconvenience and embarrass that librarian's colleagues. Why anyone would assume that users do not make judgments about nameless librarians is not clear to me; if a librarian cannot be identified by name, users might simply say "the one with the red hair" or "the one wearing green pants."

More importantly, what is so threatening about the possibility of having to learn something valuable from a co-worker? Perhaps the librarian best liked by users could help his or her colleagues to perform better by giving workshops or other skills seminars. Librarians must realize that if they "are not known to their clients by name [they] are at a distinct disadvantage in building the trust necessary to conduct the professional service for which they are responsible" (Durrance, p. 281).

Warm Deskside Manner

Studies indicate that a librarian can also use openness and warmth to encourage a user to be more forthcoming in a reference interview. A librarian who uses "self-disclosure," who reveals his or her personality and reactions to a patron, is more likely to encourage a user to return for reference help than a librarian who is not open or self-disclosing (Markham, Stirling, and Smith, 1983, p. 370). Furthermore, "patrons were more willing to work with the librarian" and "felt more satisfied when self-disclosure was used" in reference interviews (Markham, Stirling, and Smith, pp. 372, 373).

Public library users who were shown videotapes of interviews that varied in warmth and inclusion (the degree of bibliographic instruction) "were more likely to perceive the librarian to be competent and professional and to believe that the librarian would be able to provide a useful answer . . . if he or she was . . . warm [to the] . . . patron" (Harris and Michell, 1986, p. 100). These "judgments . . . were independent of the competence actually displayed by the librarians shown in the tapes. In each tape, the librarian successfully led the patron to materials which were relevant to the information needs presented" (Harris and Michell, p. 99). Evidently, more openness and warmth in a librarian's "deskside manner" will do much to change prevailing stereotypes.

Being alert to nonverbal clues is also crucial because, "according to Ray Birdwhistell, 65 percent of the social meaning in a two-person communication is carried by the nonverbal band, only 35 percent by the words spoken" (Munoz, 1977, p. 220). An awareness of people's gestures, facial expressions, posture, and positioning is needed to conduct a reference interview and to understand all the subtleties of a patron's message. If misinterpreted body language means "public service librarians fail to communicate with users, then . . . all the resources of the library . . . have come to very little purpose" (Murphy and Nilon as quoted in Boucher, 1976, p. 31).

Librarians who listen to the message of these user studies should encourage patrons to ask for reference help and to be more forthcoming while doing so. Although only one study (Taylor's) cites the librarian's image *per se* as the deciding factor in whether a user will come to the reference desk, other research does seem to indicate that the negative image is causing a problem. The dislike and lack of confidence that are felt "instinctively" by the patron are probably rooted in the stereotype of the disapproving librarian, just as the wariness, suspicion, and lack of trust probably are. Since the approachability, identity, warmth, openness, and body language of the librarian have been found to affect users strongly, they could be taken as indicators of the improvements needed.

Changing Users' Attitudes

Librarians must make their identity, approachability, and receptivity clear to patrons. A major study of the image of librarians and its effect on users' attitudes toward the reference interview is certainly needed. However, based on the rather superficial inventory done here, it is possible to make some recommendations for change.

The problem of users' lack of trust and confidence can be ameliorated by librarians identifying themselves. Herbert White points out that "the distinction between professional librarianship and what anyone who works in a library does has never been clearly understood by our public or emphasized by us" (White, Feb. 1, 1986, p. 58).

Canadian librarians might do well to institute a national library and librarians' week that stresses the role of the librarian, unlike the U.S. National Library Week which White finds disappointing because of its lack of coverage of professionals (White, Oct. 1, 1986). The role of librarians in community life might be one theme. Outreach programs (such as literacy and multicultural projects), reference success stories, special services (such as on-line searches), and the cultural importance of the National Library of Canada could all be "advertised."

Individual libraries could set up displays—not necessarily connected with national library week—to explain the education librarians receive, their responsibilities, "hot" topics in librarianship, the anatomy of a reference interview and the type of reference questions librarians are asked. Most importantly, the displays could show photographs of the librarians with an explanation of what they do and, if the librarians are agreeable, their names (or pseudonyms) and a generalized account of their education and interests. Library technicians could also be identified and their education and skills highlighted. The displays could be changed periodically so that librarians need not "show all" at once.

Name tags with an appropriate label ("reference librarian" or "library technician") are critical to building a feeling of trust and confidence. None of us would dream of consulting a lawyer or doctor who refused to give his or her name; no wonder patrons are hesitant about taking a chance on someone they do not know and who may or may not be a librarian.

With identity badges, referrals could "be made by name rather than . . . department. 'Mrs. Shields in Business can help you with that better than I can. Let me call and tell her you're on your way,' will maintain a stronger professional-client relationship than referring the user to 'Business' " (Durrance, p. 282). If patrons know which librarian helped them, they can phone back to check a fact or confirm information, which may allay the feeling of a lack of confidence or trust.

Librarians might also consider, as an experiment, booking appointments for reference interviews to be held in an office. Users might feel more confident if they had the librarian's undivided attention. Appointments would also emphasize that the librarian's time is valuable and that the service is professional. This is not to suggest, however, that the "come-one-come-all" service at the desk be stopped.

Reference librarians can do several things to increase their approachability and reduce patrons' wariness. Administrative duties can be rotated, either daily or weekly, so that a reference librarian on desk duty does not have to look harassed or unapproachable. "If [the librarian] is required to file a certain number of catalog cards, prepare book orders, or check invoices while manning the desk, he will never be able to change the image of the preoccupied librarian" (Swope and Katzer, pp. 164-165).

The reference desk might be physically rearranged to make it more inviting to patrons. Often "the worst barrier to the ideal reference situation is the reference desk itself" (Swope and Katzer, p. 161). "Do Disturb" signs or anything else that would encourage users to be less fearful of requesting assistance or of interrupting the librarian's administrative duties should be used.

To combat the users' sense of dislike and suspicion, reference librarians can learn to be more receptive. Library administrations should consider sponsoring seminars on self-disclosure and openness—perhaps including body language analysis—so librarians can adopt techniques "with the public [that] will alleviate many of the misunderstandings and misconceptions that occur daily" (Anderson, 1985, p. 61). Perhaps a reference librarian who is particularly adept at dealing with users could lead a workshop (or a series of workshops). A free-floating reference librarian who circulates among users might help to foster a sense of warmth and caring and stimulate interest in reference services. Traditional bibliographic instruction programs also seem to make patrons feel more at ease.

A few humorous jabs at our image might help to reduce users' dislike. The Louisiana Library Association marketed "Image Busters" T-shirts at its spring 1986 conference which show a severe matronly woman—hair in bun, bifocals perched atop her nose, and finger pressed to her lips in the traditional "shushing" posture—inside a red "forbidden" circle with a diagonal slash across it. Such a shirt could be used in a display or draped in a strategic place at the reference desk.

Efforts like this, however, should focus attention on the right thing: the stereotype should be mocked, not the woman depicted in it. There are, after all, some librarians who may superficially fit the stereotype but are tremendously capable. (One need not be a feminist to see that this image is misogynistic, but the historical response to it is even more disturbing. "In their crusade to disavow this image, librarians, male and female, betrayed a belief that there was something distasteful about women growing old, being plain, never marrying" [McReynolds, p. 30]). Humour is a powerful weapon, and if reference librarians use it wisely, it could play a part in changing the stereotypes.

Conclusion

Pauline Wilson's *Stereotype and Status* (1982) is the most comprehensive work on the image of librarians yet produced. She says librarians should "stop writing about the stereotype . . . unless they have something to say that will be helpful rather than hurtful" (p. 186).

By focusing on the ways image obscures users' understanding of librarians and reference work and by suggesting ways we can combat that misunderstanding, it is hoped that this article has added something useful to the debate. The matter of cardinal importance is that the image not get in the way of librarians' ability to offer valuable services to the patron. "It is irritating when the work of librarians is trivialized and when we become the butt of ridicule based on our presumed characteristics. When we contribute to that image by our failure to outline even the most fundamental role for professional librarians it becomes stupid and suicidal" (White, Oct. 1, 1986, p. 66).

References

Anderson, A. J. "Service with a Scowl." *Library Journal*, vol. 110, Aug., 1985.

Blatchford, Christie. "Librarians are wild!" *The Toronto Sun*, Feb. 28, 1986.

Boucher, Virginia. "Nonverbal Communication and the Library Reference Interview." *RQ*, vol. 16, Fall, 1976.

Bourkoff, Vivienne R., and Julia Binder Wooldridge. "The Image of Libraries and Librarians: Is It Changing?" *Public Library Quarterly*, vol. 6, Winter, 1985-86.

Durrance, Joan. "The Generic Librarian: Anonymity versus Accountability." *RQ*, Spring, 1983.

Harris, Roma M., and B. Gillian Michell. "The Social Context of Reference Work: Assessing the Effects of Gender and Communication Skill on Observers' Judgments of Competence." *Library and Information Science Research*, vol. 8, Jan.-March, 1986.

Hatchard, Desmond B., and Phyllis Toy. "The psychological barriers between library users and library staff." *Australian Academic and Research Libraries*, vol. 17, June, 1986.

"Image: How they're seeing us." *American Libraries*, Jan., 1985.

"Image: How they're seeing us." *American Libraries*, Dec., 1985.

"Image: How they're seeing us." *American Libraries*, May, 1986.

"Image: How they're seeing us." *American Libraries*, July-Aug., 1986.

Katz, William A. *Introduction to Reference Work, Vol. II: Reference Services and Reference Processes*, 3rd ed. McGraw-Hill, Toronto, 1978.

Line, Maurice B. "Student Attitudes to the University Library: A Survey at Southampton University." *Journal of Documentation*, vol. 19, Sept., 1963.

McReynolds, Rosalee. "A Heritage Dismissed." *Library Journal*, vol. 110, Nov. 1, 1985.

Markham, M. J., K. H. Stirling, and Nathan M. Smith. "Librarian Self-Disclosure and Patron Satisfaction in the Reference Interview." *RQ*, Summer, 1983.

Martell, Charles R. "Myths, Schooling, and the Practice of Librarianship." *College and Research Libraries*, vol. 45, Sept., 1984.

Merrill, Martha. "Truth in Advertising—Not for Librarians!" *The Southeastern Librarian*, vol. 34, Spring, 1984.

Munoz, J. "The Significance of Nonverbal Communication in the Reference Interview." *RQ*, vol. 16, Spring, 1977.

Orwen, Patricia. "Pay equity to phase out female wage ghettos." *The Toronto Star*, March 7, 1987.

Romanko, Karen. "A Librarian Lets Her Hair Down." *Publishers Weekly*, vol. 230, Sept. 12, 1986.

Swope, Mary Jane, and Jeffrey Katzer. "Why don't They Ask Questions?" *RQ*, vol. 12, Winter, 1972.

Taylor, Robert S. "Question-Negotiation and Information Seeking in Libraries." *College and Research Libraries*, vol. 29, May, 1968.

White, Herbert S. "Respect for Librarians and Librarian Self-Respect." *Library Journal*, vol. 111, Feb. 1, 1986.

White, Herbert S. "The Trivialization of National Library Week." *Library Journal*, vol. 111, Oct. 1, 1986.

Wilson, Pauline. *Stereotype and Status: Librarians in the United States*. Greenwood Press, Westport, Conn., 1982.

INFORMATION AND MADNESS

John Swan

> Information. What's wrong with dope and women? Is it any wonder the
> world's gone insane, with information come to be the only real medium
> of exchange? [1]

These words are uttered by one Semyavin, an exasperated black marketeer
in the midst of *Gravity's Rainbow*, Thomas Pynchon's great, mad epic of
eroticism and paranoia. We may feel we know better than Semyavin what
is wrong with traffic in drugs and sex—not that our world is any less
addicted to this commerce than his war-ravaged Germany—but we would
do well to take a hard look at his second question.

Librarians (we read) are information specialists, information scientists, information brokers, information professionals, information gurus,
guardians, gatekeepers. This—nobody dares deny it—is the Information
Age. The ruling assumption here is that there is truth in Semyavin's assertion. If we protest that information must be our salvation as much as it
is our madness, then the questions become even more difficult: What can
we do to make it serve as the former rather than the latter, apparently
dominant role, and what can librarians do to be part of the solution rather
than the problem?

The Age of the Librarian?

If the Information Age ought logically to be the Age of the Librarian, there
are many signs that the logic hasn't panned out, from low salary and funding levels to the closing of library schools to the considerable evidence that
in the vigorous national debates about educational and cultural priorities
libraries are an afterthought. This is not a balanced picture, to be sure.
There is much positive energy in the manifold current efforts of librarians
"to enhance learning and ensure access to information for all" (in the
words of the laboriously crafted American Library Association Strategic

Long-Range Plan). The massive shift to the new information technologies is the most obvious demonstration of this energy. The change is necessary, inevitable in any case, and rife with actual and potential advantages for librarians and everyone else.

There are no doubt many reasons for the failure of the Age of the Librarian to materialize, but the computer is not in itself one of them. The issue here is not our actual use of the evolving information technology, but our basic relationship to the information being processed.

On the simplest level, there is the problem of role identity: If the essence of our mission is to connect people with information, and this is also the essential function of the ever-more-powerful information machines, then the greater our commitment to these new tools, the more tenuous our existence as a profession apart from them. Our identity becomes less and less distinct from that of the computer specialist or, indeed, from the user friendly machines themselves. As usual in these matters, F. W. Lancaster puts forth the sharpest projection:

> Ultimately . . . libraries as we know them seem likely to disappear. Facilities will still exist to preserve the print-on-paper record of the past, of course, but they will be more like archives, or even museums, providing little in the way of public service. As for the electronic sources, libraries may have an interim role to play . . . to subsidize access to electronic publications. . . . In the longer term, it seems certain that the library will be bypassed. That is, people will have very little reason to visit libraries in order to gain access to information resources.[2]

Librarians Without Libraries

Lancaster's prediction applies to libraries, not librarians. What he calls the "disembodiment process," the ability to access information without resorting to library shelves, will eventually render those shelves obsolete. Librarians themselves will become specialists in various subject fields and forms of "information analysis"—"information consultants" who will outlive the "crumbling institution" of the library. Many do not agree with Lancaster, of course, but the alternative visions of the future, while often strong in advice for adapting and changing, are not based on arguments for a unique identity. Clyde Kendrick is typical in this:

> The doomsayers who predict the dispersion or demise of the library are wrong. As knowledge continues to multiply, the need for expertise—to collect, categorize, store, sort, retrieve, and advise and comfort bewildered users—will also multiply.[3]

Maybe so, but nothing in this necessitates a library or librarians as traditionally conceived, given that the machines will be able to step into most of the information provider/mediator roles—machines properly fed and cared for by the new breed of information specialists who have little in common with their building- and paper-confined predecessors. The dynamic of our information-bound identity is such that the librarians of the future who work as before in libraries will be doing so largely because particular populations won't be able to afford the machines and education required for immediate, unmediated access to information.

Information Activism

Not that there is anything wrong with concentrating on the needs of the have-nots. In *The Cult of Information*, Theodore Roszak's eloquent jeremiad on the influence of a computer- and information-dominated culture, the author speculates that this traditional association of libraries (public, that is) with the less-moneyed may be a major reason that libraries are "the missing link in the electronic age":

> The major commercial thrust behind the cult of information is to sell computers. Library sales count for little compared to the prospect of putting a privately owned microcomputer into every home. . . . The personal computer has been dressed up as an affluent, middle-class appliance. . . . Its use in the library associates it with ideas of public budgeting and thrifty purchasing, a sensible investment meant to serve a distinctly lower status populace. In its democratic outreach, the library contacts a clientele that may even include the genuinely poor, whom the data merchants do not regard as any sort of market at all.[4]

Computers can and are being enlisted in the service of the poor, and libraries should be engaged in information activism that offers access to the new technology as well as other forms of information and education. But if our identity centers more and more exclusively on the role of ombudsman for the information poor, as our other roles wither in the face of electronic progress, then we are likely to lose what power we do have. As noble and necessary as this role is in itself, librarians would find themselves circumscribed as information welfare workers, with little say except as the humblest of consumers in the information decision making.

From the Instant-Everywhere

It is not enough, then, to be content with a future as information workers for those who cannot help themselves. It is not enough, in fact, to define our roles in terms of information itself, or even information connected to the people who need it. As a number of observers have noted, the value of information itself must be examined.

While knowledge is orderly and cumulative, information is random and miscellaneous. We are flooded by messages from the instant-everywhere in excruciating profusion. In our ironic twentieth-century version of Gresham's law, information tends to drive knowledge out of circulation. . . . The latest information on anything and everything is collected, diffused, received, stored, and retrieved before anyone can discover whether the facts have meaning.[5]

Returning to the initial cry of our frustrated black marketeer, this relentless flood of facts to feed the Information Society is a symptom of radical disconnection, of collective madness.

But librarians and our allies in the index and database trades can protest that we tame and render orderly that which Daniel Boorstin refers to as random and miscellaneous. Our power to store and retrieve is unparalleled and growing stronger. For those who choose to ground their professional identity in this power, the essential role of the librarian may remain simple: connect people with the information they want, show them the possibilities and the routines (in the increasingly unlikely case that they are actually physically present).

For these people, the nature of the job will change along with the technology. They will (they do) contribute mightily to the revolution in information management that both enhances our mastery and renders null all the distinctions between librarianship and any other form of information processing.

Note a sample of the language of information mastery used by one of the managerial leaders of the new age of librarianship:

Compression techniques to wring out redundancy are available. One solution to the problem of ever-increasing amounts of information to absorb and integrate involves developing more comprehensive categories of information. . . . Library/information scientists have long worked to establish coping mechanisms that will reduce redundancy and effect compression through indexing, abstracting, extracting, classifying, and systematizing. Automatic sentence parsers and comparative algorithms may also assist this process.[6]

The managerial mandate is clear: "The essence of an organization is its information system," and in order for the library to function efficiently and responsively as the hub of the system, it must align itself entirely with the goal of information efficiency. Whether or not it is making us mad, whether or not it is driving knowledge out of circulation, information commands our total professional loyalty; our role, in this commanding view, is to speed its flow.

Efficiency as a Goal

Information efficiency as a goal may be admirable, but as a professional identity for librarianship it is fatally simplistic. We define ourselves as master navigators of the sea of information, when in fact we show every indication of drowning in it. Libraries great and small are forced by economic necessity to reallocate their resources to make room for the computer. Even large and well-supported research libraries have to choose, making cuts in acquisitions and channeling an ever larger portion of the flood of publications into electronic formats rather than onto shelves—generally accompanied by choruses of praise for the efficient solution of problems of space, preservation, labor, and access, all those messy burdens associated with paper.

Many such changes in libraries and librarians are basically a response to the pressure of what Boorstin calls the "instant-everywhere." Our identity is inevitably bound up with this vulnerability to the currents of the present (call it "responsiveness"), as public libraries seek to portray themselves to their taxpaying public as sources of instant information and up-to-the-minute best sellers, and academic libraries invest heavily in systems of remote electronic access and other means of sparing the modern scholar the pain of actually setting foot in the library.

Emerging or Submerged?

This relationship between professional identity and power is at the bottom of the worried dialogue among library science educators about just what it is that they teach. The four basic questions posed by Ann Prentice at a recent conference underline the dilemma: "Are we an emerging discipline? What is a discipline? How do we relate to other disciplines? Who cares?"[7] In fact, most librarians don't care, preferring to practice their trade rather than analyze it. But there are very compelling reasons to care, dramatized in the words of a university provost to a library school dean: "Your school is stumbling into some very valuable turf—somebody better protect it or it will be taken away."[8] If protecting our turf means committing ourselves more and more exclusively to electronic access, the question remains whether the result will be an emerging or a submerged discipline.

We already share the information access turf with some very powerful partners—and competitors. Like these "information professionals," we are subjected to profound challenges and changes occasioned by the technological revolution, but unlike them, we face losing our professional identity altogether. Being absorbed by assorted better-defined and likely better-paying nearby information professions may not seem such a terrible fate —unless there is something essential that librarians and libraries do that would be left undone when there are no more librarians and libraries.

In his keynote address to the ALA members assembled in San Francisco in the summer of 1987, Roszak returned to the theme of his book, warning librarians of the dangers inherent in a society in thrall to the Cult of Information, and locating our particular strength in our role as "cultural generalists rather than information specialists." In his most telling phrase, he described the librarian as "a living mind, a human presence" in the world of information.

This may serve as a clue to the essence of our profession—if there is one. I refer not so much to the already familiar instruction and support services that are the most recognizably human elements in connecting people with information. These activities, however admirable, will not long retain an important place in a society that finds its highest priority in the efficient transfer of precisely chosen bits of information to exactly the right end user. "Right" here means sophisticated, or at least well-connected, as in a recent OCLC strategic planning document predicting a powerful future for "value added services":

> providing the needed information in the most useful form will become a deciding factor for sophisticated users regarding which information sources or services are used. Giving such users a book or pile of journals or journal articles will not suffice. They will demand and get the precise pieces of information and conclusions they need and will be willing to pay for such services.[9]

For these people traditional librarianship just will not do. And if we continue to focus our highest professional aspirations on this clientele only, "value added" will also mean subtracting the living, thinking librarians from all points of actual patron contact.

A Human Context for Information

But there is a larger implication in the relationship between librarians and their patrons, and a more pervasive potential loss if the librarian and the library are driven—or reconfigured—out of existence. The presence of librarians and their buildings in the scheme of things is not only to provide the connection to people, but to provide a human context for information itself. Pynchon's black marketeer Semyavin was right: A world hooked on information to the exclusion of everything else *is* insane. The users who insist always on the instant retrieval of their own precise line of information, shorn of any context except their preconceived notion of their needs, *are* living an unhinged existence.

It is not necessary to go far to find evidence that many of our most sophisticated information users—doctors, lawyers, nuclear engineers, shuttle rocket designers, foreign policy experts, presidents—are performing at levels far short of the golden promise of the vast wealth of information so easily available to them.

Adding another voice to those of Boorstin and Roszak, Oscar Handlin recently wrote of the threatened condition of the library and the unique nature of what it offers:

> The machines that supply databases and bibliographies with superb efficiency do one thing only: they repeat what is put into them. To a question asked, they return a programmed answer. Libraries, however, like teaching, can do more than provide information on request. Information is not knowledge, any more than knowledge is wisdom. . . . Really creative work permits or compels students, teachers, and scholars to look for answers to questions they cannot formulate. . . . To serve that long-term, reflective purpose, the research library—however large or small —presents its users, not single books or bits of information . . . but collections. . . . A collection is evidence of a mind at work, making choices in the light of some view of knowledge—past, present, and future.[10]

Significantly, Handlin expresses a distrust of librarians:

> The librarians attempt to cope; but the libraries are too important to leave it to them.[11]

We tend to align ourselves with power—"presidents, deans, and provosts" —and with the goals of managerial efficiency these forces usually represent. The managers are right; information is power. But a lot of powerfully insane forces are loose in the world because powerful people are manipulating information without regard to any but the most narrow perspective.

Context is Everything

Librarianship as we have known it so far has confronted the world of information from exactly the opposite point of view: context is everything. The human presence which we express is in effect the profound insistence on a human scale. The signal difference between information and knowledge is in the degree of connectedness, perspective, human value. Knowledge and wisdom require information in a human context. The hierarchies of the Library of Congress and Dewey classifications and the various protocols of access that we depend upon do not in themselves constitute wisdom, but—for all their occasional insanities—they do provide a grounding, and they do reflect the broad and deep perspective that is fundamental to the library.

Whether or not a librarian is literally present to help a patron, a person who uses a library encounters information in its broadest cultural context. Often the search is an impatient chase after just the sort of isolated piece of data that the "value added" information industry could spit out instantly. Often the search is conducted in near total ignorance of what the library systems are all about. But if it is conducted in a library, and if the transaction has any meaning at all for said patron, then something more has happened than the mere transfer of information. To some degree, however humble, that person experiences the human context out of which the chosen book, record, article, phrase, or statistic has come. Again, librarians knowledgeable about the organizing and synthesizing potential of the new technology may protest that the truly interactive workstation and the development of "hypertext" electronic publication promise quantum leaps in the power of the individual to create a context for information, to summon vast chunks of culture to a screen, juxtaposing and rearranging at will. But channeling quantities of pre-programmed resources onto a screen is still an act of linear, logical manipulation. It surely offers its own kind of creativity, but it is not the learning experience offered by the library.

The new information machines require those entrusted with them to conceive of information in ways both physically and intellectually different from that stored on paper in libraries. These different media are not mutually exclusive, of course; we live in a society that is showing itself very capable of conceiving of information as both symbols on a page and as a disembodied collection of stored signals. But the priorities of this society and this profession are still that one medium may well win a fatal dominance over the other. And for us, the "informatization" of society has the inherent ability to separate librarians from libraries, from books, and from their patrons.

The library is special and necessary in the world of information because by its very nature it counters the decontextualization and the disembodiment that is an inevitable part of the electronic metamorphosis of information. It is true that information is not a physical thing, and neither are accumulated knowledge and wisdom. But the library and its contents are the closest physical analogues we have to this precious immateriality; they offer the most compelling reminder of, and the freest access to, the whole fabric of memory and knowledge. Information that is torn from that fabric is a dangerous medium of exchange.

Information as Obsession

In the chaos and ruin of the Zone, the post-war Europe of *Gravity's Rainbow*, all of the traditional contexts and connections have been disrupted. A strange, mad welter of conspiracies, underground networks, and palpable paranoias have rushed in to fill the void. In that world, information is the object of the deepest obsessions.

It may just be that our Information Society carries within it a similar drive that will master us, and that we will then no longer have any use (except in scattered cultural backwaters) for information that comes in the packages which the library offers. Perhaps another kind of human presence will assert itself in that new age, something beyond us librarians and our buildings. It would be better, however, if we asserted ourselves now as the unique providers, not merely of information, but of a vital context, a foundation in collective sanity, for information. If this sounds more than a little quaint in the face of the new information science, that may just mean that we have our work cut out for us, among ourselves as well as among our patrons, who still have libraries and librarians to serve them.

References

1. Pynchon, Thomas. *Gravity's Rainbow.* Bantam, 1974, p. 300.
2. Lancaster, F. W., "Future Librarianship: Preparing for an Unconventional Career," *Wilson Library Bulletin,* May 1983, p. 749.
3. Kendrick, Clyde, "The University Library in the Twenty-First Century," *College and Research Libraries,* March 1986, p. 127.
4. Roszak, Theodore. *The Cult of Information.* Random, 1986, p. 172-173.
5. Boorstin, Daniel. *Gresham's Law: Knowledge or Information?* Library of Congress, 1980, p. 3.
6. Daniel, Evelyn, "An Examination of Faculty and Administrative Knowledge Workers and Their Major Information Support Units," *Campus of the Future: Conference on Information Resources,* OCLC, 1987, p. 42.
7. "Protecting Our Turf," Report on the January 14-16, 1987 ALISE conference, *LJ,* March 15, 1987, p. 44.
8. *Ibid.,* p. 44.
9. "Strategic Planning Scenario Assumptions" in *SONAC* (SUNY OCLC Network Advisory Committee) *Letter* No. 51, July 23, 1987.
10. Handlin, Oscar, "Libraries and Learning," *The American Scholar,* Spring 1987, p. 214-215.
11. *Ibid.,* p. 218.

THE RARE BOOK
LIBRARIAN'S DAY

Daniel Traister

I.

In the autumn of 1975, I entered library school, where I was pleased to find a program especially designed for the preparation of rare book librarians. I was less pleased to hear my instructor inform my class, at its first meeting, that jobs in rare books generally went to rich WASP males. But I am a baseball fan and know that .333 is a respectable major league batting average. So, even though I failed both "rich" and "WASP," I gambled on "male"—and, I suppose, I have won my little bet.

I am the Curator of Special Collections—that is, the person in charge of the rare books and manuscripts department—at the University of Pennsylvania's Van Pelt Library. I have a title on my door, though no Bigelow on my floor. People call on me to write articles, organize conferences, even give speeches, and that is very flattering (more flattering than remunerative, to be sure). Several libraries have paid me money, and one continues to do so, for what they are pleased to consider my services in areas of interest to them. I work in an atmosphere that reeks of older books, and I get to do so in a setting—that is, in a library—with which I have been long enamored.

But almost none of what I do is what I had expected to do when I entered library school a bit more than a decade ago, nor does it bear much resemblence to what I thought I would be doing when, some eleven months later, I became the second boy on my block with four degrees.

How can I describe my ordinary day? Most readers of a journal such as this one already have ideas about rare books and what it is like to work with them; some may even have polite notions about the people who do so. I do not want to imply that these ideas are wrong, although I suspect that they may be inadequate. Rare books, we know, are the *sexy* part of the library world, the stuff of scholarship. They are what *research librarians* work with, and require specialized knowledge, bibliographical expertise, historical sensibility, and high moral standards of their guardians. The status of rare books librarianship is high. Those of us who work in this field are perceived—though perhaps we merely perceive ourselves—as an elite breed. This is certainly the view I learned in library school. It seems to have spilled over into the larger world.

As for our colleagues who toil in the mire of circulation or general reference—well, surely *their* horizons extend no further than *Choice* cards and RLIN terminals. They expatiate nauseatingly upon 590 and 620 fields. They carefully weed from their collections older books—those that date from before the Vietnam War. They do not know tree calf from russia, have never heard of Jenson or Mardersteig, and think that Palatinos get forty-six miles to the gallon in E.P.A. highway driving tests. Some must never even *see* a book or a periodical—let alone *read* one; God forbid! No doubt they spend their days thinking about computers, systems, circulation tapes, acquisitions records, retrospective conversions (a concept that has always struck me as peculiarly Mormon), or other bits and pieces of the detritus of inventory control which differ not at all from whatever it is that happens in Filene's basement or in the world of the stockboy at the neighborhood grocery. They work wholesale, down there in the trenches, with their seven thousand readers a day—most of whom are in the library for this week's issue of *Time* or last month's *Harper's*.

Rare Book's three thousand readers a year, by contrast, work with the raw materials from which new knowledge will derive. Surely, their research needs our expertise: our exquisitely refined knowledge of books and manuscripts, bindings, type faces, illustrative techniques—and our knowledge of what books and manuscripts are *for*. We read our books and study them. We create bibliographies of them. Recognizing the relatedness of all special collections, we seek tools to make their joint resources widely accessible—and we began doing this long before our colleagues in general collections tumbled to the advantages of cooperative interlibrary networks. We study and interpret the history of books and printing. We contribute to the history of libraries. We understand the role of books in the cumulative augmentation of knowledge upon which scholarly progress is founded —and we know in our hearts that it is in *our* part of the library that the books and manuscripts which support this augmentation are found. These views of our trade are fostered not only by our library shcool education but also urged on us by such great librarians as Ian Willison of The British Library and Paul Raabe of Wolfenbüttel's Herzog August Bibliothek.

We patiently gather our books and manuscripts, buying them or cajoling donors into giving them to us; we see them catalogued; we try to publicize their presence in our institutions; and we love them. We love them, as we love our readers, retail, not wholesale. Our library may have three and a half million volumes and serve seven thousand readers a day, but we care for only a hundred and fifty thousand volumes and serve five readers a day—and we try to learn as much about all of them as we can. We read and write about our incunabula, our renaissance bookbindings, Shakespeare's First Folio, Elzevier imprints, Jonathan Swift's publications, nineteenth-century American publishing or book illustration, the first editions of William Carlos Williams; we caress each lovely book. We calendar, catalogue, list, encapsulate, or otherwise massage our medieval manuscripts, our Lope de Vega holographs, our eighteenth-century account books, our Benjamin Franklin papers, our nineteenth-century diaries, our twentieth-century literary papers. We swim in a sea absolutely gelatinous with primary sources.

No *Time* for us. Nor *Time* readers, either: *our* readers are bibliographical sophisticates, adding to the sum of knowledge. They edit reliable texts, the basis of all work in the historical humanities, or seek new information from forgotten books of the past which we have worked hard to preserve and to make available. Rare book librarians are guardians of an old scholarly tradition, *philology*—as defined by such people as Curtius, Spitzer, and Auerbach—and our readers are practitioners of that most venerable of scholarly crafts. We work closely with them, one on one, trying to meet or to anticipate their needs, interpreting to them both our own closed collections and those collections for which our colleagues at other institutions care. Together, we and our readers walk hand in hand toward Scholar's Heaven, the great British Library in the sky.

Or so one might suppose. And yet, for reasons I do not entirely understand, my days are not spent in philological or bibliographical trailblazing. Several of the booksellers I am privileged to know do much more such bibliographical work than I manage.

Maybe it should astonish or distress me that my readers, when they call upon me at all, usually do so to ask what the funny little letters at the bottom of the page mean—I'm talking about Ph.D's in literature who teach at serious universities but have never learned what a signature is, by the way, and (as Anna Russell once remarked) I'm not making this up, you know.

Or they want to know why some twit has just refused them permission to photocopy our exemplar of the first issue of Pope and Swift's *Letters* (London, 1740-41; Teerink 1580), no other copy of which seems to exist anywhere.

Or they would be gratified if I sent a note to the National Endowment for the Humanities informing that august body that the X Papers will indeed be available for Y's inspection during the summer of 1986, when Y hopes that NEH will support his or her Philadelphia excursion. (I always do. Anyone foolhardy enough to *want* to spend a summer in Philadelphia deserves to.)

I do have a reader—one—who comes in to see me every so often to talk about his latest discovery in our sixteenth- and seventeenth-century classical texts, whose provenance among *Mitteleuropa* classicists of those centuries he investigates as a kind of hobby. Not once, however, has he asked me to assist him in his investigations. Since I know nothing about the subject, he has not hurt my feelings by this failure to acknowledge my expertise.

My doors are not beaten down by scholars who want to walk hand in hand with me towards a new learning. Only two scholars have even suggested that I buy a book for their use. One suggested something so breathtakingly impossible that I have politely pretended to forget all about it. The other appeared utterly astonished to learn that I actually *bought* one of the books he suggested (the other had already been sold when I reached the bookseller). It had not occurred to him that I might take his suggestion seriously. I hope he was pleased.

No one has ever seriously suggested that I do anything even approaching "research" in the collections for which I am responsible. The only people I have met silly enough to assume that I do such a thing on my own are disgruntled faculty members, my acquaintances at other institutions, who envy me my opportunity to pursue my own interests among miles of stacks filled with the books I love. "Isn't it pretty to think so?" as Jake Barnes remarks somewhere or other.

I don't suppose that any of them ever believes me when I say that, during my first five years as a rare book librarian, I looked up exactly two references for my own scholarly use. In fact, they were the same reference, from John Harington's 1591 translation of Ariosto's *Orlando Furioso*. I looked it up once when I was writing whatever I was writing, and once again to check my reference when I was proofing the galleys. Fortunately: for, first time around, I'd got the reference wrong.

If my days are not spent dipping my head into the scholarly trough, what, then, *do* I do? This is a question I have often asked myself. I have chosen one day—October 24th, 1985—to recall, as best I can, for your edification.

II.

I woke up a bit before seven, shaved, showered, ate breakfast, and drove off to pick up some books from a suburban donor. I spent the time from 9:45 till a bit after noon choosing from among the donor's books. Then, with a chauffeur's help, I loaded some of them into my car during a light rain.

Back at Penn, I parked in a borrowed space behind the Library and brought the books up to the sixth floor with the help of a colleague returning from lunch as I arrived. Because I had to thank the donor and arrange for appraisal of the gift, I asked a student assistant to begin listing the books. I would then have forgotten about them but for the unanticipated arrival of the Chair of my Library's Friends group, a friend of the donor's family. She wanted to see the books; she also wanted to go to lunch. I hadn't planned on such a lunch. But I am a good boy, and so I went, taking along a member of my staff who had not yet met our Friend's Chair socially.

Lunch took about an hour longer than the sandwich I'd have sent out for. Back at my office, I found my door littered with little pink message slips: I had received phone calls while away. I had, for instance, to call the librarian at The Lewis Walpole Library in Farmington, Connecticut—a branch of the Yale University Libraries—about some ex-Walpoles that had turned up at Penn. We were on the verge of trading them to Farmington for non-Walpole copies of the same books, and I had to make arrangements to get them to Yale, along with a supposed ex-Walpole book from a neighboring library, whose Curator I also had to call.

There were other messages and mail, as well. I shuffled through them as best I could. Most I did not get to. The building supervisor showed up—twice—to talk about one thing or another. I got to ponder a budget which we were writing as part of a grant application. I spent about five minutes typing an expense account and enclosing receipts to cover reimbursement for a trip to New York. I got a call from a colleague at Brown asking when I could meet with him and two other colleagues in New York about a conference the four of us are planning for 1987. None of us was going to be free for the better part of the coming month.

Finished with him, I spoke with another person on his staff about the needs of a genealogist who had approached Brown for an early American manuscript which Penn owns. I agreed that she could use our manuscript, and he promised to tell her so.

Most of the letters in my mail that afternoon didn't get read; most of the junk didn't get tossed. I did manage to distribute that day's batch of booksellers' catalogues to my colleagues; it is useful to have someone read them while they are still fresh.

I was now 4:30. I left to attend the opening at a neighboring institution of an exhibition to which we had loaned several items. I took a colleague with me. At the exhibition I met several people from our own Friends group, including several donors, and I spoke with as many of them as I could, while trying not to neglect the people who had mounted the show, other librarians who, like me, were visitors from neighboring institutions, or my own colleague. The opening lasted till eight, but my colleague and I lasted only till six. We returned to "my" parking spot behind our Library, for we, too, had an event that night.

The Philadelphia area Penn alumnae held their monthly meeting that evening at the library. One of its attractions was to be a visit to Special Collections. While I had visited our suburban donor and the neighboring institution's exhibition, my colleagues had pulled a number of obvious objects for us to speak about: a Shakespeare First Folio; Audubon's *Birds of America*; a copy of Martyn's *English Entomologist* lacking *all* of the plates but noteworthy nonetheless since it comes from the library of William Beckford and contains, instead of the plates, the original watercolors from which the plates were allegedly made; a letter from Thomas Jefferson on the occasion of Benjamin Franklin's death; a manuscript poem on women by Elizabeth Barrett Browning; and other more or less similar stuff. We had to set it all up in preparation for the group's scheduled seven o'clock arrival.

However, they didn't arrive at seven. They were half an hour late and arrived bearing food which they insisted on eating before their tour. Their delay gave us a chance to pull some additional materials which seemed likely to interest the people whom we were now seeing for the first time. But their delay also forced my colleague, who had a train to catch, to leave before she got to speak; she had cancelled a dinner invitation in order to stay at Penn that evening. I spoke for her as well as for myself. And then, after the group had left, put the books away and cleaned up the space in which it had met.

I got home towards eleven. I looked at the *Times* and, since it had recently resumed publication following a strike, the *Inquirer.* I ate some soprassata and a yogurt; I'd had no supper, and this was it. I peeked at my children. They were sleeping. I spoke with my wife. Somewhere around midnight, I went to sleep.

Let me make a few quick points about the day I've just described. One thing that may not be obvious is that my attendance at both the donor's home and the exhibition represents *work*. These are not occasions when one walks up to a bookcase and sweeps everything in sight into a large sack, or says hello to a few folk and runs for the hors d'ouevres and bourbon. Along with the donor were a daughter-in-law, who is a member of the Council of my Library's Friends group, a grandson, and a sister. At the opening, I met both our Friends and people who might become my Library's Friends. One person I saw is already one of our donors, as well as an eminent member of Penn's faculty. He remarked that he'd expected to see me there. If Woody Allen is right that ninety percent of success consists in just showing up, then I am glad he did see me: he thinks of me as "active," which he clearly values, and it is therefore important for my Library that I live up to his expectations. One must always be ready to talk graciously—and, if possible, amusingly—about topics that may or may not be of interest, to people whom one may or may not ever see again. This is not the sort of work for which a library school education prepares one.

When I parked behind my Library after returning from the donor and, later, from the exhibition, I was parking illegally in a space that is not mine. Here is another small lesson that no one ever taught me in library school: make friends with your building administrator. If it is raining, and you want to park in a space that is not yours, and will need help in getting cartons of books upstairs—or if you just need lightbulbs changed, or toilet paper for the restrooms on your floor—a friendly staff may be more valuable than a foundation grant.

I involved several colleagues in most of my activities on the day I have described. Development and promotion of one's staff is the ongoing responsibility of *any* librarian. Today's employee may be tomorrow's opposite number—and *should* be, if you have done your hiring well—and she will remember if you have helped or hindered her advancement. Better, then, to help. Better for you right now, in fact: the better your staff look, the better you look. My staff *all* look better than I do. As much as possible, I want them participating in the meetings I go to: they keep more details in their heads than I can, and always save me from my own vast ignorance.

The matter of a trade of books with Farmington deserves special mention. While it is worthwhile to cooperate with one's colleagues, it is worth remembering that cooperation with other institutions is also not a bad idea. A bookseller has privately berated me for letting Yale have Penn books that, because of their provenance, are worth more than the books we got in exchange. I have, he thinks, failed in my fiduciary responsibilities to my institution. But in fact our books *belong* at Farmington, where Walpole's library is, as far as possible, being reconstructed; Penn needs the texts, but not this particular provenance. My directors had the option of asking Yale to pay for the difference between our ex-Walpole and their non-Wolpole copies of these books, and to pay for their respective appraisals, as well; I am glad they didn't take that option. It might have made the matter so complicated that Yale would merely have marked its copy of Hazen to indicate that these books were at Penn, and that would have been that. Libraries are not booksellers. We support serious scholarship, generally at our own expense. It is not our role in life to turn a profit. All this, by the way, is an issue that had been considered for a long time before my October 24th phone call to Farmington—since 1982, in fact. Libraries move with a kind of ponderous grace when they move at all; the events of any one day are more often than not the results of events on many other days.

One last point. After the alumnae group finished its visit, who put back the Audubon by himself? Lugging Audubons around is a fine substitute for visiting a Nautilus exercise machine. And who returned the reading room chairs and tables to their proper positions for the next day's readers? And who was never told in library school about the work-related benefits of a strong back?

III.

And that's it. *A Day in the Life.* The bulk of my work on October 24th had nothing to do with what most people may suppose rare book librarians do, and bore almost no resemblence to what my library school education had led me to expect of a career in rare book librarianship. My day certainly included nothing that coud be called "research" by even the most generous of definitions.

Of course, everybody has such days on occasion. Surely this one was not typical.

But my point is that this day was *precisely* typical—except for the fact that, during it, I got to look at some books when I was at our donor's house. Precious little of most of my days has anything to do with books.

My day was spent, in case I have to make this explicit, *talking to people*, in person, over the phone, or in writing, while trying to keep my staff as unencumbered as possible so that some of my department's work might get done. It's dirty work, there's a lot of it, and *somebody* has to do it. My job is administration, making a place work—or, if not that, then at least making a place give the *impression* that it works.

That is my job. I get paid to talk. To talk, to impress, to let my staff work with our books, our manuscripts, and our readers (all tasks I used to love doing myself) without being burdened by the demands of all the people to whom I talk for them. Make us look respectable. Give the world —or that stunningly tiny portion of it which might, for a brief moment, care—the feeling that, at Penn, those folks in rare books know what they're doing.

It's not quite so simple as it sounds. To be fair, my job does involve something more than just the talk to which I referred exaggeratedly above. But for most of it, nothing in my library schooling prepared me, any more than it prepared me for the reality of my typical day.

Do we know what we're doing? Beats me. We collect books and manuscripts in a variety of areas. We hope they're appropriate, although they get such little use that, nine cases out of ten, we never find out. We try to make them as accessible as possible. We encourage readers to come make use of them. Our rule of thumb is simple: if it walks, talks, and doesn't smell too bad, it can be issued a book or a manuscript. This laxity doesn't help much: we still don't get many readers. Maybe that's not so bad. In a world in which all of the historical humanities are in trouble, it's surely not our fault.

But while it's not our fault, it *is* our problem. In fact, it's *my* problem. For better or worse, I care about my institution's books, about collecting and caring for the materials with which scholars may advance knowledge in a variety of disciplines, and about seeing that they get used in ways that will justify our expensive existence to the people who pay for my department and its bills. These are all matters I learned to care about in library school, matters that my background had already prepared me to care about. They're what make my job different from managing the inventory in Filene's basement, apart from being less well paid.

But it's a problem about which I do almost nothing. What I do do isn't too terribly different from managing the inventory in Filene's basement. I worry about what—and what not—to purchase for our collections. And how to pay for what we buy. Or I worry about dealing with donors.

I worry about staff members. They get colds, retire, have accidents or family problems. I *have* to worry about them, if for no other reason than that our work and their vacation schedules may be affected. My job demands no more by way of *human* concern, though if I feel that, too, then maybe I collect points with Heaven.

I worry about water leaks; the possibility that use of my department's facilities for luncheons or dinners will bring us vermin who like to eat what we like to eat but who will settle, *in extremis*, for books and papers; payroll forms; new online catalogues and the ways in which our collections are represented in them; publication projects that involve our holdings; new shelving; organizing manuscript collection data; staff development, evaluation, raises, promotions; supervision of student assistants; reading room regulations; photocopying prices and restrictions; conservation; exhibitions and the reconstruction of exhibition space; annual reports; Friends of the Library newsletters, events, and fundraising appeals; an annual series of bibliographical lectures run by my Library; book funds; insurance; security installations; and departmental and library-wide meetings on a variety of issues.

Of course, I don't *do* most of these things. My life is spent in avoiding work. My staff does them. But I do worry about them. Occasionally, I even have to lift, carry, hew, and haul, or stand back as my four female colleagues do these things, living in hope that ruptures are a sex-linked health hazard.

I worry, in short, about keeping the collections for which I am responsible running for the benefit of the scholars whose research and publications justify the enterprise. Not my research—theirs. It's a service profession, as the name of the library school I attended—Columbia University's School of Library Service—reminds us.

And these are the matters that occupy my days. There are other librarians, in and out of special collections, who must dispose of twenty-four hours more cleverly than I. I admire my colleague, at another institution, who writes about paper history. Another has made herself expert on the history of book illustration techniques. A third is a leading incunabulist. A fourth knows more about early American bookbinding than anyone. A fifth studies Mathew Carey. A sixth thinks Very Big Thoughts about the nature of The Book.

I don't do these things. I think small thoughts. When I have time to think. That's not as frequent as I wish. But my guess is that, for most people in this field, thought and the time it requires are luxuries beyond price. One result is that not enough people know about the resources in our care.

My staff and I care for approximately a hundred and fifty thousand printed books, many hundred of thousands (if not millions) of pieces of paper, and about four to five thousand readers a year. We are four-and-one-half professionals, assisted by two-fifths of a secretary and approximately two FTE student assistants during the fall and spring semesters and an additional two or so FTE students during the summer. I wish we did research. But the amount of work we have just keeping up—or trying to keep up—with what must be done day in and day out to keep abreast of our readers and the requirements of our collections for improved access, improved environment, improved security, and continued growth precludes much by way of spare time for research. We may *receive* relatively few readers—but even though I didn't see one of them on October 24th, my day was more than filled by work intended to *serve* readers.

Rare books librarianship—"research librarianship," as popularly conceived—sounds like a fine field and an exciting one. I admire my colleagues in it, and I remain grateful both for the training I received which prepared me to enter this field and for the generosity of spirit which has permitted several people to think me fit to romp in it, too. But, on many days, I am far from certain that it is the field I am in. Or even one that exists.

IV.

In 1954, J. H. Hexter's essay, "The Historian and His Day," appeared in the *Political Science Quarterly*, later to be reprinted in his book, *Reappraisals in History*, first published in 1961. In preparing this essay, I have borne Hexter's in mind. From it, I have taken my title, slightly modified to rid it of the stench—unconscious, I devoutly hope—of sexism with which it was originally tainted.

Hexter contrasts two schools of thought about history prevalent when he wrote. The first he called "present-minded." Its advocates are "realists" who "recognize that every generation reinterpretes the past in terms of the exigencies of its own day." The second school he called "history-minded": "idealists," they argue that we ought "not to intrude our contemporary value systems and preconceptions and notions into our reconstruction of the past" and that is the historian's duty "to understand the past in its terms, not our own."

Just as Hexter contrasted two views of historiography in his essay, I have been contrasting two views of rare books librarianship, less explicitly than he, I confess. One view is "idealistic." It is the view of the high calling that special collections, or research, librarianship represents, and it has a generally unarticulated corollary that the practice of special collections librarianship reflects the high nature of the calling. The otherview is "realistic" and it is the view implicit in the description I have offered of my job and its typical day.

Hexter ends his essay by pointing out that neither the present- nor the history-minded view of the historian's calling is adequate. Both viewpoints reflect aspects of historical practice that any historian who takes seriously what he or she is about must engage. I fear that I have no similar reconciliation to propose, even though I value the calling of special collections librarianship highly while also understanding the compelling necessities that underlie at least my own experience of its daily practice.

It may not be true at all research libraries, but it is, I think, true at most that special collections are understaffed as well as underfinanced. They *must* be, if libraries are to pay for the services which the vast majority of their users require. There is no parity between a few thousand readers a year and several thousand readers a day. No arguments based on a notion of the relative "quality" of readership—a quality I for one would hesitate to measure, having experienced more than my share of lousy scholarship, and written some of it, too—will make this disparity disappear.

Understaffing and underfinancing mean more work per person for the people who staff special collections. If these people believe (as my colleagues and I believe) in the importance of their collections to scholars seeking to advance knowledge, and if they take their work to mean keeping their institutions open, growing, and reasonably well-administered, then the amount of research they do is going to be pretty small.

This is true at Penn, whose collections are much more important, much richer, and, so far as I can tell, much less well-studied than most people realize, and where my colleagues, at least, are well-prepared properly to value and study our holdings. The four of them hold at least eleven degrees, with one more of which I am aware in progress, and it is my well-founded impression that, between them, my colleagues know something about a large number of topics. But they don't do much research even in our own holdings or on topics in their areas of special expertise: mostly, they try to keep their heads (and mine) above water. That alone proves to be a moderately time-consuming task; I certainly hope that our readers would agree that it is an important one.

Moreover, librarianship is, at all levels, an administrative field. Because its salaries are notoriously inadequate, it forces people to seek increasingly responsible (and therefore time-consuming) administrative positions simply so that they may feed themselves and their families without too much deprivation. Most library administrators I know do not have the time to add to the history of books, printing, and libraries or to create bibliographies that open up new fields of study; these are not issues we think

about. Nor, quite simply, are they our jobs. The decent administration of
a library is an important job: it is worth doing well. I know very few people
who have taken on administrative duties who do not feel strongly that,
however distant such duties may be from what they set out to accomplish
in a field, administration both deserves and requires one's whole-hearted
attention.

Yet both traditional bibliography (in the manner of Greg, McKerrow,
Bowers, and Tanselle) and the new *histoire du livre* (Martin, Darnton, and
Eisenstein) will suffer if practicing librarians do not contribute the expertise gained in their quotidian workaday experience with older books and
manuscripts. And those scholars who require the resources of special collections will suffer if not served by staff able to interpret complex, closed-
stack collections on the basis of extensive knowledge of and familiarity
with their collections—knowledge which current conditions rarely permit
them to acquire. The kind of person most attracted to and best prepared
for work in a special collection will chafe if this sort of research is impossible. I suspect that it very nearly is.

Not quite. But very nearly. Some institutions are so rich that they have
staffs numerous enough for some to pursue scholarly investigation of their
own collections. Others are so terrifyingly underutilized that their staff do
research because they face few other demands for their attention. People
need and like to work, as well as to love, as Freud knew.

But most institutions are neither rich nor terribly underutilized. They
are used just heavily enough to keep staff hopping, and financed just badly
enough so that any research which staff manages is minute—or done in
whatever passes for "free time." This is a loss not only of the talents of
the staff. It is also damaging, finally, to the morale of a good staff. And,
perhaps most important, it puts an effective damper on the investigation
and dissemination of important and useful information about books, publishers, libraries, and collections from which the entire world of historical
scholarship might benefit—and benefit in a very high degree.

I wrote about this matter in a different context some years ago, query-
ing a few so-called "research librarians" about the amount of research they
actually do, and then counting, as well, the contributions published by
librarians in several bibliographical journals. The results of that informal
survey were not encouraging. By most measures, American rare book and
manuscript collections present an impressive picture. Well-stocked, increasingly well-staffed, and well-administered, they are far easier to use
and far more responsive to their society and its needs than many of their
European counterparts. They are not for these reasons altogether happy
places, however.

I may be wrong, but it seems to me that both scholars and rare book
libraries *need* "research librarians." Libraries like Penn's—like *many* of
Philadelphia's libraries, for that matter, which together constitute one of

the great unknown scholarly resources of this country—deserve the public attention which the studies of research-oriented staff could bring them. Right now, several Philadelphia area libraries, supported by an imaginative grant from The Pew Memorial Trust, are preparing an exhibition scheduled for 1988 of this region's rare books and manuscripts. Such exhibitions are welcome. But they will not be enough. Flash is better than nothing, to be sure. But despite the endeavors of one of the flashiest librarians in Philadelphia's history, and numerous brilliant exhibitions, one of the greatest American research libraries remains underutilized and underappreciated in its own hometown; even Edwin Wolf could, more or less singlehandedly, do only so much to spread the news of The Library Company—just as, a bit further west, Rudolf Hirsch could, more or less singlehandedly, do only so much to spread the news of Penn.

One could conclude by remarking that rare book librarianship is, after all, not a field of high romance; it is a job. It is not a field which *requires* scholarship, and obviously it does not always, within working hours, leave scholarship much scope—though, goodness knows, scholarship will never hurt. It is a job in which one performs crucial services for *other* scholars— and for *very* few even of them.

But our great libraries will never be as well-used as their resources cry out for them to be till we return a bit of high romance to their staffing. That means, I think, finding ways to support staff research in their collections. Training for special collections librarians needs a clearer definition of "research librarianship." The expectations of those who enter the field will be constantly disappointed by reality if its daily necessities are not more realistically emphasized.

Not until I started to work in a research library did anyone breathe a word of that reality to me. Ninety percent of librarianship, I was told by a man who gave me a drawer full of catalogue cards, involves filing. You might as well find out now if you like it.*

---

*This essay was originally presented in somewhat different form before audiences at Columbia University's School of Library Service (1985) and the Franklin Inn Club, Philadelphia (1986). I am grateful to Terry Belanger and David Holmes for the invitations which gave me the occasion to write it. I have not tried completely to efface the evidence of its original oral delivery. I want to thank my colleague, Kathleen Reed (Special Collections, Van Pelt Library), for the critical care with which she read earlier versions of this text.

THE ONE-PERSON LIBRARY: AN ESSAY ON ESSENTIALS REVISITED

Guy St. Clair

A special issue of *Special Libraries*, the primary journal for librarians working in the special library and information services community, is an appropriate venue for an updated look at one-person librarianship. It is especially appropriate that this special issue deals with continuing education, for this is an area in which the subject of one-person librarianship has been given major emphasis.

In the 11 years since the appearance of "The One-Person Library: An Essay on Essentials" (published in *Special Libraries*),[1] an enormous amount of attention has been given to this specific category of library management. Not only has this decade plus one year produced a book[2] and a continuing newsletter,[3] professional awareness about the subject has been raised to new levels. Today there is no need to define the term (as was the case in 1976, when to talk about "one-person libraries" was to elicit a quizzical look on the listener's face), and one-person librarianship is recognized as a legitimate subject for serious consideration in professional discussions. There has been the establishment in the United Kingdom of an organized support group for library professionals who work alone (the "One-Man Band" Section of AS-LIB), and in the United States, under the auspices of the Library Management Division of the Special Libraries Association (SLA), there appears to be an effort being made to form a roundtable or discussion group to address the specific needs of one-person librarians. If this latter effort is successful, it could have significant membership-growth implications for SLA, especially if the Association should choose to direct some of its marketing attention to this large group of librarians and information professionals. The American Library Association, through its journal, *American Libraries*, is now offering frequent articles of special interest to the small (but not necessarily one-person) library, and *Library Journal* has a regular column for the librarian who is employed in a single-staff or minimally staffed library. Clearly, an effort is now being made to serve the professional needs of the one-person librarian.

What has brought about this increased awareness and, concurrently, the reaction from within the profession that this is a level of library management that should be addressed? First of all, one-person librarians have now been recognized to be a sizable part of the profession. Although numbers are hard to come by, there is research which demonstrates that approximately one-third to one-half of all librarians work alone.[4,5] Then, too, if we follow the standard definitions now accepted for defining "special libraries," we can conclude that many of these single-staff librarians work in what we would call "special libraries." Certainly Wilfred Ashworth's definition of a special library ("one which is established to obtain and exploit specialized information for the private advantage of the organization which provides its financial support")[6] is one that accurately describes the organization in which many one-person librarians are employed. When we consider the number of law firms, small businesses, consulting firms, accounting firms, or even the various single-staff departmental or branch libraries of some of the larger businesses and corporations, we can see how these one-person librarians are engaged in managing an informational unit devoted to the retrieval and exploitation of "specialized information."

Similarly, when we consider additionally the noncommercial organizations wherein single-staff libraries are found, organizations such as museums, art galleries, churches and synagogues, clubs and professional associations, historical societies, and the like, the now-standard definition of a special library, as posed by Emily Mobley and Elizabeth Ferguson (both, incidentally, leaders in the special libraries community) becomes just as well the description of a one-person library: "A special library is characteristically a unit or department of an organization primarily devoted to other than library or educational purposes. A special librarian is first an employee, a staff member of the parent organization, and second, a librarian. 'Special' really means library service specialized and geared to the interests of the organization and to the information needs of its personnel."[7] Many of those employed in these organizations, perhaps a majority of them, work alone as one-person librarians, and the "special" library service is provided without the aid of other professional library or information personnel on the staff. It just might be argued that it is in the special libraries community that we find a level of concern about professionalism and the value of information (and the service that provides it), which leads to—or certainly contributes to—the increased awareness of the professional needs of the single-staff librarian. If this is the case, then one-person librarians have not only their numbers to thank for their new-found recognition, but the special libraries community as well.

Of particular importance, as part of this raised awareness within the profession, there has been an upsurge of interest in one-person librarianship as a subject for study in the continuing education and professional development activities offered for librarians. In fact, the professional development of single-staff library management skills has become something of a growth industry in itself, with local groups, state systems, professional associations, and even commercial vendors offering seminars, workshops, lectures, and certification courses for librarians who work alone. Nowadays, librarians in all types of libraries—from corporate to medical, from historical to those in educational institutions, from private to academic—can find programs about managing the single-staff library. It is important to note, as a point of some pride, that the effort has been led all along by SLA, which offered the first of these continuing education courses on one-person librarianship. SLA is now recognized as the authoritative professional association for those single-staff librarians who wish to belong to an organization that takes seriously the development of the particular skills they need for the successful performance of their professional duties.

We do not need to look far to determine why continuing education programs about one-person libraries are popular. Librarians who work alone are daily confronted with a full agenda of tasks, each of which must be analyzed and implemented in the most efficient and professional manner possible. These information specialists are expected to provide a high level of library service, and they must provide it under the circumstances of professional isolation, a situation that requires a unique combination of skills and talents not generally considered in their professional training. They have not been taught how to run a library alone. Likewise, there are many employers of librarians who, for a variety of reasons not the subject of this essay, do not choose to employ professionally trained graduate librarians and information specialists to be in charge of their libraries, and these people, too, have not been trained in the skills needed for running a single-staff library. Finally, there are those librarians, graduate trained or not, who, after some experience and time in multi-staff library situations, find themselves working in a one-person library. They also have not been prepared for this specific type of library management. It is for the training of these three groups of single-staff librarians that continuing education and professional development programs have evolved.

For most of the continuing education courses, the topic of the course —managing the one-person library—is dealt with broadly to incorporate the subject as it is considered by many working one-person librarians. For this group there is a need to discuss, in a structured format, the problems of professional isolation. But the discussions of their worries about being alone are coupled with considerable emphasis on the pleasures that come from the unique independence to be found in a library in which one works without staff. Attention is generally given to basic management techniques for working by one's self in a library or research-oriented office, and to the role of the library in the parent institution (as well as to the role the librarian or information professional is expected to play). Additional consideration is given to specific techniques of particular value to the single-staff librarian, and subjects such as time management, the value of planning, basic budgeting concepts, basic automation concerns, and similar topics are dealt with. In these courses and seminars, whenever possible, much attention is focused on group participation. Case studies, both those brought in by the instructor or lecturer and those brought to the course by participants, are analyzed for the benefit of the entire group.

There are, of course, those one-person librarians for whom such basic considerations are not particularly useful. They have worked in their libraries long enough to have mastered for themselves the techniques and skills for the successful management of the one-person library. Still, these librarians working alone sometimes feel out of touch with the profession, and they, too, want to benefit from this new interest in single-staff libraries. Attempts are being made to provide these librarians with continuing education and professional development programs, and there has been some progress, especially in those programs offered by SLA, where the one-day program has evolved into a two-day course, with basic concerns studied on the first day. For those who wish to continue, or who have been in the field long enough to prefer a more indepth approach to single-staff library management, a second day of advanced work is offered.

For the advanced or experienced one-person librarian, there are other continuing education programs that can be considered, and these are often attended as a second day of study following or preceding the general one-day course. Practically all of the professional associations offer advanced programs in such subjects as time management, automation and new technology, how to use volunteers and other nonstaff assistants, creative management techniques, practical research methods, budgeting, space planning, the cost of information, and the like. Additionally, library systems, usually in cooperation with a state library agency or a regional network, will offer seminars and workshops on subjects of special interest to one-person librarians. In offering these courses, they are finding that many of the participants have already had some exposure to a basic program on the subject and are looking for more specific instruction. Certainly more of these will be offered in the future.

We come, then, to the conclusion that for many in our profession the subject of one-person librarianship is an important one. Why is this? What is it about this particular type of library work that distinguishes it from what other librarians do? Primarily, the difference is one of focus. Librarians and information specialists who work alone, or as the only professional in the library or information center, are characteristically required to direct their energies to a total picture of service. For them, the luxury of limiting their work to only one part of the library's activity, such as technical services, readers' advisory, or the answering or referral of reference queries, is not a workable option. The single-staff librarian must quickly become adept at performing all of these professional tasks, and, at the same time, he must be willing to carry out routine clerical tasks, which, in a multi-staff library setting, would more than likely be performed by someone reporting to him. Finally, as a manager, he must delicately balance these two seemingly contradictory sets of skills, while he performs as an adminstrator: he must know the basics of good office management, maintain interdepartmental cooperation with some finesse, be able to interact with vendors (for the benefit of the parent organization that employs him), and be skilled, at the very least, in the basics of financial planning and implementation. These are not skills that come automatically with one's graduate education and, speaking frankly, for many in single-staff libraries, they are not skills which come easily or naturally. They must be developed, and it is in continuing education seminars and workshops —where one can interact with other one-person librarians under the guidance of a professional colleague—that one-person librarians learn to appreciate in themselves the very skills that, in a larger library, are divided among the staff.

This is not to say that most one-person librarians are introspective and timid souls who find themselves reluctantly being called upon to be library administrators against their will. Those types of individuals, it would seem, do not bother to seek out new skills and new experiences. They continue their passive and short-sighted single-staff roles, doing as little as possible and not concerned—as their supervisors are certainly not concerned—with the limitations of their work. In fact, it is just the opposite types who seem to be working in most of the one-person libraries today, and these are the very people who are coming to the professional development programs. Not only are they not particularly introspective (and certainly they are not shy), they are so full of themselves that they cannot contain themselves in their professionally isolated situations. They are bursting to learn new ideas, new techniques, new skills, indeed, to learn anything that will enable them to grow in their jobs, to make their jobs, full as they are of routine and not necessarily stimulating tasks, as exciting and as interesting as they can be, given the normal limitations of size and service in the type of library that is small enough to be managed by only one person. Thus, we have one-person librarians who are enrolling in continuing education programs not solely to enable themselves to provide better service for their users, but to provide themselves with better, more interesting jobs. It's one of the oldest tricks in the game, and it always works: when the job has become too routine, too dull, how better to improve the situation than to look for new challenges? And what better challenge could there be than to take a good look at the job itself, and learn new skills and new attitudes that will enable you not only to provide better service, but to have a better job. It's a challenge many one-person librarians take willingly, and they use their continuing education courses and professional development programs as a logical route to making their work more rewarding.

If focus is one reason the subject is important, we might also suggest that the subject is important because, in addition to the many numbers of one-person librarians employed in special libraries, there is also recognition in the profession that one-person librarianship just might become a standard for library staffing in the future. Certainly we can see this happening in many of those institutions in which special libraries supply the organization's informational needs. If there is any level of librarianship that would seem to be secure, it is the single-staff library. Regardless of what happens to employment patterns in the profession as a whole, it seems logical that the numbers of librarians working alone will increase. Certainly they won't decrease, simply because managements will find that they get more value for their money by employing one highly skilled and effective librarian/information specialist instead of a team—however small —of generalists who are not as skilled. Such is the optimistic scenario many of us envision for the future, and it is one that, so far, seems to be happening.

We are often asked, "What makes a good one-person librarian?", "What qualities are required?", and "Can these qualities be learned in continuing education programs?" There are, of course, many ideal qualities to be sought in any librarian. Things like curiosity, good recall, the ability to teach, a quality education, and good oral and writing skills are basic— or should be—for any professional library job, especially if the work brings the librarian in contact with users and readers. For many of us, the personal qualities put forward by former SLA President Shirley Echelman in her award-winning essay "Libraries Are Businesses, Too!" [8] are especially essential: an analytical intelligence, self-confidence, flexibility, a sense of humor, patience, and a high frustration threshold.

Although her essay was not particularly directed to librarians who work alone, Echelman's six personality qualities are equally, if not more, necessary for those who manage single-staff operations. Any one-person librarian is advised to consider these qualities, and whether or not he possesses them, when he is thinking about his work and his suitability for it.

In addition to these characteristics, however, the one-person librarian must also bring to the job certain other qualities that may or may not be required for success in other types of library work. Primarily, the single-staff librarian must be something of a visionary, an idealist, one who can look at the library or information service and think about what (within the limitations of the library's stated mission) that service can be. Planning skills are essential. The one-person librarian must have the ability—and determination—to find some time each day to plan and organize the next items on the daily or weekly agenda. In addition, he must work with the parent organization's management, administrators, clerical staff, users, library committee, and, in some cases, even interested outsiders—all non-librarians—to study and plan, and perhaps to implement, the library's direction for the future. As part of this process, the one-person librarian must be able to work with others in the organization, not just as librarian —for we are all trained to do that—but as staff member, employee, and part of the organizational team. He is, for the good of his company and for his own work, required to be involved and to build an alliance, a union, with those who are interested in the library and the work that goes on there. And if the interest itself has to be created, so be it. A talented and enthusiastic one-person librarian can create interest in the library, if he is doing a good job.

By working as a team member, by understanding and appreciating what is going on in the parent organization, and by enthusiastically participating in it, the one-person librarian is making a case for the library. When this happens, when the librarian or information professional is discovered to be one who understands the library's role in the parent organization and is perceived not as someone different or as an outsider, the librarian is going to have the respect and appreciation of the other staff, and automatically part of the problem of isolation is removed. The professional isolation, the separation from other librarians, is still there, but it is pleasantly tempered by the recognition that, while he is the only librarian, the librarian is but one employee. Such self-recognition does much to put one's work in a happier perspective.

The answer to the question "Can these ideal qualities be learned in continuing education programs?" is easier to provide. The personal qualities cannot be taught, and it is not the purpose of the professional development programs to teach people how to be patient, or to have self-confidence, or to learn analytical skills. Certain other skills and techniques can be taught, however, and when basic management and planning skills are combined with the personal, when the attending librarians are encouraged to look inside themselves to determine how they can use their personal attributes in their work situations, the result is hopefully a better librarian and better service for the organization that is employing that librarian.

Continuing education and professional development programs look at those areas that can be developed. Once the librarian has discovered that he has the interest and the motivation to try to change some of the ways he does things in his library, he is able to learn techniques used by others and can then adapt them for implementation in his own library. Thus, while the librarian may, for years, simply plod along trying to perform his tasks in whatever haphazard manner he might casually have come up with, once he learns something about the basics of planning and time management, he may very well find that he does, indeed, have time to do everything he is expected to do in his small library. Similarly, if his sense of professional isolation literally prevents him from performing effectively, he will learn, as he thinks about some of the basics of networking and forming connections, that he has access to other professionals who just might be willing to share some of their ideas, interests, or even resources with him. He could, of course, learn these things on his own, but it is difficult when he is a few years out of graduate school, the only professional librarian in the organization, not exceptionally motivated at the job, and, especially, has begun to feel a sense of dullness about his work. Continuing education courses and professional development programs are designed to help ease that difficulty.

One thing the courses do not teach is how to become a two-person library. There are occasionally those who come to the continuing education and professional development programs with the idea that they will go away armed with the facts and information they need to persuade management to permit them to add staff. Other work has been done in this area,[9,10] and the addition of staff is not the focus of these programs. In fact, the purpose of these courses is to encourage the single-staff librarian to rethink the work he does in his library. By adopting some of the techniques and attitudes considered by the group, he will be able to organize his work and, in fact, perform on his own the tasks that he thinks require more staff. This is not to say that there are not one-person librarians who are overworked and who do not have enough time to do the things they are expected to do. What we are saying, however, is that, from a management point of view, there very well may not be the need for more than one person to provide information for the organization. If that is the case, it is our goal in the continuing education programs to suggest the means by which one-person librarians, working in their libraries as presently structured by management (that is, in one-person libraries) can use their time and their energies most effectively for the benefit of the parent organizations that employ them.

Finally, the subject is important as a basis for continuing education courses and professional development programs because they bring about, for the one-person librarian, a route to renewed professional affirmation. Because of the isolation of the situation, without frequent contact with other professional information people on a daily basis, single-staff librarians often find themselves suffering from a lack of professional affirmation. Or, if not from the real thing, there is often a perception that they are not appreciated or considered professionals by their colleagues in the organization that mutually employs them. By attending the programs that are offered to them, they accomplish several things. First, by convincing management that the programs are beneficial for the organization and will result in better services in the library or information unit, the librarian is keeping management aware that the library is a serious part of the organization and, in fact, that the librarian's profession is serious enough about the high quality of library services that it offers its practitioners these opportunities to learn and grow. Second, the methods and techniques brought back from the programs and implemented (even minimally) into the daily workings of the library will indeed produce benefits for the organization, benefits that are bound to affect staff and management's perception of the value of the librarian. Third, the librarian, himself, receives professional affirmation simply by being at the workshop or seminar and interacting with others who are in the same type of work situation. There is great solace in learning, when you work alone all the time, that there are others in the professional community who share the same concerns and rewards that you have in your work.

What is suggested here is that continuing education courses and professional development programs are indeed a benefit of our profession that, while actively pursued by many, could be of benefit to many others, especially to those who work alone in their libraries. As professional librarians, we can be expected to have a "commitment to an active pursuit of continued growth and learning," suggests Sheila Creth, assistant director for Administrative Services at the University of Michigan Library. "Articles, conferences, and workshops abound with the theme of change in society . . . indicating that professionals are well aware of the scope and pace of change anticipated in the environment. While much of the predicted change appears exciting, questions are also raised about a loss of tradition and a loss of influence and control over library decisions and activities. . . . As change surrounds us and affects every aspect of our professional lives, we can choose to keep pace—indeed, set the pace— by acquiring the knowledge and skills needed for the future." It is not enough, obviously, to go to work each day, discharge one's duties until time to leave, and then forget one's profession until seated at the desk the next day. Professionalism requires a commitment, and that commitment for one-person librarians must include a willingness, as Creth suggests, "to invest time and energy and dollars in our own continued education and a demand of . . . administrators to provide staff development programs and to support continuing education activities through release time and financial support." [11] Such commitment does not come easily for the one-person librarian, already frequently overextended in order to meet the rigorous demands of a difficult job. Nevertheless, with planning, with commitment, and with just a modicum of assertiveness more than he had planned to bring to the job, even the busy one-person librarian can find ways to stretch his mind by participating in continuing education courses and professional development programs. The committed one-person librarian, hearing about these offerings, will consider whether they can be of value to him. If they can, he finds a way to attend, for, as Creth writes, "There are no obstacles to pursuing continued learning that cannot be overcome; there are only excuses." [12]

References

1. St. Clair, Guy. "The One-Person Library: An Essay on Essentials." *Special Libraries 67* (no. 5/6): 233-238 (May/June 1976).
2. St. Clair, Guy, and Joan Williamson. *Managing the One-Person Library.* London and Stoneham, Mass.: Butterworths, 1986.
3. *The One-Person Library: A Newsletter for Librarians and Management.* (OPL Resources, Ltd., P.O. Box 948, Murray Hill Station, New York, NY 10156) Volume 1-, 1984-.
4. Serjean, R. "Librarianship and Information Work: Job Characteristics and Staffing Needs." *British Library R&D Report 5321 HC* (London, 1977).
5. East, Harry. "Changes in the staffing of UK special libraries and information services in the decade 1972-1981: a review of the DES census data," *Journal of Documentation 39:* (no. 4): 247-265 (1983).
6. Ashworth, Wilfred. *Special Librarianship,* Clive Bingley, London, 1979, p. 6.
7. Ferguson, Elizabeth, and Emily R. Mobley. *Special Libraries at Work.* Hamden, Conn.: Library Professional Publications, Inc., 1984, p. 4.
8. Echelman, Shirley. "Libraries Are Businesses, Too!" *Special Libraries 65:* 410 (Oct./Nov. 1974).
9. Mintz, Anne P., and Amy Ribouli, "Effect of Growth in a Business Library: The Addition of a Second Professional." Unpublished paper presented at the 77th Annual Conference, Special Libraries Association, Boston, June 1986, and described in *The One-Person Library: A Newsletter for Librarians and Management 3* (No. 6): 5-6 (October 1986).
10. Collins, Susan. "Determining Effective Staffing Levels in Special Libraries." *Special Libraries 75* (no. 4): 283-291 (October 1974).
11. Creth, Sheila. "National Adult and Continuing Education Week: Changes in Academic Libraries and The Need for Upgrading Professional Skills." *College and Research Libraries News* (no. 10): 658 (November 1986).
12. *Ibid.*